# The Astrology of Fate

# The Astrology of Fate

## Liz Greene

SAMUEL WEISER, INC.

York Beach, Maine

First published in 1984 by
Samuel Weiser, Inc.
Box 612
York Beach, Maine 03910

Fifth printing, 1995

Library of Congress Catalog Card Number: 84-51742

ISBN 0-87728-636-1
MV/JC

Cover illustration by Liz Greene.

Printed in the United States of America

The paper used in this publication meets the minimum
requirements of the American National Standard for
Permanence of Paper for Printed Library Materials.
Z39.48-1984.

*To John, with love*

Death is certain, and when a man's fate has come, not even the gods can save him, no matter how they love him.

**Homer**

And God-the-Mind, being male and female both, as Light and Life subsisting, brought forth another Mind to give things form, who, God as he was of Fire and Spirit, formed Seven Rulers who enclose the cosmos that the sense perceives. Men call their ruling Fate.

*Corpus Hermeticum*

One should not speak of fate. It is too paganish a word.

**Oliver Cromwell, to the First Protectorate Parliament**

Free will is the ability to do gladly that which I must do.

**C. G. Jung**

# Contents

# Introduction

---

*What is ordained is master of the gods and thee.*

**Euripides**

Once upon a time, it is said, there lived in Isfahan a young man who spent his days as servant to a wealthy merchant. On a fine morning the young man rode to market, carefree and with his purse jingling with coins from the merchant's coffers to buy meat and fruit and wine; and there in the market-place he saw Death, who beckoned to him as though about to speak. In terror the young man turned his horse about and fled, taking the road that led to Samara. By nightfall, filthy and exhausted, he had reached an inn there, and with the merchant's money procured a room, and collapsed upon the bed with mingled fatigue and relief, for it seemed he had outwitted Death. But in the middle of the night there came a knock at the chamber door, and in the doorway stood Death, smiling affably. 'How come you to be here?' demanded the young man, white-faced and trembling; 'I saw you only this morning in the market-place in Isfahan.' And Death replied: 'Why, I have come to collect you, as it is written. For when I saw you this morning in the market-place in Isfahan, I tried to say that you and I had an appointment tonight in Samara. But you would not let me speak, and only ran away.'

This is a short, sweet folktale, and one might read many themes into it. But among its deceptively simple lines is surely embedded a comment about fate: its irrevocability and yet, paradoxically, its dependence upon the will of man for its fruition. Such a tale, because it is paradoxical, invites all manner of philosophical and metaphysical speculation, of the sort with which sensible people do not occupy themselves. For example: If the servant had stayed and spoken with Death, would he have still had to die in Samara? What if he had taken another road? *Could* he have taken another road? If not, then what power, inner or outer, directed him to the appointed place? What if, like the knight in Bergmann's *The Seventh Seal*, he had challenged Death? Or, in short, that queer conundrum which the East has always treated with such subtlety, yet which the West has persisted in reducing to an either-or, black-and-white choice: are we fated, or are we free?

I have found that the word fate is often quite offensive to many people in this enlightened twentieth century. Death has at last been separated from its original unity with fate, and has been transformed into a clinical, rather than a metaphysical, phenomenon. But this was not always so. Fate was called *Moira* by the Greeks, and was from earliest times a *daimon* of doom and death, a great power older than the oldest gods. Greek philosophy had quite a lot to say about fate, which we shall explore in due course. But mentioning fate now seems to imply a loss of control, a sense of powerlessness, impotence and humiliation. When Cromwell told his Parliament that they should not speak of fate, he gave voice to a sentiment that has pervaded our social and religious outlook ever since. The history of philosophy hinges upon the profound issue of man's fate and freedom; yet modern philosophical writers such as Bertrand Russell see 'fatalism' and its inevitable creative children – the mantic or divinatory arts – as a kind of taint spawned by Pythagoras and Plato on pure rational thought, a stain which discoloured the otherwise brilliant fabric of the classical Greek mind. Wherever there is a concern with fate, there is also a concern with astrology, for the concept of Moira evolves from the vision of an orderly, interconnected cosmos; and astrology in particular finds disfavour with the modern school of philosophy embodied by Russell. As Professor Gilbert Murray says, 'Astrology fell upon the Hellenistic mind as a new disease falls upon some remote island people.' Russell quotes this passage in his *History of Western Philosophy*, and caps it with one of his own:

> The majority of even the best philosophers fell in with the belief in astrology. It involved, since it thought the future predictable, a belief in necessity or fate.[1]

Christian theology too found this subject of fate a great problem. The denial of Moira, or *Heimarmenê* as it is sometimes called in early astrological texts, has been a popular Christian theme for many centuries, and it does not require a mind of great brilliance to suspect that this denial rests on grounds somewhat subtler than the argument that fate is paganish. Although medieval Christians from Boethius to Dante acknowledged the pagan tradition of the goddess of fate side by side with the omnipotence of the Trinity, the Reformation brought with it a conviction that the very idea of such a figure was an insult to God's sovereignty. God sometimes works with a grace which nullifies the influence of the heavens, says Calvin hopefully, and people are often made new by the experience of conversion. Just as the Reformation threw out the 'cult' of Mary, it likewise threw out the other numinous feminine power in the cosmos. And as Cromwell bade us, since the seventeenth century we have not spoken of fate.

The theological argument which replaced the ancient goddess and which is still viable today is the doctrine of God's Providence. Even Calvin's gloomy children will argue if one calls by the name of fate the predestined salvation of the elect in which they believe. Those of a more scientific bent revert to the terminology of 'natural law'; but the irony of this is that Moira, as she emerged in the thought of Anaximander and the more 'scientific' Ionian school of Greek philosophy which Russell favours over those gullible and mystical Platonists, is nothing more nor less than natural law, raised to the status of deity.

> Moira, it is true, was a moral power; but no one had to pretend that she was exclusively benevolent, or that she had any respect for the parochial interests and wishes of mankind. Further – and this is the most important point – she was not credited with foresight, purpose, design; these belong to man and the humanised gods. Moira is the blind, automatic force which leaves their subordinate purposes and wills free play within their own legitimate spheres, but recoils in certain vengeance upon them the moment that they cross her boundaries . . . She is a representation which states a truth about the disposition of Nature, and to the statement of that truth adds nothing except that the disposition is both necessary and just.[2]

Anaximander and his fellows envisioned the universe as portioned out into a general scheme of allotted provinces or spheres of power. The word Moira itself means 'share' or 'allotment'. The universe was first a primary and undifferentiated mass; when the four elements came into being, they received their 'allotment' not from a personified goddess, but from the eternal motion within the cosmos, which was considered no less divine. But interpreting natural law as a *numen* does not appeal to us today. And when we consider other aspects of natural law such as heredity and the phylogenesis of disease, we are scarcely prone to see these processes as anything to do with fate.

It has even become acceptable, in some circles, to speak of *karma*, while avoiding the word fate. Karma, it would appear, is a nicer term because it implies a chain of cause and effect, with some importance given to the individual's choices in a given incarnation. Fate, on the other hand, seems, in popular conception, to be random, and the individual possesses no choices at all. But this was never the philosophical conception of fate, not even in the eyes of the Stoics, who were as their name suggests exceedingly stoical about the lack of freedom in the cosmos. Stoicism, the most fatalistic of philosophies, acknowledged fate as a cause and effect principle; it merely postulated that we humans are generally too blind and stupid to see the results implicit in our actions. According to the Indian formula, man sows his seed and pays no attention to its growth. It then sprouts and eventually ripens, and each individual must eat of the fruit of his own field. This is the law of karma. It is no different from Heimarmenê, which is eloquently described below by Professor Murray:

> Heimarmenê, in the striking simile of Zeno [the founder of Stoicism], is like a fine thread running through the whole of existence – the world, we must remember, was to the Stoics a live thing – like the invisible thread of life which, in heredity, passes on from generation to generation of living species and keeps the type alive; it runs causing, causing forever, both the infinitesimal and the infinite ... rather difficult to distinguish from the Pronoia or Providence, which is the work of God and indeed the very essence of God.[3]

It is not only difficult to distinguish fate from Providence; it is equally difficult to distinguish it from karma and from natural law. This situation bears an irresistible similarity to the use of words like 'copulation', 'fornication' and 'intercourse' in order to avoid saying you-know-what.

Psychology too has found other, more attractive terminology when confronting issues of fate. It speaks of hereditary predisposition, conditioning patterns, complexes and archetypes. All these are useful terms, and no doubt more appropriate for the twentieth century; I shall use them myself throughout this book, and it is probably fitting that our view of fate should have evolved, over three or four millennia, from a personified goddess to a property of the unconscious psyche. But I am struck over and over by the repugnance those in the helping professions seem to feel – in particular the psychiatrist, who ought to be able to see the connection when he pronounces the prognosis of schizophrenia incurable and declares it to be hereditary – when the word fate is served up cold upon a plate without sauce or garnish. It is not surprising that the modern astrologer, who must sup with fate each time he considers a horoscope, is made uncomfortable and attempts to formulate some other way of putting it, speaking instead, with elegant ambiguity, of potentials and seed plans and blueprints. Or he may seek refuge in the old Neoplatonic argument that while there *may* be a fate represented by the planets and signs, the spirit of man is free and can make its choices regardless. Margaret Hone is a typical voice on the subject:

> Synchronisation with a planetary pattern *apparently* denies free-will entirely . . . Inasmuch as a man identifies himself with his physical self and the physical world about him, so he is in-dissolubly part of it and subject to its changing pattern as formed by the planets in their orbits. Only by the recognition of that which he senses as greater than himself can he attune himself to what is beyond the terrestrial pattern. In this way, though he may not escape terrestrial happenings, by the doctrine of free and willing 'acceptance' he can 'will' that his real self is free in its reaction to them.[4]

Jeff Mayo, on the other hand, appears to belong to the 'blueprint' school:

> You may think that if the future can be foretold we have no free-will, we are enmeshed in an irrevocable fate we cannot escape. The astrologer *cannot* predict every event . . . An astro-logical aspect with regard to the future can correspond with any one of a variety of possibilities, mostly dependent upon the 'freedom of choice' of the individual concerned, yet the aspect still foretells the actual *trend* of circumstances, or the *nature* of the individual's reaction to the situation.[5]

These two voices are characteristic of astrology's current reaction to the problem of fate. Either fate is merely a trend, a set of possibilities, rather than something more definite, or it is indeed definite but only applies to the corporeal or 'lower' nature of man and does not contaminate his spirit. One is a pragmatic approach; the other, a mystical one which can be traced all the way back to Plato. Both, however, are open to challenge. On the one hand, it would seem, in my experience, that some very specific events in life are fated and unavoidable, and can hardly be called a trend or attributed to the individual's active choice. Some of the case histories in this book illustrate this rather painfully. On the other hand, it would seem that the inner life of man – the spirit of which Margaret Hone writes – is as coloured by fate as his outer life, in the form of unconscious complexes which even influence the nature of the God he worships, and which shape his choices far more powerfully than any act of conscious volition. In fact, the concur-rence of inner complexes and outer circumstances suggests that the division into 'physical' and 'spiritual' which Hone is making is an arbitrary one. I do not pretend to have an answer to these dilemmas, and I would not suggest that either of these two very accomplished and experienced authors is 'wrong'. But I am left with the feeling that something is being avoided.

Fate means: it has been written. For something to be written with such immovability by an utterly unseen hand is a terrifying thought. It implies not only powerlessness, but the dark machinery of some vast impersonal Wheel or highly ambiguous God which takes less account than we would like of our hopes, dreams, desires, loves, merits or even our sins. Of what value are the individual's efforts, his moral struggles, his humble acts of love and courage, his strivings for the betterment of himself and his family and his world, if all is ultimately rendered pointless by what has already been written? We have been fed, for the last two centuries, on a highly questionable pabulum of rational self-determination, and such a vision of fate threatens an experience of real despair, or a chaotic abreaction where the spinal column of the moral and ethical man collapses. There is equally a difficulty with the more mystical approach to fate, for by severing the unity of body and spirit in order to seek refuge from the strictures of fate, the individual creates an artificial dissociation from his own natural law, and may invoke in the outer world what he is avoiding in the inner.

Yet to the Greek mind, as to the mind of the Renaissance, the vision of fate did not destroy the dignity of human morality or human soul. If anything, it was the reverse. The first religious poet of Greece, Hesiod, states simply that the course of Nature is anything but careless of right and wrong. He implies that there is a definite and sympathetic connection between human conduct and the ordered law of Nature. When a sin has been committed – such as the unconscious incest of Oidipus – all Nature is poisoned by the offence of man, and Moira retaliates with immediate catastrophe brought down upon the head of the offender. Fate, to Hesiod, is the guardian of justice and law, rather than the random predetermining force that dictates a man's every action. This guardian has set the bounds of the original elemental order, within which man must live because he is part of Nature; and it waits to exact the penalty of every transgression. And death, because it is the final statement of Moira, the 'allotment' or circumscribed limit beyond which mortal creatures cannot pass, is not an indignity, but a necessity, issuing from a divine source.

It would appear that since the Reformation we have lost much of this sense of connection with Nature and natural law; we have forgotten what we knew of the meaning of fate, and so the vicissitudes of life, including death, are to us in the West an offence and a humiliation. When an old person dies, we no longer speak of 'natural causes' or a death due to old age, but rather, written on the death certificate, 'cardio-respiratory failure', thereby implying that, had it not been for this failure or mistake, death would never have taken place. But I do not think we have lost our fear of fate, although we mock it; for if the modern individual were so truly enlightened beyond this 'paganish' concept, he would not surreptitiously read astrology columns in the newspaper, nor evidence the compulsion to ridicule whenever possible the spokesmen of fate. Nor would he be so fascinated by prophecy, which is fate's handmaiden. Nostradamus' *Centuries*, those bizarre visions of the future of the world, have never been out of print, and each new translation sells in astronomical figures. As for the ridicule, it is my feeling that fear, when unadmitted, is often cloaked with aggressive contempt, and rather stringent attempts to disprove or denigrate the thing which threatens. Every palmist, astrologer, card reader and clairvoyant has met this peculiar but unmistakable onslaught from the 'skeptic'. And it occurs, sadly, not least within the field of astrology itself. The outlines of this spectre can be glimpsed in the more determinedly 'scientific' astrologer's attempts to prove his study solely through a tidal wave of statistics, ignoring or refusing to recognise those mysteries which elude his computations, pleading shamelessly for recognition of his science (if that is what it is) from an obdurate scientific community, and ultimately apologising for even calling astrology by its own name, replacing this with such tongue-twisters as 'cosmobiology' in the hope that it will render him more respectable. I am not insulting valid research in pursuit of clarity or truth by this observation, but am rather calling attention to an attitude of what seems to me fanatical overcompensation that throws the baby out with the bath water. The community of modern astrological practitioners often seem terribly ashamed that they must traffick with fate.

Astrology, in company with the Tarot, palmistry, scrying, and perhaps also the *I Ching* which has now firmly entrenched itself in the West, are the modern carriers of the ancient and honourable role of seership. This has been, from time immemorial, the art of interpreting the clouded and ambiguous intentions of the gods, although we might now call it the clouded and ambiguous intentions of the unconscious; and it is directed towards the apprehension of *kairos*, the 'right moment'. Jung used the term synchronicity in connection with these things, as a way of attempting to shed light on the mystery of meaningful coincidence – whether it is the coincidence of an apparently unrelated external event with a dream or inner state, or an event with the pattern of cards, planets, coins. But whatever language we use, psychological or mythic, religious or 'scientific', at the heart of divination is the effort to read what is being, or has been, written, whether we explain this mystery by the psychological concept of synchronicity or the much older belief in fate. For the uninitiated layman with no experience of such things in their enormous multilevelled subtlety, acquaintance with Moira is limited to predictions in sun sign columns, and occasional visits to the funny old lady in Neasden who lives with seventeen cats and was *actually right* about my mother's operation. In these expressions our typically concrete Western interpretations of fate are evidenced in all their schizoid glory. Either we believe wholeheartedly that next week will indeed bring the unlooked-for windfall, the new lover, the bad news by post, the promotion; or, sometimes at the same time, we jeer cruelly at the friend who is stupid, ignorant, gullible enough to think he or she could actually get help from that sort of ridiculous mumbo-jumbo. Novalis' statement that fate and soul are two names for the same principle is, of course, incomprehensible in the face of such concretisation. Yet the astrologer, who ought to know better, may still be found making his concrete pronouncements, and not only about the new lover and the bad news by post: zodiacal signs and planetary aspects mean behaviour and behaviour only from this literal perspective, with not a thought to the inner 'soul' of which Novalis speaks.

It is not my object to convince the layman of either the mantic arts or of fate. What concerns me is the approach of the astrological practitioner. I am not happy with either the 'trend' approach to the horoscope, or the Neoplatonic 'fate affects the body but not the soul' approach. For me, the former evades the issue of the mysteriously meaningful events that provoke individual development, and the latter evades the issue of individual responsibility. From what I have observed in my analysands and my astrological clients, there is certainly something – whether one calls it fate, Providence, natural law, karma or the unconscious – that retaliates when its boundaries are transgressed or when it receives no respect or effort at relationship, and which seems to possess a kind of 'absolute knowledge' not only of what the individual needs, but of what he is *going* to need for his unfolding in life. It appears to make arrangements of the most particular and astonishing kind, bringing a person together with another person or an external situation at precisely the right moment, and it appears to be as much part of the inner man as the outer. It also appears to be both psychic and physical, personal and collective, 'higher' and 'lower', and can wear the mask of Mephistopheles as readily as it can present itself as God. I make no pretence of knowing what 'it' is, but I am unashamedly prepared to call it fate. And I feel that if we understood this thing better we might be of far greater assistance to our clients, not to mention ourselves.

The purpose of this book, like the Greek Fates themselves, is threefold. Firstly, it is intended to confront and question the issue of fate in some detail. I have no answers to the fundamental problem of whether we are fated or free; no such conclusion is ever definitively reached in this exploration. I am inclined, when faced with such an enormity, to feebly answer, Both. I do not know what fate is in a defined metaphysical sense, or a theological one; philosophy and religion concern themselves with this problem in far more erudite terms than I am capable of. When Apuleius of Madaura speaks with certainty of dual fate – fate as energy and fate as substance – or when Chrysippos proposes that even our thoughts are fated, I am hardly in a position to challenge them. There have been many attempts to define fate over the centuries, and sometimes the conclusions differ. I do not know with any certainty whether it is possible to alter fate, or whether fate itself alters, or what 'altering' might mean, although I have raised some questions about just what it is that 'transforms' during processes such as psychotherapy. Nor do I know whether some people are more fated than others, although it would certainly seem so on a literal outer level. But sometimes it is the asking of the question that opens doors, rather than the determined search for an unambiguous answer.

Questions that deal with such bottomless issues as man's freedom or lack thereof, however, have a tendency, if taken seriously, to invoke in the questioner a rather uncomfortable ambivalence. It seems as though it is safer not to ask, but merely to ignore or mock; for, having asked, one has, in the act of composing the question, torn the protective skin off a deep and mysterious human dilemma and source of suffering. Once conscious of that dilemma, if no immediate answer is forthcoming, one is suspended between the opposites like someone hanging on a cross. This problem translates itself in human terms in a deceptively simple question: if one is struck powerfully by impulses or desires which erupt from the psyche, does one act them out because they are fated, or does one try to repress or control them? Or might there be a third possibility, which grants the inevitability of the experience but also tests the whole man in terms of his moral choices? This is no easy question, as any psychotherapist knows, for sometimes an individual cannot help himself, and sometimes he can; and sometimes he ought not to help himself, and sometimes he must. This very dilemma in fact permeates the story of Christ's betrayal and crucifixion. Such a suspension may deepen and enrich, but it can also paralyse. Deepening and stretching are not for everyone; otherwise we would probably not, as a collective, shy away so obviously from the question. Suspension robs us of certainty, whether it is on the side of morality or amorality, fate or freedom. And how many of us would dare, like

Socrates, to acknowledge the root of all wisdom in the knowledge
that we do not know?

The second purpose of this book is an attempt to understand the
repugnance and even anger which the subject of fate invokes,
particularly in my fellow astrological students and practitioners
and in my fellow analysts. There is no modern profession which
brings an individual closer to the experience of fate than the
practice of the horoscopic art, save that of the psychotherapist. The
discussion of 'blueprints' and 'trends' is valid enough for the
individual whose life has not been violently touched by fate: the
healthy person, physically and psychically, who is 'at a crossroads'
or wants vocational guidance or is 'seeking direction' or wants to
'learn more' about himself. But these are not the only clients who
come for astrological advice. If they were, our work would always
be pleasurable, and never challenge us. Yet there are the people
tormented by some inner *daimon* or compulsion, struggling futilely
against what they experience as their own evil; who have been
twisted almost beyond recognition by childhood experiences
which they did not choose; who have been broken open by some
numinous or transpersonal experience which demands a sacrifice
of something they hold most dear; who have been physically
maimed by accident or illness or congenital defect; who have
suffered unjust losses and unearned separations, or have been
caught up in collective horrors like wartime Germany or post-war
Czechoslavakia or Northern Ireland; who have been raped,
robbed, pillaged and used; who have gone, are going or will go
mad because their mad families have elected them as symptom-
bearers and scapegoats. Nor is the gifted individual free of suffering, for the possession of talents and insights and even what we
call 'luck' marks a man as surely as deformity does, and separates
him from the community into an isolation of the spirit which
equally demands an answer of some kind. I do not find it easy to
come up with specious phrases when facing this catalogue of
apparently unmerited human vicissitudes. I was once told during
a workshop, by a woman with a voice of smug certainty, that
people are never given more than they can bear. A brief visit to a
hospital or a psychiatric ward tends to render this sort of pro-
nouncement nonsensical. I cannot talk glibly about karma as many
astrologers do, and imply that it was something to do with one's
previous incarnations so not to worry, just close your eyes and
think of England; nor can I imply that the individual 'made' these
things happen out of what was merely a 'trend', because he is
personally stupider or more culpable than most. I must admit
honestly that I do not know, and because I do not know I have
engaged in an attempt to understand more deeply the nature of

whatever 'it' is. As with many people, the presence of extreme suffering invokes in me the question of meaning. But for me, the roads of human perversity and catastrophe do not ultimately lead to the comforting paternal arms of a benign Judaeo-Christian God whom we must not question; nor do they lead to the indictment of society as the source of all ills. Rather, they lead to fate.

It is my feeling that all genuine vocations or 'callings' have about them, shadowy and often unseen, an archetypal or mythic figure, in itself fascinating and compelling although unconscious, which in some way is the symbol of the inner meaning or 'rightness' of that vocation. Or it could be put another way: the human imagination formulates these figures spontaneously as a means of articulating some mysterious sacredness or numinosity about a particular function in life which the intellect cannot fully comprehend. Jung thought that these figures were archetypal images, perceptions of innate human patterns or ordering processes the source of which remains a mystery and the experience of which conveys a sense of the divine. Take, for example, the doctor. We may know perfectly well that he is fallible, that he has a habit of not answering his telephone at weekends, that he overcharges (if he is in private practice), that he too falls ill, that he cannot cure the incurable. Yet we resonate not to the individual doctor when we panic over an illness, but to the Shaman, the Priest-Healer, the lame Asklepios who has received his wisdom from the gods and is himself a god, and who is holy priest to the desperate cries of both the body and the soul. It has been suggested by Jung and others that the Healer is an inner figure, who may be met in dreams and who embodies that profound mystery of the psyche's and the body's capacity to heal itself. But we do not think in terms of inner archetypal figures; we reach for the telephone to get the doctor. The rather callous playboy recently and barely graduated from medical school, with a disastrous marriage and neglected children and a myriad sexual, financial and emotional problems is not the face we see in the consulting room: but something shining, powerful, able to instil hope in the face of hopelessness, offering calm acceptance even of imminent death.

The more perceptive doctor knows about this Doctor too, and is well aware that healing, in many instances, depends upon the inner image being constellated; for if it is not, the patient will not get better, despite the technical skills and knowledge of the practitioner. Inner Doctor and outer doctor thus work hand in hand, although often no one, in particular the doctor and the patient, is the wiser. If we did not place this divinely, or archetypally, inspired trust in our medical practitioners, it is doubtful that we would ever visit them, save for the broken bones and minor

bruises of everyday life. And the doctor himself? Granted, he may
acquire handsome financial remuneration in America, and in
England if he manages to acquire a Middle Eastern practice in
Harley Street; and he obtains also the status which his credential
offers, and a place in the community, and a sense of security in the
'network' of his colleagues. But the moral as well as the technical
standards of the medical profession are demanding to an excessive
degree, and it is no joy to deal with necrotic tissue and disintegration and death every day; not to mention what the Prince of Wales,
in his address to the British Medical Association, referred to as 'the
stricken spirit who comes . . . with his sick soul disguised as an
ailment of the body'. What justification can the doctor offer to his
own soul, when he must finally confront it, if there were not some
Other glimmering behind his often genuine but frequently insuffi-
cient dedication and desire to help, whether he calls it compassion,
or integrity, or service, or a need to live a meaningful life?

Analytical psychology speaks with justification of the dangers of
identification with an archetype. The doctor is not the Doctor and
is better off remembering this, lest he run the risk of inflation and
even potential psychosis if the divine image overwhelms the
conscious ego's sense of human fallibility and limitation. But these
archetypal figures, when approached with consciousness and
humility, nevertheless demand an offering from their children. To
eat of godly flesh requires a return, which those who pursue 'jobs'
rather than the inspiration of calling do not have to make. It is
perhaps the sense of this which forms the inner logic of the
Hippocratic oath in medicine. This act of returning something to
the god – the act of recognising something sacred for which one is a
vessel of some kind – differentiates the vocation from the job, or
differentiates the individual's feeling about his job. The ner-
vousness felt in esoteric circles about charging money for horoscopes or 'spiritual teaching' is a valid intuition, albeit sometimes
grossly misplaced, that somewhere Someone is owed something.
And what figure stands behind the astrologer, if not fate?

> The finished shape of our fate, the line drawn round it. It is the
> task the gods allot us, and the share of glory they allow; the
> limits we must not pass; and our appointed end. Moira is all
> these.[6]

All the scientific knowledge in the world will not erase that
which has been there from the beginning, older than the oldest of
gods. Science too carries a mythic background which exercises
numinous power; otherwise we astrologers would not be so
intimidated by it, nor the scientific community so ready to use the
word as though it were a religious truth any doubt of which

constituted heresy. And, paradoxically, the mythic backgrounds of both astrology and science are united in the same figure:

> Such genuine religious feeling as is to be found in Homer is less concerned with the gods of Olympus than with more shadowy beings such as Fate or Necessity or Destiny, to whom even Zeus is subject. Fate exercised a great influence on all Greek thought, and perhaps was one of the sources from which science derived the belief in natural law.[7]

The same mythic background indeed, though clothed in a new gown. I sometimes wonder whether astrologers, when they can no longer trust anything but statistics, are not in part merely changing the Old Harlot's dress to assuage their own insecurities, as well as offering valuable contributions to a rational understanding of their study. Yet deeply disturbing though it may be to confront these ancient forms while still retaining our twentieth-century's hard-won knowledge of the physical universe and of man's greater choices within it, nevertheless it is this very conflict which I believe to be the modern astrologer's fate, if you like: the conflict with which he must struggle, full of ambivalence yet with Parsifal's question forever on his lips. Whom do we truly serve? Fate or freedom? The passively fatalistic astrologer and his opposite, the self-satisfied rationalist who looks no further than mechanical cause and effect and talks about 'mastering' the chart, perhaps miss the point – and, sooner or later, may betray the gods, the client and themselves.

So, in summary, the second purpose of this exploration is to try to bring into clearer perspective that figure with which we must deal, which seems to provoke such ambivalence: the ancient shape of fate, from which we have become estranged. In order to facilitate this effort, I have found it useful to draw from a very old past to trace man's images and stories about fate. Much of this may seem irrelevant to the modern astrologer. Yet myths, as Jung was at great pains to point out, are the eternal patterns of man's soul. They are alive and well in our dreams, in our fantasies, in our loves and hates, in the fabric of our lives; and not least in the more sensitive astrologer's consulting room, where the practitioner with any receptivity to the unseen and unspoken psyche may sense the white-gowned forms of Clotho the Spinner, Lachesis the Measurer, and Atropos the Cutter hovering dimly over the zodiacal wheel.

The third purpose of this book is, in a sense, to conjure; to invoke. By this I mean that any symbol, astrological or otherwise, cannot be truly grasped by the intellect alone. There are more elusive yet equally productive roads by which the 'map of the heavens' might be approached, and I have therefore attempted to deal with some of our astrological symbols not only conceptually but also, perhaps more importantly, in the language in which they are wont to clothe themselves. Hence, to the undoubted frustration of the more pragmatic reader, astrological interpretations are hopelessly mixed herein with fairy tales, myths, dreams and other oddities, along with more respectable references from philosophy and psychology. I find it difficult to summarise a sign or planet with a keyword, and even more difficult to deal with it as a statistic. How can one measure the places where fate enters a life? There is case material included, however, to help ground the flights of fantasy, in hope of demonstrating the workings of fate in actual people's lives.

I have found that fate is as liquid and elusive a word as love. Plato thought they were the same; and it is worth noting in passing that in Old Norse, the word for the fates is identical with the word for the sexual organs. Novalis wrote that fate and soul are two names for the same principle. Man's oldest image of fate is the image of a woman; so let us begin where we may first find her.

# PART ONE

*Moira*

# 1

# *Fate and the Feminine*

---

*Das Ewig Weibliche zeiht uns inan.*

**Goethe**

She may be met in the old, wild, barren places: heath and treeless mountaintop, and the mouth of the cave. Not always one, she is sometimes three, emerging out of mist or clothed in it. Banquo, stumbling upon the apparition with Macbeth at his side, cries:

> *What are these,*
> *So withered and so wild in their attire,*
> *That look not like th' inhabitants o' the earth,*
> *And yet are on't? Live you? or are you aught*
> *That man may question? You seem to understand me,*
> *By each at once her choppy finger laying*
> *Upon her skinny lips: You should be women,*
> *And yet your beards forbid me to interpret*
> *That you are so.*
> *. . . You can look into the seeds of time,*
> *And say which grain will grow and which will not.*

The curtain opens upon the first act of Wagner's *Götterdämmerung* 'amid gloomy silence and stillness', and there, crouched upon the crag before the cave that is at once the womb and the tomb, the passage outward into life and downward into death, are the tall female forms swathed in dark veil-like drapery:

> *Let us be spinning and singing;*
> *But where, where tie the cord?*

Daughters of Nyx the goddess of Night, or Erda the Earth-mother, they are called Moirai or Erinyes or Norns or Graiai or Triple-faced Hekate, and they are three in form and aspect: the three lunar phases. The promising waxing crescent, the fertile full face and the sinister dark of the moon are in mythic image the three guises of woman: maiden, fruitful wife, old crone. Clotho weaves the thread, Lachesis measures it, and Atropos cuts it, and the gods themselves are bound by these three, for they were first out of inchoate Mother Night, before Zeus and Apollo brought the revelation of man's eternal and incorruptible spirit out of the sky.

> The spindle (of the universe) turns on the knees of Necessity; and on the upper surface of each circle is a siren, who goes round with them, hymning a single tone or note. The eight together form one harmony; and round about, at equal intervals, there is another band, three in number, each sitting upon her throne: these are the Fates, daughters of Necessity, who are clothed in white robes and have chaplets upon their heads.[8]

Plato's intricate geometric vision of the cosmos, with Necessity and the Fates enthroned at the centre governing all, is echoed by Aeschylos in *Prometheus Bound*:

> Chorus: Who guides the helm, then, of Necessity?
> Prometheus: Fates triple-formed, Erinyes unforgetting.
> Chorus: Is Zeus, then, weaker in his might than these?
> Prometheus: Not even He can escape the thing decreed.[9]

And the philosopher Heraclitus, in the *Cosmic Fragments*, declares with less than his usual ambiguity:

> Sun will not overstep his measures; if he does, the Erinyes, the minions of Justice, will find him out.[10]

Greek thought, as Russell states, is full of fate. It can, of course, be argued that these sentiments are the expressions of an archaic culture or world view which died two thousand years ago, prolonged through the medieval epoch because of ignorance of the natural universe, and that we know better now. In one sense this is true, but one of the more important and disturbing insights of depth psychology is the revelation that the mythic and undifferentiated consciousness of our ancestors, which animated the natural world with images of gods and *daimones*, does not belong to chronological history alone. It also belongs to the psyche of modern man, and represents a stratum which, although layered over by increasing consciousness and the hyper-rationality of the last two centuries, is as potent as it was two millennia or even ten millennia ago. Perhaps it is even more potent because its only voice now is the neglected dream-world of childhood, and the incubae and succubae of the night which are better forgotten in the clear light of morning. We understand, from our much more sophisticated knowledge of the physical universe, that the sun is not a 'he', and that it is not the snake-tressed screaming Erinyes who prevent it from overstepping its measures. At least, the ego understands: which is to say, that is only one way of looking at it.

The language of myth is still, as ever, the secret speech of the inarticulate human soul; and if one has learned to listen to this speech with the heart, then it is not surprising that Aeschylos and Plato and Heraclitus are eternal voices and not merely relics of a bygone and primitive era. Perhaps it is now more than ever important to hear these poetic visions of the orderly nature of the universe, because we have grown so dangerously far from them. The mythic perception of a universe governed by immutable moral as well as physical law is alive and well in the unconscious, and so too are the Erinyes, the 'minions of Justice'. Fate, in the writings of the Greeks, is portrayed in images which are psychologically relevant to us. Fate in the archaic imagination is, of course, that which writes the irrevocable law of the future: beginnings and endings which are the inevitable products of those beginnings. This implies an orderly pattern of growth, rather than random caprice or chance. It is only the limits of human consciousness which prevent us from perceiving the full implications of a beginning, so that we are unable to foresee the inescapable end. The second century gnostic text, the *Corpus Hermeticum*, phrases this with beautiful succinctness:

> And so these two, Fate and Necessity, are bound to one another mutually, to inseparable cohesion. The former of them, Heimarmenê, gives birth to the beginning of all things. Necessity compels the end of all depending from these principles. On these does Order follow, that is their warp and woof, and Time's arrangement for the perfection of all things. For there is naught without the interblend of Order.[11]

It is a very particular kind of fate with which we are dealing here, and it is not really concerned with predestination in the ordinary sense. This fate, which the Greeks called Moira, is the 'minion of justice': that which balances or avenges the overstepping of the laws of natural development. This fate punishes the transgressor of the limits set by Necessity.

> The Gods had their provinces by the impersonal appointment of Lachesis or Moira. The world, in fact, was from very early times regarded as the kingdom of Destiny and Law. Necessity and Justice – 'must' and 'ought' – meet together in this primary notion of Order – a notion which to Greek religious representation is ultimate and unexplained.[12]

In order to grasp the particular flavour of Moira, we must dispense with the popular conception of preordained events that have neither rhyme nor reason but which happen to us out of the blue. The famous 'you will meet a tall dark stranger' formula of the parlour teacup reader or the newspaper astrology column does not have very much bearing on the profound sense of a universal moral order which the Greeks understood as fate. This moral order is very different from the Judaeo-Christian sense of good and evil, too, for it does not concern itself with man's petty crimes against his fellows. To the Greek mind – and, perhaps, to some deep and forgotten stratum of our own – the worst sin that man could commit was not any found later in Christianity's catalogue of deadly vices. It was *hubris*, a word which suggests something including arrogance, vitality, nobility, heroic striving, lack of humility before the gods, and the inevitability of a tragic end.

> Before philosophy began, the Greeks had a theory or feeling about the universe, which may be called religious or ethical. According to this theory, every person and every thing has his or its appointed place and appointed function. This does not depend upon the fiat of Zeus, for Zeus himself is subject to the same kind of law as governs others. The theory is connected with the idea of fate or necessity. It applies emphatically to the heavenly bodies. But where there is vigour, there is a tendency to overstep just bounds; hence arises strife. Some kind of impersonal super-Olympian law punishes *hubris*, and restores the eternal order which the aggressor sought to violate.[13]

When an individual is afflicted with *hubris*, he has attempted to overstep the boundaries of the fate set for him (which is, implicitly, the fate portrayed by the positions of the heavenly bodies at birth, since the same impersonal law governs both microcosm and macrocosm). Thus he strives to become godlike; and even the gods are not permitted transgression of natural law. The core of Greek tragedy is the dilemma of *hubris*, which is both man's great gift and his great crime. For in pitting himself against his fated limits, he acts out an heroic destiny, yet by the very nature of this heroic attempt he is doomed by the Erinyes to retribution.

These themes of natural law and the transgression of fate-imposed limits could, and do, fill volumes of drama, poetry and fiction, not to mention philosophy. It would seem that we curious human creatures have always been preoccupied with the difficult question of our role in the cosmos: are we fated, or are we free? Or are we fated to attempt our freedom, only to fail? Is it better, like Oidipus or Prometheus, to strive to the utmost limits of which one is capable even if it invokes a tragic end, or is it wiser to live moderately, walk with humility before the gods, and die quietly in one's bed without ever having tasted either the glory or the terror of that inexcusable transgression? Obviously I could go on for several thousand pages on this theme, which is what most philosophers do. As I am not a philosopher, I shall instead focus my attention on the curious fact that the 'minions of justice', in whatever mythology or poetry one finds them, are always female.

Perhaps one of the reasons why there is an inevitable association between fate and the feminine is the inexorable experience of our mortal bodies. The womb that bears us, and the mother upon whom we first open our eyes, is in the beginning the entire world, and the sole arbiter of life and death. As a direct psychic experience, father is at best speculative, but mother is the primary and most absolute fact of life. Our bodies are at one with our mothers' bodies during the gestation that precedes any independent individuality. If we do not remember the intra-uterine state and the convolutions of the birth passage, our bodies do, and so does the unconscious psyche. Everything connected with the body therefore belongs to the world of the mother – our heredity, our experiences of physical pain and pleasure, and even our deaths. Just as we cannot remember that time when we did not exist, a mere ovum in the ovary of the mother, so we cannot conceive of the time when we will no longer exist, as though the place of emergence and the place of return are the same. Myth has always connected the feminine with the earth, with the flesh, and with the processes of birth and death. The body in which an individual lives out his allotted span comes from the body of the mother, and those characteristics and limitations ingrained in one's physical inheritance are experienced as fate: that which has been written in the hieroglyphs of the genetic code stretching back over aeons. The physical legacy of the ancestors is the fate of the body, and although cosmetic surgery may alter the shape of a nose or straighten a set of teeth, yet we are told that we will inherit our parents' diseases, their predisposition to longevity or the lack of it, their allergies, their appetites, their faces and their bones.

So fate is imaged as feminine because fate is experienced in the body, and the inherent predispositions of the body cannot be altered regardless of the consciousness that inhabits the flesh – just as Zeus cannot, ultimately, alter Moira. The instinctual drives of a species are also the province of Moira, because these too are inherent in flesh and although they are not unique to one family or another they are universal to the human family. It seems that we cannot overstep that in us which is nature, which belongs to the species – however much we repress it or feed it with culture. In this sense Freud, despite himself, emerges as one of the great affirmers of fate as instinct, because he was compelled to acknowledge the power of the instincts as a shaper of human destiny. The instinct to procreate, differentiated from what we call love, exists in every living species, and that it operates as a force of fate may be observed in the compulsive sexual encounters and their consequences which punctuate virtually every human life. It is no wonder that the Norsemen equated fate with the genitals. Likewise the aggressive instinct exists in us all, and the history of war, which erupts despite our best intentions, is testimony to the 'fatedness' of that instinct.

The soul too is portrayed as feminine, and Dante's great poetic edifice to his dead Beatrice stands as one of our most awesome testimonies of the power of the feminine to lead man out of mundane life and into the heights and depths of his inner being. Jung has a considerable amount to say about the soul as *anima*, the inner feminine which can lead a man both into the torments of hell and the ecstasies of heaven, igniting the fire of his creative individual life. Here fate seems to come from within, through the passions and the imagination and the incurable mystical longing. Whether an actual woman carries this role for a man in life or not, the soul will nevertheless drive him towards his fate. This soul sets limits, too: she will not permit him to fly too high into the remote realms of intellect and spirit, but will ensnare him through the body's passions or even the body's disease. In myth it is the goddesses, not the gods, who preside over disease and decay – as Kali does over smallpox – and in the end they restore even the most spiritualised of men to the dust from whence he came. These inadequately covered connections are perhaps some of the threads which link the mythic image of fate with the feminine. However we wish to understand this triple face of fate, she is imaged as an eternal presence, spinning the cycles of time, the birth gown, the nuptial veil, the shroud, the tissues of the body and the stones of the earth, the wheel of the heavens and the eternal passage of the planets through the eternal zodiacal round.

We meet the feminine face of fate also in the humble fairy tale of childhood. The word 'fairy' comes from the Latin *fata* or *fatum*, which in French eventually translated into *fée*, enchantment. So fate not only avenges the transgression of natural law; she also enchants. She spins a spell, weaves a web like the spider who is one of her most ancient symbols, transforms a prince into a frog and sends Briar-Rose into a hundred-year sleep.

A long time ago there were a King and Queen who said every day: 'Ah, if only we had a child!' but they never had one. But it happened that once when the Queen was bathing, a frog crept out of the water on to the land, and said to her: 'Your wish shall be fulfilled; before a year has gone by, you shall have a daughter.'

What the frog had said came true, and the Queen had a little girl who was so pretty that the King could not contain himself for joy, and ordered a great feast. He invited not only his kindred, friends and acquaintances, but also the Wise Women, in order that they might be kind and well-disposed toward the child. There were thirteen of them in his kingdom, but, as he had only twelve golden plates for them to eat out of, one of them had to be left at home.

The feast was held with all manner of splendour, and when it came to an end the Wise Women bestowed their magic gifts upon the baby: one gave her virtue, another beauty, a third riches, and so on with everything in the world that one can wish for.

When eleven of them had made their promises, suddenly the thirteenth came in. She wished to avenge herself for not having been invited, and without greeting, or even looking at anyone, she cried with a loud voice: 'The King's daughter shall in her fifteenth year prick herself with a spindle, and fall down dead.'[14]

Who then are these 'Wise Women' who are gracious and generous if acknowledged, yet vengeful and merciless if ignored? 'Little Briar-Rose' is a fairy tale, and therefore a tale about fate. I cannot resist associating those numbers twelve and thirteen with some very ancient things, for there are thirteen lunar months in a year and twelve solar; and the king in this fairy tale, being a king and not a queen, has opted to set the solar measure above the lunar. Thus his own problem with the feminine is visited upon his daughter in the form of a punishment, and the Erinyes, in the guise of the thirteenth Wise Woman, claim their retribution.

It seems to be fate, rather than accident, which accomplishes the strange transformations in fairy tales, and it is a fate which above all else resents being unrecognised or treated without humility. Nor is this resentment ever questioned on a moral basis within the tale. No character in the story ever says, 'But it isn't reasonable or humanitarian that the wicked fairy put a bad spell on Briar-Rose.' The spells, enchantments and curses pronounced by the fairies are part of the life portrayed by the tale; the hero or heroine may seek to transform or overcome them, but they are never ethically challenged, for they are not *wrong*. They are *natural*, i.e. they are the reflections of a natural law in operation. One never meets a wicked male fairy, either; occasionally an evil dwarf may be encountered, but he is almost always in the service of a witch, as the Kabiroi once served the Great Mother.

The Grimm Brothers collected their fairy tales primarily from Western Europe, and from the German-speaking peoples in particular. The Wise Women who make their appearances in these stories are close cousins of the Teutonic fates, the Norns, who dwell beside the spring of destiny beneath the roots of the World-Tree Yggdrasil, and water it each day to preserve its life. Well into medieval times, when the old Teutonic gods had been ousted by the power of the Church, the legend persisted all over north-western Europe of a group of supernatural women who could determine the destiny of a newborn child. These were called Parcae in Latin, and were generally three in number; and it was even a common custom for women to lay three places at table for them. Sometimes they were called the Norns.[15] The implication here is that something *other* than heredity plays a part in the shaping of a life. It is not mother, but Mother and her emissaries, who bestow gifts and curses on the newborn child.

So it is a kind of fate, these witches and fairies who give us an ugly beast who is potentially a gracious prince, or a sleeping princess concealed by a curtain of thorn bushes who needs time, and a kiss, to awaken; and we might be permitted to transform these things only if the magic formula is found to lift the spell. But the wisdom of fairy tales does not offer sociological reasons for how things got to be that way in the first place. It was a fairy, it is our fate. Idries Shah, in his commentary to his collection of *World Tales*, writes:

> So Fate and magic are always associated in traditional tales; and the kind of 'fairy' found in modern Western story-books, usually for children, is only one form of this concretised Fate.[16]

The procedures necessary to the overcoming or transformation of fairy tale spells and curses are highly ritualised affairs. The will alone can do nothing. Even where cleverness serves as the way through, it must be cleverness coupled with timing, and with assistance from strange and often magical sources. Frequently the help comes from those same dastardly fairies, or their minions, who cast the spell in the first place. Sometimes it is the heart which works the transformation, as the love of Beauty does for her Beast; sometimes it is the passage of time, as is the case with Briar-Rose. Sometimes the hero must travel hopelessly on a long and weary journey to the world's end, beset by darkness and despair, to find the miraculous object which will redeem the kingdom. But the resolution of the spell or curse depends upon faculties other than the rational ones, and no resolution can be accomplished without the secret collusion of the fairies, or the fates, themselves. This intimates another mystery about our feminine face of fate: While it may oppose neglect or punish transgression of natural law, yet it works in the hidden dark towards a relationship with the alienated will of man, before the rift becomes too great and the tragic end is invoked. The motifs of fairy tales are humbler and seemingly more mundane than the glorious pageants of the world's great mythic sagas. Yet in some ways they are more relevant to us because they are more accessible, unpruned and raw and closer to ordinary life. And they suggest, where myth does not, that a bridge might be built between man and Moira, if respect and effort and the appropriate propitiatory rites are offered.[17]

Numerous explorers of the untrodden pathways of the psyche have attempted to understand the curious fact that man, brushing close to the profound inner compulsions which represent his necessity, calls his fate by a feminine name and clothes it with a feminine face. Most important of these explorers is Jung, who wrote at great length in various of the volumes of the *Collected Works* about fate as he experienced it in his own life and in the lives of his patients. Sometimes he refers to instinct as compulsive, and seems to equate it with fate of a biological or natural kind: The flight of the wild gander is its fate, as is the bursting of the seed into seedling, sapling, leaf, flower, fruit. So too is the 'instinct' to individuate, for a man to become himself. Fate, nature and purpose are here one and the same. My fate is what I am, and what I am is also why I am and what happens to me.

Jung also wrote about the spectrum of instinct and archetype, the former as the determinant of physical or natural behaviour, the latter as the determinant of psychic perception and experience. Or, put another way, the archetypal image – such as the image of the three Fates themselves – is the psyche's experience or perception of instinctual patterning, embodied in figures which are numinous or godlike.

> The instincts form very close analogues to the archetypes – so close, in fact, that there is good reason for supposing that the archetypes are the unconscious images of the instincts themselves; in other words they are patterns of instinctive behaviour.[18]

Instinct and archetype are therefore two poles of the same dynamism. Instinct is embedded in, or is the living force expressing through, every movement of every cell in our physical bodies: the will of nature that governs the orderly and intelligent development and perpetuation of life. But the archetype, clothed in its archetypal image, is the psyche's experience of that instinct, the living force expressing through every movement of every fantasy and feeling and flight of the soul. This image that is older than the oldest of gods, the primordial face of Moira, is the psyche's perception of the immutable law inherent in life. We are allotted our share, and no more. Jung pressed close to a mystery which the intellect has great difficulty in containing: the unity of inner and outer, of body and psyche, of individual and world, of outer event and inner image. He speaks of the archetype on the one hand as an inherited mode of functioning, an inborn pattern of behaviour such as we may observe in all the kingdoms of nature. But it is something else as well.

> This aspect of the archetype is the biological one ... But the picture changes at once when looked at from the inside, that is, from within the realm of the subjective psyche. Here the archetype presents itself as numinous, that is, it appears as an *experience* of fundamental importance. Whenever it clothes itself in the appropriate symbols, which is not always the case, it puts the individual into a state of possessedness, the consequences of which may be incalculable.[19]

It is just these 'incalculable consequences' which appear to enter life as events fated from without. Here is the crippling illness, the strangely timed accident, the unexpected success, the compulsive love affair, the tiny mistake which results in the overturning of a life's entire structure. Yet it would seem that the source of this power is not without, or rather, not solely without; Moira also lies within.

One can read in Jung's work an increasingly formulated connection between fate and the unconscious.

> 'My fate' means a daemonic will to precisely that fate – a will not necessarily coincident with my own (the ego will). When it is opposed to the ego, it is difficult not to feel a certain 'power' in it, whether divine or infernal. The man who submits to his fate calls it the will of God; the man who puts up a hopeless and exhausting fight is more apt to see the devil in it.[20]

The connection is also increasingly drawn between this 'will not necessarily coincident with my own' and the Self, the central archetype of 'order' which stands at the core of individual development. Fate, nature, matter, world, body and unconscious: These are the linked threads which are woven on the loom of Moira, who rules the realm of flesh and substance and the instinctual drives of the unconscious psyche, of which the ego is a latter-day child.

The Indo-European root *mer, mor*, means 'to die'. From it also come Latin *mors*, Greek *moros* ('fate'), and possibly Moira, the goddess of fate. The Norns who sit under the world-ash are well-known personifications of fate, like Clotho, Lachesis and Atropos. With the Celts the conception of the Fates probably passed into that of the *matres* and *matronae*, who were considered divine by the Teutons . . . May it perhaps point back to the great primordial image of the mother, who was once our only world and later became the symbol of the whole world?[21]

On the symbolic representations of the Mother archetype, Jung writes:

All these symbols can have a positive, favourable meaning or a negative, evil meaning . . . An ambivalent aspect is seen in the goddesses of fate . . . Evil symbols are the witch, the dragon (or any devouring or entwining animal, such as a large fish or serpent), the grave, the sarcophagus, deep water, death, nightmares and bogies . . . The place of magic transformation and rebirth, together with the underworld and its inhabitants, are presided over by the Mother. On the negative side, the Mother archetype may connote anything secret, hidden, dark; the abyss, the world of the dead, anything that devours, seduces and poisons, that is terrifying and inescapable like fate.[22]

I have quoted Jung at length because I believe these passages are fundamental to an understanding of the feeling of fatality or blind compulsiveness which so often accompanies emotional entanglements and the events those eruptions or affects precipitate. Depression, apathy and illness are also perhaps masks the Erinyes wear. Needless to say, the relation to one's personal mother is undoubtedly significantly connected with one's feeling of choice and inner freedom in adult life, for the bigger and blacker mother is, the more we fear fate. But mother is also Mother, who here seems in part to embody the unconscious in its guise of 'origins' or 'womb' or 'unknown depths'. The argument is unanswerable as to whether man formulates his psychic images of goddess, serpent, sea, sarcophagus, because of his body's cloudy memory of the sea of the uterine waters, the serpentine umbilical cord which gives life yet may strangle, the tomblike darkness and constriction of the birth canal, the life-giving comfort of the milk-laden breast; or whether he experiences pleasure or terror, comfort or compulsion, longing or hatred, and exaggerates a 'merely' biological experience with godlike images because of the archetypal or numinous figure of which the biological experience is merely one concrete manifestation. This is, of course, the old spirit-matter problem: Which comes first, the chicken or the egg? Do we imagine gods because we must invest meaning into the vagaries and vicissitudes of physical life, or is physical life experienced as innately meaningful because there are gods? Of course, I cannot answer this question. Certainly Jung, in his efforts to formulate psychologically in these uncharted waters, tried to steer the middle course: Both are aspects of one reality, and cannot be separated. If instinct is one end of a spectrum which encompasses an archetypal or 'spiritual' level as well, then fate is not just the fate of the body, but of the soul too. The experience of the power and life-and-death-dealing nature of the personal mother is linked in the psyche with the numinosity of Moira, divine life-giver and death-dealer. That is perhaps all we can say: There is a link.

Two other writers are worth perusing on these themes. One is Johann Jakob Bachofen, a nineteenth-century Swiss jurist and social philosopher, whose poetic approach to myth is a refreshing counterpoint to the *Concise Oxford Dictionary*'s overwhelmingly subtle definition of myth as 'an untrue story'.

Thus the activity of nature, its skilful creation and formation, were symbolised in spinning, plaiting and weaving; but these labours were related in still other ways to the work of tellurian creation. In the weaving of two threads, could be seen the twofold power of nature, the interpenetration of the two sexual principles prerequisite to all generation. The sexual was still more manifest in the working of the loom. This physico-erotic relation also comprises the idea of *fatum* and destiny. The thread of death is woven into the web of which every tellurian organism consists. Death is the supreme natural law, the *fatum* of material life, to which the gods themselves bow, which they cannot claim to master. Thus the web of tellurian creation becomes the web of destiny, the thread becomes the carrier of human fate, Eileithyia, the midwife, the good spinstress, becomes the great Moira who is even older than Cronus himself. The loom, carrier of the supreme law of creation written in the stars, was assigned to the uranian deities in their sidereal nature; and finally, that human life and the entire cosmos were seen as a great web of destiny.[23]

Apart from his obsession with the word 'tellurian', Bachofen really ought not to be paraphrased, so I have quoted him at length. Here in his intricate web of connections we may begin to see where astrology itself – Heimarmenê, the 'planetary compulsion' or natural law of heaven and earth – is part and parcel of the celestial body of the Great Mother. This is a creation myth that predates Yahveh of the Old Testament, for here the original creative power

in the cosmos is the great goddess Moira. The harmonious ordering
of the celestial spheres is her design, and the awesomeness of this
tremendous image makes gentle mockery of our common conception of a fate that can be read in the tea-leaves. It is this image which
I feel we touch and invoke when we ponder the horoscopic wheel,
for this ancient image lies in ourselves. Perhaps it is in this way that
the body experiences itself as having an allotted span. The image of
Môira is not wiped away as the rational intellect climbs to its
impressive heights. Archaic though she is, she has simply receded
into the underworld from whence she issued long ago, where the
spinning and weaving continue unrecognised and uninterrupted,
only to emerge into the light of day as an experience of 'my fate'.

I will quote one further passage from Bachofen, because we will
find it relevant later.

> In the Ogygian dark depths of the earth they weave all life and
> send it upward into the sunlight; and in death everything
> returns to them. All life repays its debt to nature, that is, to
> matter. Thus the Erinyes, like the earth to which they belong, are
> rulers over death as well as life, for both are encompassed by
> material, tellurian being ... In their other aspect the friendly
> Eumenides are the terrible cruel goddesses, hostile to all earthly
> life. In this aspect they delight in catastrophe, blood and death,
> in this aspect they are accursed monsters, bloodthirsty and
> hideous, whom Zeus 'has ruled outcast'. In this aspect they mete
> out to man his merited reward.[24]

When the Erinyes enter the stage in the last play of Aeschylos'
*Oresteia*, they wear this darker face:

> *Our mission's bloodright, we're not sent*
> *ever to harm the innocent.*
>
> *Show us your hands. If they're not red*
> *you'll sleep soundly in your bed.*
>
> *Show us your hands. Left. Right.*
> *You'll live unhunted if they're white.*
>
> *Show us your hands. There's one we know*
> *whose hands are red and daren't show.*
>
> *With men like him whose hands are red*
> *we are the bloodgrudge of the dead.*
>
> *The she-god of life-lot gave us these powers,*
> *ours, ours, forever ours.*
>
> *When we came into being, they were marked out, the confines.*
> *We and the Olympians have no intimate contacts.*
> *Food's offered to either but not both together.*
> *We don't wear white robes, they don't wear black ones.*[25]

I have no doubt that we too, in this century, like Zeus, have ruled them outcast. Since the dawn of the Christian era our gods have only worn white robes. Yet these things remain as eternal images in the depths. I have seen them too often in the dreams of virtually every analysand with whom I have worked, to believe otherwise. In Aeschylos' tragedy they torment Orestes into madness for the slaughter of his mother, although Apollo himself demanded that slaughter; and Aeschylos gives us a very interesting insight into the manner in which this retributive aspect of fate, which punishes the transgressor against natural law, might be observed in modern man. Even a century after Aeschylos, men no longer believed in those dreadful ladies with talons for feet and snakes for hair and vultures' wings and the voices of screech owls. The Western world left them behind long ago. But a visit to the local psychiatric hospital can effectively reintroduce us to their current dis-embodied manifestation. I would suggest that the individual, man or woman, who transgresses too brutally the natural law of his own being may perhaps pay the price in what we now choose to call 'mental illness'. There is nothing fair about this, for such transgressions are generally made unconsciously, and one cannot blame the individual for that of which he is ignorant. But the Erinyes are not fair, either, in the way they deal with Orestes; he has no choice, and is compelled to commit his murder by the god Apollo, yet he must pay the price nevertheless. I personally find it sometimes more creative to consider the Erinyes, guardians of natural law, than to revert to terms which I do not fully under-stand, such as schizophrenia, but no doubt anyone who pays attention to the Erinyes today is a schizophrenic. Be that as it may, I feel that it is of immense value to consider, when working as an astrologer, what natural laws are represented by the horoscope, and in what sphere a 'transgression' is being perpetrated, know-ingly or unknowingly; and whether and how that transgression might be redressed, lest the Erinyes hound that individual from within or from without as a 'bad fate'.

The third writer who has contributed major insights into this mysterious complex of fate-unconscious-mother-world is Erich Neumann. In *The Great Mother*, he writes:

> The life feeling of every ego consciousness that feels small in relation to the powers is dominated by the preponderance of the Great Round that encompasses all change. This archetype may be experienced outwardly as world or nature, or inwardly as fate and the unconscious . . . Thus the terrible aspect of the Feminine always includes the uroboric snake woman, the woman with the phallus, the unity of childbearing and begetting, of life and

death ... In Greece the Gorgon as Artemis–Hekate is also the mistress of the night road, of fate, and of the world of the dead.[26]

We might remember at this point Macbeth's bearded witches, who are phallic women: the feminine which contains its own procreative or generative power. These women create and destroy life according to their own laws, not those of a spouse or consort or king. Mother Night or the goddess Necessity gives birth to the Moirai and the Erinyes parthenogenically, that is, without the benefit of male seed. The passage quoted above contains something I feel to be extremely important for the astrologer to consider: that the individual who is most terrified of fate, and is most threatened by what he experiences as its darker, more destructive soul- and life-destroying propensities, is the individual in whom the sense of ego, the sense of 'myself', is weakest. This carries a certain implication for the student of astrology himself, for many of us learn our art for this very reason, and we share this problem with our clients. An awareness of this shared problem can be immensely creative, but an unconsciousness of it plays right into the hands of the Erinyes, and reinforces the fear of fate.

When the Erinyes sing that 'food's offered to either but not both together', they articulate a common dilemma: Either we live in terror of fate because we have not yet found any sense of genuine individuality, or we repudiate the very idea of fate for precisely the same reason. Thus the astrologer not only colludes with his client; he colludes with the virulent skeptic as well, who is afraid of the same thing. Like the secret identity of the psychiatrist with his mad patient, the problem of fate binds us not only to those who fear the retributive aspect of life, but also to those who reject anything but the autonomy of rational consciousness. Although I am not clear about the ramifications of this, I suspect it is part of the reason why astrology so often falls foul of the collective, why the passionate accumulation of statistics has become necessary, and why the individual astrologer so often feels persecuted by 'normal' people. Now I am not suggesting that a firm sense of personal identity makes fate go away. I would not be so stupid as to suggest that; nor, I suppose, would Neumann. But the coming to terms with 'my fate' in a creative, rather than a fear-stricken way, perhaps rests largely upon the individual's sense of being an individual.

Neumann goes on to write:

> The male remains inferior to, and at the mercy of, the Feminine that confronts him as a power of destiny ... The symbol of Odin hanging on the tree of fate is typical for this phase in which the king-hero was characterised merely by an acceptance of fate ... This fate may appear as a maternal old woman, presiding over

the past and the future; or as a young, fascinating form, as the soul.[27]

The author is at pains to point out that when he refers to the 'masculine ego' he does not mean men, but rather the centre of consciousness in both men and women, which is 'masculine' in the sense that it is dynamic, motivated towards differentiation. In short, it is sunlike in contrast to the diffuse and shadowed lunar depths of the unconscious. I am quite certain that the sun, astrologically considered, is a point in the horoscope which is perhaps more accessible to men in general, because it represents a masculine motivation which is goal-oriented; but the sun means the same thing in a woman's horoscope, and is still the symbol of differentiated ego-consciousness in both sexes. In this sense Neumann is not in the least concerned with 'sexist' issues, and it would be absurd to interpret him as such. He is speaking about a dilemma which both men and women face: the sense of impotence and powerlessness which we all experience in the face of those compelling eruptions of the psyche which come upon us like fate. On the other hand, it is quite irresistible to see implied in this passage one of the archetypal roots of that terror which so often creeps into male–female relationships, where the woman seems, by projection or perhaps in truth, to be the carrier of fate for the man; who, angry and frightened of 'the powers' over which he has no control, attempts, like Zeus, to rule her value outcast.

> The primordial mystery of weaving and spinning has also been experienced in projection upon the Great Mother who weaves the web of life and spins the thread of fate, regardless whether she appears as one Great Spinstress or, as so frequently, in a lunar triad. It is not by accident that we speak of the body's tissues, for the tissue woven by the Feminine in the cosmos and in the uterus of woman is life and destiny. And astrology, the study of a destiny governed by the stars, teaches that both begin at once, at the temporal moment of birth.[28]

The problem of the frightening power which the ego experiences as a property of the unconscious is, as I have said, not a sexist issue. It seems to be a human issue, and I have met as many women running in fear of their own depths as I have met men dominated by the same fear. Yet perhaps fear is the beginning of wisdom, as the Old Testament teaches us, because this fear of the power of fate is at least an acknowledgement. I am therefore inclined to question the value of telling a client who has come for a horoscope reading that a birth chart 'merely' suggests potentials which he may overcome or master as he chooses. I am not suggesting that we should regress to an archaic level, where the ego reverts back to the primitive terror and passive acceptance of fate which characterises both ancient cultures and the modern infant. We have struggled for several millennia to be able to do something more than that. But *hubris*, in turn, does not eradicate the archetypal image of fate that dwells in the depths of both the client's psyche and the astrologer's. Nor will such an attitude spare the client his fate.

The feminine fate which we have been exploring is, in a sense, the psychic parallel to the genetic patterns inherited from the family line. Or, in a broader sense, it is the archetypal image for the most primitive instincts that coil within us. This is a fate of allotment, of boundaries or natural limits which cannot be crossed. It is the circle beyond which the individual may not pass in his lifetime, despite whatever limitless potentials he may sense in himself, because generations have built that circle stone by stone. Fate and heredity therefore belong together, and the family is one of the great vessels of fate. We shall see more of this later. Moira when viewed in this light is one of the innate urges within the psyche, both individual and collective, and her role is to uphold justice and law in the natural realm of the instincts. Since our basic urges are represented in astrological symbolism by the planets, it is reasonable to suppose that the ancient retributive principle of Moira is portrayed in the horoscope by one of the planets, as well as by whatever signs and houses are connected with that planet. It is also reasonable to suppose that, since we have ruled fate outcast and pretend these days that she does not exist, we would likewise be ignorant of this dimension of her significator within astrology. In a sense, we might also consider that the image which presides over retributive fate is the image of an instinct for setting pro-scribed boundaries within oneself. Moira is the guardian of mother-right within the individual, and she is as necessary to the equilibrium of psyche and body as other, more extroverted and more transcendant urges.

I have found it very productive, when interpreting astrological symbols, to be at times unashamedly non-rational, and to work with the images which such symbols invoke, rather than concep-tualising or reducing to keywords those ancient and sacred figures which for so many centuries were perceived and experienced as gods. We still do not really know what they are. It is more acceptable now, for the purposes of collective evaluation and comprehension, to call them drives, or motivations, or archetypal urges. But I feel that the astrologer, like the analyst, can benefit from Jung's method of amplification to get closer to the essence of astrology's language. We might go even further and envision the experience of a planet as an encounter with a deity, a *numen*, rather than thinking in terms of motivations or urges. For are these things not the same? Perhaps it is not always wise to appropriate everything within as though it were 'mine', i.e. the property of the ego. Our innate urges are ultimately no more subject to dissection and rational control than Plato's *daimones*, which are given to each individual at birth and shape his character for a lifetime. It might be important to acknowledge, particularly when we are dealing with such things as fate, that there are aspects to our 'motivations' which are beyond ourselves, transpersonal, autonomous, even infernal or divine.

Meeting a planet in a sign and house is like entering a temple and meeting the manifestation of an unknown god. We may meet that deity as a concrete 'outer' experience, or *via* another person who is the mask through which the god's face peeps; through the body; through an ideology or intellectual vision; through creative work; as a compelling emotion. Often several of these are experienced together, and it becomes difficult to see the unity between what is happening in life outside and what is happening within. Nevertheless, the planet bridges the abyss between 'outer' and 'inner' and provides us with our meaningful connection, for the gods live in both worlds at once. To meet the personification of all that we have so far explored, distilled into the image of Moira, is to meet that which is compulsive and primordial. It is a confrontation with death and dismemberment, for Moira breaks the pride and will of the ego into little pieces. Because she is unchangeable, we ourselves are changed. She is stronger than the ego's desires and determination, stronger than the intellect's reason, stronger than duty and principles and good intentions; stronger even than one's faith. Plato envisioned her enthroned at the centre of the universe, with the cosmic spindle laid across her knees and her daughters, who are differentiated reflections of her own face, guarding the limits of natural law and punishing the transgressor with deep suffering. Moira's wisdom is to be found in despair and depression, powerlessness and death. Her secret is the thing which guides and supports the individual when he can no longer support himself, and which holds him fast to his own unique pattern of development.

> The innate urge to go below appearances to the 'invisible connection' and hidden constitution leads to the world interior to whatever is given. The autochthonous urge of the psyche, its native desire to understand psychologically, would seem akin to what Freud calls the death drive and what Plato presented as the desire for Hades . . . It works through destruction, the dissolv-

ing, decomposing, detaching and disintegrating processes necessary both to alchemical psychologising and to modern psychoanalysing.[29]

This description by James Hillman suggests that the thing which guards the circumscribed boundaries of nature also seeks knowledge of its own spinning: my fate seeking unfoldment of itself. This goddess of fate as 'minion of justice' is, it seems to me, most emphatically represented in astrology's planetary pantheon. Within the horoscope, I would say that what the Greeks knew as the Erinyes, the retributive face of Moira, we would call Pluto.

# 2

## Fate and Pluto

---

*Hades, death-god holds assize*
*on a man's deeds when he dies*

*death-god Hades won't forget*
*the deed of blood and the blood-debt.*

**Aeschylos**

If we wish to approach astrological symbols through amplification with other images and symbols rather than through concrete definition, then it is now in order to look at myth's offerings on the subject of Hades–Pluto, and on the theme of underworld rulers in general. The Greek lord of the underworld was originally known as Hades; the epithet 'Pluto', which means 'riches', is a later appellation which the Romans then used to describe him. James Hillman is illuminating about this change of names:

> Pluto, especially, is important to recognise in our euphemistic references to the unconscious as the giver of wholeness, a storehouse of abundant riches, a place not of fixation in torment, but a place, if propitiated rightly, that offers fertile plenty. Euphemism is a way of covering anxiety. In antiquity, Pluto ('riches') was said as a euphemistic name to cover the frightening depths of Hades.[30]

In much the same spirit, the Erinyes, the terrible avengers of the Mother, were called Eumenides, 'the kindly ladies'.

We astrologers also use euphemisms. 'Transformation' is a resonant word, redolent of numinosity and deep psychic purpose, and most encouraging to the client who has an approaching transit or progresssion involving Pluto. But it is, unfortunately, the sort of word which we like to call upon when the meaning of a planet is vague or merely intellectual, or when the experience foreshadowed in the horoscope augurs crisis and suffering for the client. It is not at all easy to watch another person undergoing necessary suffering. For one thing, our compassion cries out that it should not be necessary, for our feeling values are not often in sympathy with Pluto's ruthless law. For another, we see ourselves mirrored in that other's incipient disintegration or loss. Pluto is particularly difficult to work with unless one has some trust in fate; but how can one trust it, unless one has spent time in despair, darkness, rage and powerlessness, and has found out what supports life when the ego can no longer make its accustomed choices? I have never found anything cheerful or funny about the transits and progressions of Pluto, no matter how psychologically know-ledgeable the client is. Insight cannot spare suffering, although it can prevent blind suffering. Obviously a great deal depends upon the depth of the individual, and also on the condition of Pluto in the birth horoscope. If there is no insight, the transit or progression might hopefully pass without too much fuss registering on consciousness, if the person is sufficiently obtuse. Often there is a great release of energy which accompanies the movements of Pluto: things which have lain long dormant or died early in life are resuscitated and burst forth. Often it is the passions that form this eruption, and such a release of life can be immensely creative. But this kind of experience, although hindsight perceives its value, is frequently painful, frustrating, confusing, disorienting and frightening, and rarely passes without some kind of sacrifice or loss, willing or unwilling, or some kind of confrontation with what is most brutal and 'unfair' in life. Even the stout-hearted Scorpionic types, who are ruled by Pluto and therefore have some innate inkling of the goddess Necessity and the inevitability of endings and beginnings built upon the corpses of dismembered pasts, are not immune to the natural ego fear of that which is overpowering and cannot be placated by will or reason. Death and passion leave irrevocable changes in their wake, whether on a corporeal or a psychic level, and what has died cannot be put back again.

> Sometimes it may appear that the decree of fate allots some positive good to men; but from the totality of its functions there can be no doubt that its character is not positive but negative. It sets a boundary to limit duration, catastrophe to limit pros-perity, death to limit life. Catastrophe, cessation, limitation, all forms of 'so far and no farther', are forms of death. And death is itself the prime meaning of fate. Whenever the name of Moira is uttered, one's first thought is of death, and it is in the inevitabi-lity of death that the idea of Moira is doubtless rooted.[31]

Although one may know that life will return again invigorated in a new form, richer and more vital, still the thing which has reached its appointed end suffers in the dying, and will not itself ever return to life. Anguish, fear and deep grief often accompany these deaths, and whatever 'part' of us undergoes such a transition, we experience it inwardly as the whole of us if we are conscious of it at all, identifying with it and its suffering: the inevitable accompaniment of any deep change in the psyche. The mind speaks encouragingly of transformation and renewal, yet something still asks: What if there is no renewal? How can I believe hopefully in something which I cannot see and do not understand? What have I done to earn such a fate: where does my fault lie? What if the blank emptiness simply goes on and on? Any experience of deep depression carries with it the firm sense that nothing will ever change. It might therefore be appropriate, along with the encouraging statements of future potential inherent in movements of Pluto, for us to recognise also the mark of an initiation into the irrevocable, and a need for genuine reverencing of depression and despair. Empathy and respect for another's process of dying, literal or metaphorical, is a necessity with Pluto, although this is not usually the gift of the more Uranian astrological counsellor. Death makes everyone uncomfortable; even with the medical profession the business of telling someone, or his family, that he is dying is a fraught affair, and it is not surprising that many doctors cannot cope very well with such a confrontation. This is no less the case on an inner level, for the odour of internal death touches off one's own fears.

Myth tells us that Hades is the lord of depths, the god of invisibles. He is brother to Zeus, therefore ranking equally with the ruler of heaven. He is the dark but equally potent twin of the all-merciful sky-father. In fact he has the greater status, since his law is unchangeable while that of Zeus can be gainsaid. Hades was given virtually no altars or temples where he might be worshipped; one simply recognised that death is everywhere in life, and each living thing contains within its mortal body its own altar, its own inevitable seed of death that is born simultaneously with physical life. Hades cannot be seen by men in the upper world, for he wears a helmet which renders him invisible. This is the hidden connection, the secret fate, the 'world interior to what is given'. We cannot perceive Hades, but he is everywhere at all times, inherent in the beginning of every thought, feeling, inspiration, relationship or creative act, as its preordained and inevitable end.

The male figure of Hades as underworld lord is a relatively late formulation. The primordial chaos from which life emerges and to which it returns belonged in the beginning to the Great Mother, or the goddess Nyx. All the denizens of the depths – Doom, Old Age, Death, Murder, Incontinence, Sleep, Dreams, Discord, Nemesis, the Erinyes and the Moirai, the Gorgons and the Lamia – spring from her womb. Another of her faces, ancient triple-headed Hekate, goddess of fate, magic, childbirth, witchcraft and the eternal round of the fluctuating moon, is overthrown by a more patriarchal culture and remains only in the figure of Cerberus, the tricephalic dog who guards the further shore of Styx. The earliest images of the goddess are those of a phallic Mother, a self-fertilising deity who bears the Moirai without male seed. In the end this goddess vanishes into her own depths, and the phallic power is represented as a male deity: Hades. Although he is a god, he is the dark son, servant and executor of the unseen Mother. In Sumerian myth, which predates classical Greek myth by many centuries, it is the great goddess Ereshkigal who rules the realm of the dead. Her name means 'Lady of the Great Place Below', and it is her image above all which I feel can help us to amplify the planet Pluto in order to better understand it. Ereshkigal has male gatekeepers and minions, and a male vizier called Namtar whose name means 'fate'; but these are her servants, who do her bidding.

For the following material on Ereshkigal I am indebted to Sylvia Brinton Perera's book, *Descent to the Goddess*, which offers a good deal of fascinating insight into this archaic goddess of the underworld. This material is relevant enough to confirm my feeling that in the astrological Pluto we are confronting something feminine, primordial and matriarchal. When the goddess Inanna, the Sumerian Queen of Heaven (the early form of Ishtar, Aphrodite and Venus), descends into her sister Ereshkigal's realm, the Lady of the Great Place Below treats her bright and beautiful sibling according to the accepted laws and rites for anyone entering that kingdom: Inanna is brought 'naked and bowed low', while pieces of her clothing and regalia are ritually stripped at each of the underworld's seven gates. That rite of entry is a process I have observed on many occasions concurrent with the transits and progressions of Pluto – the gradual loss of everything which one has previously used to define one's identity, and the 'bowing low' of humiliation, humility and eventual acceptance of something greater and more powerful than oneself. Ms Perera writes from her experience as a Jungian analyst, focusing on the initiatory journey of women who have suffered a dissociation from their own feminine centre. I am writing here also from my experience as an analyst, and likewise from my experience as an astrologer; and I have observed that this descent, with its loss of landmarks and props and attachments, seems to occur in both men and women under the transits and progressions of Pluto.

There is much of the Gorgon and the Black Demeter about her: in her power and terror, the leeches on her head, her terrible life-freezing eyes, and her intimate connection to nonbeing and to fate ... Ereshkigal's domain, when we are in it, seems unbounded, irrational, primordial, and totally uncaring, even destructive of the individual. It contains an energy we begin to know through the study of black holes and the disintegration of elements, as well as through the processes of fermentation, cancer, decay, and lower brain activities that regulate peristalsis, menstruation, pregnancy and other forms of bodily life to which we must submit. It is the destructive–transformative side of the cosmic will. Ereshkigal is like Kali, who through time and suffering 'pitilessly grinds down all distinctions in her indiscriminating fires' – and yet heaves forth new life ... Unreverenced, Ereshkigal's forces are felt as depression and an abysmal agony of helplessness and futility – unacceptable desire and transformative–destructive energy, unacceptable autonomy (the need for separateness and self-assertion) split off, turned in, and devouring the individual's sense of willed potency and value.[32]

I cannot think of any better description than this of the feeling–tone of Pluto.

I would now like to return to Hades, the rampant phallus of the Mother. Whenever myth portrays his entry into the upper world, he is shown persistently acting out one scenario: rape. This suggests something further about the experience of our planet Pluto. Its intrusion into consciousness feels like a violation, and we, like Persephone, the maiden of the myth, are powerless to resist. Where Pluto is encountered, there is often a sense of violent penetration, unwished for yet unavoidable, and in some way necessary to the balance and development of the individual – although one might not see it that way at the time. Ereshkigal, too, is a rapist of a kind to those whose faces are turned against her:

To matriarchal consciousness she represents the continuum in which different states are simply experienced as transformations of one energy. To the patriarchy death becomes a rape of life, a violence to be feared and controlled as much as possible with distance and moral order.[33]

The myth of Persephone's rape is also a relevant one in terms of understanding Pluto, for it is her virginal innocence which draws the desire of the dark lord of the underworld. Persephone is a springtime goddess, the not-yet-violated face of her mother Demeter, mistress of the harvest. She is the archetypal maiden, the fertile ground not yet sowed with seed; her emblem is the waxing crescent of the moon, which promises future fulfilment yet who is eternally in a state of potential. She is bound to her earth-goddess mother, to the five senses and the world of form. She also reflects the bright surface of life that promises future joys through the eyes of uncontaminated youth. Thus she is an image of a particular kind of human perception and outlook, full of possibilities but still unformed.

The unimpeachable bond between this pair of mother and daughter goddesses suggests something of the divine unity between mother and infant, the wonderfully innocent and pro-tected world of babyhood where there is as yet no separation, no aloneness, no conflict and no fear. This is the world before the Fall, before the cord is cut, and there is no death because there is not yet individual life. Parts of us may remain in this uroboric embrace well into later life, for Persephone is not just an image of chronological youth, nor of literal maidenhood. As we become increasingly sophisticated in external knowledge and accomplishments, so we increasingly forget those rites and rituals which facilitate the separation of the youth from the mother at puberty. The wisdom of the primitive tribe with its elaborate ceremonies to announce the advent of adult life and responsibility has been lost to us in the West for a long time. So we remain, ageing Persephones hopefully picking flowers, until some critical transit or progression of Pluto comes along. Persephone, although her name – oddly – means 'bringer of destruction', is untouched by life. Her abduction is cruel, yet governed by necessity; and she herself secretly invokes it, by picking the strange death-flower which Hades has planted in the meadow for her fascination. It is the plucking of the flower which heralds the opening of the earth beneath her and the arrival of the dark lord in his chariot drawn by black horses.

The issue of the flower seems such a small thing, yet I believe the process of Pluto works in this way. One can see, in retrospect, the small thing by which the gates are opened. Persephone colludes with her fate, even in her voluntary eating of the pomegranate, the fruit of the underworld, which is a symbol of fertility because of its multitude of seeds. She is an image of that aspect of the individual which, however terrified, still seeks the union which is a rape and an annihilation. In the Orphic mysteries Persephone bears her lord a child in the underworld, just as Ereshkigal in the Sumerian myth bears a child after she has destroyed her sister Inanna and hung her, dead and rotting, on a peg. Persephone's child is Dionysos, the underworld counterpart to the bright redeemer from heaven whom Christianity has formulated in the figure of Jesus Christ. Both are born of virgins, by divine fathers. But Dionysos, who redeems through the ecstasy of eroticism, is a much more ambiguous child. It seems that the myth expresses something about the fertility of any encounter with Pluto; it is full of fruit. An enriched sense of the vitality and sensuality of the body is certainly one frequent facet of Pluto's fruit. There may also be other children who spring from this experience of ravishment: a new outlook which is deeper and broader, a new discovery of inner resources, a more profound sense of one's own purpose and autonomy. All these things must be paid for, through the rupturing of the psychic hymen which protects us through our innocence.

These are frightening depths indeed. It is not surprising that we use euphemisms, nor is it surprising that Scorpio, Pluto's sign, has always had such a dubious reputation. It can be somewhat tricky finding the right wording for the client, let alone for oneself, as Pluto slowly moves towards a lengthy conjunction of sun, moon, ascendant, Venus, indicating that the halls of Hades will be thrown open to receive the unwilling guest at his own unconscious request.

Next, there is the question of what is down there. Myth offers a remarkably precise geographical portrait of the Great Place Below. Ereshkigal's realm possesses seven gates, and a peg upon which to hang the visitor. Landscapes such as these are inner landscapes. They belong to a 'place' to which we 'go' *via* moods, feelings, dreams and fantasies. We might first consider the entrances. These are usually caves and fissures, cracks in the earth and the mouths of volcanoes. Through the holes and fissures of consciousness, through one's uncontrollable emotional eruptions and anxieties and compulsive fantasies and phobias where the ego is swamped by something 'other', one tumbles down, increasingly denuded of pretences at each gate. This is known in the analytic world as *abaissement du niveau mental*, the lowering of the threshold of consciousness which occurs through dreams, fantasies, delirium, affect, even slips of the tongue and inexplicable omissions and amnesia. Pluto's favourite entrances, I believe, are the volcanoes, where some apparently insignificant event triggers a great gush of alien and often terrifying rage, jealousy, hatred, fear or murderousness, that reveals that we are not quite so civilised as we seem. The untamed creature which bursts forth is, like Ereshkigal, full of vindictive spite over wounds we did not even know we had. The volcano is often located wherever Pluto is found in the horoscope.

The Greeks, like the Sumerians, envisioned an elaborate rite of entry into the underworld; but their mythic scenario is different. The souls of the dead must cross the river Styx, ferried by the ancient boatman Charon who demands his coin in exchange.

Here, as at Ereshkigal's gates, something must be given, something of value that is one's own possession. Money is one of our images of value, worth, ego-identity and ego-property. That which we hoard, it seems, must be given away during the descent – the regalia and clothing with which we define ourselves and our accustomed sense of worth, our unimpeachable self-esteem, our high price. The feeling of worthlessness, of falseness and disgust at one's own emptiness, of disillusionment at the vacuity of the trappings which used to mean so much, is something I have heard repeatedly expressed by those undergoing Pluto transits and progressions. This is not limited to the so-called 'bad' aspects, but applies to the trines and sextiles as well. It would seem that acceptance of this sense of being stripped and humbled and empty is a necessary prerequisite for the acolyte at the gates.

Following is given the dream of a man who came for a horoscope reading while transiting Pluto was making a long conjunction with his natal sun in Libra placed in the tenth house. He was a successful publisher of scientific textbooks, with an international company which provided him with a considerable income and a respected place in society. With this persona he had always identified, for it gave him his sense of achievement and importance. That it also provided him with a means of fulfilling his mother's dream of a successful and brilliant son had not yet occurred to him as a primary motive in his choice of career, although many astrologers might view with suspicion the unity of identity between mother and child which the tenth house sun suggests. He told me of his dream during the course of the chart interpretation, because I had referred to some of the images and feelings connected with Pluto that I have mentioned above: death, deadness, depression, isolation and entombment.

> I dream that I have died and am now awaiting some kind of rebirth or resurrection. Instead of a head, there is a fleshless skull between my shoulders. It is horrible to feel this skull. I am dead, rotten, unacceptable. In a room to the right, all the books and journals I have published are displayed like trophies in glass-topped cases. Some friends come to invite me to dinner, but they are appalled by the sight of my skull. I try to explain that I am dead but that another life awaits me. But they only show disgust and leave me alone. In another room my funeral is in progress. My mother is weeping wildly over my coffin. She cannot see me, or the part of me that remains. For her I am totally dead.

This dream does not really require interpretation. It describes itself quite adequately as an inner image of the experience of Pluto and as a profound comment on the meaning of this period in my client's life. Although he found the dream uncomfortable and disturbing, nevertheless he said that it had left him with a sense of hope during a period of great depression and despair. In short, the dream conveyed to him – and he was not undergoing any form of psychotherapy, but gleaned the insights himself – a feeling that his depression was *necessary* in some way which he could not fathom. The image of the skull is not merely an image of death; it appears with great frequency in alchemical symbolism and is that part of the human being which does not decay as the body does. It is the *caput mortuum*, the dead head which is left after the purifying fire has burned away the dross. In his external life, the situation which seemed to be triggering my client's depression was his decision to sell his company and put his energy into farming a large tract of land which he had bought in Australia. He had expected to be joyous and enthusiastic about this venture, but became depressed and anxious instead. This unwelcome mood, which came upon him like a rape, made no sense until he began to understand that such a decision meant the death of the power of the mother in his life, with all the inner implications such a separation entails.

> When ghosts descend to Tartaros, the main entrance to which lies in a grove of black poplars beside the Ocean stream, each is supplied by pious relatives with a coin laid under the tongue of its corpse. They are thus able to pay Charon, the miser who ferries them in a crazy boat across the Styx. This hateful river bounds Tartaros on the western side, and has for its tributaries Acheron, Phlegethon, Cocytus, Aornis and Lethe ... A three-headed or, some say, fifty-headed dog named Cerberus, guards the opposite shore of Styx, ready to devour living intruders or ghostly fugitives.[34]

Black poplars, as Robert Graves points out in a later passage, are sacred to the death goddess. The names of these underworld rivers are evocative and also explicit: Styx, which means 'hated', contains waters which are deadly poison, yet which can also confer immortality; Acheron means 'stream of woe'; Cocytus means 'wailing'; Aornis means 'birdless', Lethe 'forgetfulness', and Phlegethon 'burning'. All these images are redolent of the feeling of the astrological Pluto.

The poison of Styx is like the acid of deep-buried resentment, which is a typically Plutonian manifestation. This unforgiving bitterness connects us with the figures of the unforgiving Erinyes, the minions of justice. There is certainly a poison of vengeance in Pluto, the raving ghost of Klytaemnestra who whips the Erinyes into pursuit of her son Orestes. No compassion is here, and no healing; only black, unending hate. We know from our traditional astrological texts that Scorpios are good haters, and do not forget slights and injuries. Nor does Pluto. The experience of the planet often plunges an individual into his own previously unrecognised potential for deep, abiding, unrelenting hatred. Moira as nature does not forget an insult, nor ignore violation. The spirit of the Christian myth, with its figure of mercy and compassion, is the direct antithesis of Ereshkigal, who is the black heart of nature who cannot forget her suffering. Tolkien embodies this poisonous heart of nature in the figure of Old Man Willow in *The Lord of the Rings*:

> Tom's words laid bare the hearts of trees and their thoughts, which were often dark and strange, and filled with a hatred of things that go free upon the earth, gnawing, biting, breaking, hacking, burning: destroyers and usurpers ... But none were more dangerous than the Great Willow: his heart was rotten, but his strength was green; and he was cunning, and a master of winds, and his song and thought ran through the woods on both sides of the river. His grey thirsty spirit drew power out of the earth and spread like fine root-threads in the ground, and invisible twig-fingers in the air, till it had under its dominion nearly all the trees of the Forest from the Hedge to the Downs.[35]

The river of hatred and poison that encircles the underworld is like Old Man Willow at the heart of the forest, and it is not always conscious in the individual. More often we do not know of its existence, and think of ourselves as decent people who can forgive another his transgression; but we suffer instead from mysterious ailments and emotional disturbances, and subtly sabotage our partners, parents, friends, children and ourselves without fully recognising that somewhere we may feel them as 'destroyers and usurpers' who must be made to pay.

Perhaps here too a ritual is appropriate, and myth certainly offers us one. Ereshkigal's hatred is softened by Enki's mourners, two small creatures that the fire god Enki fashions out of dirt from beneath his fingernails. These little mourners descend to the underworld and mourn alongside Ereshkigal while she suffers and vents spite. They recognise her grief, listen to it, empathise; they do not judge her, nor call her ugly or wicked or hateful, nor try to get her to 'do' anything about it. They represent a quality which I feel to be essential in dealing with Pluto, which many psychotherapists call an ability to 'be with' someone. It is the providing of a container for the poisonous waters without the necessity of 'changing' things. The Erinyes too are placated, in the myth of Orestes, by this same gentle recognition. Athene listens to them, does not argue or condemn, but offers them an altar and honourable worship in exchange for Orestes' life.

The discovery of one's own poisonousness is one of the less attractive aspects of a confrontation with Pluto. Enki's mourners, and Athene, provide us with a mythic model of a kind of self-recognition that steers between harsh self-judgment and sodden self-pity. This entails a recognition of the necessity or inevitability of hate, through empathy with the injured thing. From Ereshkigal's point of view, life is thoroughly rotten. She has been raped and thrown outcast into the underworld, and everyone, particularly her free and joyous sister Inanna, must suffer for it. The little mourners neither agree nor disagree, neither do they blame nor rationalise. They simply listen, and accept her grief and bitterness. Pluto's rage, when it erupts from within or approaches from without, is terrifying, perhaps more so when it is encountered within because one becomes afraid of destroying those things one loves. For this reason the rage is repressed, and gnaws away in the underworld of the psyche. The mourners in the Sumerian myth offer an alternative both to repression and to the acting out of spite in externally destructive ways which ultimately do not heal the wound. To put oneself in the stance of the mourners is more difffficult than it seems, however, for even if one is able to face this vindictive and destructive instinct in oneself, it is irresistible to try to 'transform' it. The ego is fond of wanting to change everything it finds in the psyche according to its own values and standards, and Pluto's poison provokes a predictable response: Now that I have seen my ugliness, I find it despicable, and must cure it. But Enki's mourners are not concerned with curing Ereshkigal. They can see both sides of the issue: the necessity of rescuing Inanna, and the legitimacy of Ereshkigal's rage. The fire god Enki, who fashions these creatures, is the Sumerian counterpart to Loge in Teutonic myth and Hermes in Greek. He is on no one's side, but has the scope to see the entire pattern, and can love all the protagonists because they are part of the grand theatre. I feel that it is questionable whether Ereshkigal is truly 'curable' anyway. Certainly she is not likely to respond to the demands of the ego, but only when she herself wishes it, if she ever does at all.

Lethe is the river of blessed forgetfulness, in which the souls of the dead are submerged before they return to the world for another incarnation. Those who believe in reincarnation as a concrete philosophy may take this as the blessing of Pluto: that we mercifully do not remember our fates when we are born. Or we may take it more symbolically; Not only do we mercifully forget what has been written for us at birth, but we also do not remember very well what it was like down in the Great Place Below when a Pluto experience has passed. Having managed to emerge from the underworld, like Orpheus we are commanded by some inner voice not to look back, and when the transit or progression is over we cheerfully announce how very productive, enriching, and growth-inspiring it all was. We do not recall this place, for if we did, we would lose our courage for the future and the next turn of the Great Round. Lethe is the gift of Pluto; it is an image of psychic resilience, and the capacity to forget pain. It is not that Pluto does not offer riches. I think it is that we, of necessity, must forget later the price we paid for them, lest we be poisoned by Styx and never forgive life. I have also found that experiences of Pluto often coincide with a remembering of what has been forgotten, a rediscovery of grief and rage and hatred that has been numbed and driven under-ground by the ego for the sake of its survival.

The psychotherapist is familiar with the miasma of hatred and injured rage, both of parents and of self, which erupts when the unconscious abuses, rejections and humiliations of childhood emerge into the light of day. Where Pluto is found in the horo-scope, there is often a forgetting, a necessary repression, and a liability to sudden recollection and the volcanic eruption of poison on an object who may be no more than a catalyst. There seems to be a relationship between Pluto and what Freud meant by repression (which is not performed purposively by a determined act of consciousness, but occurs as an instinct of survival, through a kind of unconscious censorship). These are the things which we must forget for a time, in order to live.

> There are 'repressed' wishes in the mind . . . In saying that there are such wishes I am not making a historical statement to the effect that they once existed and were later abolished. The theory of repression, which is essential to the study of the psychoneu-roses, asserts that these repressed wishes *still* exist – though there is a simultaneous inhibition that holds them down.[36]

One may make some educated guesses as to the nature of the repressed 'wishes' of Pluto, as well as the very good reasons for the 'simultaneous inhibition' which blocks their entry into conscious life. Freud, who had Scorpio on the ascendant, formulated them very well in his concept of the *id*. They are too violent, too vengeful, too bloodthirsty, too primitive and too hot for the average individ-ual to feel much comfort or safety in their intrusion. Along with 'wishes' may be included memories, experiences of great emotional intensity which are forgotten along with their objects. Thus large slices of childhood fall beneath the censor's knife – those slices which reveal the savage face of the young animal struggling for self-gratification and survival.

Along with the poison, potentials too can be repressed, lest invoking the one might unleash the other. The child who is subjected to mother's possessive rage or father's freezing disinterest each time he sits down to play with clay or paint, and commits the outrage of withdrawing into his own individual psyche, will grow up to become the 'uncreative' adult who for some unfathomable reason cannot even attempt to bring pencil to paper, but would rather live in the grey twilight of unlived and unexpressed life, envious of all those can express themselves better, rather than risk the recall of the price paid for those initial creative efforts. The child who draws his parents' jealousy down upon him because he is too clever, too beautiful, too much himself, will grow up into the adult who sabotages himself each time he is threatened with success in life, rather than risk the terrifying competition of parents without whose support he cannot live. One does not wish to disturb the blankness, the forgetting, even if it means that nascent growth or the development of a talent is sacrificed. This is better and easier than confronting the violent feelings of one's parents, one's siblings, and oneself. Later, often under transits and progressions involving Pluto, we remember what we have forgotten, the fear and the pain and the longing and the rage. Then a return is required, to the same place, through the same depression and grief and self-disgust. But the journey later is a spiral rather than a circle, because it is the child within the adult who remembers, and the adult can, perhaps, help the child to tolerate and contain the pain.

Tartaros is sometimes the name given in myth to the whole of Hades' realm. More often it refers to a kind of sub-realm, a borough as it were, which is close in nature to the medieval concept of Hell. It is from Tartaros that the brood of Mother Night issues to torment living men and avenge family curses and sins against the matriarchal line. In Tartaros the souls of the wicked are fixed in unchanging torment throughout eternity. Yet it is a radically different world from the Christian Hell. Torment in Tartaros is portrayed through images of frustrated desire, rather than random sadistic torture. The sins are different, too. If one travels with Dante through the circles of the *Inferno*, one meets a predictable catalogue of medieval sinners: the adulterer, the usurer, the sodomite, the blasphemer. One also meets some familiar pagan faces, for Dante's Christianity was not all that Christian: Fortuna or Fate with her Wheel, and Cerberus, and three-headed Dis (Hades). But Dante's underworld is a reflection of the Middle Ages' obsession with the damnableness of worldliness and sexuality.

In Tartaros things are different. Men's sins against men, particularly the carnal ones, are not worthy of the name. *Hubris*, on the other hand, earns the just reward. The mythic figures imprisoned in Tartaros are men and women who have overstepped their boundaries, transgressed natural law, insulted Moira and defied the gods. They have lusted after a goddess, mocked a deity, or boasted that they were greater than the Olympians. Pluto's law is not that of social and legal constructs, nor concern for the civilised behaviour of the group. A rapist himself, he does not judge the sexual urges of others. He is not Saturn, and is unconcerned with what men do to men in the world of form. He is not a patriarch, but rather, a matriarch. So Sisyphus rolls his rock eternally up the hill and must eternally watch it roll down to the bottom again, for ever and ever, because he has betrayed Zeus' divine secrets. Tantalos reaches eternally for the water and the fruit which are eternally just out of reach, because he has insulted and mocked the gods. Ixion spins eternally on his fiery wheel, because he has attempted to rape Hera, the queen of the gods. All these images are formulations of frustration, endless despair, burning from within (like the river Phlegethon), humiliation and *nemesis* as a reward for inflation and pride.

> To be put on the wheel in punishment (as Ixion) is to be put into an archetypal place, tied to the turns of fortune, the turns of the moon and fate, and the endless repetitions of coming eternally back to the same experience without release . . . Rings are closed circles and the circle closes on us whether in the marriage band, the crowning laurel, or the wreath on the grave.[37]

The irrevocable turn of fate, whether toward gain or loss, is characteristic of Pluto. So too is the experience of frustrated desire. That which we want more than we have ever wanted anything before, but which is the one thing we cannot have, or can only have through a great sacrifice or the death of some cherished part of ourselves: all this is typical of Pluto. Naturally the sexual arena is one of the most obvious places where this kind of experience occurs. So is the arena of power and position. Power and sexuality, power or loss of power through sexuality, are themes which are intrinsic to Pluto. This seems to be what the Norsemen knew when they duplicated that word for fate and genitals. I do not think it is always clear whether the power lies in one's own hands or another's, for the powerful one and the one who submits to him are aspects of the same figure, just as Persephone belongs to Hades. The craving and greed and desire emanate from both, and wherever Pluto is found implicated in a situation where one must submit to another who is more powerful, it is probably valuable to remember that when this planet is involved one is never blameless. Confronted with Pluto, we meet our abhorrent compulsions, our unsatisfiable passions: the impossible repetitive pattern of struggling with something only to meet it again and again. Tartaros describes in mythic language human darkness, greed and pathology. It encompasses illness, cruelty, burning, obsession, icy coldness and perpetual thirst. These tormented figures tell us something else about Pluto: He reminds us over and over of the incurable thing, the place of the unhealable wound, the psychopathic side of the personality, the Gorgon's twisted outraged face. It is the thing that never gets better. One of alchemy's images for this greedy, desirous, violent, unredeemable side of nature is the wolf, which must be placed in the alembic with the king. The wolf destroys the king, and is then itself burned over a slow fire until nothing is left but ash. If these things do truly change, they do so only through fire; and the king, who embodies the ruling values and belief systems of the ego, must die first. Pluto is therefore a great and divine balancer of *hubris*. Without him man would believe himself to be God, and would in the end destroy himself: a situation that grows increasingly likely with the passage of time. Faced with Pluto as the infant is faced with the mother, one experiences the unpassable circle of the limitations of the soul, the limitations of fate. These are not the worldly limits of Saturn, but the deepest savouring of one's vulnerability and mortality.

> The circular states of repetitiveness, turning and turning in the gyres of our own conditions, forces us to recognise that these conditions are our very essence and that the soul's circular motion cannot be distinguished from blind fate.[38]

Pluto, it would seem, governs that which cannot or will not change. This is a particularly painful issue in an age of self-help therapies and a growing belief that one can make oneself into anything, given the right techniques, books or spiritual leaders. Humility before the gods is an antique virtue, promoted not only by the Bible but by the Greeks as well. 'Nothing in excess' – not even self-perfection – was carved before the door to Apollo's temple at Delphi, along with 'Know thyself'. These were the chief requirements the gods asked of men. But it is just this issue that Pluto forces us to confront. It is ironic, and paradoxical, that the genuine acceptance of the unchangeable is often one of the keys for true and deep change within the psyche. But this little piece of irony, which would have suited double-tongued Apollo, does not appear to be learnable in any school but life's fires. Therefore it remains a secret, not because nobody will tell it, but because nobody will believe it, unless he has survived the fire.

Thus Pluto, as a symbol of retributive fate, rules the place where the will no longer avails. Therapies and meditations and diets and encounters do not reach here; and the decision is no longer whether I should do right or wrong, but whether I should sacrifice my left arm or my right. This god is an image of our bondage, our humbling and our rape. I feel that the issue of *hubris*, the offence against circumscribed limits and against fate, lies at the core of the meaning of the planet. Echoes of this theme are also to be found in myth in connection with the sign of Scorpio, for the scorpion in earliest Sumerian and Babylonian and Egyptian myth, as well as in Greek, is invariably the creature sent by an angry deity to punish somebody's *hubris*.

Since its first expressions in Greek and Latin, the Scorpion myth has been connected with the disaster that struck Orion, the great hunter whose *hubris* led him to offend the gods. The Scorpion attacked and killed him, emerging suddenly from the bowels of the earth – from beyond the world to which Orion, the one attacked, belongs. As far as I know there is no astrological text in which this element of sudden destructive aggressiveness does not appear as an essential characteristic of Scorpio. Astrological symbolism expresses this by assigning Scorpio to Ares (Mars), the fiery and aggressive god, lord of violent and dramatic catastrophes; thus immediately giving Scorpio the central significance of a breakdown in equilibrium by the irruption, from the shadows, of an unknown assailant ... Scorpio, the sign of the creature rising from chthonic moistures, is in fact characterised more and more clearly as the sign of dross, of primitive nature, chaotic, discordant, damnable, and revealing itself by sudden and dangerous irruptions.[39]

This attractive description seems to coincide with what we have seen of Pluto. It is almost superfluous to add that, in the Orion myth, the giant scorpion which destroys the great hunter for his *hubris* is sent by Artemis–Hekate, 'mistress of the night road, of fate, and of the world of the dead'.

# 3

# *The Astrological Pluto*

*Nature loves to hide.*

**Heraclitus**

I would now like to look more carefully at Pluto in the horoscope. Somewhere within the birth chart will be found the entry into the Great Place Below, 'in a grove of black poplars beside the Ocean stream'. In one form or another, each of us has met or will meet the feminine image of retributive fate which punishes *hubris* and redresses family sin. Pluto moves very slowly through the zodiac, taking a leisurely 248 years to complete his round. Because so many people are born with Pluto in a given sign, he will stamp an entire generation with a particular compulsion, a particular kind of obsession, and a particular form of recompense.

It is difficult to talk about generations in any way other than in generalisations, because some individuals seem to embody the *zeitgeist* or spirit of their time, and others do not appear to express it at all. It is even more difficult for me to elaborate from living examples about Pluto's generational themes, because I have never met anyone living with Pluto in Aries, Taurus, Scorpio (at least, not yet), Sagittarius, Capricorn, Aquarius or Pisces. My direct experience of Pluto is limited to those with him placed in Gemini, Cancer, Leo, Virgo and Libra, and, at the time of writing, those with Pluto in Virgo and Libra have not yet reached maturity and exhibited the potential of the planetary placement in full. That is not even half the zodiac. I can only attempt to capture a feeling of the ways in which an entire group will flock to one banner, respond in similar fashion to external and internal challenges and pressures, express the same deep subterranean needs and visions, by an observation of cultural trends, fads and fashions, and, most importantly, the collective fate which such a group must fulfil. I do not wish to attempt this through theory alone, and shall therefore limit my description to those groups of which I have the most experience. It cannot be accidental, any more than any astrological coincidence is accidental, that the generation born with Pluto in Cancer, spanning the years between 1914 and 1939, have passed through two wars and the complete destruction and transformation of everything that meant home, nation, family and clan. With this group, the sacrosanct inviolability of family and country as the justification of everything came to an end. These are the people whose children became drop-outs and runaways, and who suffered the overturning of the family unit as primary law. Perhaps obsessive overvaluing or idealising is what, in part, constitutes the *hubris* that invokes the wrath of the denizens of the Great Place Below. To offer anything such blind obedience, be it family, nation or even relationship 'for the sake of the children', is a form of excess. As John Cooper Powys once wrote, the Devil is any God who begins to exact obedience.

I have certainly seen this intense and blind commitment to family and country with great frequency among those who have Pluto in Cancer, and also the tragic bewilderment and disillusionment when families and countries were torn apart during their lifetimes. It is as though this group is marked as the battleground where old values and ethics have been burned in the purifying fire, freeing the collective of a little more blindness and unconsciousness in the sphere of family and roots. What heritage and blood and duty to nation meant to these people is something those born later will perhaps never comprehend, because those values belong to a generation which has suffered greatly and been transformed out of this destruction. If there is such a thing as a lesson to be learned, then perhaps it is about the dangers of interpreting our obsessions on a concrete level. But I am more inclined to see it not as a lesson, but as a necessary fate, so that something might be freed or deepened within the collective: a bridge over which the next generation may walk. Whatever 'home' or 'family' or 'nation' means, those with Pluto in Cancer have been coerced by the events of their times into either understanding these terms differently and more deeply, or living with a canker of bitterness and longing for a past which can never exist again.

Nor do I feel it to be accidental that the generation born with Pluto in Leo – the so-called 'me' generation, spanning the years between 1939 and 1958 – have made a god of individualism and the right for individual expression and destiny, while they have grown up in a world where political ideologies lean increasingly towards the group, the collective, rather than the individual. In this world technology has become so sophisticated that individual gifts are being rendered superfluous because a computer can do it better; and a shrinking world economy and disappearing planetary resources have put the tools and means for such individual expression out of many people's reach. During the lifetimes of those with Pluto in Leo, half the nations of the world have espoused a form of socialism or communism which frustrates with utter ruthlessness the Leonine conviction of the sanctity of individual differences and individual worth.

Generations too have fates, are afflicted with *hubris* and over-attachment, are raped by necessity, are recompensed with eternally frustrated desire; and serve as pointers to the rest of us about the laws of allotment and mortality. I believe that Pluto represents a force in the collective psyche as well as in the individual: an impersonal order, a Moira that reminds us perpetually of the limits of nature which we transgress at our peril. Uranus and Neptune too are great collective *daimones*, dynamic 'gods' within the body of the collective, that give birth to streams of new ideas and streams of new religious visions. Pluto is to me the symbol of Moira within the human soul, sounding the drumbeat of recurrent historical cycles and heralding the end of expansion in the sphere of a particular sign: the finishing of a chapter begun 248 years before. It marks the ordained end, the advent of fate.

Although each person is bound to the fate of his generation, he meets Pluto primarily through a particular house in the horoscope, and through the planet's aspects to more personal planets. So the grim law of nature confronts us through very personal domains of life, and appears as 'my fate'. An astrological house is like a stage upon which the actors play. The scenic backdrop is skilfully painted to represent 'money', 'home', 'friends', 'partners', 'health', 'children'. I have written elsewhere of the multilevelled meanings of the different houses, so I will not elaborate them here. The sets, within a basic theme, can take on different colorations. But it is an interior painter who designs these backdrops which are the houses; they, like the geography of Hades, are really inner landscapes which we project upon outer objects. The subjective manner in which we perceive the outer world is coloured by the signs and planets tenanting a particular astrological house, and each person sees a different vision. Thus, with Pluto placed in a given house of the horoscope, some sphere of life becomes the place where one meets the retributive justice connected with ancestral sin, the limitations of nature visited congenitally upon the individual through what appears to be 'my problem', 'my incurable wound'.

Meeting Pluto in the seventh house, for example, means meeting Moira through the partner, the 'other'. The circumstances may vary enormously. Divorce is common, as are love triangles, painful rejections, experiences of dominance and submission

within relationship, complete sacrifice of relationship due to con-
victions or circumstances, death of the partner, confrontation with
madness in another, marriage to one who brings a great emotional
or concrete burden, sexual problems and power battles. All these
enactments are typical of Pluto in the seventh. The variations are
enormous, but the theme is single: relationships are the place
where one is subjected to something far more powerful and
inevitable than one's own will and choices. Sometimes the individual may elect to work with others who are caught in Pluto's web,
and this is another way of meeting him in the sphere of relationship. Here we find the doctor, the psychoanalyst, the psychiatrist
and even the politician, who must deal with a world no less mad
than that which his medical counterparts must meet. There is as
much compulsion in these 'chosen' professions as there is in the
more fraught world of the Plutonian love affair; but one has the
illusion that it is a 'job'.

The intrinsic meaning in all these variations seems to be the
same: there is nothing one can do, save to trust to fate. It is this
feeling of powerlessness which seems to pervade any encounter
with Pluto, and here the powerlessness is experienced in relation
to another. Either the partner imposes a fate about which the
individual can do nothing, or the individual himself is made in a
certain way and cannot, however hard he tries, alter his needs or
patterns in relationship. All personal encounters are turbulent,
and the deeper the meeting, the less it is within one's control. Thus
the deepest changes take place through these encounters. I have
noticed that many seventh house Pluto people form the habit of
avoiding deep relationship, lest fate be invoked and those
emotions which belong to Ereshkigal's domain be unleashed. Yet
fate will not be cheated, and seems to come upon the person
sooner or later, no matter how strenuous the avoidance. I have also
seen many situations where the primordial emotions of the underworld are projected upon the partner; this is an extremely popular
way of experiencing Pluto in the seventh house. It is the partner
who is vicious, violent, treacherous, overpowering, castrating,
devouring, paralysing, manipulating, cruel. I do not need to
emphasise the degree to which one's own unconscious behaviour
can draw such primitive emotions from even the most civilised of
companions. Naturally it is not really the other who is all these
things, but rather, a deity, a primeval power in life which one
perceives *via* the other. This is the power that forces us to accept
the uncivilised face of nature as a necessary ingredient of experience. And this terrifying other would never enter one's life disguised as partner, lover, friend, or 'public' (for that is another stage
backdrop belonging to the seventh house) if that deeper Other did

not abide somewhere within, the invisible enchanter and rapist of the soul. The partner may leave, betray, cheat, restrict, die, or present painful and often insurmountable difficulties. But it is through that partner that an archetypal power is encountered. We are free in every place but this, where we meet Necessity.

I do not wish here to elaborate house by house the manifestations of Pluto in the horoscope. It is not my intention to provide a 'cookbook' for the interpretation of this planet, but rather, to focus on the feeling and meaning of Pluto in a more general way. The reader can no doubt work the rest out for himself. The confrontations with power and powerlessness, loss and frustrated desire, and the potential healing that arises from the acceptance of Necessity are characteristic of Pluto in every house. Some houses, such as the seventh and tenth, tend to present us with people and objects, while others, such as the eighth and twelfth, tend to present us with inner objects and emotional states – the noncorporeal actors in the play. But the encounter is the same. The goddess Necessity, whose Greek name is Ananke and whom we met in Plato's cosmic vision, is another image worth exploring for amplification of the astrological meaning of Pluto. Necessity in Greek myth is always spoken of and experienced in what James Hillman calls 'pathologised modes'.

> Pathologised experiences are often connected directly with Ananke (Necessity) ... At core, necessity means a physically oppressive tie of servitude to an inescapable power. The family relationships and the ties we have in our personal worlds are ways in which we experience the force of necessity. Our attempts to be free of personal binds are attempts at escaping from the tight circle of Ananke.[40]

A quality of chronic, repetitious suffering or restriction, which circles back again and again just when one thinks oneself free of it, is something I associate with Pluto's effect on the spheres of life represented by the astrological houses. There is never any final solution, but rather, a spiralling which takes the individual deeper and deeper into himself. This might also be described as a feeling of being fettered to something, just as Ananke in Plato's vision 'fetters' or compels the heavens to circle according to her law. For example, I have known many people with Pluto in the ninth house who feel fettered in this fashion to what they understand as God, the 'oppressive tie of servitude' to an aspiration which may be anything but beatific. The seventh house I have already touched upon, and the sense of being fettered to a partner is characteristic of this placement of Pluto. I have also seen Pluto work through the fourth house in this way, binding the individual to his heredity and his family myths in such a way that these cannot be psychologised away or forgotten even if thousands of miles are placed between the individual and his family of origin. In the tenth, Pluto often wears the face of the personal mother, while behind that fleshly face is the Great Mother who binds her child with unbreakable cords that often lie within the body itself. The tenth is also the house of 'the world', and this too is the body of the mother; and it not only fetters the individual to positions of responsibility within it, but punishes ferociously any transgression beyond the appointed limits. I am thinking here, among others, of Richard Nixon, who has Pluto in the tenth house in Gemini and who, I suspect, is no more corrupt than most American politicians. But it was his fate to get caught, and to become the public scapegoat of an outraged 'world'. Nor was Watergate the first taste of Ananke that Richard Nixon experienced; his political career is criss-crossed with the repetitive tracks of failure just at the moment of achievement, and subsequent resurrection, and subsequent failure. As Aeschylos' Prometheus complains:

> *Oh woe is me!*
> *I groan for the present sorrow,*
> *I groan for the sorrow to come, I groan*
> *questioning when there shall come a time*
> *when He shall ordain a limit to my sufferings.*
> *What am I saying? I have known all before,*
> *all that shall be, and clearly known; to me,*
> *nothing that hurts shall come with a new face.*
> *So I must bear, as lightly as I can,*
> *the destiny that fate has given me;*
> *for I know well against Necessity,*
> *against its strength, no one can fight and win.*[41]

Not even a god, says Plato, can cope with Necessity.

When I have discussed the various placements of Pluto in the horoscope with my clients, I am struck by the fact that the usually productive psychological approach of trying to bring the unconscious elements into consciousness does not, in the end, make all that much difference. It may, however, interiorise the dilemma, so that Pluto is not met so blindly through outer events and people. Also, digging deep to unearth the background experiences which form the web of bondage to the past may release a profound sense of 'rightness' or meaningfulness. But the fate does not go away. That is not to say that psychological insight is irrelevant with Pluto. It seems to be quite the reverse, for it is just this compulsion to find the roots of a problem which introduces the individual to the reality of Moira. But once the bottom of the barrel has been scraped, and the personal outrages, hates, hurts, poisons, separations and griefs of childhood have been contacted and expressed and even forgiven, there is still the barrel itself, with the already written shape of the individual's bondage. If one is fettered to God with Pluto in the ninth house, then one remains fettered to God. It is just that the overlay of personal father and mother, childhood church, inculcated moral teachings *et al.* may no longer cloak the stark and purposeful nature of the chain.

What, then, does one tell the astrological client, or oneself? Athene soothes the ire of the Erinyes by granting them an honoured place in the divine hierarchy: an altar and respectful worship. She overturns the dictum that 'food's offered to either but not both together'. Enki's little mourners soften the hideous suffering and rage of Ereshkigal by listening, by being receptive, by waiting without judgement. Whether there is more that we can do is another issue. There is a history of effort not only to avoid or escape fate in the stream of Neoplatonic philosophy, but also to transform it; or, perhaps more accurately, to transform the individual's relationship with it. We shall examine this more deeply in due course. But much of the work of transformation, if that is indeed what it is, also lies in the mythic formula of honouring, listening, accepting and waiting. I do not believe there is any other way to learn respect for one's inner laws. Any more cerebral or wilful methods do not seem to reach the halls of the Great Place Below, and may anger further an already furious power. From what I have seen of Pluto, I would find it funny if it were not often so painful, when there is talk of 'mastering' or 'transcending' this planet.

I would now like to explore in greater detail some of the aspects of Pluto. I must repeat that I am not attempting to provide a 'cookbook' of interpretations, so not every aspect of Pluto with every other planet is mentioned. Rather, I am seeking further insights into the issues of individual fate which the planet seems to reflect. An astrological aspect between two planets – no matter whether it is a conjunction, square, opposition, sextile, trine, sesquiquadrate or quintile – makes those planets lifelong bedfellows. Or, put another way, the gods, or motivations, which the planets represent, cannot be separated, but blend together and fight together on both internal and external levels until death parts them and the individual. So we must consider what sort of bedfellow Pluto makes, and what he does, in bed or out, to those planets which he aspects. Hades and Ereshkigal, of course, provide us with some very succinct imagery, for we have already seen how they are prone to greet visitors to their domain. Rape, death, suffering, bondage and resurrection are their themes.

The aspects of Pluto to the sun, moon and ascendant, especially the conjunctions, squares and oppositions, seem to turn up with great regularity in the charts of those into whose lives fate has noticeably intruded. Whether this is an external fate – illness, congenital defect, death, encounter with armies or alien governments – or an internal one – madness, in oneself or a close relation, nightmare, obsessions and compulsions – these are not the people with whom one can talk for long about 'blueprints'. Although the circumstances vary, there is usually a sense of confrontation with something irrevocable, which *must* be met and acknowledged. There may be some choice about where this meeting takes place; I have worked with many sun–Pluto people, for example, who have elected to confront the diseased and the mad and the primordial through the medium of the helping professions, or through politics. But this is perhaps a mature decision (if it is truly a decision at all), made in the second half of life, to deal with something which the individual has had to accept as his necessity. These are often the very people who have suffered from Pluto earlier in life, and who have managed to fight through to the healing aspects of the destruction. But if the Plutonian realm is shut out by an individual in whom the planet figures strongly, then it seems that trouble ensues. I have seen sun and moon contacts with Pluto in a good many cases of psychotic breakdown, where the enemy is not corporeal but lies in the violent depths of the person himself.

Sometimes sun–Pluto and moon–Pluto are lived out through a violent or disturbed husband or wife, an ill mother, a problematic child, a sterile womb, an inherited illness. Pluto, when he is manifesting in this form, is not much fun. But I believe these differing faces of bondage are purposeful, in the sense that Moira is purposeful. Something is taken away, so that another thing might grow in its place. The seeds of this bondage generally lie several generations back, so that the sins of the parents are well and truly visited upon the children; and it becomes the children's task to attempt some kind of understanding. If one does not take up this challenge, then there is only a black despair and a rage against life. I have come to feel that when Pluto is strongly marked in the birth horoscope, the individual is faced with the task of redeeming or carrying something for the larger collective, which only he is able or equipped to do; or, put another way, he is faced with the expiation of ancestral sin, and must become a bridge over which something ancient and undifferentiated and outcast may walk to find a welcome in consciousness. Collective fate here intrudes upon the life of the individual, and may demand great effort and sacrifice. There is also redemption in this kind of encounter with fate, for the 'ability to do gladly that which I must do' relates the ego to an eternal and interconnected cosmos. This transformative effect of Pluto seems to offer a renewal of life through seeing life with different eyes. It is in its own way a profoundly religious experience, although it has little to do with any heavenly spirit and is much more related to the support of the instincts and of the feminine pole of life. Paracelsus, the sixteenth-century physician and astrologer, put it this way:

> What then is happiness but compliance with the order of nature through knowledge of nature? What is unhappiness but opposition to the order of nature? He who walks in light is not unhappy, nor is he who walks in darkness unhappy. Both are right. Both do well, each in his own way. He who does not fall complies with the order. But he who falls has transgressed against it. [42]

Sometimes compliance with the order of nature may be beyond an individual's resources. There are extremes of loneliness, isolation and despair – embodied in Inanna's encounter with Ereshkigal – which, if the individual does not possess the ego strength to contain them, may become unbearable in the end. In some theoretical and ideal universe, one 'ought' perhaps to work with Pluto in an enlightened way. But we do not live in such a world, and I am not convinced that this is the 'fault' of 'society' so much as it is one of the sadder aspects of the patchy progress of human evolution. The man whose dream I have given below is one of those individuals whose story has made me query the speciousness with which astrology is sometimes inclined to treat the difficult aspects of Pluto in the birth horoscope. I have also reproduced his chart, although no time of birth was available and we must therefore be content with a 'flat' chart without an ascendant or house cusps. Following is the dream:

> I am in a rock quarry. In front of me is a bottomless pool of black water which goes down into the rocks. Something is floating to the surface from very far below. I am rooted to the rocks with terror and cannot move. I wake up before the thing surfaces, but I have seen it through the water. It is an Egyptian mummy, wrapped in bandages.

I cannot think of a more Plutonian image than this ancient mummy rising to the surface from immeasurable depths of black water. But the dreamer possessed no resources with which to cope with fate's demand that something be confronted. The dream, and something of the background of the young man, whom I will call Timothy S., were given to me by the psychiatrist by whom he was being treated. Not long after he had this dream, he committed

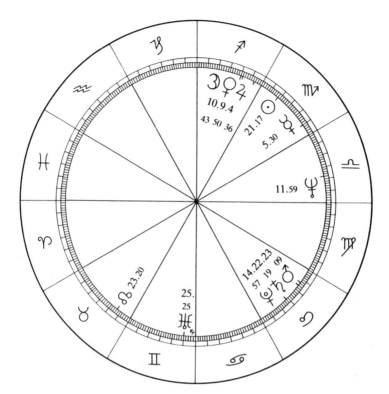

DIAGRAM 1. Birth horoscope of Timothy S.

b. 14 November 1947
no birth time given; planetary placements are for noon GMT

d. 27 June 1981
transits for date of death: (midnight GMT)

☉ 5 ♋ 16
☊ 3 ♌ 08
☽ 29 ♈ 14
☿ 27 ♊ 54
♀ 26 ♋ 33
♂ 15 ♊ 21
♃ 1 ♎ 47
♄ 3 ♎ 24
♅ 26 ♏ 39 ℞
♆ 23 ♐ 09 ℞
♇ 21 ♎ 32 ℞

suicide. His death was not one of those attention-claiming attempts gone wrong, but was a carefully organised and impeccably executed self-sentence. He did not speak of his suicidal feelings to the psychiatrist; he simply left his last session with a remark about the next appointment, waited for a day or two, and then hooked up the exhaust pipe of his car in an isolated wood, so that he might asphyxiate himself without interruption.

Timothy had a long history of psychiatric illness, and had received repeated treatment for depressive breakdown. He experienced a constant inner torment of isolation and self-loathing. He had never formed any close relationship with either man or woman; he fought constantly the incipient feelings of need and warmth toward his psychiatrist. His dwelling in the underworld was intolerable to him, but the pain of forming a relationship seemed even more intolerable. Evidently he elected to remove himself once and for all from his anguish. He left behind a document, the life history required by many psychiatric establishments, which is an eloquent statement of his Plutonian world, and of which I am grateful to be able to reproduce an extract.

> I feel at this moment hopelessly alone, scared, trapped and depressed . . . I realise this is a crisis but the new cannot be born and the old will not die, so where do we go from here? Another sleepless and tormented night; I don't know what it is that has reaped such havoc inside me but whatever is there has always been. It has always tormented me in one way or another, like a worm eating away at an apple. It has almost completely consumed me and I can go no further. What can the doctors do?

The anti-psychiatry sentiments prevalent among many astrologers and counsellors might be invoked here, but I do not feel they would apply to this situation. The man who worked with Timothy knew very well the necessity of dealing with his young patient with a greater degree of depth and humanity than is usually found within psychiatric establishments, and I do not feel, from my own conclusions about both the case history and the chart, that any blame rests here. Perhaps some deeper form of psychotherapy earlier in life might have helped. But by the time Timothy began to work with my colleague, he had already experienced years of drug therapy and ECT; and I feel that something in him had already given up from the repeated failures of the doctors to help him. Such methods, although they have their place, are not necessarily the best way to deal with Pluto. In what way Timothy had inherited a collective or family fate I do not know. Certainly many deep parental and sexual problems emerged during the few sessions before his death. But a mummy is an ancient thing, and belongs to a past which predates the failings of the personal parents. I have found that a strongly Plutonian disposition often inclines the individual towards identifying with those 'ancestral sins' that lie deep in the collective unconscious, with the result that he may provoke, or believe that he deserves, retributive justice.

Although we lack Timothy's ascendant, the planetary aspects and signs in this horoscope are quite eloquent. The sun is in Scorpio, in square to a Saturn–Pluto conjunction in Leo. Mars is also part of this conjunction, and one of the implications of this grouping is that all the violence and aggression and powerful sexuality suggested by the configuration is turned against Timothy himself. Now obviously a great many people were born with the sun in Scorpio squaring the Mars–Saturn-Pluto conjunction in Leo, and they do not all have depressive breakdowns and kill themselves. Some even become astrologers, or psychotherapists. But even the most careful sifting of the parental background would only explain why Timothy did not have the personal resources to confront the darkness in himself. It would not explain where the darkness came from, or what its intrinsic nature was. From astrology's point of view, this darkness is a given; it is a fate. Timothy was born with the necessity of living with a potent and primordial force within himself, which the collective standards of his family and his society did not equip him to understand. He was horrified by the violent sexual fantasies which plagued him and the discovery of cruelty and bestiality within himself. Here perhaps one may consider the parents; no real acceptance was given of this more primitive side of his nature. But I have not met many parents of the generation of Timothy's who would be capable of such insight and containment. One of the more important implications of astrology in this case is that we are each given different proportions of helpings from different gods. The inverted rage and passion of Mars–Saturn–Pluto in square to a Scorpio sun are not 'caused' by parental rejection or neglect. Certainly the subjective portrait of the father suggested by these aspects is not a very edifying one. But those passions were there from the beginning, as Timothy himself was perceptive enough to see.

Because Scorpio and Pluto are connected so strongly with what our culture sees as dross and discordance and unacceptable emotion, it is easy for the Scorpio individual to see himself as the embodiment of all the family's shadow side, the carrier of evil and darkness. Yet to blame the culture is absurd; for there are archetypal patterns at work within cultures as there are within individuals, and for the last two thousand years the archetypal dominants in the West have moved in a direction antithetical to Pluto. Blaming the family is equally absurd, for its members suffer the same collective problem. Not only may family members project upon the Plutonian individual the unwelcome dross in their own natures; such an individual will himself readily accept the projection, and find nothing of the light within, but only darkness. The mummified Osiris, a mythic image which emphasises the importance of Timothy's dream and of the crisis he was entering, is an image of depression and darkness, for the god lies in such a state of death after his unsuccessful battle with Set, the lord of the underworld, before the goddess Isis resurrects the corpse. The dream might imply a possibility of resurrection, as the mummy floats to the surface of the water. But for an individual who has spent his life in isolation and self-hatred, the compassionate acceptance and love of another may be too painful to bear.

At the time of Timothy's suicide, an illuminating transit was at work: Uranus, in the last decanate of Scorpio, was moving over the sun and squaring the Mars–Saturn–Pluto conjunction. Although it was not in exact aspect on the date of death, it had been stirring up the natal configuration for some time, with the implied possibility of some kind of breakthrough or resolution. Transits of Uranus, I have found, offer this chance: one may bring something into consciousness which has been buried or denied for a lifetime. It is my feeling, from this transit, that there might have been an opportunity for change. Perhaps it was this very thing that terrified Timothy, because the devil that one knows is sometimes more comforting than the new life with all its unknown responsibilities and demands.

I would not like to venture an opinion about whether anything can be 'done' when an individual has himself chosen to meet his fate in such a final way. Perhaps, in some sense, Timothy offered himself as a scapegoat or sacrifice. I had occasion to observe Mr and Mrs S. at the coroner's inquest where my colleague was required to give his report, for, being curious about Timothy's parents from my examination of his horoscope, I requested permission to attend. They were pleasant and unassuming people who simply could not comprehend what had happened, and had very obviously never, themselves, looked into the jaws of hell. Their little sins were apparent: stuffiness, prudishness, unlived shadows, a lack of real understanding of the complex creature they knew as a son. They were simple, ordinary, collective folk, not greatly different from most parents. It would be ridiculous and useless to blame them, for Pluto stretches back further than the parents, and the ancestral sins of the collective are exceedingly old. In the end, one cannot judge what this sacrificed life might have redeemed in the act of suicide, although our conscious judgments are naturally to the contrary.

Another aspect of Pluto which I have found to be particularly turbulent – perhaps because its meaning collides with popular social definitions of love and marriage – is Venus–Pluto. The problems of this aspect need to be considered whether it is found in the birth chart or in progression or transit. Once again, I do not feel there is any appreciable difference in meaning whether it is a 'good' or 'bad' aspect, save that the individual may find it easier to accept and give value to Pluto's demands if the aspect is a harmonious one. Myth is, as usual, a fruitful amplification, and in particular the myth we have already met: the descent of Inanna the love-goddess into the realm of her sister Ereshkigal, Lady of the Great Place Below.

Inanna is an earlier and less differentiated form of Venus, goddess of sexual love and fertility. She is creative and joyful, the Queen of Heaven, unmarried and with many lovers, delighting in the beauty of her own body, and also a wise judge and counsellor. She is an extroverted goddess, and Venus is an extroverted planet, seeking her fulfilment through stimulation from, and union with, beloved objects. Even quarrelling and raging in battle for the sake of the passionate experience of life which encounter with another brings is part of Venus' outward-directed world. Even in battle, Inanna is 'clean', for her whole self is given to her actions, and there are no hidden, devious motives. For Inanna, or for what the planet Venus represents within the individual, the collision with the dark realm is an exposure to that side of love which is most frequently seen in the marriage counsellor's consulting room: the power battles, manipulations, greeds, vendettas, and oppressions which are often only detectable by their smell. In this dark landscape we meet the Gorgon raging, and the unfeeling ice-man withdrawing; the Terrible Mother and the castrated son; the spider or scorpion which eats its mate after the act of love. Awareness of this side of relationship is perhaps not required of everyone. It would seem, from the size of the subscriptions, that some people can model their marriages after the pattern of ladies' journals and actually get away with such blissful ignorance – or such blissful simplicity. Or perhaps it is simply not their fate to have Ereshkigal in the connubial bed.

Not so with Venus–Pluto; for Pluto introduces Venus to what lies beneath the flowers and elegant gestures of romantic courtship. This underpinning is often not 'pretty', and certainly not 'fair'. For the individual with Venus–Pluto who has not yet reached the middle of life, the fate may not have made itself known. But it becomes apparent later, which is why the aspect has acquired a reputation for broken marriages. Venus–Pluto also has a propensity for sexual triangles. These are neither fair nor wished for, but are a fact of life, generally compulsive and conducive to considerable suffering among all the participants. Venus–Pluto is not cool or 'liberated' like Venus–Uranus, nor is it martyrlike and self-sacrificing like Venus–Neptune. In terms of personality quali-ties, it is proud, passionate, intense and often achingly loyal, just as Ereshkigal is. But the very intensity of its passion usually runs side by side with spite, vengeance, betrayal, loss, manipulation and a revelation of one's own potential for the destruction of what one loves most. It may be the fate of Venus–Pluto to be the betrayed, and equally often to be the betrayer. But it seems that the experience of betrayal is embedded in the necessity of the aspect. I have found that the square and opposition of Venus to Pluto often 'disown' the Plutonian side. One then hears the time-honoured justification: 'It's not me that's jealous and possessive/treacherous and disloyal, it's my wife/husband.' Nevertheless, despite this very understandable and very human effort to farm the unpleasing qualities of the aspect out onto others, the collision with Pluto's world of steamy and ambivalent emotions is still likely to occur within relationship, regardless of whose 'fault' it is. Leaving one relationship to find another, more trouble-free idyll, tends to simply repeat the same pattern.

Love for Venus–Pluto may be transformative, deepening, numi-nous, ecstatic, and full of meaning and richness; and there is usually a sense of fatality about it. But it is never simple, and is not permitted to remain naïve. The prettiness of Venus, reflected in Libra's courtly etiquette and Taurus' gentle simplicity, is pitted against the subtleties and secret purposes of the destroyer–rapist. Something or someone is trying to dismember the very thing one values and cherishes the most. I believe that this destroyer, which is inherent in the psyche of the individual who is born with Venus–Pluto, is not really intent upon wanton ruin. Perhaps it is intent upon self-revelation, or a discovery of the underworld of one's own emotions – an acceptance of a *daimon* more powerful than good intentions and loving thoughts. Only the Olympians can claim goodness and perfection, and even they cannot claim it all the time. What is incarnate is flawed, and shares in the violence and darkness of nature. Rather than accept this, Venus–Pluto will more often try to blame the partner for this fated intrusion into idealised love. One imagines that one sees in the other, male or female, the shadowy woman with the 'soul-freezing eyes'. It is not that Venus–Pluto is incapable of the gentler face of love. But this comes at a price. Here fate often intrudes upon love, frequently in the form of an obsessive sexual passion, or the breakdown of the sexual relationship between two people, which forces one or the other of them to begin to consider what might be meant by 'the unconscious'. I think that Enki's mourners are of some help in this situation, for such an attitude offers recognition and acceptance of the beast in oneself which it is one's fate to meet in the marriage bed, the embrace of the lover, the sexual initiation.

Death is also a form of initiation into Venus–Pluto, and sometimes the aspect makes a concrete manifestation as the death of the beloved or the cherished child or the needed parent at an age when support is most necessary. This is easy to write about, and much more difficult to endure, especially when Pluto denies or destroys the relationship one has so badly wanted through betrayal or a death which is no one's 'fault' but is simply irreconcilable. But it is sometimes helpful to remember that Inanna's death and regeneration, her suffering in the underworld and her redemption, renew life in the world above. Inanna's story is the oldest myth of sacrifice and transformation known, and far predates the story of Jesus. In its earliest form it is envisaged as a feminine journey toward a feminine goal, although it is certainly not the exclusive priority of women. This story is our most ancient promise of the necessity of grief and mourning to renew a living connection with one's own reality.

I would like to quote in relation to this aspect the dream of one of my analysands, which occurred during the long transit of Pluto over her natal Venus. In her birth chart the sun conjuncts Pluto in Leo, and both are in semisquare to Venus. At the time of the beginning of the transit, she had not in any way permitted the qualities of the sun–Pluto conjunction, with its intense sense of 'differentness' and its passionate purposefulness, to enter her life.

I am with my husband, mother and sister at a hotel in the country. We are trying to find a way into the city, but the arrangements for transportation have got mixed up. My father has gone on ahead with my son, and they are already in the city. The four of us are waiting at a crossroads to get a taxi. It begins to grow dark. One of the side roads is only a dirt track which vanishes into thick bushes and trees. Suddenly my sister sees something on the track, and becomes horribly frightened. She grabs my mother by the arm and begins to run back to the hotel, screaming at me and my husband to hurry or 'it' will get us. I peer down the track and see a blurred black shape, a kind of sinister cloud, moving towards us. I try to drag my husband by the arm, but he is very slow and stumbles as though drunk. Finally he runs into a bush. It is too late; there is no escape.

The central image of this dream, beneath its contemporary overlay, is an archetypal one, which may be met in many fairy tales: the meeting in the lonely wood, or on the lonely road, with that which is dark, evil or otherworldly. Coleridge expresses it in these lines from *The Ancient Mariner*:

> *Like one, that on a lonesome road*
> *Doth walk in fear and dread,*
> *And having once turned round walks on,*
> *And turns no more his head;*
> *Because he knows, a frightful fiend*
> *Doth close behind him tread.*

This is the encounter with the unconscious, which at first seems destructive and terrifying. The 'black shape' which approaches the dreamer from the narrow track that leads into the impenetrable forest of the psyche turned out, over the ensuing months, to embody what we have seen of Ereshkigal; for this dream heralded in my analysand, whom I will call Caroline, a near-psychotic eruption of violent rage, destructiveness, terror of separation, and an obsessive fear of uterine cancer which had no medical basis but seemed to concretise in the body the invisible corrosive enemy. I have found that many people with the element of fire strong in the horoscope tend to experience such unconscious eruptions first as a fantasy of sickness in the body. Caroline had been a 'good wife', a 'perfect mother', and was known among family and friends for her optimism, generosity and sunny nature – what one might expect from the sun in Leo. Nothing was to be seen of the greater depth of the sun–Pluto conjunction. That she had amputated certain aspects of herself in order to live up to this collective fantasy had not yet occurred to her. With Venus in Libra in the birth chart, she held very romantic ideals about love and marriage, and could not abide 'scenes' or negative emotions in her relationships. She was never angry, and almost always gave way to others so as not to be what she called 'selfish'. The darker qualities of Pluto were carried, as might be expected by its conjunction with the sun, by her father, who had run off with another woman when Caroline was very young. It will be apparent without lengthy explanation what this parental scenario contributed to her strenuous efforts at perfection.

Caroline found that it helped her to represent the uprushing black emotions in drawings, which were almost always black and red and portrayed snakelike shapes or prehistoric reptilian monsters: images of the primeval feminine, Tiamat the dragon out of whose body the world was made, Mother Night in her cold-blooded inhuman vastness, immured in the swamps of time. Looked at in a more reductive way, this black inhuman rage was also her own and her mother's rage at the sexual humiliation of a husband lost to another woman. Caroline held, beneath her bright and romantic exterior, a deep and abiding hatred of men and of life, which welded her into a unity with her superficially quiet but inwardly seething mother. As we worked on these issues, it became increasingly apparent to Caroline that the loathsome emotions, and the equally loathsome pictures she painted, might be recognised as valid expressions of vital life. The transit of Pluto, portrayed on an inner level by the dream, introduced her to a world within herself which was, in part, a family inheritance – the unexpressed poison and grief of her mother and her mother's mother and her mother's mother's mother, which all of the preceding generations had run away from but which she was now fated to encounter. This family running seems to be expressed in the dream by the father, mother, son and sister all vanishing in different directions and leaving her to deal with the 'black shape'. It is her dream, and her issue, and the others cannot help her.

In the dream, Caroline's husband is ineffectual; in fact, it is his apparent drunkenness which ultimately prevents her escape. In her actual life this situation was in fact expressed. Her husband, who was burdened with his own emotional difficulties, could not redeem her as she had unconsciously hoped he would. She was faced with her own necessity, and no rescue was permitted. Yet the advent of this experience deepened and matured her. Her sense of her own individuality and separate destiny began to emerge, as is fitting for a sun–Pluto in Leo, bringing with it both sadness and aloneness and a greater feeling of worth as an erotic and alive woman instead of merely someone's two-dimensional wife and mother. It is not surprising that what seems like a rebirth into creative life should be met with so much resistance and ambivalence, because the route – as the myth of Inanna suggests – is almost always through the darkness when Venus and Pluto are in aspect. Even the resultant relative freedom is experienced with ambivalence, because it requires the shouldering of the burden of one's essential differentness and aloneness.

Caroline's journey did not in the end destroy her marriage, as sometimes occurs with Venus–Pluto transits, and as she herself feared. In the dream she and her husband are linked and must go through the experience together. This suggests that Venus–Pluto is not concerned so much with separation on a concrete level as it is with separation from the fantasy of the ideal husband–father who will protect one from life and adore one enough to enable an escape from oneself. This psychic separation is, I feel, one of the meanings of Persephone's abduction by Hades, where she is torn from the loving and protective embrace of the mother who both shelters her and denies her the possibility of her own womanhood. This pattern is an archetypal one, a psychic necessity. If one denies or repudiates this fate, then it may be acted out upon one, and nature then may wear the face of the Erinyes.

The aspects of Mars and Pluto are also linked to sexuality and, I believe, to a feeling of fatedness, although the sexuality of Mars is not really concerned with relationship. The coupling of the two rulers of Scorpio has a reputation in many textbooks for all sorts of nasty things such as violence and obsessive desire, repression and cruelty, sadism and rape. The best that is ever said about Mars–Pluto is that it reflects a powerful will and a profound sense of self-determination. It might be appropriate to begin an exploration of Mars–Pluto with some mythic amplification, for Mars is not as simple as he first appears. He is generally interpreted as a symbol of masculinity, male directedness, self-assertion, aggression and competitive instinct. All of this is no doubt true, and the typical Arien personality, male or female, usually possesses some share of these direct and forceful attributes, whether on a physical, emotional or intellectual plane. But this describes the Arien side of Mars. He has another face, his 'night house' as medieval astrology was wont to call it, and this is the Scorpionic side of the planet; and he has kinship with Pluto in many ways. Walter F. Otto in *The Homeric Gods* gives a fine if unsettling descriptive passage on the war god Ares, whose Roman name is Mars.

> Ares is sketched as a bloodthirsty, raging demon, whose confidence in victory is nothing more than braggadocio compared with the rational power of an Athene. 'Mad' and 'insane' the gods call him; he does not know 'what is right', and turns, with no character, 'now to one and now to another'. To Zeus himself 'no Olympian god is so hated' as he, for 'he thinks only of strife and wars and battles' ... The figure of Ares derives from the antiquated earth-religion, where his savagery had its proper place among other pitiless forces. He is the spirit of imprecation, vengeance, blood-guilt. As the daimon of bloody slaughter, he still possesses fearful stature for Homer. His element is manslaughter; he is called 'the destroyer', the 'slayer of men'.[43]

Not a cheerful bedfellow; but then neither is Pluto. According to Hesiod's cosmogony of the gods, Ares is the parthenogenous son of Hera the Great Goddess. The birth of Ares occurs because Hera is infuriated with Zeus; he has had the audacity to generate the goddess Athene from his head without a female consort, and Hera must one-up him. To couch this in psychological jargon, Athene is the anima of Zeus, the feminine wisdom of the male; and Ares is a rather negative form of the animus of Hera, the fighting spirit of the female. That Ares is a mother's son immediately relates him to Hades, who is a mother's phallus. Zeus, in Homer's *Iliad*, feels that

Ares' proper place is among the Titans banished in the deepest depths of Tartaros. This war god has no dignity and no honour; he is of enormous size (700 feet tall) and utterly treacherous. In short, Ares is an image of Hera's outrage.

Ares–Mars is male in the same way that Hades–Pluto is male: Both are the masculine servants and expressions of an ancient mother-goddess who emerges from a primordial world view where the male was subordinate to the ultimate female power of procreation. Mars and Pluto obey the powers of earth and under-world rather than heaven. The repulsion that Zeus feels toward this fatherless god is something I have seen in a good many 'spiritual' men and women, Jupiterians whose loyalties lie with the realms of logic and intuition and who find this brute daimonic power terrifying and intrinsically ugly. It is not surprising that Mars alone can be a problem in a 'light' horoscope full of air. The growth movement has seized upon this as a primary difficulty in 'getting out your anger', but anger, I am afraid, is the least of it. It is no wonder, if one reads Otto's description of Ares–Mars, that a more cerebral or spiritual type finds the planet uncomfortable. Uranus also seems to dislike Mars; in myth, the sky god Ouranos is revolted by his earthy Titan children and banishes them to Tarta-ros because they are ugly. This is what Zeus would like to do to Ares, but he does not dare because of Hera's power.

It is interesting to note that the catalogue of nasties attributed to Ares is earlier given to the feminine deities, just as the underworld realm originally belongs to Ereshkigal and Hekate before it becomes the property of Hades. Inanna, the Sumerian Queen of Heaven whom we have already met, is a battle goddess; Ishtar, her Babylonian counterpart, likewise; Sekhmet, the Egyptian solar goddess, is a war leader and mistress of massacre and vengeance; and even gentle, sensuous Aphrodite, who later becomes the beloved of the god Ares–Mars, was originally worshipped in Sparta as a *numen* of bloody battle. There is something very primordial about Mars, before we even begin to look at his aspects to Pluto. I am not suggesting that there is anything feminine about him in the ordinary sense. But he seems to represent the masculi-nity of the body, rather than the masculinity of the spirit, and the body belongs, ultimately, to the Great Goddess. Ares–Mars emerges, as Otto suggests, from the earth-religion and the world of instinct with its primitive deities presided over by the feminine. Mars belongs to the old matriarchal realm of flesh, rather than the solar and Jupiterian world of mind and spirit. Erich Neumann puts it as follows:

The Earth Father, lord of all chthonic forces, belongs psychologically to the realm of the Great Mother. He manifests himself most commonly as the overwhelming aggressiveness of phallic instinct or as a destructive monster. But whenever the ego is overwhelmed by the sexual, aggressive or power instincts of the male, or by any other form of instinct, we can see the dominance of the Great Mother. For she is the instinctual ruler of the unconscious, mistress of animals, and the phallic Terrible Father is only her satellite, not a masculine principle of equal weight.[44]

Pluto and Mars in aspect seem to emphasise this chthonic side of Mars. Ruthlessness, not at all a bad trait in the appropriate circumstances, is a quality I associate with Mars–Pluto, although when the two planets are in sextile or trine this ruthlessness seems to wear a more socially acceptable face and is called 'determination'. Survival is one of nature's primary goals, and the Mars–Pluto individual is dedicated to his or her survival. There is often, also, a kind of cruelty linked with a love of power, particularly sexual power. That there is a close link between the erotic and the bloody, the sexually exciting and the brutal, is something which it is not always comfortable for the individual with Mars–Pluto to acknowledge. Venusian eroticism is pleasing and lovely because it involves expression together, but Martial eroticism involves power over another, and is unquestionably more like a rape. It is crueller, more potent and, for some people, more stimulating. As Freud puts it:

> The history of human civilisation shows beyond any doubt that there is an intimate connection between cruelty and the sexual instinct; but nothing has been done toward explaining the connection, apart from laying emphasis on the aggressive factor in the libido. According to some authorities this aggressive element of the sexual instinct is in reality a relic of cannibalistic desires – that is, it is a contribution derived from the apparatus for obtaining mastery, which is concerned with the satisfaction of the other and, ontogenetically, the older of the great instinctual needs.[45]

Freud, who had Mars and Pluto in quincunx in his birth horoscope, must have known a great deal about this dilemma himself. The sort of 'primitive animus' of which Jung writes and which is personified in the rough, silent, 'natural' man such as Heathcliffe or the ape-man Tarzan, bears kinship with the qualities of Mars–Pluto. So too does Caliban, Shakespeare's monstrous bestial male who is the magician Prospero's dark counterpart in *The Tempest*. Caliban is also a mother's son, a chthonic creature of earth. D. H. Lawrence, who had Mars and Pluto in sextile in his birth horoscope, infused these same qualities into the character of Mellors the gamekeeper in *Lady Chatterley's Lover*. The less redeeming features of Mars–Pluto may also formulate in the figure of the rapist, and this image is not an uncommon one in the dreams and fantasies – if not the actual lives – of those with natal Mars–Pluto squares, conjunctions and oppositions.

Understandably there is often a deep fear of the more primitive urges represented by Mars–Pluto aspects, although these apparently ugly male images possess a good deal of wisdom about survival and fertility, both biological and psychic, which the winged heaven-gods tend to lack. The violence and passion of Ares are frightening to the civilised ego, and are easily cut off and 'banished to Tartaros' – in other words, repressed. This can be a particularly painful issue for a man with Mars–Pluto, because Mars is bound up with a man's sense of confidence in his own virility and self-determination. The repudiation of Mars–Pluto because of its primitiveness frequently results in a sense of impotence, castration and powerlessness. This leaves a man open to dominance by women, whereupon he will usually blame his problem on his mother if he thinks psychologically at all; but the difficulty here is not so much with the mother as with the repulsion that Zeus feels toward Ares, or, put more simply, that the intellectually and spiritually inclined person feels toward his corporeal roots and fleshly desires. The horoscope of Timothy S. which I gave earlier is perhaps revealing in this context, for depression is often an inversion of violent rage; and Timothy was an individual who could not find any way of confronting or finding an outlet for the thing which consumed him.

Primitive desire is not the entire meaning of Mars–Pluto. There is another facet to this planetary combination which seems to carry with it much more of a feeling of 'fatedness'. Mars is by nature an extroverted god, just as Venus is an extroverted goddess. He seeks satisfaction of his desires and impulses through outer objects. Servant of the Great Mother though he may be, his field of activity is the external world: instinct making itself effective in the environment through the satisfaction of desire. Pluto, on the other hand, draws things in and down to his hidden realm, and is in some ways an image of the introversion of libido or psychic energy. Or, put another way, Pluto as an image of the dark maternal roots of the psyche is forever pulling us out of life and back into the womb of the Mother, either for renewal or death. The regressive tug of depression, apathy, loss of energy (which the African tribesman calls 'loss of soul'), despair and death-fantasies, are the feeling components of this constant pressure to regress and return to the Mother. Pluto demands a withdrawal of projections and attachments from the upper world. It is this quality which is in part responsible for the sense of bondage and imprisonment which accompanies transits and progressions of the planet. One cannot any longer find gratification outside, either because external circumstances deny it or because some hidden compulsion or thief within the psyche steals energy and pulls it down into the unconscious. Pluto is not only a rapist, breaking violently into outer life, but is also a robber, stealing Persephone and dragging her below with him. The rapist–robber is a common dream image accompanying the onset of depression and loss of interest in life. It is an equally common image in the dreams which cluster around the beginning of depth psychotherapy. The rapist–robber heralds the 'abduction' of the ego into the underworld. The myth makes clear, too, for whom Pluto the male rapist works; for when Hades steals his bride from her mother Demeter, he escapes into the Great Place Below through a pathway opened up for him by Gaia, the Earth Mother. This strange involvement of the Great Mother in her own daughter's rape (for Gaia and Demeter are so similar that they are unmistakably one goddess) suggests that the psyche requires this inward and downward movement for its own purposes, despite the suffering which is entailed to itself.

Intense frustration is therefore one of the more recognisable of Mars–Pluto experiences. Passions are forced into introversion, and often this seems like fate because it is the outer object of desire which appears to offer the refusal. One cannot have what one wants so badly in the outer world without the downward journey as prerequisite; yet the very intensity of the Mars–Pluto combination guarantees that one will want it very, very badly. I have seen Mars–Pluto people bash their heads again and again on the stone wall of another's rejection, never relenting, never giving up, becoming angrier and more vindictive, never relinquishing the cherished object which some invisible inner law dictates they are not permitted to have. This so often feels like fate that I can only assume it *is* fate. It can be a deeply distressing experience, because the more the Mars–Pluto person tries to utilise his power and purpose to coerce the outer world into submission, the more resistance the outer world offers. Thus the individual colludes with and perpetrates his own fate, when a more appropriate response might be to accept what cannot be changed and follow the pathway into the underworld to discover what the Lady of the Great Place Below has in mind.

This circle of intense desire and equally intense frustration is, I feel, one of the reasons why Mars–Pluto is so often repressed. Certainly it would be rare to find a person who willingly subjected himself to such pressure. I think it is this pressure which promotes the suppressed violence of the aspect, inner or outer, or draws violence to itself through displacement. If the individual is unable to make the required sacrifice on the altar of Moira, then the pressure becomes unbearable. Mars–Pluto can certainly be treacherous and manipulative; any aspect that has connections with the Great Goddess seems to manifest this shadier face of the feminine, which has a very different moral code from that of the sun and Jupiter. The morality of the chthonic world is not based upon thinking principles or ethics, but on survival and the propagation of the species. From Pluto's point of view, the arguments of morality are irrelevant. Yet the very qualities which give the Mars–Pluto person his immense survival capacities are often felt as repellent because they seem to violate conscious moral codes.

There are many parallels to Mars–Pluto in alchemy, where the animal of greed and desire and instinctual need – often a wolf, which belongs to the Goddess and which is portrayed as outcast and perpetually hungry – is imprisoned within the sealed alembic and roasted slowly over the fire until it consumes itself and is transformed. It seems as though Mars–Pluto is often forced to accept a double-bind: to acknowledge and value the primordial qualities of nature, yet at the same time to accept frustration in the expression of those qualities until they have been purified by fire. It is this aspect in particular which makes me affirm the validity of Jung's belief that the unconscious wishes to become conscious but also doesn't, and will only do so at the cost of great conflict and great effort.

In my experience, Mars–Pluto seems to appear in many people's dreams as a black man. This is no doubt a symbol appropriate only to our predominantly white Western culture. This figure of the black man was also a favourite of the alchemists, who called him the Ethiopian and believed him to be the *prima materia*, the crude stuff of life upon which the alchemical work was performed. James Hillman suggests that one may

> consider black persons in dreams in terms of their resemblance with this underworld context. Their concealing and raping attributes belong to the 'violating' phenomenology of Hades . . . just as their pursuit resembles the hounding by the death demons. They are returning ghosts from the repressed netherworld – not merely from the repressed ghetto . . . They bring one down and steal one's 'goods' and menace the ego behind its locked doors.[46]

The black man and the wolf are typically Plutonian symbols. So too is the werewolf, that strange creature of Eastern European folklore, which in legend is transformed unwillingly from man to beast under the full moon and is doomed to devour the thing it loves. Wagner used the archetypal equation of black/bestial/ underworld in his character of Alberich the Dwarf. In the *Ring* cycle, this figure is called 'black Alberich'; his realm of Niebelheim is the Plutonian underworld; and he stands in stark counterpoint to Wotan the sky god, ruler of the heavenly Valhalla. Figures such as Alberich embody the raw, primal, savage, greedy, ruthless natural man who in potential contains the seeds of gold. In *Das Rheingold*, it is Alberich, not Wotan, who through ruthless abjuration of love seizes power over the gold and forges it into a ring of power. Likewise, in Tolkien's *Lord of the Rings*, it is the dark lord Sauron who possesses not only the evil but also the strength to make and wield the One Ring. In Jung's view, the black man and the wolf are images of the unconscious itself – raw nature, full of affect and conflict, which gives birth to the ego and then struggles with it in the long process of individual and collective development. I have encountered these and similar motifs so often in the dreams of my chart clients and analysands – particularly those with Mars–Pluto aspects – that it has compelled me to consider the black–white conflicts in the outer world as, in part, exteriorisations of a deep internal dilemma between intellectualised Western consciousness and its primordial roots. The apartheid of South Africa is a favourite and highly emotive theme in the dreams of many people who are not in any way directly involved and frequently ill-informed, and the intense affect surrounding issues such as this one certainly suggest a degree of unconscious projection or identification between a collective external issue and a deeply internal one. I think this motif throws some light on Mars–Pluto and the conflicts such an aspect can provoke.

Sometimes the fate of Mars–Pluto is physical rape. In making this statement I am not in any way implying that if one has a Mars–Pluto aspect in the birth chart, then being raped – or becoming a rapist – is an inevitable 'result'. But there seems to be a relationship between the aspect and the concrete experience of rape. This subject is so emotionally charged, particularly in the wake of the feminist movement, that it would be much easier if I avoided it. But rape belongs to the Mars–Pluto realm and therefore must be mentioned here. We have already met the symbolic motif of the rapist in Pluto himself. This motif has more of a tendency to externalise itself when Mars joins him, perhaps because of the intense pressure of anger and frustration which so often accompanies the more difficult aspects. As a woman I cannot pretend to be wholly objective about this issue. But although feelings of profound rage and humiliation are to be expected in women when confronted with such an act of violence and violation, these feelings do not help us to understand why rape overtakes some women and not others. The voice of extreme feminism suggests that rape is an exclusively male barbarity visited upon helpless and blameless female victims, typical of the brutality displayed by men against women throughout history. The voice of our Judaeo-Christian culture, dominated by its patriarchal deity, suggests that it is women who are to blame, either because of the ingrained belief that the individual woman has provoked it, or because – more irrational still – some part of the collective psyche, in both men and women, still equates the feminine with the sexual and therefore with sin. This is perhaps why guilt, rather than murderous rage, is so often the immediate emotional response of the woman who has been raped, and why the passage of a rape case through the courts is such a profoundly humiliating experience for the victim.

These two extreme viewpoints may shed considerable light on the archetypal problems between men and women in terms of their anger towards each other, but both extremes become quite useless when considered in relation to the individual. I am too aware of the phenomenon of unconscious collusion, and of the enormous difficulty in making any meaningful connections between oneself and an apparently random and unprovoked 'outside' event, to lay blame in too cavalier a fashion on either masculine or feminine in this ambiguous issue. There may well be a social issue in rape; rapists, according to some surveys, tend to come from difficult and underprivileged or emotionally sterile backgrounds. But there is also the evidence of astrology, which implies that there is an individual issue as well. It is worth attempting to look at rape from a more objective standpoint, for I have seen too many Mars–Pluto contacts in the charts of women who have been raped – on one level or another – to ignore the fact that there may be something in the psyche which draws such experiences. One might even call that 'something' fate.

Rapist and victim are connected by a shared experience, and perhaps they share something else as well: a psychic background reflected by the Mars–Pluto constellation. Bradley Te Paske, in his extremely insightful book, *Rape and Ritual: A Psychological Study*, begins by quoting some of the recent American studies on rape, and points out that approximately one-third of the rapists investigated had themselves been subjected to some sexual trauma in their youth. Often these offences were perpetrated by the mother, and the implication here is clear. Rape and allied aggressive sexual acts are not exclusively the prerogative of the barbaric male, unless 'male' is extended to include the animus as well; and the theme of aggressor and victim together can relate to one individual.

Te Paske then examines the Hades–Persephone myth, and has

obviously been struck by the strange involvement of the mother-goddess in her own daughter's rape. He quotes Jung's work on 'The Psychological Aspects of the Kore':

> The maiden's helplessness exposes her to all sorts of dangers, for instance of being devoured by reptiles or ritually slaughtered like a beast of sacrifice. Often there are bloody, cruel, even obscene orgies to which the innocent child falls victim. Some-times it is a true *nekyia*, a descent into Hades and a quest for the 'treasure hard to attain', occasionally connected with orgiastic rites or offerings of menstrual blood to the moon. Oddly enough, the various tortures and obscenities are carried out by an 'Earth Mother'.[47]

There is a very disturbing implication in this mythic theme. It seems to be the Great Mother herself, in her phallic form as Hades, who is the rapist; and the rape is perpetrated upon her virginal and incipiently erotic daughter. Te Paske suggests that this situation reflects a basic conflict between the instinctual maternal feminine and the individualised erotic feminine, a conflict which, if it is great enough, can lead to the imagery and perhaps even the experience of rape.

Following is the dream of a woman with whom I worked analytically for a short time. The analysis was interrupted when she decided to move to Germany with her husband, who had been born in that country. This woman, whom I will call Angela, had experienced rape at the hands of her stepfather when she was eight years old, and twice more, both times at the hands of strangers, while in her teens. Despite these experiences she had managed to form a close and fulfilling relationship with her husband, but the sexual side of the marriage left a great deal to be desired, primarily because of Angela's quite understandable but extremely distressing fear of losing control. In her birth chart, the conjunction of Mars, Saturn and Pluto which we have already met in the horoscope of Timothy S. appears in the seventh house.

> I am in a room with a very pretty young girl of about sixteen, who is dressed in a white bridal gown. She is golden-haired, blue-eyed and very flirtatious, a sort of 'daddy's girl'. There is a dark, very tormented young man who is in love with her. He is possessed by some terrible violence, and wants to drive a knife through the girl's heart. He cannot help himself. He plunges the knife into her breast, and blood spurts everywhere. The girl is dying, and staggers into my arms. I must hold her while she undergoes her death agony. Suddenly I notice an older woman sitting in the room. She is large and very dark, and sits watching

with a strangely satisfied look. I realise with horror that this is the girl's mother, and that she has either made the young man commit the murder or at best condones it, because she does nothing to help.

This dream, which is a thinly disguised enactment of the Hades–Persephone myth, portrays the phallus as a knife, performing the act of death–marriage while the Great Mother looks on. It seems to reveal a good deal about the unconscious patterns at work within a woman who has been exposed more than once to rape. Angela was only a child when she was first raped, and could hardly be blamed for being 'provocative' in any literal sense, although most children 'try on' their incipient sexuality in the course of normal development. Yet there is a fate at work here. When speaking of the very painful issue of her childhood experience, Angela gave voice to a sentiment which I have heard on several other occasions from women who have been subjected to childhood rape: unconsciously, there is a feeling that the mother is in some way to blame. This may defy any rational consideration of the objective family circumstances, yet the feeling may be a strong one and may persist despite the sense of guilt it provokes. When Angela began to express this feeling as a fantasy, she experienced her mother as secretly fostering the rape, or carefully turning a blind eye to its occurrence, because it kept the husband quiet. Such a fantasy may have no backup in terms of actual behaviour or intention, but in Angela's case it seems that she perceived some unconscious undercurrent at work within the family situation. The sense of having no protection against the terrifying force of the rapist, and the conviction that this reflects an omission or even an intention on the part of the mother, is one of the deepest wounds around the issue of childhood rape, and is in many ways as painful as the physical act itself because of the profound feeling of betrayal. Whether this reflects a convoluted and deeply unconscious family collusion or an archetypal 'meaning', it is still a fate.

Angela's dream is not only about what happened to her body; it is also a dream of initiation occurring at a time when she stood on the threshold of relinquishing her terror of penetration by life. It points both backwards and forwards, not only raising the issue of the mother's collusion, but also highlighting the necessity of a sacrifice of the 'virginal' innocence which she clung to as her only defence against the terrible rage within. That she is able to hold the dying girl and contain her death agonies in the dream is an augury that Angela had the strength to deal with whatever emotions might burst forth. This in fact turned out to be the case, and the eruption of rage towards the mother released a good deal of the sexual inhibition that had plagued her. Her anger towards her stepfather was conscious, but expressing it had not helped her. It was only when she confronted the issue of her mother that any change or healing could begin to occur.

Te Paske is primarily concerned in his book with the psychology of the rapist, and with the significance of such a theme when it appears in the dreams and fantasies of men who are not inclined to act it out yet who encounter it as an inner event. The conclusion he draws is that rape is a manifestation of the masculine libido struggling against the stifling and suffocating grip of the unconscious imaged as Great Mother. Thus dreams of rape may not necessarily represent anything pathological, but may occur as images of a process of developing individuality. The rapist, on the other hand, is, in Te Paske's view, usually mother-bound, and seeks both revenge against the feminine and salvation through his victim during the act of rape. This is why, despite the violence and callousness of the act, so many rapists ask their victims whether their love-making was any good.

> Be the person a Charles Manson, a rapist of lesser criminal instinct, or just another conquering male, the influence of the negative aspect of the mother plays an important role in his psychology ... by viewing the psychic background of rape in terms of the pervasive fear of, and simultaneous falling under the power of, the negative aspect of the feminine, one major factor alone is emphasised.[48]

Later in the book he phrases this conclusion even more succinctly:

> In a profound sense rape attempts psychological matricide. But when the mother is too powerfully internal and too deeply unconscious to be confronted as an inner problem, the outer woman falls victim to the concrete assertion of masculine power.[49]

This assertion of masculine power and virility struggling with the castrating and devouring face of the feminine unconscious is, in astrological language, represented by Mars in conflict with Pluto. It is understandable enough in terms of masculine psychology. But the woman who is the victim of rape often has the Mars–Pluto constellation. The implication here is that the same drama enacts itself within her psyche, and externalises itself in the concrete experience of rape, although she is more likely (although not invariably) to play the role of the victim. What does this mean for the individual woman? Perhaps it is a way of expressing the problem of her own initiative and creative potential (which Jung calls the animus), held in the grip of the instinctual mother. Or, put another way, she is in a sense the innocent inheritor of a problem within the mother and the family, and is 'fated' to be the sacrifice which the mother unconsciously offers up to resolve her own dilemma between maternity and sexuality, or between blind instinctual life and individual self-expression.

In such a situation, rape is the enactment of something which has not been internally integrated yet which has built up enormous pressure within the family psyche. If the figure of Mars–Pluto is powerful within the family or within the individual, yet is repressed too forcibly, then it may break out as an exterior fate. Forensic psychiatry is unpleasantly familiar with the difficult problem of assessing an accusation of rape, for some are clear-cut but many more are highly ambiguous. Often the woman claims she has been raped, the man claims he has been invited, the couple know each other and perhaps have been lovers in the past, and the comforting panacea of moral outrage and blame – towards either party – disappears into the uneasy feeling that there is a strange unconscious collusion between rapist and victim. In the case of a child victim, or rape by an unknown assailant, this seems an outrageous implication. But perhaps the collusion exists on some level in the unconscious, and its roots lie further back than the individual. I have the feeling, from what I have seen of this aspect running through the horoscopes of families, that Mars–Pluto can imply an ancestral inheritance rather than a strictly individual problem of 'attracting' rape. It may be a family *daimon*: a turbulent and vital sexual energy that successive generations have attempted to crush and exclude because of their dependence upon respectability or socially acceptable values, or because the Great Mother dominates the psychology of the family. Then someone gets elected, unconsciously, as the scapegoat, and becomes the rapist or the one raped. Seen as an issue between mother and daughter, rape becomes something much more complex than a social issue. Te Paske is illuminating in his interpretation of Mars:

> Appropriate particularly to the theme of rape is Mars in that this figure embodies the brute, warlike and aggressive nature of man standing opposed to, and yet in love with, Aphrodite. Jung states that Mars (Ares) may be considered as 'the principle of individuation in the strict sense'. This 'strict sense' denotes the individuating principle as hot, violent, sulphurous. Mars represents power and anger in rudimentary and concrete form.[50]

In other words, Mars within a woman is no different from Mars within a man: it is the urge to actualise one's individual identity in the world. Rape as the manifestation of unconscious collusion between mother and daughter and rapist thus suggests the mother avenging herself against the daughter's urge to develop as a separate individual, or the mother fighting her own urge to develop as projected upon her young daughter. Rape as the manifestation of unconscious collusion between woman and rapist suggests something similar: the unconscious retaliating against the individual's urge to develop too far away from its maternal roots.

I am reminded here of the dream of another analysand, a young woman in her early twenties, whom I will call Ruth. She experienced many dreams of the figure of the rapist during the course of the first year of analysis. She was not a victim of childhood rape, at least not in concrete form, but was subjected to it in her relationship with a violent lover. This is a terribly common experience of rape, but such cases never arrive in court for obvious reasons. Gradually during the analysis it became apparent that this violent animus, who often assumed the most brutal and sadistic guises in Ruth's dreams, was connected as much with her own unexpressed rage and aggression as he was with her external lover. This suppressed rage Ruth tended to turn upon herself, 'raping' her own value with thoughts of worthlessness and badness. Had she been a more aggressive or harder personality, this animus would no doubt have been directed outward against others; but she is a gentle and sensitive woman, deeply introverted, and extremely idealistic in her values. Thus the inner rapist directed his destruction towards her own sense of individuality. It also became apparent that this rapist belonged as much to her parents and their marital dynamics as it did to her. In one early dream he appeared specifically as 'in the service of' her mother, who was herself an illegitimate child with a severely impoverished early life. This mother carried within herself an enormous and quite violent anger which never surfaced except in scenes of weeping and mundane marital quarrels, and in outbursts of destructive criticism against her daughter. This is truly Hera's outrage, passed down from mother to daughter as a psychic inheritance. Ruth's Mars, representing her own individual and creative potential, was completely in the grip of the mother. The father was a retired army officer, and although he was described as 'weak' in relation to his daughter, he expressed violence regularly to his sons, and perpetrated a species of covert emotional violence on Ruth. Not surprisingly, in Ruth's horoscope Mars is in square to Pluto, Mars being conjunct the midheaven – the point in the chart which pertains to the inheritance from the mother. Following is the dream:

> I am in a room with an angry, dangerous black man. I recognise him immediately from other dreams. I am terribly frightened. I

try to talk to him, and ask him why he is pursuing me. He says, 'If you show hatred to me, I will show hatred to you.'

This dream, in the light of what we have been exploring, is so transparent that it needs no interpretation. It is concerned not so much with the roots of the problem as with a potential way of dealing with it. Here the unconscious, which on the one hand portrays itself as a violent pursuer, is on the other hand offering a means of reconciliation to the ego. This 'dangerous man' cannot be reduced simply to an aggressive aspect of the dreamer. He is much more than that. He is the 'principle of individuation in the strict sense', and he is asking for a parley; and he is presumably pursuing her because she has not yet removed herself from identification with the mother's psyche. He is also an image of powerful family anger and creative potential, bottled up for several generations and formulating in a frightening way in Ruth's own psyche – and in her external life. He is, of course, her own anger as well, for she was carrying considerable rage towards men, inverted and acted out as a self-destructive pattern within her relationship life. Pluto, which is involved in the square to Mars, is placed in the twelfth house in the birth chart, which I feel concerns, among other things, the ancestral past, unseen 'causes' or pressures which have slowly accumulated before the individual's own birth (represented by the ascendant) and lying hidden behind the individual personality. Sometimes the twelfth house is called the 'house of karma', but what then is karma, if not the chain of unseen causes which pass from generation to generation and bear fruit in the present life of the individual? One does not necessarily have to believe in reincarnation to understand karma, or fate, in this sense; nor is it mutually exclusive with reincarnation either.

The violent black man in the dream seems to embody an entire family complex, an inherited fate. This fate has fallen upon Ruth to deal with, and deal with it she must if she is not to remain victimised by it. In dealing with it she unlocks her own freedom of development, for he is the goad which drives her out of the parental web and into her own creative life. It would seem that she cannot repudiate this inner rapist as her parents did, by passing it on to the next generation. Fate has, it seems, not only descended upon her in an apparently cruel and difficult way; it is also asking her for its own transformation and release. Ruth is the scapegoat, the carrier of what Hillman calls 'retributive justice connected with ancestral sins'. She has done nothing to 'deserve' this fate; she is a person of great honesty and integrity, and I am not prepared to make the blithe and, it seems to me, arrogant assumption that she must have committed some crime in a former life. I do not know if she has had a former life, nor does she; and even if I were convinced of this, it would not help her to integrate this family *daimon* into her present life. Nor am I prepared to assign any conscious responsibility. This is much more than a 'potential' or 'trend' implied by a planetary pattern. She has literally had no choice. If there is an issue of personal responsibility connected with such things, then it can only lie in the burden – taken on unwillingly – of trying to bring into consciousness something which the ego can in no sense be blamed for creating. Had Ruth been older, one might have looked at the 'lopsidedness' of her conscious attitude with some suspicion. But she has not yet matured enough to have a firm conscious attitude. As long as this young woman is caught in the family web, and attempts to cast the rapist with his rampant, vital sexuality into Tartaros, he will pursue her in dreams and in life, and she is 'doomed' to destructive relationships.

The violent man underwent many permutations since the early dream mentioned above; and so did Ruth herself. What made this possible is a great mystery, and one which we shall explore more fully later. Although the themes of abuse and rape continued at intervals in her dreams, the entire pattern slowly began to change, and Ruth was no longer a mere passive recipient. The man began to appear in more helpful guise, guiding or supporting her, as she began to make a relationship with this primitive piece of psychic life. Eventually she extricated herself from the destructive external relationship, through which she acted out the dissociated figure of the rapist. The termination of that bond occurred after a dream where the black man appeared and asked her to kill and eat him. To eat something, in a dream or fairy tale, implies digesting it, making it conscious and building it into the framework of one's own life. The theme of cannibalism abounds in Greek myth, and it is always punished rigorously by the gods, for they are jealous of their powers and strive to prevent the heroic ego from growing too fat on stolen meat. Evidently the unconscious is implying through this dream that the battle is nearly over; it is time to take responsibility for this figure through a sacrifice of the painful but nonetheless easier path of enlisting another person to act it out. Here there is no threatened punishment from the gods, but an accord between conscious and unconscious. This dream marked the beginning of a resolution of some of the more extreme problems inherent in the natal Mars–Pluto square.

Ruth first came to see me when this square was being triggered by the long transit of Uranus in opposition to Mars and in square to Pluto. Once again, Uranus implies the potential of breakthrough and realisation of something which has previously been unconscious and compulsive. The outcome of this transit of Uranus was far more edifying than the outcome for Timothy S., but it is difficult to understand why. I have given Ruth's example because it is an excellent paradigm of some of the difficulties of Mars–Pluto, for which there are no easy solutions. Perhaps there are no solutions at all, but only compromises, for there is no way that the Mars–Pluto individual can repudiate the primitive elements in his psyche. Individual development seems, with these aspects, to require a collision with that which opposes such a development, and reconciliation is possible only if the individual himself changes – 'dies', in a sense, at the moment of 'marriage'. I can only assume that if we are given such aspects in the birth chart, then they constitute a fate and an opportunity for the individual to restore dignity and value to something long ago ruled outcast.

The few descriptions I have given of some of the aspects of Pluto are not, as I warned, intended to provide easy interpretations for the astrologer. They are intended to illustrate a theme, and they are single examples of a story which I have heard enough times to be convinced that it is the primary story of Pluto. The Dark Mother of which Pluto is our astrological symbol – the world of womb, underworld, tomb, unconscious, instinct – is that ancient power which the Greeks called Moira, and she is alive and well in the twentieth century in forms which perhaps require the language of depth psychology to comprehend. Moira is certainly a vengeful goddess if the bright light of ego-consciousness repudiates her and disregards her allotted boundaries. What is harder to accept is that she will visit her vengeance upon the children of erring parents. But perhaps, from a deeper perspective, this is not so 'unfair' as it sounds, since the individual is part of, and emerges from, a family and racial and collective human background and therefore inherits the problems and gifts of the whole. This is not so very different from the religious idea that we 'inherit' sin from Adam, and are therefore culpable although we may not be individually culpable; or that we, as in Bach's *St Matthew Passion*, are simultaneously Judas, the vengeful crowd, Pilate, and the crucified Christ all at once. Aspects from the inner planets to Pluto seem to reflect the necessity to live in peace with Moira's allotments. If the aspects are harmonious ones, then this task is made easier, for one tends to be more flexible about accommodating natural law and the more primitive side of oneself and life. If the aspects are difficult, the same innate potential is present, but it cannot be actualised without some struggle and a collision with the unconscious psyche, which feels like a rape and a death. The nature of Moira as symbolised by Pluto includes all the demands of instinct: the body and its appetites, the sexual drive, the aggressive and destructive impulses. What Freud meant by the *id* with its ambivalent sexual and destructive urges, which he called Eros and Thanatos, is not very far away from our ancient goddess. The needs of the instinctual man, if Pluto is strong in the horoscope, cannot be avoided without retaliation, and the retaliation often takes the form of possession by the very thing one has been trying to avoid; but, as in the case of Ruth, it may first appear 'outside'. Yet if this primordial power is acknowledged, however 'negative' or 'lower' we may first feel it to be, then something seems to happen to both ego and unconscious. One of the boons of Pluto, so far as I have seen, is a capacity for survival and a tough inner core which may not always be 'kind' or 'selfless', but is a good deal more effective in life, and is not frightened by separation, suffering or death.

I have connected the planet Pluto with the particular aspect of fate that the Greeks imaged as a dark, ancient and stern goddess. There are other, broader sp. .eres where we might also look at this goddess, besides the particular planet we have been examining. Pluto points back to family fate, but family fate in the largest sense can only be discerned if we examine the dynamics and horoscopes of the family. This is the next sphere in which we might gain further insight into the nature of feminine fate. I would first like to end this chapter with a fairy tale. The ancient goddess Moira makes her appearance here too, although her primordial majesty is dimmed and it might take a moment's reflection to recognise her. The tale of *Mother Hölle* is perhaps a fitting summation, in fairy tale language, of Moira as Pluto. When I first encountered this tale, which is one collected by the Grimm Brothers, I wondered what the name Hölle might mean. But inquiries into German dictionaries and from German-speaking friends yielded no answers. No one knew what the word meant. Only much later, by chance, I discovered that *Hölle* is an archaic German word which means Hell.

## MOTHER HÖLLE[51]

There was once a widow who had two daughters – one of whom was pretty and industrious, whilst the other was ugly and idle. But she was much fonder of the ugly and idle one, because she was her own daughter; and the other, who was a stepdaughter, was obliged to do all the work, and be the Cinderella of the house. Every day the poor girl had to sit by a well, in the highway, and spin till her fingers bled.

Now it happened that one day the shuttle was marked with her blood, so she dipped it into the well, to wash the mark off; but it dropped out of her hand and fell to the bottom. She began to weep, and ran to her stepmother and told her of the mishap. But she scolded her sharply, and was so merciless as to say: 'Since you have let the shuttle fall in, you must fetch it out again.'

So the girl went back to the well, and did not know what to do; and in the sorrow of her heart she jumped into the well to get the shuttle. She lost her senses; and when she awoke and came to herself again, she was in a lovely meadow where the sun was shining and many thousands of flowers were growing. Across this meadow she went, and at last came to a baker's oven full of bread, and the bread cried out: 'Oh, take me out! take me out! or I shall burn; I have been baked a long time!' So she went up to it, and took out all the loaves one after another with the bread-shovel. After that she went on till she came to a tree covered with apples, which called to her: 'Oh, shake me! shake me! we apples are all ripe!' So she shook the tree till the apples fell like rain, and went on shaking till they were all down, and when she had gathered them into a heap, she went on her way.

At last she came to a little house, out of which an old woman peeped; but she had such large teeth that the girl was frightened, and was about to run away. But the old woman called out to her: 'What are you afraid of, dear child? Stay with me; if you will do all the work in the house properly, you shall be the better for it. Only you must take care to make my bed well, and to shake it thoroughly till the feathers fly – for then there is snow on the earth. I am Mother Hölle.'

As the old woman spoke so kindly to her, the girl took courage and agreed to enter her service. She attended to everything to the satisfaction of her mistress, and always shook her bed so vigorously that the feathers flew about like snowflakes. So she had a pleasant life with her; never an angry word; and to eat she had boiled or roast meat every day.

She stayed some time with Mother Hölle, before she became sad. At first she did not know what was the matter with her, but found at length that it was homesickness; although she was many thousand times better off here than at home, still she had a longing to be there. At last she said to the old woman: 'I have a longing for home; and however well off I am down here, I cannot stay any longer; I must go up again to my own people.' Mother Hölle said: 'I am pleased that you long for your home again, and as you have served me so truly, I myself will take you up again.' Thereupon she took her by the hand, and led her to a large door. The door was opened, and just as the maiden was standing beneath the doorway, a heavy shower of golden rain fell, and all the gold clung to her, so that she was completely covered over with it.

'You shall have that because you have been so industrious,' said Mother Hölle; and at the same time she gave her back the shuttle which she had let fall into the well. Thereupon the door closed, and the maiden found herself up above upon the earth, not far from her mother's house.

And as she went into the yard the cock was sitting on the well, and cried:

*'Cock-a-doodle-doo!*
*Your golden girl's come back to you!'*

So she went in to her mother, and as she arrived thus covered with gold, she was well received, both by her and her sister.

The girl told all that had happened to her; and as soon as the mother heard how she had come by so much wealth, she was very anxious to obtain the same good luck for the ugly and lazy daughter. She had to seat herself by the well and spin; and in order that her shuttle might be stained with blood, she stuck her hand into a thorn bush and pricked her finger. Then she threw the shuttle into the well, and jumped in after it.

She came, like the other, to the beautiful meadow and walked along the very same path. When she got to the oven the bread again cried: 'Oh, take me out! take me out! or I shall burn; I have been baked a long time!' But the lazy thing answered: 'As if I had any wish to make myself dirty!' and on she went. She soon came to the apple tree, which cried: 'Oh, shake me! shake me! we apples are all ripe!' But she answered: 'I like that! One of you might fall on my head,' and so went on. When she came to Mother Hölle's house she was not afraid, for she had already heard of her big teeth, and she hired herself to her immediately.

The first day she forced herself to work diligently, and obeyed Mother Hölle when she told her to do anything, for she was thinking of all the gold that she would give her. But on the second day she began to be lazy, and on the third day still more so, and then she would not get up in the morning at all. Neither did she make Mother Hölle's bed as she ought, and did not shake it so as to make the feathers fly up. Mother Hölle was soon tired of this, and gave her notice to leave. The lazy girl was willing enough to go, and thought that now the golden rain would come. Mother Hölle led her also to the great door; but while she was standing beneath it, instead of the gold a big kettleful of pitch was emptied over her. 'That is the reward for your service,' said Mother Hölle, and shut the door.

So the lazy girl went home; but she was quite covered with pitch, and the cock on the well, as soon as he saw her, cried out:

*'Cock-a-doodle-doo!*
*Your dirty girl's come back to you!'*

But the pitch clung fast to her, and could not be got off as long as she lived.

# 4

# *Fate and the Family*

---

*Never believe fate's more than the condensation of childhood.*

**Rainer Maria Rilke**

There was once a King of Lydia called Tantalos, a son of Zeus. Because of his divine birth and his boundless wealth, Tantalos became afflicted with *hubris*, and believed himself to be cleverer than the gods. In his madness he mocked them, by inviting them to a banquet in his city of Sipylos. Here he dared to set on the banquet table before the Olympians the best he had to give: the flesh of his own son Pelops, whom he had cut up and cooked in a cauldron. Thus he intended to test the omniscience of the immortals. But the gods, save for Demeter, knew of the sin, and refrained from eating. Rhea the Earth Mother, wife of Kronos, put the portions together again and made the child rise from the cauldron. Hermes recalled him to life, and Clotho, one of the Moirai, permitted it because she had not yet determined the time of the child's death.

The boy rose up more beautiful than he had been before. But he had one shoulder made of ivory, because the goddess Demeter had eaten this portion unknowingly. For that reason the descendants of the house of Pelops were distinguished by a birthmark, an unusually white shoulder or a star on the same part.

In punishment for his sin against the gods, Tantalos was confined for eternity in Tartaros, the darkest abyss of the underworld. There he was stood in a pool, with the water reaching his chin; he was tormented by thirst, but could not drink, for when he bent down, the water disappeared. Fruit trees dangled their riches over his head, but when he reached up to grasp the fruit in his hunger, the wind whisked it away. And on his descendants the curse of the Erinyes hung, for the evil had not yet been spent.

Pelops ruled as a great king with the favour of the gods, and the curse passed him by. He fathered three male children. The two

elder ones were called Atreus and Thyestes, and these sons
inherited the evil of their grandfather Tantalos. They murdered
their younger brother Chrysippos, Pelops' favourite child. So their
father cursed them and their descendants.

Atreus married a woman called Aerope, but his wife deceived
him with his brother Thyestes. Before Atreus could avenge
himself, however, events in the wider world interfered. The
people of the city of Mykenai summoned the brothers, for an oracle
had bidden the city to make king a son of Pelops. A quarrel broke
out between the brothers as to who should take the throne of
Mykenai, and Atreus drove Thyestes out and became king. But his
lust for vengeance against his brother was not yet satisfied, for the
thought still rankled that Thyestes had shared Aerope's bed.
Atreus invited his brother back to Mykenai, saying that he wished
for a reconciliation. But secretly he planned a horrible revenge. He
slew Thyestes' children, and invited his brother to eat unwittingly
of the roasted viscera and boiled flesh. When Thyestes realised
what he had eaten, he fell backwards, vomited up his meal,
dashed the table over with his foot, and pronounced a curse upon
the house of Atreus.

There were now three curses waiting to descend upon the line of
Atreus: that of the gods against the children of Tantalos, that of
Pelops against his son's progeny, and that of Thyestes against his
brother's line. Atreus had two sons by Aerope, called Agamemnon
and Menelaos. Thyestes, after his own sons had been butchered,
had left to him only a daughter. But he received a message from
Apollo's oracle at Delphi bidding him to raise up an avenger for the
murder of his children. So he raped his daughter, and raised the
son of the union, called Aegisthos, nurturing him in exile with
dreams of vengeance against Atreus' line.

Menelaos became King of Mykenai after Atreus, and his brother
Agamemnon became King of Argos. They were wedded to two
sisters, Helen and Klytaemnestra, daughters of King Tyndareos of
Sparta. Through Helen's infidelity to Menelaos with a Trojan
prince, the Trojan War began; and both Menelaos and Agamemnon became war-leaders who led the Greek armies to sack the city
of the enemy.

When Agamemnon travelled to the assembly of allied kings to
lead the Greek forces, he left behind with his wife Klytaemnestra
two daughters and a son called Orestes. The elder and more
beautiful of the daughters was named Iphigenia; the younger,
Elektra. While assembling the Greek fleet at Aulis to embark for
Troy, Agamemnon had occasion to offend the goddess Artemis
because of a prideful boast he made in her sacred wood. The angry
goddess accordingly sent bad weather, and the Greek ships could

not sail. A seer informed Agamemnon that Artemis would be placated only if he sacrified his daughter Iphigenia on the goddess' altar. So Agamemnon deceived his wife by saying that his daughter would be married at Aulis, and slew the child to win the goddess' favour.

When Klytaemnestra discovered that her beloved child had been slaughtered by Agamemnon, she swore revenge. She took as a lover that same Aegisthos who was the son of Thyestes by his own daughter. First she sent her son Orestes into exile, so that he could not defend his father. Then, when Agamemnon returned triumphant from the Trojan War, she and Aegisthos butchered him in his bath, and she set up Aegisthos as her consort to rule Argos with her.

Orestes had been banished to Phokis. The god Apollo visited him there, and commanded him to return to Argos to avenge his father's death, threatening dire punishments if he attempted to shirk the deed. So Orestes returned in disguise, and plotted in secret with his sister Elektra. First they murdered Aegisthos, their mother's lover, and then Orestes stabbed his own mother to death.

Although Orestes had obeyed the command of the god Apollo, he had violated the law of the Erinyes, defenders of mother-right and avengers of the murder of blood-kin. So the Erinyes pursued Orestes all over Greece and drove him horribly mad. Eventually he begged sanctuary before the altar of the goddess Athene at Athens. Athene, taking pity on him yet recognising also the right of the Erinyes to their prey, placed the case before the supreme court at Athens. Both Apollo and the Erinyes pleaded their causes before the human judges. When the vote was taken, it was equal; so Athene placed her deciding vote on the side of Orestes, and offered the Erinyes in exchange an altar and honourable worship in her land. The Erinyes were afterward called Eumenides, 'the kindly ladies', and Orestes returned a free man to Argos and married Harmonia the daughter of Menelaos and Helen. So the curse on the line of Tantalos was spent.

One wonders what a family therapist would think of this tale if Orestes turned up as the 'identified patient' with his presenting symptom of psychotic breakdown. Yet it is just this kind of tale that families do tell, although not usually in such florid terms as matricide and quarrels between the gods. The psychological equivalents, however, are often similar. Families are organisms, and the psychic life of an enmeshed family is a closed circle within which ancient and often violent emotional dramas are enacted in the secret darkness of the unconscious. Nothing is seen until the 'disturbed' child is taken for professional help, and then, terribly

slowly and often against strenuous opposition, the threads that
weave the tale are disentangled and what looked like an individual
'illness' becomes increasingly apparent as an unresolved family
complex. We have met facets of this problem already in the two
examples I gave of Venus–Pluto and Mars–Pluto, for in the lives of
both Caroline and Ruth, the sexual and emotional difficulties of the
parents and grandparents are somehow 'passed on' to the child,
and work as a fate in the child's life. Pluto is a particular significator
of a particular kind of experience: Moira as the Terrible Mother,
seeking vengeance for the violation or repression of her laws.
Problems of a sexual nature, or of an instinctual nature generally,
seem represented as family complexes by Pluto. But other things
besides instinctual conflicts pass down through families, and these
can bear a creative as well as a destructive face. Myth is once again
of immense value as a source of insight into the archetypal patterns
which dominate families generation after generation. The image of
the family curse, so beloved in Greek myth, is a vivid portrayal of
what passes unseen down the family line, and embodies the
experience of family fate.

A family is a system, as the relatively new field of family therapy
has revealed. As Salvador Minuchin puts it:

> The individual who lives within a family is a member of a social
> system to which he must adapt. His actions are governed by the
> characteristics of the system, and these characteristics include
> the effects of his own past actions. The individual responds to
> stresses in other parts of the system, to which he adapts; and he
> may contribute significantly to stressing other members of the
> system. The individual can be a subsystem, or part of the
> system, but the whole must be taken into account.[52]

Although much of the work of family therapy concerns itself with
the present family situation in which the individual finds himself –
and also with the present interactions and patterns which are at
work – nevertheless the 'system' of which Minuchin speaks is of
relevance both to the astrologer and the analyst. This system, in
astrological terms, is represented by the linked horoscopes of the
entire family, and this includes parents, grandparents, great-
grandparents and on into that distant past which the East so
gracefully describes as 'the ancestors'. Although most family
therapists would probably not avail themselves of the insights
available from family horoscopes, that is no reason why astrology
should not avail itself of the insights of family therapy. Seen from
the perspective of depth psychology, the 'characteristics of the
system' which are so profoundly important in influencing the
individual both in behavioural and intrapsychic terms are not so

very different from the warring gods in the drama of Orestes. In other words, these characteristics are not only the habit patterns of communication and role-assignation established over time which dictate whether mother is the one who always suffers or mediates in arguments, or whether father is always the one who acts out the anger and violence, or whether son or daughter is asthmatic, anorexic, obese or otherwise identifiable as 'the sick one'. The characteristics of the system are ultimately the archetypes, the core patterns or modes of perception and expression which can best be portrayed through mythic image. They pass from one generation to another in the same fashion as the curse of the House of Atreus. I am not in a position to comment on whether there is a genetic aspect to this psychic inheritance. But if there were, we would still have to deal with the inheritance.

One of the more striking features of the Orestes myth is the constant and changeable interference offered by the gods. Apollo, for example, takes now one side and now the other, ordering Thyestes to raise up an avenger against Atreus, then commanding Orestes to avenge his father – whose death would not have occurred if the god had not demanded the grooming of Aegisthos as a murderer in the first place. It is Apollo, too, who tells the people of Mykenai to place a son of Pelops on their throne. This constant interference on the part of the god implies a changing and developing archetypal direction which is at work within the family organism. In other words, there is a kind of intelligence at work which, although at times it provokes crises and problems and the suffering of individuals within the system, seems oriented towards a goal of some kind, or a resolution. What is also striking is that, each time this divine interference occurs, a great deal hinges upon the manner in which the human protagonists of the drama react to it. Family fate seems to be a product both of deeply unconscious archetypal factors, and also individual consciousness and responsibility. All the characters in the Orestes myth, save Orestes himself, are quite ready to react spontaneously and violently and without reflection to the promptings of the gods. It is only Orestes himself who truly embodies an inner conflict. Like Orestes, sooner or later the 'identified patient' will present himself for help with his difficulties, because at long last someone has the potential consciousness to attempt to reconcile or bridge the conflicting opposites within himself which are so often blamed on other family members. These conflicting opposites, however, are much older than the individual members of the family, and are imaged in Greek myth as gods.

It is not difficult for the more rational mind to understand the dynamics of the family in terms of behavioural patterns which have become established over several generations and which can be altered by the intervention of the family therapist. The father whose secret love affair has remained an idyllic fantasy of lost happiness may confer upon his daughter the name of the lost lover, thereby placing upon her shoulders the responsibility of being daughter–lover and soul to him and supplying the emotional fulfilment that his own marriage lacks. The mother who has suffered rejection or abandonment by her husband may transfer her rage to the son whose very maleness is an affront to her pain, raising him up to be her devoted servant–lover as recompense and turning him against his own sex in retaliation. These kinds of patterns are to be met with in most methods of psychotherapy, and the analyst encounters with regularity the mysterious tacit passing on of unlived and unconscious complexes from parent to child. As Frances Wickes puts it,

> We recognise the physical and economic dependence of the child upon the father and mother. We do not attach sufficient importance to the psychic bond which in early childhood often amounts to a condition of identity of the unconscious of the child with the unconscious of the parent. Through this identification the disturbing forces that lie below the level of conscious adult life are intuited by the unconscious of the child and give rise in their milder forms to vague fears, apprehensive fantasies, and disturbing dreams. In the more tragic instances dissociation from reality or antisocial acts result.[53]

As long as we view family interactions as causal, there is nothing strange or mystical about their importance. Even the above paragraph, although concerned with the boundlessness of the unconscious, suggests a causal relationship between unresolved parental conflicts and the child's disturbed behaviour. It is perhaps more difficult to envisage the psychic substance of the family as one substance out of which the lives of its individual members are molded, to such an extent that particular planetary aspects repeat among the charts of family members without any perceivable or understandable causal basis. Families as much as individuals are driven by mythic patterns. Inherited psychic substance is a curious concept, because whether or not there is a genetic basis or parallel to it, it is stated baldly by the aggregation of family horoscopes, and its manifestations are so often couched in dreams and fantasies rather than in physical characteristics or behavioural patterns. It is only when these psychic undercurrents begin to build up pressure for lack of integration in life that they seem to turn into the compulsions which are so disturbing in individuals, and often then there is no immediately recognisable connection with family matters. If the archetypal images are representations of instincts experienced through the psyche, then the archetypal patterns which are at work within families are representations of the very blood and bones of the family, the psychic parallel to biological heredity. The moment we consider these patterns in such a light, then we are once again within the realm of Moira, the spinner of the tissues of the body. Our families are our fate because we are made of the substance of those families, and our heredity – physical and psychic – is given at birth.

Frances Wickes places the most profound importance upon the unity of the unconscious of mother and child. Only through slow, gradual struggle does the individual ego of the child emerge – a weak, fragile, unprotected thing that can all too easily be battered and scarred by the unexpressed conflicts and frustrated energies alive within the psyche of the parent. The sins of father and mother are in truth visited upon the children, not through overt action, but through what has never emerged from primordial darkness. This is the child's Moira, his allotment. The unconscious conflicts that have remained unresolved come home to roost in the child, in the form of psychic inheritance. In later life, that secret bond between the unconscious of the child now grown to adulthood and the unconscious inheritance of the parents remains as potent as ever. It may be that astrology has a good deal to offer the analyst in terms of the selective receptivity that different children have towards these parental packages, through the connections between the horoscopes. We shall see more of this shortly. But it is the experience of many psychotherapists, including myself, that work on these family issues affects, in a strange and inexplicable way, the other members of the family. It is as though the real unity of the family psyche is revealed by one individual taking on the responsibility of working with the family complexes. The unity of substance in the family does not die with the physical death of the parents either, for they are not only actual people but images within the psyche of the child. 'The ancestors' thus remain a living inheritance, just as the genetic inheritance remains alive within the body and continues to be passed on to future generations.

There is a rather problematic issue around this 'inheritance' of psychic factors, however, and it comprises an apparent pair of opposites. I am not sure just how opposite these opposites really are, but they pose a problem not only from the point of view of the 'management' of psychotherapeutic work, but also from a philosophical point of view – or, in other words, from the point of view of fate. If painful or life-distorting experiences are 'caused' by the parent – whether by overt behaviour or, as Wickes suggests, by unconscious conflicts which find their way into the child *via*

unconscious identification with the parent – then the most enormous responsibility lies upon the shoulders of any individual who
would bring a child into the world. It is doubtful that many of us
would have children if we realised the full impact of this responsibility. Nor are we really dealing here with 'what has been written',
because presumably there is always an option on the part of the
parent to seek greater insight into himself so that he does not
burden his offspring with his own unsolved dilemmas. Much of
the work of psychotherapy, when it is conducted in depth,
involves the separation of the individual from this unconscious
identification with the parent, which may have gone on for the
whole of a lifetime and is no less potent just because the child has
grown into adulthood and the parents are, apparently, left behind.
If the parent has not taken the opportunity to assume responsibility for his conflicts, then the child become adult still can; through
a work of 'reconstruction' in the therapeutic situation, the individual's own identity can gradually emerge from beneath the blanket
of the parental world view. This is a fairly classical approach to the
matter, and would probably not offend the most pragmatic of
therapists. Jung sometimes places his major emphasis on this
'causal' approach, although he, like Wickes, is predominantly
concerned with the unconscious atmosphere rather than with
overt acts and words.

> The child is so much a part of the psychic atmosphere of the
> parents that secret and unsolved trouble between them can
> influence the child's health profoundly. The *'participation mys-
> tique'*, that is, the primitive unconscious identity of the child
> with its parents, causes the child to feel the conflicts of the
> parents, and to suffer from them as if they were its own troubles.
> It is hardly ever the open conflict or the manifest difficulty that
> has the poisonous effect; it is almost always a disharmony
> repressed and neglected by the parents. The real first cause of
> such a neurotic disturbance is, without exception, the uncon-
> scious. It is the things vaguely felt by the child, the oppressive
> atmosphere of apprehension and self-consciousness, that
> slowly pervade the child's mind like a poisonous vapour and
> destroy the security of the conscious adaptation.[54]

There is, however, another way of viewing this family inheritance, and on the surface it is contradictory to the attitudes and
approaches of many psychotherapeutic schools. This is the insight
which astrology offers, and it may be put very simply: The figures
of the parents, the unsolved dilemmas and unconscious conflicts
they contain and pass on, and the intrinsic nature of the parental
marriage, are *already* present as images within the birth horoscope.

In other words, they are *a priori*, inherent from the beginning –
what has been written. Because of these innate predispositions to
experience the parents through the perspective of the individual's
own psyche, the 'inheritance' is no longer only causal. This is a
very disturbing thought to those who take comfort in blaming their
parents' neglect, oppression, rejection, possessiveness or other
failures for their own inability to cope with life. The horoscope tells
us, in other words, that what is in the parents is also in us. There
can be no doubt that the objective parent and the inner image
connect, and perhaps even collude. But it is the inner pattern
which we must now consider, and it is this pattern which, I feel,
constitutes family fate. There is no 'reason' why signs should
repeat through family charts, or single aspects such as moon–
Uranus or Mars–Saturn, or specific house placements such as
eighth house Saturns or third house moons. But they do, despite
the lack of causal basis. 'Something' arranges these things, and
contemplating it is an awesome experience.

If mother, for example is experienced as Saturn and is therefore
felt as a cold, repressive, over-conventional or critical woman, then
in a sense mother can never really be anything else no matter how
hard she works at the parent–child relationship. The rejection is as
much on the part of the child as it is on the part of the mother. For a
period of time at least, and this often means the first half of life, that
is the child's subjective experience of mother. She may be no more
critical and cold than many another, 'better' mother, but she and
her child share the unfortunate fate of a relationship in which this
Saturnian factor is the dominant one that the child registers and
remembers. Frequently – so frequently that it is downright eerie –
the mother whose child sees her as Saturn will often be a Saturnian, either through a predominance of Capricorn in the horoscope,
or an angular Saturn, or a moon–Saturn or sun–Saturn conjunction. Thus it is a shared substance, just as it is a shared rejection. It
may even be said, and I am saying it from experience of many
examples, that the child's perception of the mother is coloured by
his own projection to such an extent that he can draw from her
those very qualities for which he blames her. Thus, the mother
with Capricorn rising, Venus in Pisces and sun in Cancer will only
register as Saturn on her child, and will begin to behave as Saturn
despite herself. The child's own behaviour and feeling, conscious
or unconscious, can push the mother into the more critical side of
her own nature, so that for reasons which defy her understanding
and may lead to considerable guilt and pain on her part as well as
the child's, she keeps behaving in a negative manner towards him.
Jung was also aware of this component of the family network,
complementary to the causal one:

All those influences which the literature describes as being exerted on the children do not come from the mother herself, but rather from the archetype projected upon her, which gives her a mythological background and invests her with authority and numinosity. The aetiological and traumatic effects produced by the mother must be divided into two groups: (1) those corresponding to traits of character or attitudes actually present in the mother, and (2) those referring to traits which the mother only seems to possess, the reality being composed of more or less fantastic (i.e. archetypal) projections on the part of the child.[55]

It has long been my feeling that insight into the *actual* personality chemistry between parent and child may be gained from examining the comparison of horoscopes – child and mother, child and father, mother and father, and so on. Insight into the archetypal image which the child projects upon the parent, and which also forms a major part of his own psychic constitution, may be gained from examining the sun and moon in the birth horoscope, as well as the tenth and fourth houses and their cusps. As I have said, these two things overlap, for the planetary significator in the child's chart is all too often echoed in the chart of the parent. The meridian of the birth chart is a representation of family fate, but it does not really describe what one's parents did to one in childhood. Rather, it is a portrait of two inner parents, archetypal or mythic in nature, which dominate the psyche of the child and remain as representations of relationship between man and woman throughout life. These are the inherited complexes, the 'ancestral sins'.

The actual parents usually bear more than a cursory relationship to these figures, and their marriage usually contains as one of its dominant themes the situation described in the child's horoscope. But the parents also possess other attributes, some of which may show everywhere except to the child. All that concerns the child is what he perceives; and if he is not to fall victim to the family pattern, then he must find a way to distinguish between the actual parents and the mythic images through which he views them. These mythic images are his fate, and he will be confronted with the necessity of working with them in his own life. But he can find a way to meet them with his own individual resources, rather than falling under the 'doom' of the parental marriage. Thus he does not sever connection with these images, but embraces them as figures which must be creatively incorporated into his development. As long as they remain 'parents' in a literal sense, however, then he is at their mercy.

The ascendant–descendant axis may be seen as a representation of individual destiny. But the meridian is altogether different. The signs and planets and aspects which are found in the two parental houses, the fourth and the tenth, are not objective portraits of the parents. They are archetypal images, gods, or 'allotments', and it is these gods which dictate the 'characteristics of the system' within the family far more than the personality differences and affinities. Ultimately I do not believe these 'allotments' to be negative, although they certainly become so if the individual attempts to dissociate himself from what they represent in the hope that he can free himself from his family. These tenth and fourth house planets cannot be escaped, any more than can the sun and moon. They are truly fate – inherited images which must be lived. If I were going to fantasise a horoscope for Orestes, I would imagine him to have, perhaps, Pluto at the midheaven in opposition to the sun at the IC, thus representing the battle between the matriarchal power of the Erinyes and the solar power of Apollo. As it is not atypical of sun–Pluto people to work out their conflicts through a breakdown of some kind, great or small, this would not be an inappropriate aspect for the Greek hero. He might also, perhaps, have Saturn conjuncting the sun and involved with the opposition to Pluto, since Apollo's dictum is a stern and unyielding law; and he would probably have Libra on the ascendant, since it took him so long to make up his mind which side of the fence he was on. But placements like these do not indicate literally that a mythic devouring mother has created havoc in a young man's life. Unfortunately, it is not so simple. No mother is merely Pluto. Even Klytaemnestra, who *is* mythic, has her story too, and in Aeschylos' tragedy she may be seen with some sympathy, a victim of her husband's brutality, infidelity and abandonment, grieving for the loss of a daughter destroyed through his pride and stupidity. Nor is any personal father purely sun–Saturn, radiant and wise and all-knowing and the giver of law. These figures do not really speak of the parents. Orestes experiences the gods through his parents. Pluto and sun–Saturn here speak of the gods themselves; and they are Orestes' fate.

I shall now make a leap from this rather bare introduction to the story of the young woman whose chart follows. The issues of family fate can best be illustrated by example.

This example is truly an 'identified patient', because she – I will call her Renee R. – suffers from the condition which psychiatry calls autism, the commonest form of 'childhood psychosis'. Renee is, of course, no longer a child, as will be evident from the birth data given; she is now an autistic adult, cared for in an institution. The psychiatric diagnosis for autism is poor. There is no treatment, and

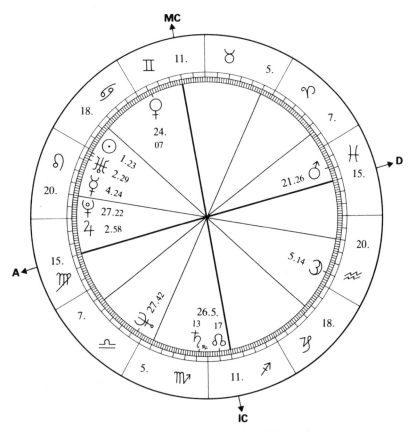

DIAGRAM 2. Birth horoscope of Renee R.

b. 24 July 1956
9.30 a.m.
London.

psychiatry considers that there is no evidence in favour of a
psychotherapeutic insight-directed approach. This diagnosis is
contradicted by the work of such analytical psychologists as
Michael Fordham, from whom we will hear more later. But it is the
accepted formula within the psychiatric establishment, which is
where most autistic children wind up. Although some improve-
ment in social behaviour is possible in later life, most adult autistics
remain severely handicapped in institutions or families, as is
Renee. The importance of environmental and emotional factors is
controversial in psychiatric studies. In other words, to put it

baldly, so far as the medical establishment is concerned, autism is a condition whose causes are obscure, whose treatment is a mystery, and whose prognosis is negative.

Following is a classification of the behavioural abnormalities of autism.

(a)  *Abnormalities of language:* abnormal response to sounds; very poor comprehension of gesture and speech; no imaginative play; poor or absent gesture; restricted social imitation; abnormal speech.

(b)  *Social abnormalities:* aloof and indifferent to people; poor gaze contact; no co-operative play (though may relish rough and tumble); no persisting friendships, weak parental attachments, no discrimination between people; indifference to social conventions, insensitivity to others' feelings.

(c)  *Rituals and routines:* rigid play (lining up toys) or preoccupation with sterile topics (bus routes, etc.); resistance to change with 'preservation of sameness' of environment (timetables, furniture placements, etc.); attachments to particular, often unusual objects or collections; tantrums when frustrated by denial of above.

(d)  *Additional abnormalities may be present:* a lack of curiosity and unresponsiveness to people in infancy (deafness is often queried); unpredictable fears, screaming or laughter; abnormal movements (finger stereotypes, spinning self or objects, toe-walking, etc.); difficulties learning manipulative tasks and orientations; hyperkinesis; self-destructive behaviour and rocking; isolated skills (jigsaws, music, computation, rote memory).[56]

This sparse clinical picture from a psychiatric textbook does not, of course, convey the feeling of the strange, disturbing ritualistic withdrawnness of the autistic child, who appears to exist in some other dimension of time and space and frustrates, sometimes violently, every effort to penetrate his inner fortress. But it does provide us with a good idea of the spectrum of behavioural peculiarities typical of autism. Some cases of autism are more severe than others, and some can be linked with organic causes such as brain damage. Renee, however, in so far as tests are in any sense conclusive, does not appear to suffer from any organic impairment. The roots of her autism are unknown. In childhood she was frighteningly strong-willed, and would go without sleep for long periods, standing rooted in a frozen posture for hours. Up to the age of fifteen, she was subject to violent rages and screaming fits. She would also subject her body to violence 'like someone pos-

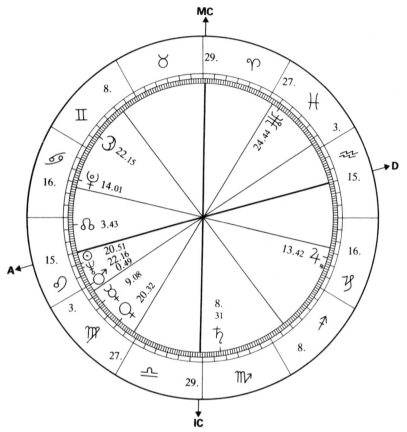

DIAGRAM 3. Birth horoscope of Mrs R. (Renee's mother)

b. 14 August 1925
5.00 a.m.
Antwerp

sessed'. She has never evidenced any capacity for normal speech, but occasionally 'echoes' a word or two of something that has been said – a typical autistic trait. By the time she was five years old she had been institutionalised. As she grew into adulthood, the rages and fits gradually subsided. Now she moves about in a zombie-like fashion, sometimes refusing to eat or sleep, simply sitting and doing nothing. It is difficult, when faced with a life of this kind, to be specious in talking about 'potentials' unused because of any conscious choice, or about freeing the 'spirit' from the 'lower nature'. Nor is any discussion of 'bad karma' from some other

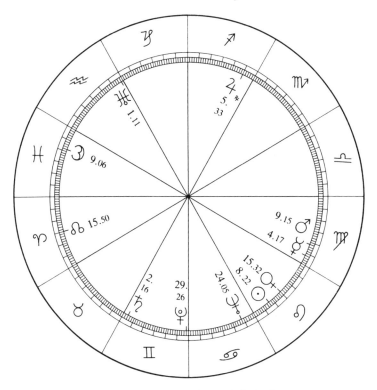

DIAGRAM 4. Birth horoscope of Mr R. (Renee's father)

b. 1 August 1912
No birth time given; planetary placements are for midnight GMT.

incarnation very edifying, save as a comfort to any among her family who might believe in it.

I shall not pretend at any point in this discussion to have found the 'cause' of Renee's autism. It remains as much a mystery to me as it does to the psychiatrists who have examined her, or to the bewildered members of her family. But if there is such a thing as family fate, then perhaps some small insight might emerge from a careful perusal of the family history and the family horoscopes, which now follow. It will also be of some value to examine what Jung and Fordham have to say about autism, in contrast to the disturbingly flat psychiatric portrait we have just seen.

Renee's mother, Mrs R., was married twice. Her first marriage was short-lived; her volatile husband vanished shortly after the birth of a daughter Rose. After obtaining a divorce on the grounds

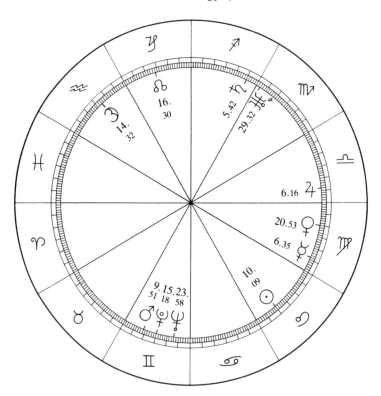

DIAGRAM 5. Birth horoscope of Grandmother R. (Renee's maternal grandmother)

b. 2 August 1898
No birth time given; planetary placements are for noon GMT.

of desertion, she then remarried, this time to a quiet, sweet-tempered, unobtrusive man. Renee is the daughter of this second marriage. So humiliated and wounded was Mrs R. by the desertion of her first husband that she never told Rose of her real father, but led the child to believe that the second husband, Mr R., had fathered both girls. Rose only discovered the true facts by accident when she was in her teens. Family secrets of this kind have a way of pervading the psychic atmosphere of the home in ways which are difficult to foresee.

Unable to face the implications of such an obviously disturbed child as Renee, Mrs R. insisted that there must be some birth defect responsible, and until Renee was institutionalised at the age of five simply could not cope with the task of looking after her. The

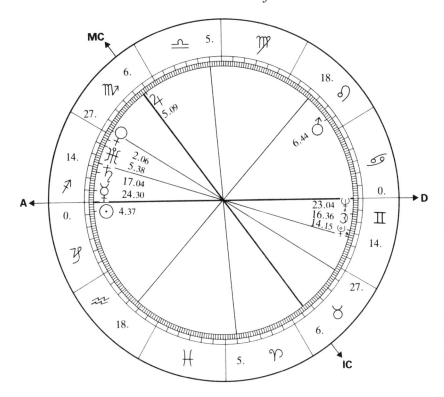

DIAGRAM 6. Birth horoscope of Grandfather R. (Renee's maternal grandfather)

b. 26 December 1898
8.00 a.m.
Amsterdam

responsibility of caring for the difficult and sometimes violent child thus fell to Rose, who was then around eleven years old. Mrs R. to this day still stubbornly refuses to consider that there might be emotional factors involved in Renee's autism, and remains convinced of the idea of a birth defect despite any number of medical tests to the contrary.

Mrs R. was herself an unwanted child, the result of an accidental pregnancy. She has had a long history of depression and physical disability, including various disturbances of the reproductive organs. She conceived her two children with great difficulty, and was frequently ill during her pregnancies. She was a 'good' child, perhaps compensating for the feeling of being unwanted, and developed into a passive, self-effacing adult. Her manner has

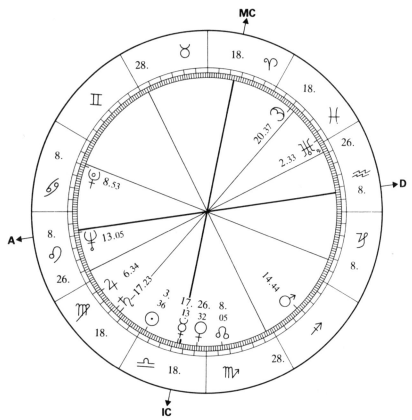

DIAGRAM 7. Birth horoscope of Aunt R. (Renee's mother's sister)

b. 27 September 1920
1.30 a.m.
Antwerp

always been apologetic and full of self-blame, and this persona was
in evidence long before Renee was born; the difficulties of raising
an autistic child have only increasd the sense of martyrdom to a
bad fate. She suffers from migraine and from stomach ulcers, both
of which conditions, alongside the chronic depressions, were her
excuse for not taking responsibility of the care of Renee when she
was small. Mrs R. has a younger sister, whose horoscope is
included under the name 'Aunt R.', since she is Renee's aunt. This
younger sister seems to have acted out much more of the
aggression and anger of the family, pursuing a dramatic sequence
of broken love affairs and abortions. There is immense jealousy

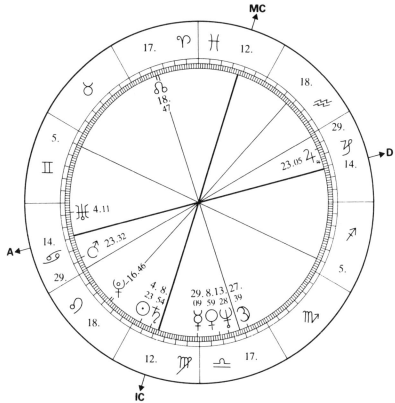

DIAGRAM 8. Birth horoscope of Rose R. (Renee's sister)

b. 28 August 1949
1.30 a.m.
London

between the two sisters. Aunt R. has always believed that her sister was the favoured child (despite Mrs R.'s belief that she was unwanted). Both vied for the love and attention of their father, who seems to have shown some sterling qualities, being a man of dignity and integrity. Their mother (whose horoscope is included under the name 'Grandmother R.') seems herself to have been a martyred type, begrudging the needs and demands of her two daughters, and offering a generally pathetic image to the world. She too suffered from numerous physical complaints.

This very brief description of a troubled family conveys one point very strongly: the women in the family, in particular Mrs R., have not in any sense dealt with their difficulties in an honest way, but have instead become victims of life. Mrs R.'s passive, self-effacing personality, which is characteristic of the sufferer of migraine and ulcers, is almost a carbon copy of her own mother's, and Aunt R., although apparently more active, is equally a sad victim of unfortunate affairs of the heart and is ultimately no less passive in attempting to deal constructively with her problems. The only family member who appears to have deviated from this pattern of martyrdom is Rose, who, perhaps in part because she was forced to face the dilemma of Renee so early, opted to take responsibility for her own life. She is the only one who is settled in a reasonably happy and stable marriage with loved children of her own. She is also the only one who has chosen to look at the problems of her family psychologically, for she has herself become a psychotherapist. These two sisters, Rose and Renee, have in very different fashions been burdened with a family fate. One has manifested this fate as autism, while the other has attempted to deal with her wound in a creative way.

We can now begin to examine the horoscopes of the family, first from the point of view of overall recurrent patterns or themes – the family 'myths' or 'characteristics of the system' – and second from the point of view of the individual horoscopes, in particular Renee's. What is immediately apparent and rather startling is the preponderance of the signs Leo and Virgo in the network of family charts. The repetition of these two signs is so frequent as to be almost absurd. Renee, Mrs R., Mr R. and Grandmother R. all have the sun in Leo. Aunt R. has Leo on the ascendant. Renee has Virgo on the ascendant, while Mrs R. has a satellitium in Virgo. Mr R. has Mars and Mercury placed there, while Grandmother R. has Venus and Mercury. Rose has the sun, Mercury and Saturn all in Virgo. This combination of Leo and Virgo extends into the horoscopes of Rose's children, for her young daughter has the sun, ascendant, Mercury and Saturn in Virgo, and the moon in Leo. Only Grandfather R. lacks planetary placements in these two signs.

Whatever else this predominance of Leo and Virgo might mean, I am struck by the juxtaposition of a fiery, energetic, self-willed and self-expressive sign with a collection of such passive, depressed and timid personalities. This fact alone is enough to set off warning bells in the objective observer. What has happened to all that fire? One might envision a family of talented, creative people such as the Redgraves; or a rowdy, competitive dynasty such as one finds in American soap operas like *Dallas*. Of all the signs, Leo is the one most concerned with individuality and the right to be oneself. This is, in a sense, a family *daimon*, a tremendously potent creative drive which, evidently, was simply choked to death. It is my feeling that this problem of the vanishing Leo is a very relevant point when we come to look at the possible background to Renee's autism.

At first glance, it might seem that Virgo is more obvious in the visible characteristics of the family portrait, at least in its less attractive manifestations: the preponderance of psychosomatic ailments which seems to burden the family members. But Virgo too is not really being expressed in any true sense, for this earthy sign is a doer and a builder. Only Rose, with the sun conjunct Saturn in Virgo, has manifested the ambition and conscientiousness to achieve anything in a worldly sense, academically and professionally. The intellectual liveliness of Virgo, like the self-expressiveness of Leo, seems to have been quite stifled in this family. At best, the Leo–Virgo blend produces the creative artist or craftsman, or the worldly entrepreneur, who combines breadth of vision with a meticulous attention to the details of earthly life. At worst, it is a frustrated, fretting hypochondriac, eternally worried about what others think and whether everything is in the safe place where it was last left: the negative side of Virgo overwhelming the bright fire of Leo. What remains, with such a souring of the dough, is, to put it very simply, suppressed rage. The fiery *daimon* stifled and dampened and inverted so that each little illness is a further means of attention-getting and covert control, turns poisonous. Although it is purely intuitive speculation on my part, I feel we do not have to look far to surmise who has been the recipient of all that poison.

Now, such a gross generalisation is my own astrological imagination playing about with a problem which most psychiatrists would deal with far more cautiously. But it is worth perusing, at this point, some of the less orthodox views on autism offered by people other than those entrenched in the psychiatric establishment. Frances Wickes offers the following remarks on autism:

> A child who has normally passed beyond auto-erotic acts may be thrown back into them by an abnormal urge to retreat. It may take any of the forms belonging to that earlier stage of development ... Regressive tendencies resulting from failure to adapt often seek compensation in power. Or it may result in a withdrawal of forces. Ordinarily (as I understand it) this regressive behaviour can be worked with analytically if the task or situation to which the child cannot adapt can be discovered. *In autism evidentially the task or situation is life itself, and the child simply refuses to develop an ego at all.*[57]

So, in Wickes' view, a child such as Renee takes a kind of quick look out (or something which is pre-ego but nevertheless sentient takes that look), and says to itself, No, thank you. Whatever is out there is evidently too terrifying, too monstrous, too threatening, too life-destroying to merit the effort. The body continues to develop, and the child lives within the penumbra of the unconscious Self. Its rituals are reminiscent of those of an animal, such as a dog circling round and round before settling itself in its basket. The ego, the complex of conscious adaptation to the environment, never separates out from the Self, although the nascent personality traits which are reflected by the birth horoscope may be glimpsed in crude and primitive form. One may well ask why Renee would have found life an impossible task. Perhaps this is related to all that furiously suppressed life in a family of Leos who cannot live. One wonders what kind of psychic charge accumulates within the collective fabric of such a repressed group of people. Perhaps if such things can be perceived by the psyche of a newborn child, then it is a sufficient reason to deny psychological birth.

Jung implies that a complex is at the core of autistic withdrawal. Although we shall have more to say about complexes and fate later on, this might mean, put very simplistically, that there is a complex of associations, images and responses which acts like a magnet in the unconscious and draws the libido, the life-energy, away from the external world and in and down to itself.

> Autistic withdrawal into one's fantasies is the same as what I have described elsewhere as the marked proliferation of fantasies related to the complex. Reinforcement of the complex is identical with increase of resistance ... The 'life-wound' is the complex, which is naturally present in every case of schizophrenia and of necessity always entails the phenomenon of autism or autoeroticism, since complexes and involuntary egocentricity are inseparable and reciprocal ... For some time I have employed the concept of *introversion* for this condition.[58]

Seen in this perspective, autism is extreme introversion, extreme withdrawal of life-energy into the unconscious towards the complex. But what, in the case of Renee, is the complex, the 'life-wound' as Jung puts it? Perhaps I can be forgiven for waxing mythical, but I would suggest that the complex has something to do with the raging lion, the angry deity who, denied outer expression for several generations, now inhabits the underworld and devours from within. I am reminded most strongly of that Greek image of the family curse, embodied in an angry power which in some mysterious fashion works from *within* the family and provokes actions which in turn promulgate catastrophe. If I view it in this way, Renee's autism is not the 'fault' of Mrs R. Rather, the entire family, Mrs R. included, is at the mercy of something which destroys from within because no single family member – save Rose – is sufficiently conscious to give it expression in outer life.

Michael Fordham, in his book, *The Self and Autism*, offers an exhaustive and illuminating study of the subject. He begins his discussion of autism by quoting Winicott and Bettelheim, two analysts who are convinced that the environment and in particular the mother are decisive in cases of secondary (non-organic) autism. Winicott considers that there has been an environmental defect, while Bettelheim goes so far as to contend that autistic children are autistic because they came into the world and were confronted with mothers who wished for their death. This is, needless to say, an extreme viewpoint, and it does not accord with Fordham's findings; nor does it accord with astrology's findings, although Fordham would probably not be pleased to find that the horoscope affirms his viewpoint.

> If autistic children live in an 'inner' world it is not by any means felt so to be – rather they live with a world of objects (and this includes parts of their own bodies) whose arrangement is often very precise and organised, though not distributed in terms of what is inner and outer. On the basis of observations such as these it seems probable that the hypothesis of a barrier protecting an inner world is simply an assumption made by adults to explain the child's inaccessibility; this is often felt by the parent as a barrier when, in terms of the child's experience, no such feeling is established because the barrier is set up not against them but against not-self-objects. He may know and feel a barrier but it is not a defence to protect an internal object.[59]

He then goes on to say:

> It is assumed that the essential core of autism represents in distorted form the primary integrate of infancy, and that idiopathic autism is a disordered state of integration, owing its persistence to failure of the self to deintegrate.[60]

As I understand this statement of Fordham's, he is not very far away from Wickes: the Self must deintegrate for the ego to form, and it does not do so, thereby preserving the original 'wholeness' of the newborn infant before relationship with the external object (mother, mother's breast) begins. The rage and anger of the autistic child is therefore directed at any outer object which does not comply with the inner self-object requirements, or, in other words, anything which is sensed as 'not me'.

As I am not experienced in the field of therapy with autistic children, I am not in a position to agree with or contradict these authors except in a theoretical way. I have quoted this material to help give a picture of the condition and its perplexities, and the findings of those who work within the field. But for the astrologer, the primary question is – or perhaps ought to be – whether such a condition as autism can be seen in any form, nascent or actual, in the birth horoscope. If not, then one is irresistibly led to the mother, and to the relation between mother and child. I do not know whether Mrs R. harboured secret unconscious wishes to destroy her child. It is certainly possible, considering her life history. She certainly seems to be damned by circumstantial evidence. But Renee herself is an equally important partner in this dialogue, so we must now turn to her birth horoscope.

At first glance, this does not seem to be a particularly 'unfortunate' horoscope. At least, it is not unfortunate in terms of the traditional nasties such as overemphasised and afflicted sixth and twelfth houses, dreadful Saturn aspects, and other astrological terrors from medieval horoscopic literature. The sun is in dignity in its own sign of Leo, and there is a grand trine, albeit out-of-sign, in the airy houses. This ought, in ordinary terms, to suggest some kind of mental facility since these are the three houses concerned with communication and exchange between people. I am only too aware of the problems of hindsight in chart interpretation. We shall all no doubt be trotting out the charts of Hitler and Oscar Wilde unto eternity to see whether one can spot a homosexual or a world dictator. I shall never be convinced that Renee's chart 'shows' autism, any more than Wilde's 'shows' homosexuality or Hitler's 'shows' mastery over most of Europe. But as autism is such a mystery even within the therapeutic field, I can perhaps be excused for piecing together a scenario which might tell a story. This I have already begun to do in considering the omnipresence of Leo in the family horoscopes and suggesting the idea of a family myth or *daimon* of self-expression and individuality which has been inverted and turned destructive.

A closer inspection of Renee's grand trine reveals a powerful, perhaps even a ruthless will. That is not, of course, in contradiction either of the typical autistic personality or of Renee herself, who stands for hours refusing food and sleep and falls into violent rages if intruded upon. The will is certainly there, but it is used for something other than extroverted activity. The frightening outbursts of temper and the attacks on those who disturb the intactness of the fantasy world are accomplished with tremendous rigidity and determination. The ego has perhaps never been born, but in its nascent state it would seem still to be a Leo, an anti-consciousness that clings to the uroboric embrace with all the tenacity of any Leo, at one with the unconscious Self and violently resistant to outer intrusion or invasion of any kind. For reasons best known to herself – or to her Self – Renee has elected to turn the fixity and determination of the sun in trine to Saturn in trine to Mars against, rather than into, the world. Thus she herself becomes omnipotent, all-powerful, and anything which threatens this experience must be negated or destroyed.

Saturn in the third house in Scorpio also tells a tale. At best, this placement is not communicative. At worst, it is virtually inarticulate. Whatever 'normal' might mean, Saturn found in the third house is not one of your party chatterboxes. It can display great suspicion of the environment, and evidences Scorpio's habitual nose for the shadow. If there is an angry *daimon* around, or, as Bettelheim suggests, an unconsciously murderous mother, then Saturn in Scorpio will find it, even where no one else will. Even moderately murderous mothers – those in whom some basic ambivalence is to be found towards the child, a common and probably 'normal' situation – become Terrible Mothers for Scorpio. The third house is also traditionally the house of siblings, and carries the suggestion here of dependency upon and hostility towards Rose, who was eleven when Renee was born and was coerced into taking care of her. Saturn is in square to Mercury, another contact which is suggestive of a withdrawn, non-communicative nature. These qualities are comfortable and may even be attractive in someone in whom the ego is strong enough to express them in a related way. An ordinary interpretation of this third-house–Mercury–Saturn link-up might touch on hesitancy in expression, and a certain self-doubt in terms of intellectual confidence. But one might also point out the tact, depth and thoroughness inherent in the aspect. But in Renee's case, what we have is virtually a caricature of the individual who cannot speak, cannot learn, and cannot permit any infringement of the environment into her private world.

We are, so far, no closer to discerning autism in Renee's chart, although certain configurations such as the Saturn–Mercury aspect 'fit' in an exaggerated way the condition of this unfortunate woman. Perhaps even more important than the Saturn–Mercury square is the square of Saturn to Pluto in the twelfth house. This square is a very close one, and in light of all we have seen Pluto in the preceding chapters, it ought to suggest something 'fated' at work in Renee. I have mentioned that the twelfth house concerns the collective psyche of the family, with its past 'sins' and unlived complexes. Pluto placed in the twelfth supports my feeling that tremendous violent anger lurks in the atmosphere within this family. It is a kind of 'pick-up' of the collective shadow, a peculiar sensitivity to the dark destructiveness which lies below the threshold of conscious individual expression and which has been carried forward into the present from the ancestral past. Renee's third house Saturn in Scorpio suggests a sensitivity to the immediate environment, but Pluto in the twelfth squaring this Saturn suggests a deeper sensitivity, and one which even in a 'normal' child might suggest night terrors and great fear of the unseen destructiveness which the parental psyches carry. Although this aspect does not declare 'autism' any more than any other horoscope placement does, it certainly emphasises what might be the 'impossible task' with which Renee was confronted.

Another configuration of undoubted importance is the T-cross between the sun, moon, Uranus, Mercury and Neptune. With this very tense grouping we may glimpse some of the qualities which express themselves through Renee as violence and destructiveness. This is also no doubt part of the 'life task' which Renee cannot or 'will not' take on, for accommodating such diverse and powerful feelings as those reflected by two outer planets colliding with sun and moon is a problem which even in a strong ego would very likely give rise to intolerance of restriction or opposition of any kind. Given this predisposition in Renee, nascent from the beginning, one can only speculate on the response if someone of her strong-willed and explosive nature encounters something equally strong-willed and explosive in the environment. Although the family as we have seen it evidences some pretty pathetic, repressed personalities, somewhere in the psychic atmosphere all that buried Leo lurks. It is both within Renee and outside her. Even if we consider Bettelheim's more extreme view that the autistic child refuses development because of the intuited murderous feelings of the mother, what if both mother and child possess a murderous rage?

The full moon in Renee's chart echoes the chart of Grandmother R., who was born under the same Leo–Aquarius full moon. Mr R. has the sun in Leo in opposition to Uranus in Aquarius, although he does not seem to have expressed it. Mrs R. has the moon in square to Uranus. These parental contacts of sun and moon to Uranus are both reflected in Renee's chart. So there is not only Leo, but Uranus to contend with as well. Beneath the exterior this family psyche is like a mine-field. Sun and moon aspecting Uranus are not placements which are overly conducive to co-operative interchange and adjustment to others. If the individual with such aspects is a more social or gregariously inclined type, then the more abrupt and iconoclastic Uranian qualities are often repressed, and are lived out through a partner or friends who are 'peculiar'.

Renee's moon–Uranus opposition is particularly relevant, because the moon has a special bearing on the image and experience of the mother in the individual's horoscope. The moon represents our roots; it is a symbol of that aspect of the pyche which contains and supports life. In this sense it is also an image of the physical body, the container of the psyche, and also of the mother, who is our physical container during pregnancy and our psychic container during childhood. The moon tells a story about the individual's feeling of safety in life, both from the point of view of how he experiences his childhood and how he experiences his own physical self as a safe place in which to live. It will be immediately apparent that Uranus is anything but a safe container. The experience of the mother is not nurturing or supportive. It is felt as unpredictable, unreliable, sometimes kind and comforting but suddenly and without reason hostile or perverse. The difficult aspects of Uranus and the moon pose a great dilemma for a woman, because the maternal moon and its instinctual world become disturbed and threatened by the compulsion to break free. The woman with moon–Uranus may experience a lack of safety through her own mother; and her mothering, in turn, may be fraught with ambivalent feelings. It is as though she is not quite comfortable about being a woman at all, because Uranus fights violently against the biological bondage of the moon. Ambivalence and even rage toward the ordinary functions of the female body are often the by-product of an unresolved moon–Uranus dilemma. In some people I have seen the great tension and fear of disruption expressed in symbolic ways such as fear of flying in aeroplanes, or a fear of electricity, or a fear of fire. The body anticipates sudden death or harm, which is the moon's reaction to the intrusion of Uranus, just as Uranus feels the moon to be a trap and a tomb. It is therefore not surprising that Mrs R. experienced such difficulty in conceiving her children, and suffered from recurrent ailments during her pregnancies. It is as though she consciously wanted a child but unconsciously rejected it, and the conflict was suffered in the body rather than in consciousness. I have often seen this with moon–Uranus women: Rather than endure the conflict and make the necessary steps to give both sides of it value in life, they often identify with the 'good mother' role, thus harbouring immense unconscious anger towards the child who has bound them to their female bodies. This, perhaps, is what Bettelheim means by the mother who secretly wishes to destroy her child. Torn between being a woman and being the asexual spiritual being symbolised by Uranus, this aspect is a frequent contact in the charts of those who suffer sexual disfunctions, gynaecological problems and difficulties or delays in childbearing.

The moon–Uranus opposition in Renee's chart could be taken as an indicator of her basic experience of her mother. In turn Mrs R. also has the aspect, in the form of a square. So she too experienced instability in the relationship with her own mother, Grandmother

R. This interpretation is confirmed by the fact that Grandmother R. conceived by accident and did not want her child. We are here confronting a family inheritance which has worked its way down from grandmother to mother to daughter, and has probably even earlier roots. It is like a Greek family curse, which if it remains unconscious simply leads to the next generation suffering from the same problem. How much the accumulated psychic stuff of several generations of angry women is connected with Renee's inability to develop a functioning ego is an open question. But the problems of this aspect are certainly suggestive of great insecurity and a feeling of being 'uncontained' in life. One of the more interesting facets of the moon–Uranus contact is that the 'container' is not only the mother; it is the individual himself or herself, the body containing the conflict of feelings, the personality containing its unruly elements. Moon–Uranus is not only a portrait of a person who has difficulty in feeling 'safe'. It also pictures a person who fears that he cannot himself contain his own explosiveness. The aspect has always had a reputation for 'bad-temper', but this is something more than ordinary irritability. The fear of explosions, fire, sudden accidents, aeroplane crashes and other 'phobic' manifestations is really a projection upon outer objects of the disruptive tendencies within the individual himself. The container which is faulty is not only the mother; being unmothered, it is the individual who often has a low tolerance for anxiety and cannot stand ambivalent emotions. It is perhaps relevant here to remember Renee's sudden rages, erupting out of nowhere, exhausting themselves and then vanishing, as well as the obsessive ritualising of objects and actions which are so eerily like the primitive rituals that keep the dark forces of the inimical gods at bay.

We may now examine another 'inherited' contact in Renee's chart, the square between the sun and Neptune. In Mrs R.'s chart, the sun is conjunct Neptune in the first house. Grandmother R. has the two planets in semisquare. This is another configuration which appears to follow the maternal line. Mr R. has neither sun nor moon aspecting Neptune. Aunt R. has the moon in Pisces, which is (if the pun may be excused) a watered-down version of moon–Neptune, which does appear in Grandfather R.'s chart as well. Neptune is a planet which is antithetical in meaning to Uranus, because it is connected with the realm of feeling rather than thought, and embodies the archetypal image of the victim and the issue of redemption through suffering. In terms of Mrs R.'s chart, the sun–Neptune expresses much of her overt behaviour in life, and appears to have virtually dominated her. What is visible is not the dynamic Leo, nor the turbulent moon–Uranus, but the self-effacing and sacrificial stance of Neptune, to whom love and suffering are inseparable and for whom life is barren if there is no one to offer up one's soul to. This tendency to give up one's own identity and live through sacrifice to others is perhaps one of the reasons why someone as strong as Mrs R. elected to live the life she did. Any hurt – such as the abandonment by her first husband – is seen not as a source of anger or of self-examination, but an affirmation that life is a place of suffering and sacrifice. Renee also has this dilemma in her horoscope. The unresolved conflict between the self-will of Uranus and the self-sacrifice of Neptune has landed firmly upon her, and once again it is tempting to surmise that perhaps this is one of the insurmountable life-tasks from which she has, on some profound level, elected to withdraw.

Like Apollo and the Erinyes in the myth of Orestes, two power-ful deities here demand satisfaction. Both are represented by outer planets, which to me suggests that neither is prone to being wholly integrated into individual consciousness. Both have the autonomy and force of a god, for they are embodiments of great collective drives and myths. Neptune is essentially a feminine planet, and is connected with the archetypal image of the suffering woman. This is the 'mediatrix' such as is portrayed by the figure of the Virgin Mary. The sentiments of Neptune are nicely expressed in Bach's *St Matthew Passion*:

> 'Tis I whose sin now binds Thee!
> With anguish deep surrounds Thee
> And nails Thee to the tree.
> The torture Thou art feeling,
> Thy patient love revealing,
> 'Tis I should bear it, I alone.

Neptune opens the floodgates to the experience of the suffering of the world and the agony of the spirit incarnated in flesh. The longing is for release from the body's prison and union with the divine source, whether this is taken in a spiritual sense as God or in a reductive sense as the original unity of mother's womb. There-fore the Neptunian person is inclined to experience the mortal passions as full of sin and grief, himself as guilty, and his expiation as the only possible means of cleansing and atonement. Renee's mother perhaps 'needed' a disturbed child, for her meaning in life is inextricably bound up with suffering. So, too, would Renee's have been, although the strongly Leonine and Uranian influences in the horoscope would have fought this necessity of suffering. This alone might provide reason enough not to bother. Uranus is a male planet, and carries the inspiration and detached breadth of vision of the heaven-gods of myth. Renee, like Orestes, has within her horoscope an apparently irreconcilable conflict. Jung felt that such conflicts, although they tend to generate suffering, are immensely creative and conducive to the development of a true individuality. But Renee was not in a position to benefit from Jung's wisdom. It is as though, sensing the turbulence and difficulty of the life mapped out for her, she decided, if I phrase it in more esoteric language, not to incarnate at all.

I am certainly inclined to speculate quite deeply upon the connection of Mrs R.'s suffering and internal conflict with Renee's autism. It is as though Orestes, confronted by the angry and demanding deities who dog his family, decided not to return to Argos to fulfil Apollo's command, but simply curled up in a ball in Phokis, the place of his exile, and never spoke again. But why does Renee lack the strength of Orestes? This question is a reasonable one to ask of the horoscope, because if the horoscope indicates basic propensities of character, then surely the capacity to cope with conflict ought to be indicated in the chart. Strength of will, as we have seen, is certainly evident. But containment is not. Perhaps Renee's inability to struggle with the battleground into which she was born is connected in part with her Virgo ascendant, not the bravest or toughest-skinned of signs. I have found over and over again that Virgo, like its opposite sign Pisces, can be extremely mediumistic and sensitive to the atmosphere of the environment. The difference is that environmental undercurrents register emotionally in Pisces, whereas in Virgo they tend to register in the form of physical symptoms. Virgo has few defences against the invader, save that of the habits and rituals so beloved by the sign and the incisive intellect which, once development has begun, serves as a bastion against chaos. Autism, in a horrible sort of way, is a caricature of this ritualism with its rigid repetitive actions and compulsive ceremonies. Obsessive ritual is a fascinating expression of the ancient primitive tendency to perform magical actions to protect oneself – or the community – against the invasion of the chaos of the archetypal world. The overpowering unconscious force of so much familial Leo would be enough to drive even a 'normal' Virgo into frenzied rituals, and probably into eczema, asthma, and stomach troubles as well. Mrs R.'s first house is a frightening barrage of unlived vital life, dominated by the pathos of a negative Neptune. In trying to imagine this formidable woman playing such a passive and acquiescent role, I am disturbed by the potential of violence that must lie beneath the surface and which permeated the psychic environment of the baby Renee, with her thin-skinned Virgo ascendant. Perhaps the autistic child makes a kind of statement: 'I am very sorry, but I am not coming out. The world is far too terrifying and destructive, I myself am far too terrifying and full of destructiveness, and my defences are too weak, so thank you very much but no thanks; I shall remain unborn.'

Rose, Renee's half-sister, has somehow managed to escape the nightmare which Renee herself apparently perceived too early and too well. There may be many reasons for this. Seen psychologically, when Rose was born, Mrs R. had not yet suffered the disillusionment of the lost husband, and had not yet fully crystallised in her martyr's stance. Seen astrologically, Rose's chart does not evidence the same turbulent conflicts as Renee's. Here the moon is in trine to Uranus, which suggests that in Rose the conflict between motherhood and freedom is an issue which, although difficult, stands a far better chance of reconciliation. Trines imply a greater possibility of integration of two warring psychic drives. Here also the sun is in sextile to Uranus, a softer aspect than the conjunction which appears in Renee's chart. This makes the wilfulness of Uranus more manageable and more able to be integrated and expressed as an independent spirit still able to live within existing social boundaries. Most important, perhaps, is the absence of Leo in Rose's horoscope. Only Pluto is placed in the sign, and Pluto does not figure strongly either in its house placement or in its aspects to other planets. Neptune too is relatively quiet, only conjuncting Venus; so whatever sacrificial tendency is implied, it is more likely to surface as romantic idealism and the sacrifice of wildly idealistic love-fantasies, rather than as a sacrifice of the identity itself as is so often the case with the sun. The T-cross involving the moon, Jupiter and Mars is certainly difficult, and does not possess the best of tempers. But these are inner planets, and are a good deal more readily digested. Uranus and Neptune threatening the sun and moon from opposite sides are a far more formidable combination in Renee's chart than Mars and Jupiter colliding with the moon in Rose's. There is a similarity, for the problem of sacrifice versus self-assertion is suggested by both. But Rose's T-cross is child's play compared with the terrible collision of the other planets in Renee's chart. Finally, the conjunction of the sun and Saturn in Virgo is also an important indicator of a kinder fate. Although it seems to reflect the loss of the father – which, consciously, Rose did not know about, but which is stated baldly here in the birth horoscope – it offers in compensation a toughness and capacity for survival and containment which none of the other women in this family seems to possess. Rose has the gift of self-preservation, and this is perhaps partly why she alone has managed to build a life for herself rather than becoming a football tossed blindly between archetypal powers.

Obviously there are many more connections among these family horoscopes which might be mentioned. They are a striking example of the repetition of patterns within families which I have seen so many times in my experience of working as an astrologer. Family fate does indeed seem to be portrayed, in part as a synchronicity of repeated signs and aspects which form a kind of statement of psychological heredity. Whether one wishes to take a causal or an acausal approach to the problem of the 'family scapegoat' or 'identified patient', it is apparent in the study of interlocked family charts that the individual is not so separate as he might think. For this reason Orestes stands as the great mythic symbol of family fate. At the core of his dilemma is ambivalence, a collision of opposites portrayed in the drama as the deadly battle between matriarchy and patriarchy, between body and spirit, between mother and father. This conflict drives Orestes mad. He is caught between two archetypal dominants, the solar god Apollo who rules the realm of light and consciousness, and the chthonic Erinyes who serve the underworld powers and the realm of instinct. When conflicts within a family proliferate without resolution for generation after generation, then the individual may find himself in Orestes' shoes: heads, they win; tails, you lose. There is no recourse but the path of suffering in order to find any redemption or freedom for the succeeding generations, but this suffering needs to be conscious rather than blind. I cannot conceive of any dilemma which has so much of the feeling of fate. Whatever factors might have contributed to the unlived life of a woman like Renee, this myth surely reflects the terror and confusion which life can hold for one who is the inheritor of such conflicts.

Orestes cannot solve his own dilemma. He can appeal to the gods who first got him into it, with trust that they will ultimately get him out of it if they possess any justice at all. Although we have seen how Apollo plays tricks and interferes with the development of the House of Atreus, nevertheless Orestes, like Job, has a patient faith in the divine powers which is the cornerstone of his salvation. His fate lies with Apollo, and he accepts it. At no point does he acquire *hubris*; perhaps for this reason Athene finally casts her vote on his side. When he confronts his mother with drawn sword, Klytaemnestra says: 'My blood will hound you.' Orestes does not pretend to be braver or more righteous than he is. He simply replies: 'My father's blood already hounds me. So what can I do?' He is not weak, but he has humility. He passes through exile and pursuit always believing that in the end Apollo will fulfil his pledge and provide a solution. This is an initiation of a most profound kind: the defeat of the Terrible Mother which requires great suffering for its creative resolution. Here family fate coincides with individual fate, for Orestes fights for his own individual freedom but the journey towards this freedom means a thorough embrace with the sins of the family. He must become a murderer like the rest, must violate blood-kin like the rest, and must become as tainted as his progenitor Tantalos. Alternatively, he might have been like Renee, and would never have been born.

The process of development of complexes within families has a feeling both of teleology – movement towards a goal – and of inevitability, just as the curse of the House of Atreus has an inevitability. If one looks backwards from the conflicts and compulsions of one's own drama, one may glimpse the family myth, twisting and winding through father and mother, grandparents and great-grandparents, endlessly uncoiling like the Stoics' vision of Heimarmenê, into the racial collective unconscious. The myth of Orestes and his family seems to suggest that whatever we are as individuals, part and parcel of that personal identity is our inheritance, which sits upon us like fate and must be met and grappled with in an individual way. It cannot be repudiated nor run away from; it is not enough to model one's life on 'anything but mother or father', for in so doing we are as surely dominated by them as if we tried to be exactly like them. One may do what one can do, or wishes to do, with an inheritance; but the inheritance itself cannot be ignored or given away, for our families are our allotment, our Moira.

# 5

# *Fate and Transformation*

---

*The force of fate does not penetrate the mind unless the mind of its own accord has first become submerged in the body, which is subject to Fate ... Every soul should withdraw from the encumbrance of the body and become centred in the mind, for then Fate will discharge its force upon the body without touching the soul.*[61]

**Marsilio Ficino**

Marsilio Ficino, Florentine philosopher, astrologer and magus, offered in the second half of the fifteenth century the above advice about freeing oneself from fate. In his horoscope at birth, according to his own calculation, Saturn was rising in Aquarius in square to the sun and Mars in Scorpio, a vicissitude about which he ceaselessly moaned to his friends because he claimed that it always made him depressed. That is not surprising since, in terms of modern depth psychology, what he is advocating is dissociation. I do not need to elaborate upon what this passage reveals of Ficino's own personal conflict between reason and nature. Those natal squares between the rational control of an Aquarian Saturn and the combustible passions of a Scorpio sun and Mars phrase it quite nicely. Ficino's advice is not unfamiliar to the modern astrologer, for we have already met it in the words of Margaret Hone; nor is it unfamiliar to those who espouse a Theosophical or 'spiritual' approach to astrology. In essence it is the voice of Platonic doctrine, astrology's constant companion on its hoary journey from Babylon, Egypt and Greece to the present day. From Plato's time through the Neoplatonists of the early Christian era and the Renaissance to Robert Fludd and William Lilly in the seventeenth century, and again from the 'rediscovery' of astrology at the beginning of this century to the followers of Blavatsky, Steiner and Bailey today, astrology and the 'perennial philosophy' have travelled hand in hand.

In the preceding pages, we have been preoccupied with a particular facet or experience of fate: Moira, the archetypal representation of fate as instinct, body, family inheritance. The Platonic philosopher, confronted with the darkness of matter and the dark feminine face of Moira, tended to look towards the master's serene and peculiarly masculine wisdom to cope with her challenges. Put simply, the ancient dictum runs as follows: If you wish to free yourself from the fate which is written upon the physical form by the heavens (Heimarmenê), then you must free your mind from the bondage of earthly things, for although Moira rules the world of the senses, she cannot rule what Plato called the 'intelligible' world of the spirit, of which the human essence is a divine spark and offspring.

So much for free will. It exists, for the Platonist, only in the non-corporeal. The body, brimming with passion and the seeds of mortality, is full of fate. It is possible to countenance this development in the history of philosophy as a valuable and necessary progression from the fatalistic Mother-cults of pre-classical Greece and the Middle East, which viewed life as nothing but an emanation of the Mother and therefore as expendable. Man as *magnum miraculum*, a being worthy of dignity and honour, emerged finally in the Renaissance because of the gradual strengthening of the spirit against Moira, first in the increasingly powerful figure of Zeus, and ultimately in the spread of Christianity. But this counterbalancing of fate with spirit simply leaves fate in the body and in life. In terms of a modern individual's psychic life, it represents to me a dissociation of spirit and body, which leaves nothing in the middle, and poses enormous problems not only for the body which is then forced to carry the burden of 'sin' but also for the inner man who is then beset by compulsions and affects which he cannot understand. The violent split which occurred in the pre-classical Greek era between the Mother goddess and the sky gods can be viewed as a natural development of human consciousness. It is imaged in myth as the hero overcoming the dragon, and retrieving the jewel of immortality from its head. But the work with horoscope consultations and analysis has convinced me that this Platonic (or Christian, for they are not so dissimilar as they might at first seem) solution to the problem of fate is no longer efficacious. We have come full circle now, and synchronous with the discovery of Pluto I feel we are facing, individually and collectively, the repercussions of that split and the necessity of a resolution on an internal level.

Alchemy and magic, during their flowering in the first centuries of the Christian era and during their second flowering in the Renaissance, seem to have been, in part, methods devised for the transformation of substance. In other words, they addressed themselves to the altering of fate itself. Alchemy in particular certainly sidled up to the heretical issue of tampering with nature, and, by implication, transforming Moira and accomplishing through human effort what God Himself could not do. But alchemy focused its operations upon 'physical' substance. Although Jung has amply demonstrated that alchemy dealt as much with the psychic substance of man as with the substance of metals, the alchemists themselves could not acknowledge what they were really doing because they were unconscious of it.[62] The dominance of Moira was therefore not really questioned by collective consciousness for a good many centuries, either by the Platonists or by the Church, which, calling Moira by another name and attributing her control of the body to Original Sin, advocated the same thing as Plato: directing one's energy and one's efforts towards the spiritual life. As the *Corpus Hermeticum* puts it:

> Tat: There, O Father! the discourse concerning Fate ... is in danger of being overthrown. For if it is altogether fated to this person to fornicate or commit sacrilege, or to do any other evil something, why is he punished, he from necessity of Fate having done this deed?

> Hermes: All men are subject to Fate and to generation and change; for these are the beginning and the end of Fate; and all men indeed suffer things fated, but those with reason of whom we have said that the Mind is Guide, suffer not in like manner with the others, but having departed from Vice, not being evil, suffer not evil.[63]

Approaching fate from the point of view of 'splitting' (I am here using a psychological term to describe what I understand as a dissociation between the mental/spiritual aspect of man which is 'good' and the physical/instinctual aspect which is 'bad') is, of course, that of Eastern thought as well. The same formula is offered to free oneself from the wheel of perpetual rebirth and bondage to karma. The East too has an alchemical tradition, but, as in the West, this tradition remained shrouded in secrecy, and the full psychological implications of what it really dealt with have had to wait until Wilhelm's *Secret of the Golden Flower* was published in the West with Jung's psychological introduction and commentary. Plato's vision of the sensible or corporeal world as a shadowy, imperfect reflection of the 'intelligible' world of Divine Ideas is very close to the Eastern vision of man trapped in the world of *maya* through many incarnations, striving to release himself from the Thousand Things by merging with the One. He cannot alter karma, but he can 'defuse' it – withdraw his identification with his suffering body – and influence the fatedness of future incarnations by freeing his spirit, accepting the blows of fate with calm detachment, and centring himself upon his inner unity with the divine.

Now, I am not in any way implying that this is a 'true' or 'false' doctrine. I have no idea whether the physical world is *maya* and the spirit the only eternal verity, and I am not a theologian and cannot argue the point theoretically. But it is a universal doctrine, and has been with us for an exceedingly long time. The similarity of Platonism with Eastern thought is not really surprising, since Plato absorbed most of his doctrine from Pythagoras, Parmenides, Heraclitus and Empedocles, who were in turn strongly influenced by the religious and philosophical currents travelling from Egypt, Babylon and points East. It is also not surprising that the essentially dualistic manner of coping with the fate that lives in the body is the main viewpoint taken by astrologers today, if they are not preoccupied with the mechanistic aspects of the study. Given that a horoscope maps out a fate of some kind, the client understandably wishes to know, first and foremost, what he can do about it. The more spiritually inclined astrological practitioner responds by splitting the human being into above and below, with the very attractive suggestion that identification with the above can make the vicissitudes of the below more tolerable – and might even thin them out a bit. Marsilio Ficino in the early stages of his long career was really just another Neoplatonic astrologer trying to come to terms with his bad Saturn aspects through becoming spiritual and rising above it all. But Ficino's views altered considerably during the course of his long life, probably because of his exposure to magical and alchemical texts. Because of him, the prevailing views of the Renaissance also changed, and inaugurated for future centuries the possibility that man might have an active hand in God's cosmos and might therefore validly attempt to make a different relationship with fate. Ficino, it would be no exaggeration to state, started the Florentine Renaissance virtually single-handed, for it was he who translated Plato into Latin and made Neoplatonic texts available to the Aristotle-steeped West for the first time since the beginning of the Christian era. Even more importantly, he translated other Greek works – philosophical, astrological and magical – which had been buried in Constantinople since the sack of Rome by the Goths, and which were utterly unknown since the Church had spread its influence throughout Europe.

One of these works was a compilation, in Greek, of gnostic and hermetic texts which actually dated from the first three centuries AD, but which Ficino mistakenly believed to be far older – contemporary with Moses. These texts, which to Ficino became a kind of alternative Bible, were eventually called the *Corpus Hermeticum*, and they were reputedly written by a great and ancient sage called Hermes Trismegistus. If there ever was such a person, the *Corpus Hermeticum* cannot have been written by him, since it is compiled of several different authors' work over a period spanning three centuries. But such scholarly dissection was not available in fifteenth-century Florence. Ficino believed in Hermes, and before long, so did everybody else. Embedded in the *Corpus*, among the familiar Platonic doctrines about sensible and intelligible worlds and astrological hierarchies and the role of Fate and Necessity in ordering the material cosmos, there lay the declaration that one could transform fate through magic. This, as I mentioned earlier, was a belief cherished by alchemy, and the magic of the *Corpus* is essentially alchemical. It is upon the metals, the raw substance of the earth, that the Great Work is performed, and it is the spiritual essence within the metals which is set free from Moira. This alchemical magic is also astrological, in that it depends upon a concordance of the heavens for the development of the work. As Marie-Louise von Franz puts it:

> The whole of alchemy depends upon the *kairos*, and he [Zosimos, an alchemist] even calls the alchemical operation the *kairikai baphai*, the *kairos* colouring. His theory is that chemical processes do not always happen of themselves, but only at the astrologically right moment; that is, if I am working with silver, the moon, which is the planet of silver, must be in the right position, and if I am working with copper, Venus has to be in a certain constellation, otherwise these operations in silver and copper will not work ... Taking the astrological constellation into consideration is what is meant by this idea of *kairikai baphae*. *Kairos* therefore at that time and in this connection means the astrologically right time, the time when things can turn out successfully.[64]

The insight at which Ficino arrived, which marks a turning point (albeit unnoticed at the time) in philosophical thought and is also relevant to our understanding of fate, is that alchemical magic is not only applicable to the metals of the earth. It is also applicable to man. Ficino therefore attempted to inaugurate a new astrology, and he is sometimes mistakenly assumed to have opposed astrology because of his rather virulent tracts and letters against his fellow astrological practitioners. But if one actually reads these tirades, it becomes apparent that it is not astrology itself he is opposing. For Ficino, in his maturity, astrology was debased by being used as a prognosticator of fate. He thought it should serve a different function. A bad transit, for the average medieval astrologer, meant a time when fate would deal a blow to the individual which might be averted (it was considered worth the effort) but probably could not be, and must therefore be accepted in true Platonic spirit. To Ficino, a bad transit began to emerge as a *kairos*, a right moment when a new relationship might be made with fate through what he called 'natural' magic.

The pagan mind would never have dreamt of challenging Moira in this way; it would have been the worst kind of *hubris*. Plato championed the inner freedom of man's spirit, but his awesome respect for fate is obvious by the central role he gives it in the ordering of the universe. The Church had from its beginnings always entertained a lively revulsion towards magic, and had slithered away from the problem of fate in general and astrology in particular during the Middle Ages by nominally condemning the astrologer while secretly fostering his services, and by calling fate Divine Providence, which no one was supposed to question anyway. But Ficino understood the *Corpus Hermeticum* to be a sacred text as old and authoritative as the Bible, and to him Thrice-Greatest Hermes seemed to be saying that man was a magus, a great miracle, who was entitled to tamper with the cosmos because he participated in the nature of both God and Moira together.

> From the two natures, the deathless and the mortal, He made one nature – that of man – one and the self-same thing; and having made man both somehow deathless and somehow mortal, He brought him forth, and set him up betwixt the godlike and immortal nature and the mortal, that seeing all he might wonder at all.[65]

Man according to this vision, is no mere passive receptacle for the forces of fate. Nor is he a lowly being contaminated with Original Sin who can only be redeemed through the doctrines of the Church. He is not driven by his despair to seek escape from the corruption of flesh and ancestral sin through redemption by the spirit. He is a proud and noble co-creator in God's creative cosmos, and by his efforts he can reunite God and Moira so that body and spirit are no longer rent in twain. The following passage from the *Corpus* became the rallying cry for the enlightened Renaissance magus:

> And so, Asklepios, man is a *magnum miraculum*, a great miracle: a creature worthy of worship and honour. For he shares in the nature of God as though he himself were God. He shares the substance of the *daimones*, for he knows he has a common origin with them.[66]

Naturally all this had a profound effect on Marsilio Ficino. From being a Platonist, he became a Hermetist. Four centuries before Jung, he took the dictates of the *Corpus* in an entirely new way. Ficino's system of 'natural' magic managed to offend neither Moira, the Church, nor astrology – a delicate operation, but then, Aquarius is known for its ability to get on with everybody. The key to Ficino's magic was *the imagination*. As we might define it today, it dealt with the transformation of man's nature through experience of, and interchange with, the world of images which we would now call the fantasy products of the unconscious. This interchange had to occcur at the *kairos*, the astrologically propitious moment. As Charles Boer states in his introduction to Ficino's *Book of Life*, Marsilio was the first depth psychologist.

The *Book of Life* includes a number of recipes for medicines, meditations, music and talismans by which the Divine Images might be experienced and the fates gently persuaded in one's favour. Ficino's increasing philosophical sophistication is discernible in a letter written several years after the extract quoted at the beginning of this chapter:

> Then if the Fates cannot be avoided, they are foreseen and foretold to no purpose. Yet if they can be avoided by some method, the inevitability of Fate is falsely maintained by astrologers. They will probably say, I suppose, that this also is in the Fates, that once in a while one thing out of many may be foreknown and guarded against. Thus it follows that among the Fates there will be contention, so that one will be determined to harm a man and another to protect him.[67]

This seems to accord with what Jung says of the inherent ambivalence and paradoxical nature of the unconscious. On the one hand, the unconscious as Mother holds back her child, threatening to devour him if he seeks to develop beyond her allotted boundaries. On the other hand, the unconscious as *anima* or soul spurs the individual into extending himself into life and challenging the bondage of family fate and primitive instinct. Ficino was very angered by the sort of astrology that allowed no room for a little contention among the Fates. Once he had got his hands on the *Corpus Hermeticum*, he was convinced that images had the power to alter or mediate the effects of planetary fate on the physical plane. Here we are in the terrain of analytical psychology, where the symbol has an almost magical capacity to mediate between the blind world of instinct and the rational world of the ego through a transformation of libido or psychic energy. In the *Book of Life*, Ficino wildly quotes every magical and Neoplatonic authority he can find – Ptolemy (whose *Tetrabiblos* and *Almagest* form the basis of modern astrology), Plotinus, Iamblichus, Porphyry (whose system of house division is still in use today), Firmicus Maternus (whom we shall meet later), and of course Hermes Trismegistus – to back up his conviction that if one makes a magical talisman either physically or, more importantly, psychically – which is composed of the proper correspondences with the heavenly bodies, and which is comprised of traditional (i.e. archetypal or mythic) images – then in some way the divine stuff of the cosmos in its 'natural' state of harmony might be drawn down into the talisman and directly affect the 'body of the world' (or the body of the magus) which otherwise is so sadly subject to the blows of fate.

Those readers who have any experience of work with dreams, active imagination and guided imagery will no doubt have already recognised where this apparent digression into Renaissance magic is leading. Ficino was a humble man, and in no way filled with the inflation of later magi such as Cornelius Agrippa and Giordano Bruno, both of whom forgot that all alchemical works, mineral or human, must be performed *Deo concedente*, that is, according to the will of God. Such a quality is, of course, the only safeguard against *hubris* and its *nemesis*, whether one is a Greek hero, a Renaissance magus or a modern astrologer or analyst. Ficino never thought it was he who accomplished the magic. He thought it was the gods, or the quarrelling Fates who could not agree about whether they wanted to be persuaded. What Ficino's system of magic represents from a psychological point of view very much concerns us now, because if one considers the horoscope as the written law of the heavens, or, put another way, as one's fate, then there are different levels upon which that fate might enact itself. These different levels are perhaps intimately connected with the inner attitude of the individual and with his relationship, or lack thereof, with the world of images and symbols. In other words, fate may be an inner psychological pattern as much as an issue of the body. This is apparent in the preceding chapter, in the fate of Renee R.

For Ficino, as for his master Plato, the real world was not the corporeal one, but the world of Ideas, *eidolos*, or, as Jung might put it, the archetypes of the collective unconscious. Fate is natural law. In this sense it is archetypal, an ordering principle or pattern. Moira represents the innate mortality and justice of the world of the instincts. But the world of the instincts is a blind world, a realm of bodily compulsions and evolutionary necessity. It is violently resistant to any transgression or attempt to bend its boundaries because survival itself then seems to be threatened, and the natural order broken. The Fates themselves quarrel, according to Ficino; *prima materia* is in a state of conflict, confusion and collision of opposites within itself. But this blind world of instinct is not really separate from the world of *eidolos* or archetypes. As we have seen, Jung believed that the dominant archetypes such as the Great Mother, the Wise Old Man, transformation, the Trickster, the anima *et al.*, are images of instincts, the self-portrayal of innate human patterns of development that possess both an organic behavioural determinism and a psychological experience of meaning.

For Ficino, the world of images – whether these were derived from dreams (his own) or myth (Greek and the synchretistic mythic variations of the first centuries AD) – were a kind of middle ground, a place in between the abstract and inaccessible world of imageless Ideas and the dense world of Moira-bound matter. For Jung, likewise, symbolic products of the psyche hold the border-land between the formal world of the archetypes and the daylight world of consciousness. These images are the 'stuff' in between, the *anima mundi* or soul of the world. They and their ground of psychic substance fall under the governorship of Hermes, lord of borders and roadways and crossroads, who in alchemy is called Mercurius. The planets, in Ficino's new astrology, are not only physical bodies in space but images within the psychic world of man, and also metals within the earth itself. Somewhere in the 'intelligible' world are the Ideas which correspond to these mortal expressions. The planetary images as Ficino conceived them are the bridge between worlds, through which the individual can slowly unite what is below with what is above, so that, in the words of the *Corpus*, the miracle of the One may be accomplished. This raises a very profound question about exactly what 'happens' when the astrologer interprets a horoscope to a client, for both astrologer and client inhabit, for that time, the 'middle ground' that unites the above and the below.

Ficino's *anima mundi* bears a strong relationship with the 'objective psyche' as Jung calls it, the indefinable world-stuff which stretches across the boundaries between psyche and body, between spirit and substance, which belongs to both and to neither, and which is accessible to us through the images of our dreams and fantasies. Work on this stuff in accordance with one's natal pattern, suggests Ficino, and one builds the connecting link (or participates in a link which is already existent but unexperienced) between God and his creation, between Ideas and corporeal reality, between archetype and instinct, between freedom and fate. As Frances Yates puts it in her study of Renaissance hermetic magic:

> Hence such Images would become forms of the Ideas, or ways of approaching the Ideas at a stage intermediary between their

purely intellectual forms in the divine *mens* and their dimmer reflection in the world of sense, or body of the world. Hence it was by manipulating such images in this intermediary 'middle place' that the ancient sages knew how to draw down a part of the soul of the world into their shrines . . . There is, further, in Ficino's words, the notion that the material forms in the world of sense can be, as it were, re-formed, when they have degenerated, by manipulation of the higher images on which they depend.[68]

I must admit that I cannot find any great difference between the 'manipulation' of images in the intermediary 'middle place' to draw down part of the world-soul into a religious shrine, and the same process applied to the building and ornamentation of our great contemporary religious edifices. The word 'manipulate' is a problematic one, for although the Renaissance magus (a title Ficino timidly backed away from, although later magi such as Agrippa gloried in the title) believed he had the right to work with the stuff of God's cosmos, it would seem from the actual fate of some of them that God's cosmos – or the unconscious – had a tendency to hit back against too much identification with the magician's role. *Hubris* and *nemesis* are evidently laws which are still in force, even if some connection is made with the world of images and the meaning of fate is interiorised. Pico della Mirandola, Ficino's disciple, was murdered, and Giordano Bruno was burned at the stake. These hazards of the profession notwithstanding, one cannot help admiring the spirit in which these men challenged the blind adherence to superstition and dogma which surrounded them. Ficino himself seems to have been an unusually self-effacing man, particularly unusual for a Scorpio, but perhaps his efforts at self-understanding and relationship with what we would now call the unconscious did indeed bring him greater harmony. He was certainly very long-lived, unusual for his time, and pursued a remarkably tranquil life. But *hubris* has a tendency to formulate very quickly when entering this mysterious terrain of the inner images which bind us to our fates. This is an incessant problem for the psychotherapist, and for the astrologer as well. Our modern equivalents for Ficino and his peers are the workers in psychology and astrology, in particular those who traverse the circuitous path of the unconscious psyche; and our dangers are perhaps even greater than our Renaissance predecessors, because they could shift the 'cure' onto the magical talisman, while we are faced with the necessity of not taking personally the archetypal projections of our clients while still feeling that we can in some way be effective or helpful.

Apart from the difficulties of entering into the intermediary 'middle place', there is the problem of comprehending what it might mean. Does fate really transform? Or is it the attitude of the individual towards whatever is his necessity that changes, and therefore creates a new relationship with fate which is permeated with a subjective sense of meaning and choice? Perhaps this is what Jung means by free will being the ability to do gladly what one must do, for the operative word is 'gladly', implying a discovery of meaningfulness which makes the fate feel 'right' and what one would have chosen oneself. Or is it that fate dictates a pattern which cannot be altered but leaves open the possibility that the pattern may manifest itself in several different modes, through several different levels of experience? Whatever the answer might be – and I do not possess it – something certainly seems to happen through encounter with that 'middle place'. It is this 'something' which I would now like to explore further.

The vitality and truth of these difficult and abstruse concepts is to be found in actual lives, and in the ongoing process of individual work on the psyche in conjunction with the planetary transits which formulate as images in dreams and as events in outer life. Earlier I quoted the dream of a young woman whom I called Ruth, who was pursued in her inner and outer life by the figure of a violent man. I mentioned that the dream figure changed as our work on it progressed, and that he began to assume a more helpful guise. At a certain point in the process the man appeared in a dream asking to be killed and eaten, and this coincided with Ruth's decision, and capacity, to break away from a destructive and stifling relationship in which she had felt paralysed and unable to either respond or leave. This change occurred during the long transit of Uranus in opposition to natal Mars and squaring natal Pluto. 'Something' obviously happened. But what?

I will now give a lengthier summary of some of the developments in Ruth's analysis. Her birth chart is reproduced below.

This case history is neither bizarre nor spectacular. Although its subject is an unusual person with many creative gifts and a deep degree of sensitivity and receptivity to the inner world, the problems from which she has suffered are, at core, basic human problems whose patterns are archetypal. The failures and successes within the analysis are also not spectacular, and Ruth has not been 'cured' because there was nothing to cure her of. But the dreams which follow provide an unusually vivid picture of a small portion of that awesome process which Jung refers to as the individuation process, and which is also, in my view, a process of coming to terms with fate. The dream below occurred at the beginning of the analysis, and dreams that occur at this time are

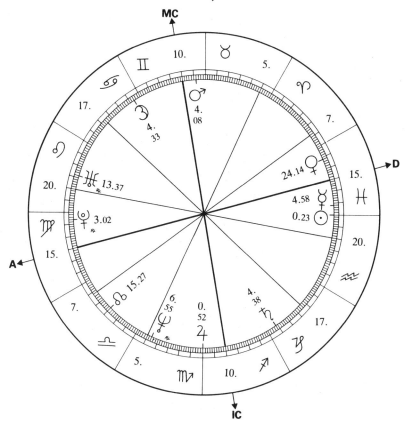

DIAGRAM 9. Birth horoscope of Ruth

b. 19 February 1959
6.40 p.m.
London

often deeply significant because they encapsulate the individual's problem, its archetypal background, and its potential for resolution. They are the road signs for further exploration of the 'middle place'.

I am in a small boat with a man. The sea is very violent and a storm is raging. It is quite dark. The boat is not very sound. The man seems to be steering the boat toward some rocks. I know that if we crash into the rocks we will be killed; the boat is not strong enough to take the impact. I cannot tell whether the man is trying to destroy us, or whether he does not realise how deadly the rocks are. I try to get him to steer the other way, but he seems determined and is much stronger than I am. I wake up in panic, not knowing whether we will hit the rocks or not.

This dream communicates a subjective experience of great danger. How this situation might translate itself in Ruth's outer life is not yet clear, but the violent waters of the unconscious and the threatening rocks of external reality have between them placed her in a very precarious position. On a personal level, I understood this dream to be speaking of the 'ship of life', the individual consciousness or ego, and here it is not very sound. Ruth's relationship with her physical reality was not very stable at the time we began work, and her sense of being 'contained' in life was minimal. The man is a highly ambiguous figure; he may be attempting to destroy her, or he may be attempting to rescue her, but she is not prepared to trust his guidance, for it seems to her that the direction in which he is steering her can have no outcome other than destruction. One of Jung's definitions of the animus is that, in a woman's psyche, the unconscious personifies itself as a masculine figure, portraying its creative and directional attributes. So, in the context of this dream, one might say that it is the unconscious which steers her towards the threatening rocks, and it is difficult to know whether this intent is destructive or redemptive.

The damaged boat, which seems to represent a damaged ego or container, is not surprising when we consider Ruth's horoscope. The opposition of the moon in Cancer and Saturn in Capricorn across the parental houses suggests that neither parent was able to provide her with any sense of security, since they were so busy being unhappy themselves. The atmosphere in Ruth's childhood was a critical and destructive one. I have already mentioned something of the mother's own unhappy circumstances. Having the moon in Cancer in the house which governs the mother, Ruth's extraordinary sensitivity to the unspoken emotional currents of her environment and of her mother in particular left her peculiarly vulnerable to the underworld of her parents' psyches, and she could not be deceived as to the actual appalling state of affairs existing within the parental marriage and within the mother and father themselves. Pluto placed in the twelfth house, as I have already mentioned, also gives a great sensitivity to the collective darkness which lurks behind the individual's birth, the 'ancestral sins' which have been accruing for many generations. Ruth experienced this insight as 'bad', a response not untypical of many children, for if nothing is brought out into the open and the child experiences destructive undercurrents he will often take them for his own. This is exacerbated in Ruth's horoscope by the sun in opposition to Pluto, for this 'family darkness' is within her as well as within the parents; and a child cannot be expected to differentiate, but will simply accept the entire package as though it is his own fault and his own creation.

Ruth's relationship with her mother was permeated by a feeling of rejection and criticism. She knew that she was hurt and angry because of this treatment, and her feelings of outrage were very conscious. About her father she was much more vague. He seemed 'weak' to her, but she did not have any clear feeling of who he was, or what she felt towards him. Another early dream brought up into the light facets of her relationship with her father which were far more disturbing and shed considerable light on some of the components which had built up the image of the terrible pursuing man in her dreams.

> I am in my room with a baby kitten which I am taking care of. My father suddenly comes in through the door. I hardly recognise him, for he seems terribly angry and has black horns on his head. He sees the kitten playing on the floor and kicks it all the way across the room. I rush after it weeping, frightened that he has killed it, and even more frightened that he will become violent towards me.

This dream, needless to say, provoked considerable upset and anxiety in Ruth. She was forced by the contents of the dream to confront the 'real' situation existing between her and her father: that very great anger lurked beneath his 'weak' surface, and that this anger had been directed against her young femininity, suggested by the kitten she is taking care of. His violence is directed against her instincts, her female development. The horns on his head are a curious image; Ruth first associated them with the devil, but as we discussed the dream further she also connected them with the horns of a bull, suggesting a terrifying phallic power in her father of which she had been utterly unconscious. Put simply, the dream seems to be suggesting that the father's repressed sexuality, poisoned with rage, was directed against Ruth herself. It is an image of psychic rape, for he enters her 'room', her own psychological space, and injures the helpless young animal which she is attempting to nurture and care for.

Ruth's earlier dream about the boat, when we add the insights gained from the second dream, seems to describe something more than a dangerous situation where the frail ego, not very well adapted to the demands of outer life, is being buffeted by violent and powerful unconscious drives and emotions. It is not surprising, in light of the nature of Ruth's unconscious perception of her father, that she does not trust the man in the boat, for the father is the first hook upon which a young girl projects the animus. If the father is violent and treacherous, then the directional power of the unconscious seems to be so likewise. The sea journey she is attempting to make in the dream emerges as an initiatory journey, an attempt to make the passage away from the parental background and out into her own life. This is the mythic *nekyia*, the night-sea journey, here taking place in a leaky boat with a highly ambivalent captain.

Bearing this initial dream in mind, my early work with Ruth was focused upon the strengthening of the boat – in other words, the strengthening of her relationship to ordinary life, through reductive work on her parental relationships and through fostering as much as possible her trust in her relationship with me. This work did not directly confront the problem of the violent man, who meanwhile appeared in threatening form regularly in her dreams, sometimes with her father's face, sometimes with a stranger's. Ruth was too terrified of him to be able to deal with him as a psychic factor in herself. But as her sense of her own reality increased, the image of the violent man began to change. This coincided with her capacity to voice rage towards the father who had dealt with her so brutally on such a completely covert level. Following is a dream which shows the first inklings of a change.

> I am wandering through the wards of a hospital. There is a man lying sick on a bed in the middle of a corridor. He is completely covered with syphilitic sores. He watches me malevolently, and I know that he is going to try to infect me with his sickness. Perhaps he has already, for I realise that he has touched me as I brushed past. I see a kind of cafe table set up, where my mother and father are sitting. My father looks ashamed and cannot look at me in the face, but my mother is gloating.

Here a new facet of this troublesome and frightening autonomous psychic force emerges: the man is 'sick', rather than evil and violent, and is in a hospital needing attention and treatment. He has 'infected' Ruth with his venereal disease – i.e. with his sense of sexual shame and guilt. The shame-faced father at the table Ruth immediately connected with the sick man, as though they were in some way the same person; when she allowed herself to fantasise about this dream, she concluded that this was her father's sexual sickness passed on to her, for her to 'carry'. She felt that her mother gloated because it was preferable for Ruth to carry the guilt and suffering. This is a particularly ugly image of a 'passing on' of something from parents to child. The sense of dirtiness which Ruth felt about her own body seemed to be directly described by this dream, and the source from which it stemmed. One of the more optimistic features of the dream is that the 'sick' man and

Ruth's father are separate people, although linked by the 'passing on' of the sickness; and this suggests to me the possibility of an increasing separation between the father and Ruth's 'inner' man.

Sometimes Ruth's dreams connected the violent man with the father, and sometimes with the mother. That the attributes of anger, violence and darkness are related to both parents is reflected by the grand cross in Ruth's chart, involving the Mars–Pluto square already discussed, the sun, Mercury and Jupiter. This grand cross has one axis along the meridian, which to me represents the axis of parental inheritance. It is a shared problem, a family complex, and the 'release point' of this grand cross is through Ruth's sun in Pisces in the sixth house, this being the most personal point of the configuration. Thus the problems of suppressed rage, violence and sexual 'shame' interfere with, challenge and ultimately stimulate the development of Ruth's own identity.

During the period in which Ruth and I worked with these and other dreams, her outer life was still dominated by the violent relationship in which she had become enmeshed. Connections began to emerge between the man with whom she lived and the father who had terrified her, and her mother, on such a subterranean level. The full impact of the battle between mother and father became visible to her, and as this material was brought to the surface by the dreams and discussed, Ruth was gradually able to distinguish the outlines of her own identity from the battlefield in which she had been born. The following dream, much later in the analysis, reflects the degree to which Ruth has begun to make a more creative relationship with the animus, who first appeared in such ambiguous guise piloting her boat:

> I am in a house, which has been demolished and is under reconstruction. The entire interior has been gutted, but the work of rebuilding is progressing slowly. I am in what will be the living room, trying to get across the room to the other side. But the floorboards have been ripped out, and there is a gaping black hole. A long way down I can see black water. As I stand paralysed at the edge of the hole, a man emerges from the cellar. He is one of the workmen, a black man dressed in a miner's tin hat. He reassures me and shows me some strong boards which have been laid across the opening, over which I can safely cross to the other side.

This dream needs no interpretation. It describes itself very precisely. What is most relevant is that the black man – Hades–Pluto, the pursuer and rapist – here emerges from the watery pit of the underworld, and rather than dragging Ruth down with him is instead offering her safe passage.

I will mention one final dream in the long, circuitous series
which followed and heralded the equally long, circuitous process
of Ruth's gradual separation from the parental darkness and the
increasing acceptance of her own complex nature.

> I am in a vast underground network of shops, like a big Amer-
> ican shopping complex. I see a jewellery shop with some attrac-
> tive pieces in the window. The place is filled with very beautiful,
> precious objects everywhere, but they are far beyond the price I
> can pay. The man in the shop smiles at me, and gives me an
> exquisite gold ring.

This dream too needs no elaboration. I will merely repeat that the
word 'Pluto' in Greek means 'riches'. Here he offers freely,
without extracting a price; presumably this is because Ruth has
been willing to pay the price already, that of relationship with him.

These sparse fragments from a lengthy and often difficult analytic process seem to offer some insight into the problem of fate and
transformation. They reflect something which frequently occurs
not only in analytic work, but in life itself, through any creative
meeting with the unconscious. Something does indeed happen. I
do not feel that it is the analyst who 'makes' it happen, for the
analyst is only the facilitator who provides a safe place in which the
individual can meet the denizens of his own unknown nature. The
process runs itself, and it seems to require a *kairos*, an astrologically
propitious moment. This process, which Jung understood as
individuation, does not have to take place within the psychotherapist's consulting room; this only becomes relevant if the disturb-
ance between ego and unconscious has become too great, and the
individual can no longer contain what is erupting from within. But
whether in therapy or in life, this process is not without suffering,
for the encounter with the inner images challenges and hurts the
ego, forcing the individual to re-evaluate many things. This is, in a
sense, an encounter with one's fate. The grand cross present in
Ruth's horoscope, involving the difficult Mars–Pluto square and
sun–Pluto opposition, suggests that the violent man, in some
form, is Ruth's fate. She cannot escape him, for he is written into
her horoscope at birth. He is both a collective and an individual
fate, and is an integral part of her psyche. The aspect between
Pluto and the sun guarantees this; it is not just Ruth's past, but her
present and her future which she must share with him. But the
determined destructiveness with which he first presented himself
is connected, in part, with the network of Ruth's family relationships, and with the degree to which neither parent would give this
psychic figure room or value or expression. He was already
inflamed and violent before Ruth was born. Had she made no

effort to confront this figure, she would have been fated to meet him perpetually in her outer life. Yet the effort was not wholly choice; in a sense, the psyche itself coerced her into this confrontation.

That Ruth decided to enter analysis is not the decisive factor, for many people decide to undergo some form of psychotherapy who are not able, despite the efforts of the therapist, to form such a relationship with the inner world; and others form it without benefit of external help. Much of the key to the changes which occurred in Ruth seems to lie in Ruth herself, and her willingness to accept responsibility for some part of the violent life in which she had become caught. This willingness seems an obvious thing, but it is exceedingly difficult and painful when one's circumstances seem so clearly to be somebody else's fault. It is possible that the very configuration which corresponds to the destructive figure of the man is the same one which has given her the depth and insight to learn more about him. This is the double edge of Pluto, who both destroys and heals.

I would not be inclined to suggest, from the material given above, that Ruth's fate has changed. I do not feel it has, any more than her birth horoscope has changed. Pluto, and the dark man, will be with her all her life. But it is his manifestations that have changed, although he is still capable of great anger and violence; and Ruth's outer life has changed in accord with the inner movement. She no longer needs to act this destructiveness out, and is therefore able to make relationships in which she is treated with some respect for her own value – because she is better able to value herself. Ruth has also begun to see other possibilities for the expression of her 'dark' animus, for she had, when younger, entertained the idea of entering medical school, and this aspiration has now begun to renew itself. Thus she is preparing herself for meeting the image of death, and the image of healing, in an entirely different form. Pursuing a creative career in which she can work with and for this archetypal image is very different from being pursued by it in nightmare and in life. Interestingly, this aspiration to embed the Plutonian figure in such a vocation reflects the traditional reading of the sun placed in the sixth house. Thus the sun, the symbol of the ego consciousness, is not quite such a leaky boat, for it can now carry her over the water.

Developments such as these raise innumerable unanswerable questions. If something like the figure of the violent man – echoed by the Mars–Pluto square in the horoscope – can 'change' during a transit of Uranus, what is it that really changes? Is it really the violent man, or is it Ruth's attitude towards him, or is it both? If this can happen for Ruth, can it happen for anyone? To the first question, I would be inclined to answer, both, although I do not really know; to the second, I do not know. There are some things which seem irrevocable, such as drastic illness, deformity and death. All the psychologising in the world will not interiorise these manifestations of fate. Nor will all the psychologising in the world help Renee R., nor did it help Timothy S. But one's relationship with these unchangeable things can change, and it is possible to find meaning in what at first seems to be cruel chance or a malicious fate. Outer and inner reflect each other, and if an inner meaning emerges linked with an act of outer fate, then one's relationship with that fate has changed. Sometimes the form in which the fate manifests changes too. There is a great mystery here which I cannot begin to fathom.

Some attempts at dealing with the inner world succeed, and others fail, and it is difficult sometimes to know why. Sometimes an individual will choose (if that is the right word) not to meet his fate on any level other than the concrete one; thus, in a sense, he fates himself. I am reminded here of a woman who once came to see me because she was having great difficulties with her husband. Both husband and wife had the sun in Pisces, but I did not obtain any other birth data from her. The husband was a psychiatric patient, who had suffered a number of breakdowns. During their long married life she had played the role of devoted nurse and helper. That she loved him deeply was without question; but love can sometimes have Plutonian undercurrents, although it is no less love. This woman was the strong, sane partner, her husband the sick, alienated one; thus they had, unconsciously, agreed long ago. But the husband decided to enter psychotherapy, rather than perpetuate his endless cycle of breakdown, medication and temporary rehabilitation. Perhaps Uranus was at work in his chart; but whatever astrological configuration was affecting him, it seemed he suddenly decided to try to get to the bottom of what was the matter with him. This situation had begun to bear fruit, and his wife had begun to panic, for this sick and apparently helpless man began gaining some insight into some of his repressed anger towards her and towards the mother–son relationship into which their marriage had crystallised long ago. As this anger came to the surface, my analysand became frightened that after so many years she might lose him. She brought me the following dream at our second meeting:

My husband and I are driving to Jung's house, where we will be shown a film. At first the journey is comfortable. But the landscape becomes unfamiliar, and I become uneasy. Then I realise with horror that the car is driving itself. We arrive at

Jung's house. My husband walks through the front door. The film is being run in colour, or so we have been told, but when I glimpse it it seems to be in black and white. I cannot go through the doorway, because a sick woman is lying across the threshold. I do not want to go near her, but cannot step over her to join my husband.

My analysand told me that the sick woman reminded her of a woman she had known in childhood, a rather tragic figure who had been in and out of mental institutions and finally committed suicide. She was visibly distressed and repelled when talking about this dream-woman, and said that she felt no desire at all in the dream to offer any help. She just wanted to go away. The rapidity with which this dream-image had surfaced caused me to ask her whether she felt this woman might have anything at all to do with her. Her reply was very vehement. She stared at me for a moment, and said: 'I don't want to know who she is. I don't want to help her. I don't want to have anything to do with her.' After this meeting, I never saw the woman again. The interview shook me, because I felt that at the moment I had asked her the question, she understood, on some profound level, the choice which lay before her, although I had not offered any interpretation of any kind of the dream, or of her difficulties. She could not cross the threshold into Jung's house – for it was analysis she had come to see me about – because the sick woman blocked her path. Her own sickness, which was acted out by her sick husband, prevented her from any further development. Interestingly, the dream suggests that her vision of life is rendered colourless because of this problem, for she can only see in black and white a film which everyone else perceives in Technicolor. Or perhaps this is a comment on her capacity to understand things only in a 'black and white' sense. But she would not take responsibility for this inner woman. I am quite certain that in making this choice – however understandable a choice it is, considering the pain inherent in such a self-confrontation – she invoked an external fate, for her marriage was already disturbingly shaky. The likelihood of an actual separation is increased, if not inevitable, for the husband had already begun to find other women interesting, and if he continued to grow in insight and no longer needed to be the 'sick' one, he would probably find another woman who could support his masculinity rather than colluding in its castration. This is a sad and deeply ironic case, because from the point of view of the outer world, the wife was a model of patience and compassion, and if she is abandoned the outer world will blame the husband. Nor will my analysand ever really understand why such a thing should happen to her. But one cannot make another person's decision for him; nor can one spare another suffering. I have rarely seen so vivid an example of an individual confronting his fate and turning away.

Whatever Ficino's 'natural' magic might have been, it was certainly an attempt to make a connection with the ancient images that emerge from the depths of the psyche. Ficino thought this might help the Fates to look with more favour upon man. Psychotherapy is certainly a place where encounter with fate occurs; but perhaps the modern world has produced such things as psychotherapy because we have lost the capacity to make our own connections naturally through myth and religion and ritual. So we must seek our gods within, and, in seeking them, find instead ourselves and our fates. Something happens when a connection is made between an outer event and an inner image. If the astrological patterns shape our fate, then they describe not only 'body' but also 'soul', for this fate is inner as well as outer. For this reason I have never been happy with the Platonic approach to astrology, such as Margaret Hone suggests. Nor is this fate potential in a general way, dependent on whether a person is clever enough to utilise it. Ruth's violent man is not a general potential. He is a compulsion, and she had no choice but to encounter him and try to come to terms with him. His image is that of the rapist, and this archetypal image has manifested in very concrete terms in her life. That is hardly 'potential' in the sense that Jeff Mayo describes it.

I would now like to digress into the past again, and trace the viewpoint of astrology towards fate before Ficino began to meddle with it. Ficino's contribution is still with us, for the line passes down from him to his disciple Pico della Mirandola, and thence to Cornelius Agrippa and Paracelsus, and from Paracelsus to Goethe, Mesmer and eventually Jung. But Ficino's insights did not affect the whole of astrology, for many of his peers clung to the old way of viewing fate, with the old Platonic solution to its problems. This viewpoint our own modern astrology has inherited. The horoscopic art of the Middle Ages to which Ficino himself was heir sprang from two primary sources. Ptolemy's *Tetrabiblos* and *Almagest* comprise the first, and Ptolemy, as might be expected, was firmly steeped in the Platonic tradition:

> The movement of the heavenly bodies, to be sure, is eternally performed in accord with divine, unchangeable destiny.[69]

Ptolemy is not the only founding father of astrology, and perhaps he is not the most important. Julius Firmicus Maternus wrote his *Mathesis* in the fourth century AD, when Greek and Roman paganism, Near Eastern and Hellenised Egyptian mystery cults, Jewish and early Christian gnosticism and kabbalism,

Persian dualism and early Church Fathers were all weaving their myriad colourful religious strands together in a great patchwork of syncretism, the likes of which were not seen again until Ficino's Renaissance and not afterward until Jung. Like Ptolemy, Firmicus was a committed Platonist; unlike Ptolemy, he was also a Christian gnostic, and it is not surprising that his particular astrological viewpoint was equally if not more popular than Ptolemy's in the Renaissance because he acknowledged the importance of the Trinity. The *Matheseos Libri VIII* (Eight Books on the Theory of Astrology) stands as the final and most complete work on astrology in the classical world. It was the primary channel for classical astrology into medieval and Renaissance thought. Firmicus borrowed from Ptolemy as well as from numerous Near Eastern sources, and he has a great deal to say about fate. His recommendations about predictive astrology became part and parcel of the Renaissance astrologer's stock in trade. Although we modern astrologers quite naturally wish to disown all that medieval claptrap, particularly the claptrap about fate, there is one very annoying obstacle to such disowning. Those fatalistic Renaissance astrologers were unusually accurate in their predictions. But there is an even more fascinating aspect to it all. The configurations upon which they based their predictions, which worked unerringly in the concrete world five hundred years ago, have lost their reliability. Thus we are faced with the problem of the changing – or transforming – manifestations of fate in the collective over history, and it is this theme which I would like to explore further. To do this, I must first tell a story.

In the Year of Our Lord 1555, His Most Christian Majesty King Henri II of France, then aged thirty-seven years, was warned by an astrologer to beware of death during single combat in an enclosed space through an injury to the head, in the summer of his forty-second year. The astrologer in question was one of the better-known savants of the time, an Italian called Luca Gaurica, Latinised, acccording to the fashion, into Gauricus. Signor Gauricus published a great work in three volumes on the principles of astrology. Called *Opera Omnia*, it may still be read in the British Library, if one can struggle with his Latin; unfortunately it has never been translated. *Opera Omnia* expounds not only the casting and interpretation of natal horoscopes, but also judicial (horary) and political (mundane) astrology as well. Included among the example horoscopes is that of the unfortunate King Henri II. Gauricus had successfully predicted crises and deaths in the lives of numerous rulers and noblemen, including the defeat of King François I at the battle of Pavia and the demise of the Duc de Bourbon on the walls of Rome during its sack in 1527. Therefore his warning to the King of France was treated with some respect. This tells us several things about the astrology of the time. It was, apart from Ficino's followers, predictive rather than characterological, it was respected in all the courts of Europe despite the Church's nominal repudiation (many notable princes of the Church were themselves astrologers), and it passed the responsibility for human benefits and catastrophes firmly into the broad lap of Moira. Gauricus did not dabble in Ficino's 'natural' magic. If he prophesied that King Henri was going to die, then die he would, although the prediction was couched, according to etiquette, as a 'warning'. Even the King himself did not think to question it, but replied that he would as soon die an honourable death in open combat as in any other, possibly ignoble, fashion. (The King was an Aries, which might have had some bearing on his courageous but rather foolhardy response.)

Another astrologer contemporary with Gauricus also issued a 'warning' about King Henri's death. This was Michel de Notredame, whom history knows as Nostradamus, and who inserted into the *Centuries*, his monumental opus of prophecies about the fate of the world published in 1555, the following verse:

> Le Lyon jeune le vieux surmontera,
> En champ bellique par singulier duelle,
> Dans cage d'or les yeux lui crevera,
> Deux classes une puis mourir mort cruelle.

This means, roughly: The young lion will overcome the old on the tournament ground in single combat. Through the cage of gold (the King was known to wear a gold helmet) his eyes will be pierced. Two wounds become one, and then a cruel death.

This prophecy, although not mentioning the King by name, appeared in the same year that Gauricus made his prediction. King Henri was instantly recognisable not only by his gold jousting helmet, but by the golden lion which formed its crest. This second astrological warning was also taken with complete seriousness and preparations were begun for the next monarch, albeit tactfully and without any overt fuss. Astrologers and seers, by the grace of God or the Devil (it was not certain which) were privy to the secrets of Fate, and could foresee what had been written.

Needless to say, King Henri died, in the summer of his forty-second year, on the tournament ground, during the celebrations honouring his daughter's marriage to the King of Spain. His opponent's lance *accidentally* splintered during combat, and the King had *accidentally* forgotten to fasten the visor of his helmet. The splinters passed through the helmet's visor, pierced both eyes, and entered his brain. He died a particularly cruel and painful death, after a prolonged agony of ten days. Everyone mourned, and praised the accuracy of Gauricus and Nostradamus, and prepared for the new reign. It is difficult for us now to understand the passive acceptance of prediction and fate that permeated the astrology of the sixteenth century. But it is equally difficult for the modern astrologer, anxious to demonstrate to his client that the interpretation of the natal horoscope is about 'potential', to justify the uncanny accuracy of these and other similar Renaissance predictions. It is very necessary for us in the twentieth century to look at the horoscope psychologically, for we live in a psychological age and our insights into ourselves may well be the only hope of salvation; yet it would seem that it was indeed possible, a mere four hundred years ago, to predict with absolute accuracy the length of a man's life and the manner of his death.

Below is reproduced King Henri's horoscope as it was cast by Gauricus.[70] Following this is a computer-calculated version of the same horoscope, based on the birth data given by Gauricus. It will be immediately apparent, if the two are compared, that the astrologers of the sixteenth century were by no means stupid in their calculations, however impoverished they were by the lack of scientific instruments. Although the ascendant and the following house cusps seem rather strangely distorted in Gauricus' version, the positions of the planets themselves are accurate to within a degree or two. I am not sure which house system Gauricus used, since he gives his own tables in the *Opera Omnia*; probably it was Porphyry, who was popular at the time. Or perhaps it was his own. The moon is the only badly misplaced planet in the chart, being four degrees out, while the Caput Draconis or ascending node is exact. Gauricus, of course, did not know about Uranus, Neptune and Pluto. He based his predictions on the seven known heavenly bodies, the nodes, and the Pars Fortuna (Arabic parts were then in vogue), which happens in Gauricus' version of the horoscope to be in exact conjunction with the ascending node. His sources are Ptolemy, Arabic literature on the fixed stars and parts, and the *Mathesis* of Julius Firmicus Maternus.

I shall quote Firmicus because my Latin is not good enough to quote Gauricus; and moreover, they say the same thing. Firmicus' work appeared first in Venice in a printed edition in 1497, during Gauricus' youth. He spends several pages arguing against the detractors of astrology and the refutors of fate:

Who is it who brings death to one unborn, to another on the first day of life, to the child a little while after, to the youth, to the old man? Let something be discovered which may teach us, which may show us, struggling as we are, the path of truth. Surely it is

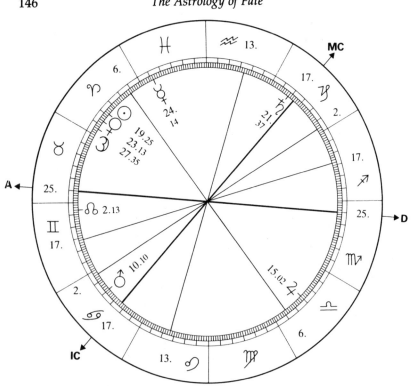

DIAGRAM 10. Birth horoscope of King Henri II of France

b. 31 March 1519 (o.s.)
10.28 a.m.
St Germain-en-Laye

(planetary placements according to Luc Gauricus, *Opera Omnia*)

Fate and the necessity of human death which distributes at its own discretion a time of living to all living things born on the Earth, denies a longer span to some, allows it to others. It makes no sense for one to admit the necessity of Fate and afterwards to deny it.[71]

Firmicus, and Gauricus in his turn, believed the astrological practitioner to be the mouthpiece of Fate, and he writes in the *Mathesis* a considerable amount about the responsibilities entailed in such a delicate role. He does not pussyfoot about the difficulties of the twelfth house, in which, according to Gauricus' version of King Henri's nativity, the sun, moon and Venus are placed. The twelfth

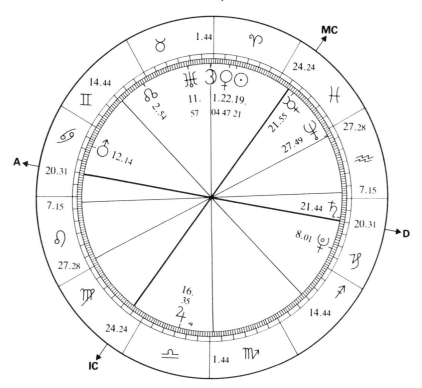

DIAGRAM 11. Birth horoscope of King Henri II of France
(calculated by computer)

house in the *Mathesis* is called *cacodaimon*, the Evil Spirit. Firmicus does not care for the sixth house either, in which Gauricus places King Henri's Jupiter:

> In this house we find the cause of physical infirmities and sickness. This house is called Mala Fortuna [Bad Fortune] because it is the house of Mars.[72]

Nor does he appreciate the psychological potential of the sun in square to Saturn, a close aspect in His Most Christian Majesty's horoscope:

> The native will die a violent death if Saturn is in opposition or square aspect to the sun. Violent death is also indicated if Saturn and Mars are in square aspect to the moon.[73]

Since King Henri has the moon as well as the sun in square to

Saturn in Gauricus' map, the poor King does not appear to have too many options open to him. On forecasting the length of life, Firmicus states:

> When you look carefully at the Giver of Life, that is, the ruler of the chart [for Firmicus, this is not the ascendant ruler, but rather the ruler of the sign which the moon enters after she has left her natal sign] and you see in what house it is located ... and you also consider the ruler of the sign in which the Giver of Life is situated ... you will easily be able to delineate the whole character of this life.[74]

King Henri's ruler, whichever way it is looked at, is Venus, according to Gauricus' ascendant; and she is in the sign of her detriment in the horrible *cacodaimon*, the twelfth house. Venus in turn is squared by Saturn and opposed by Jupiter in the house of what Firmicus calls Bad Fortune. If I had lived in the sixteenth century, I would not have bet any money on King Henri either.

The rather gloomy approach which Firmicus and his later followers adopt toward 'malefic' configurations is one which offers no flexibility of any kind to fate. This is perhaps because the idea which we now possess of 'inner' reflecting 'outer' was not a part of the sixteenth century's consciousness, save for rare souls like Marsilio Ficino. I would imagine that Gauricus, had King Henri asked him for further advice, would have told the monarch to look to the state of his soul, since not much could be done for the state of his body. Although the fate which Gauricus and Nostradamus foresaw for the King is not really Moira in the sense of retribution for ancestral sins or transgression of natural boundaries, it is Moira in her role as *daimon* of doom and death, and it is nevertheless a fate which lies in the physical substance of the world and the individual. Something was fated to be enacted during the summer of the King's forty-second year; it would never have occurred to Gauricus that this fate might enact itself on any level other than death in single combat through a head wound. Perhaps it *could* not enact itself on any other level because there was, for that King at that time in history, no other level.

Following now is a list of the transiting planets on the day that King Henri's joust reached its unfortunate climax. I have listed only the seven planets that Gauricus would have considered, in order to get a fuller sense of what he interpreted with such grim finality. After this list is a complete sequence of all ten heavenly bodies in their positions on the day of the King's actual death ten days after the accident (if such a word is appropriate). These have been calculated by computer.

The following unpleasant cosmic arrangements may now be

DIAGRAM 12.  Transits for the date of King Henri's joust
30 June 1559
(planetary placements at noon GMT)

☉ 17 ♋ 09
☽ 17 ♉ 08
☊ 4 ♈ 32
☿ 17 ♋ 39 ℞
♀ 17 ♌ 20
♂ 5 ♐ 09
♃ 18 ♓ 03 ℞
♄ 2 ♊ 29

DIAGRAM 13.  Transits for the date of King Henri's death
10 July 1559
(planetary placements at noon GMT)

☉ 26 ♋ 42
☽ 9 ♎ 05
☿ 13 ♋ 03
♀ 29 ♌ 19
♂ 5 ♐ 46
♃ 17 ♓ 49 ℞
♄ 3 ♊ 30
♅ 12 ♍ 15
♆ 28 ♉ 00
♇ 9 ♓ 00

considered: Transiting Saturn was precisely conjuncting the Pars
Fortuna and the ascending node of the moon. The Caput Draconis
or 'north' node of the moon received much more publicity in
medieval and Renaissance astrology than it does now; the astrologers of the time acquired their view of the moon's nodes from the
Arabs and the Indians, who feared the Caput greatly. It was
believed to be a fated and terribly dangerous point in the horoscope. In India the Caput or Head of the Dragon is called Rahu, the
Terrible Demon or Gorgon, who swallows the sun. This is related
to the fact that the conjunction of sun, moon and ascending node
results in a total solar eclipse. Ketu, the descending or 'south'
node, called Cauda Draconis (Tail of the Dragon), is likewise a

dangerous point, and a demon in Indian myth. Saturn conjuncting the Pars Fortuna by transit in the first house, wherein 'is found the life and vital spirit of men', is bad enough; Saturn conjuncting the Caput is disastrous.

I believe this is what Gauricus would have seen, although I would not see it that way myself. King Henri's grand cardinal cross, consisting of Jupiter in square to Saturn in square to sun–moon–Venus (the moon is not actually involved, but Gauricus thought it was) in square to Mars (which is not technically opposite Saturn, but through the idea of 'translation of light' current at the time is considered to complete the grand cross), is, to begin with, a nasty enough sight for a sixteenth-century astrologer grounded in Firmicus. It was being triggered, during the period between the fatal joust and the King's death, by the transiting sun and Mercury. Notwithstanding his sad death, King Henri's life was an exceedingly unhappy one. His youth was spent in a Spanish dungeon as hostage to the Emperor Charles V, his father disliked him intensely and avoided him as much as possible, his mother died when he was very young, he was married against his will to a woman he found physically repulsive, and he was perpetually, although not surprisingly, depressed. The best that can be said is that he played a good game of tennis. To Gauricus, the sun and the chart ruler in Aries afflicted by the baleful Saturn and Mars meant injury to the head, since Aries is traditionally the ruler of that part of the body. There are two possible explanations for the blindness prophesied by Nostradamus. One is the location of King Henri's reputed ascendant near the stars of the Pleiades, considered by the Arabs to endanger sight. The other is the location of the King's Mars on a nebula called the Eyes of the Crab, located in the sign of Cancer, also believed to endanger sight. In addition to the threatening transits of Saturn, sun and Mercury, the transiting sun also reached the IC calculated by Gauricus, the point in the horoscope which traditionally represents the 'end of life'. And there had been an eclipse earlier in the year, around the time of the King's birthday, which fell on the sun–moon–Venus conjunction in the *cacodaimon*, the terrible twelfth house. Putting all this together, we can get some sense of why the two astrologers thought the King's death to be inevitable.

Now, I have presented this summary of a day in the life of King Henri for several reasons. Firstly, I feel it is an excellent example of the mainstream of astrology's attitude towards fate, the attitude which now provokes such animosity or splitting among modern practitioners. But more importantly, I wish to draw attention to the unfortunate fact that both Gauricus and Nostradamus were right about the King. However, although I have not to my recollection ever seen a horoscope identical to that of King Henri, I have seen frequently enough the configurations which Firmicus and Gauricus would have considered baleful. They do not translate themselves so literally now. While the sun in square to Saturn might have meant violent death in Firmicus' time, and even in Gauricus', it does not appear to manifest in such a manner today. Sometimes it does, and sometimes it does not. This curious but highly significant shift is, I feel, a reflection of some profound change, not only in the attitudes of astrology from the more literally predictive to the more psychological, but also in the manner in which fate enacts itself. I have observed grand cardinal crosses involving sun, Mars, and Saturn where one corner lay in the twelfth house, and I have watched 'malefic' transits over such points, including the moon's nodes. At these times my clients did not die, either of wounds to the head or anything else. They certainly went through some rather painful and difficult experiences, including illness, accidents, depressions, marriage break-ups and so on; and one attempted suicide. But the response to planetary pressure such as Gauricus might have understood as fatal seems to vary a good deal more today than it did in the sixteenth century. A good example is the chart of Ruth, who has a grand cross involving the sixth and twelfth houses, as well as the meridian. What happened to her, was, after a fashion, a kind of death; but it was an inner one, and yielded some very creative results. Sun–Saturn squares and Mars–Saturn squares are certainly prone to engage in battle when they are triggered, and often 'in an enclosed space' in a symbolic sense. But the battles may be inner ones, and so too may be the deaths.

I suspect that we are here confronted with that mystery which esoteric tradition calls the planes of consciousness, or what might also be referred to as levels of expression for psychic energy. Jung writes about the 'canalisation of libido' in Volume V of the *Collected Works*, and suggests that psychic energy tends to transform from instinctual compulsion to meaningful inner experience through the mediation of the symbol. In other words, psychic energy 'introverts' if the image which corresponds to the outer compulsion emerges within the individual and if he is able to contain that compulsion through the mediating power of the image. In the end, the compulsion may still demand actualisation. On the other hand, it may not. This process is often an extremely fraught one. It is also the path by which Buddhism teaches that a man may loosen his attachment to the Thousand Things. To give a very crude and simple but common enough example: A man is experiencing the transit of Neptune over his natal Venus. His dreams herald the transit by manifesting erotic imagery, and mysterious unknown women who are trying to seduce him or guide him somewhere.

One day while travelling home from the office to his wife and family, he sees on a street corner a miraculously beautiful sixteen-year-old girl. (The film *10* portrays this dilemma most amusingly.) Does our hero pursue the anima, or does he attempt the painful, frustrating and anger-provoking path of trying to internalise her? Or does he attempt both? That she appears at this time in his life is an act of fate. His response has ultimately nothing to do with conventional morality, because different responses may be appropriate for different people. But it deals in part with the issue of transmuting instinct into inner image, which may become a new and creative aspect of the individual himself. Sometimes this can only occur if the actual concrete woman is met and related to. But there are a great many choices inherent in this kind of situation, and perhaps there are more of them today than there were five hundred years ago, because we have allowed into our vocabulary and into our consciousness the reality of the 'inner image'. Obviously there is no legitimate answer to the question of what our hero must do; it depends upon the man, his wife, and the sixteen year old. Some people are horribly predictable. But the predictability is not so predictable as it once was.

The profound passage that we have made from King Henri's time to our own is not merely a passage of technology and greater knowledge of the physical universe. We have also introjected many of the gods and *daimones* which people the outer world of the primitive and which still, during the Renaissance, resided in 'outer' things. This process has impoverished our religious rituals, but it has also enriched our inner lives, and it has given us more choices to counterbalance Moira. Ficino believed that one could transform at least certain aspects of fate through magic, but Ficino was in a very small minority in his time. His consciousness was much closer to ours. In general, the sixteenth century did not know the word 'inner', or the concept of 'individuality', let alone that of 'individuation' or the reality of 'psyche'. A man was, in the most profound sense, his persona; he embodied his position in society, be it king, duke, priest, artisan or peasant. His inner being, such as it was, consisted only of what he had been taught to feel and think and believe. The great writers and artists of the time shine like suns in the darkness of this collective unconsciousness, although such a writer, writing the same books now, would have some difficulty finding a publisher because he would be quite 'ordinary'. Anything aberrant within the individual was usually believed to be the work of the Devil, and madness was a possession by evil spirits. King Henri was probably not aware that he had a psyche, or an unconscious, personal or collective. Saturn in square to the sun did not suggest to Gauricus, as it does to me, that the King suffered deep insecurity and a sense of profound failure, both as a king and as a man, that he feared the judgment of society upon him, that he had been emotionally crippled by the utter ruthlessness with which his glamorous and much-beloved father, King François I, had treated him, and that he had a very violent and destructive streak to his nature which, denied any external expression save conventional battles and jousts, ultimately turned inwards upon itself. To Gauricus, there was only one way the chart could manifest itself: outwardly, through an unfortunate life and a violent end. For the King, there was only one level through which the transits activating his chart could manifest: through his physical body, in an actual duel with an actual opponent, because concrete reality was all that he possessed. King Henri was fated in this literal way because he himself was literal. He had never read Ficino, and had no patience with poetry or with introspection. He never questioned either his feelings or his motives, but allowed himself always to be led by others, and rarely proclaimed any initiatory action of his own. There were no Jungian analysts to help him, or Transpersonal Psychology workshops, or meditation groups, or EST, or Assertiveness Training. Although the hermetic movement fostered by Ficino knew of these things by other names, King Henri was a man of his time and not one of their brotherhood. There was only one kind of death which he could meet.

It would seem that although fate may not alter in its intrinsic pattern or in its timing, it may alter in terms of its clothing, its level of expression. This is suggested by the story of King Henri, and by the stories of my analysands.Whether we cultivate the Eastern viewpoint of non-attachment in order to attain freedom from the Wheel, or the psychological viewpoint of withdrawing projections in order to experience ourselves as individuals with some degree of choice in life, we are ultimately the inheritors of Ficino and the alchemists, who believed that the transformation of one's own substance was the only possible answer to fate. Paradoxically, this entails an embrace of one's fate. The twentieth-century individual with aspects like those of King Henri in his natal horoscope, who has done a little humble tampering with Nature in terms of insight into himself, is, in my experience, both more and less predictable than the individual who, like King Henri, identifies completely with his persona and can find reality only in the external definitions of his role in society. He is less predictable because more levels are open to him; he is more predictable in that, in my experience, he becomes more like his birth chart, and in particular, more like his sun sign. I should emphasise that this kind of inner work does not seem to alter the individual's innate pattern. If anything, it brings it into sharper relief. We are what we are, and fortunately or unfortunately cannot write an angry letter to *The Times* requesting a new horoscope. Nor does the timing of transits and progressions change. The rate of growth of the organism is inherent in the organism, for this is Moira, and I have not found that 'tampering' through introversion and relationship with the unconscious either accelerates or slows down that rate of growth. Rather, it may make it more meaningful. I am not very impressed by that school of astrology which believes one can 'transcend' the horoscope through psychological or spiritual techniques, or 'work through' one's karma with American-style rapidity by a little Sanskrit chanting and a quick name change and a turban. But perhaps one can experience the horoscope 'inside' as well as 'outside', and that seems to make a difference in terms of the subjective quality of life. As I have tried to show through the example of Ruth and her violent man, there may be some wisdom in glimpsing the inner psychic image which mirrors the outer event. This inner image may sometimes change, or 'feels' different as the ego changes its attitude toward the image. It is rather like a dance: both partners gradually learn to move more gracefully together, not stepping on each other's feet quite so often, remaining separate yet somehow a unity, and slowly – over a lifetime – becoming comfortable enough to actually listen with pleasure to the music.

That fate which in King Henri manifested as the violent concretisation of a violent natal configuration might, in the modern individual, find a somewhat altered, or at least a more meaningful, expression. The transits which so alarmed Gauricus and Nostradamus – such as Saturn over the ascending node, or the sun over the grand cross – might offer an opportunity for confronting something violent within oneself, as well as – or, perhaps, instead of – confronting something violent in the outer world in the form of an opponent's lance. And if the outer world does produce its lance, one may still find the experience inwardly rewarding, even the process of death. If I allow my imagination free play, I would envision those three robed female forms who are really one, offering several alternatives, provided that what they have written is accepted in essence. I once worked with a man who is a very gifted writer, who periodically expressed his anxiety and ambivalence towards his analysis and toward me by visiting, one after another, an entire stable of psychics, palm-readers and clairvoyants to find out 'what was going to happen' to him. This inevitably occurred when the pressure and heat of the analytic confrontation, and the unknown depths of the unconscious, pushed him into his intense fear and mistrust of life. He has the sun in Virgo, and such urgent need to know precisely the future course of physical events is a characteristic way in which the sign copes with anxiety. On one occasion, because I was not amenable to drawing up his horoscope on the spot and offering him an instantaneous summary of his future, he attempted to 'punish' me by visiting an Indian astrologer who would give on demand what I, the bad mother, was refusing him: a guarantee of safety. He returned in some perplexity, horoscope in hand. It seemed that the Indian astrologer had mentioned two dates in the past which he interpreted as the fathering of two children. The dates, my analysand told me, were certainly accurate; but as he was unmarried with no children that he was aware of, he was rather baffled, because these dates coincided with the publication of two very successful 'thrillers' which had set him going on his literary career. I did not inspect the horoscope, because I felt at the time that the issue of trust on which we were working needed to emerge out of the relationship and not out of the horoscope. Therefore I do not know what configurations provoked such an interpretation on the part of the other astrologer. But I would guess that he had seen some progression or transit involving the fifth house. This house, however, does not stipulate on which level we create. How was this astrologer to know, literal as he was, that the creative act for my shy, introverted and partnerless analysand might take a different form? That he had to produce children at these two junctures of his life was, perhaps, his fate. But the ambiguity hinges upon what kind of children these were going to be.

The strange and paradoxical relationship between the ego which must maintain its sense of autonomy and the demands of Moira, is not easy to define. Perhaps, ultimately, it is impossible to define. Family inheritance such as we have seen in both Renee R., the autistic child, and Ruth, the haunted woman, is certainly what I would understand as Moira. In the first case, it seems as though nothing can be done, although, in theory, many autistic children might be helped by a more insightful therapeutic approach. In the second case, something has been done, but precisely what is hard to delineate in any literal way. Nothing can be done for Ruth either, in so far as she is the person she is, and therefore has the psychic bedfellow she has. But this bedfellow showed a certain willingness to try other positions, as it were, than rape, provided Ruth showed an equal willingness to experiment with him. In a similar vein, the aspects and sign and house placements of Pluto in the horoscope are givens, which cannot be altered. But the individual's understanding of the planet's requirements can deepen, and its expression can therefore be more meaningful and less terrifying. It would seem that consciousness, in the sense that Jung means it, is the fulcrum upon which the relationship between fate and freedom balances, for this quality of consciousness permits fate to unfold in a richer and more complex tapestry which is at the same time both more supportive of the ego and, paradoxically, more honouring of the unconscious. Our dream images and the children of the imagination may enact their combats and promote the death of the old king within the psyche, and these processes may necessitate suffering and sacrifice, sometimes in the external world as well as in the inner. But perhaps they can occur with a sense of meaning and a paradoxical willingness – the ability to do gladly that which I must do. I would not be so flagrantly obtuse as to suggest that we in the twentieth century are no longer fated. But I view with interest the change from Gauricus' astonishing level of concrete predictive accuracy – even with an inaccurate horoscope – to the more muddled and uncertain predictive accuracy of the present-day astrologer. This gives me the feeling that we stand on the threshold of opening up possibilities of understanding Moira as an inner archetypal figure, as well as the great law of nature which circumscribes physical life.

# 6

## The Creation of the World

*The Creation of the World*

... The Earth, the Sky, and the Sea were once mingled together in the same form, until a compelling music sounded from nowhere and they separated, yet remained one universe still. This mysterious music announced the birth of the soul of Eurynome; for that was the original name of the Great Triple Goddess, whose symbol is the Moon. She was the universal Goddess and she was alone. Being alone, she presently felt lonely, standing between blank earth, empty water, and the accurately circling constellations of Heaven. She rubbed her cold hands together, and when she opened them again, out slid the serpent Ophion, whom from curiosity she admitted to love with her. From the fearful convulsions of this act of love rivers sprang, mountains rose, lakes swelled; it caused all manner of creeping things and fish and beasts to be born and populate the earth. Immediately ashamed of what she had done, Eurynome killed the serpent and sent his ghost underground; but as an act of justice she banished a mulberry-faced shadow of herself to live underground with the ghost. She renamed the serpent 'Death', and her shadow she named 'Hekate'. From the scattered teeth of the dead serpent sprang up the Sown race of men, who were shepherds, cowherds and horseherds, but neither tilled the soil nor engaged in warfare. Their food was milk, honey, nuts, and fruit, and they knew nothing of metallurgy. So ended the first Age, that had been the Age of Stone.

Eurynome continued to live in Earth, Sky and Sea. Her Earth-self was Rhea, with the breath of gorse-flower and amber-coloured eyes. As Rhea one day she went to visit Crete ... In Crete, out of sun and vapour, feeling lonely again, Rhea contrived a man-god named Cronus to be her lover. To satisfy her maternal craving, she then every year bore herself a Sun-Child in the Dictean Cave; but Cronus was jealous of the Sun-Children and killed them, one after the other. Rhea concealed her displeasure. She said smilingly to Cronus one day: 'Give me, dear one, the thumb and fingers of your left hand. A single hand is enough for such a lazy god as you are. I will make five little gods out of them to obey your instructions while you recline here with me on the flowery bank. They will guard your feet and legs from unnecessary fatigue.' He accordingly gave her his left thumb and fingers, and out of them she made five little gods called the Dactyls, or Finger Gods, and crowned them with myrtle crowns. They caused him a deal of amusement by their sport and dancing. But Rhea secretly instructed the Dactyls to hide from Cronus the next Sun-Child that she bore. They obeyed her and deceived Cronus, putting an axe-shaped thunder-stone in a sack and pretending that it was Rhea's child which, as usual, they were throwing into the sea for him. This gave rise to the proverb, that the right hand should always be aware of what the left hand is doing. Rhea could not herself suckle the child, whom she named Zagreus, without rousing the suspicions of Cronus; and therefore the Dactyls brought a fat sow to be his foster-mother – a circumstance of which Zagreus afterwards did not like to be reminded. Later, because they found it inconvenient to drown his infant voice with loud drumming and piping whenever he cried, they weaned him from the sow and took him away from Mount Dicte. They consigned him to the care of certain shepherds who lived far to the west, on Mount Ida, where his fare was sheep's cheese and honey. So the second Age, that had been the Golden Age, drew to a close.

Rhea hastened on the new Age by fostering agriculture, and by teaching her servant, Prometheus the Cretan, how to make fire artificially with the fylfot fire-wheel. She laughed long to herself when Zagreus castrated and killed his father Cronus with a golden sickle that Prometheus had forged, and still longer when he tried to disguise himself as a starved and bedraggled cuckoo and pleaded to be nursed back to life in her bosom. She pretended to be deceived, and when he resumed his true shape she allowed him to enjoy her. 'Yes, indeed, my little god,' she said, 'you may be my loving servant if you wish.'

But Zagreus was insolent and answered: 'No, Rhea, I will be your master and instruct you what to do. I am more cunning than you, for I deceived you with my cuckoo disguise. And I am also more reasonable than you. By an act of reason I have just invented Time. Now that Time has begun, with my Advent, we can have dates and history and genealogy instead of timeless, wavering myth. And recorded Time, with its chain of detailed cause and consequence, will be the basis of Logic.'

Rhea was astonished and did not know whether to crush him to atoms with one blow of her sandal or whether to lie back and scream with mirth. In the end she did neither. She said no more that this: 'O Zagreus, Zagreus, my little Sun-Child, what strange notions you have sucked in from the dugs of your foster-mother, the Sow of Dicte!'

He answered: 'My name is Zeus, not Zagreus; and I am a Thunder-Child, not a Sun-Child; and I was suckled by the She-goat Amalthea of Ida, not by the Sow of Dicte.'

'That is a triple lie,' said Rhea, smiling.

'I know that,' he answered. 'But I am big and strong enough now to tell triple lies, or even sevenfold lies, without fear of contradiction. If I am of a bilious temper, that is because the ignorant shepherds of Ida fed me with too much honeycomb. You must beware of my masterful ways, Mother, I warn you, for from now onwards, I, not you, am the Sole Sovereign of All Things.'

Rhea sighed and answered happily: 'Dear Zagreus, or Zeus, or whatever you care to be called, have you indeed guessed how weary I am of the natural order and tidiness of this manifest universe, and of the thankless labour of supervising it? Rule it, Child, rule it, by all means! Let me lie back and meditate at my ease. Yes, I will be your wife and daughter and slave; and whatever strife or disorder you bring into my beautiful universe by any act of reason, as you call it, I will forgive you, because you are still very young and cannot be expected to understand things as well as I do. But pray be careful of the Three Furies that have been born from the drops of blood falling from your father's severed genitals; make much of them or they will one day avenge him. Let us have recorded Time and dates and genealogy and history, by all means; though I foresee that they will cause you far more anxiety and pleasure than they are worth. And by all means use Logic as a crutch for your crippled intelligence and a justification of your absurd errors. However, I must first make a condition; there shall be two islands, one in the Western Sea and one in the Eastern, which I shall retain for my ancient worship. There neither yourself nor any other deity that you may divide yourself into shall have any jurisdiction, but only myself and my serpent Death when I choose to send for him. The western shall be the island of innocence, and the eastern that of illumination; in neither will any record be kept of time, but every day shall be as a thousand years, and contrariwise.'

Then at once she made the western island rise from the waters, like a garden, at a day's sail from Spain; and she also cast a cloud about the severed member of Cronus, and the Dactyls conveyed it safely to the eastern island, which was already in existence, where it became their companion, the jolly fish-headed god Priapus.

Then Zeus said: 'I accept your condition, Wife, if you agree that your other self, Amphitrite, shall surrender the Sea to my shadow brother Poseidon.'

Rhea answered: 'I agree, Husband, only reserving for my own use the waters that extend for five miles about my two islands; you may also rule in the Sky instead of Eurynome, with possession of all the stars and planets and of the Sun itself; but I reserve the Moon for my own.'

So they clasped hands on the bargain, and to show his power Zeus dealt her a resounding box on the ear, and danced in menace an armed jig, clashing his thunderstone axe against his golden shield so that the thunder rolled horribly across the vault of Heaven. Rhea smiled. She had not bargained away her control of three most important things, which Zeus never afterward succeeded in wresting from her: wind, death and destiny. This is why she smiled.

# PART TWO

---

# *Daimon*

# 7
# Fate and Myth

myth, mith, n. a figment; a commonly held belief that is untrue,
or without foundation.

**Chambers Twentieth Century Dictionary**

There was once a King of Thebes called Laios. This Laios had, in his
early manhood, caused mortal offence to a friend and host called
Pelops. While staying at his friend's palace, he carried off the
man's son, Chrysippos, and forced the boy with a sexual assault.
Out of shame Chrysippos killed himself; and Pelops, outraged,
cursed Laios King of Thebes, that he might never himself beget a
son, or, if he did, then by that son he should be slain.

In time Laios chose as his wife Iokaste, a princess of the house of
Echion. Three times the Delphic oracle warned him that he must
die without issue, if he were to avert catastrophe to himself and to
Thebes:

> King of the glorious chariots
> Of Thebes, do not defy the gods; beget no son.
> If ever your seed sees the light, your son shall take
> Your life, and your whole house shall drown in kindred blood.[76]

But Laios was not inclined to heed the warning, and while drunk
one night forcibly consummated his marriage. The fruit of the
union, a male child, was sent by the guilty father to be exposed on a
hillside; thus compounding Pelops' curse with the wrath of Hera,
protectress of children, and Apollo, protector of young boys, from
whom the threatening oracle had come.

The child was exposed in winter, nailed to the earth with an iron
spike through his feet. For this he was later called Oidipus, which
means 'swell-foot'. A Theban herdsman took pity on the child and
spared his life, handing him over to another herdsman from
neighbouring Corinth; who in turn presented the baby Oidipus to
the childless King and Queen of Corinth, to rear as their own.

The boy grew to sturdy manhood, with a strong body, fiery red hair, and an imperious temper. He believed himself to be the true son of King Polybus and Queen Periboia of Corinth. But one night he was insulted by a drunken guest at a banquet, who reproached him for his lack of resemblance to his parents and accused him of being a foster-child. Oidipus secretly set forth to inquire at the Delphic oracle for the answer to the question of his parentage; but the god did not answer the question, threatening him instead with the awful doom of becoming his mother's husband and his father's murderer. He did not dare return to Corinth, but instead took another route, travelling north.

Laios, King of Thebes, was meanwhile in great despair, for Hera's wrath at the King had caused her to send against Thebes a monster out of Ethiopia, called the Sphinx. This creature was easily recognised by her woman's head, lion's body, serpent's tail and eagle's wings. The wise prophet Teiresias warned Laios to sacrifice at Hera's altar to beg forgiveness. But the King did not heed the seer, and set out instead to consult the Delphic oracle once again, taking the route south.

The son's path crossed that of the father in a narrow pass where it was impossible to make room. 'Traveller, give way to the King!' cried Laios' herald to the stranger. Oidipus' rage boiled over; he refused to step out of the King's path. One of Laios' horses trod on his foot, and the old King struck him on the head with the forked goad he used to drive his team. In fury, ignorant of whom he was striking, Oidipus smote his father dead with his staff, and the herald as well. Then, consumed with murderous anger, he bit the corpse of his victim, and spat out the blood.

In time Oidipus came to Thebes. After the death of Laios was discovered, the Queen's brother Kreon ruled there. The Sphinx continued to terrorise the city. She had settled on Mount Phicium, close to the gates, and asked every Theban wayfarer a riddle taught her by the Three Muses:

> On two feet, yet on four, there treads the earth,
> Yea, and on three, a creature of one name.
> Alone it changes shape of all that walk
> On ground or fly in air or swim the sea.
> But when it goes supported on four feet,
> Then is the speed the feeblest in its limbs.[77]

When the unfortunate wayfarer could not answer the riddle, the Sphinx strangled him and threw his corpse off Mount Phicium. Among the dead was Kreon's own son. Thereupon Kreon made a proclamation, that Iokaste and the kingdom should be his who overcame the Sphinx.

When the Sphinx confronted Oidipus with the riddle, he replied:

> *Of Man thou tellest. When he goes on mould*
> *Four-footed first he creeps, a babe new-born;*
> *In age a staff, third foot, must him uphold,*
> *All heavy-necked, with curved eld forlorn.*[78]

When the Sphinx heard this, she cast herself down from her mountaintop, and Oidipus married Iokaste and became King of Thebes.

Thus Oidipus became a sage, and also the most foolish of all the kings in the world. He received as the prize of his victory his own mother, and begat on her four children. But after a time a heavy plague fell upon Thebes, and it became apparent that some god was angry. When the Delphic oracle was consulted, Apollo replied: 'Expel the murderer of Laios.' Oidipus, in his blindness, pronounced a curse on Laios' murderer, and sentenced him to exile. The seer Teiresias admonished the King that the accursed thing in Thebes which he sought was in fact himself. In due course the herdsmen were found, who revealed their story. When Oidipus at last perceived that the oracle had truly foretold his fate, and that he had become the husband of his mother, the slayer of his father and the brother of his children, he blinded himself with a golden pin. Iokaste in her turn hanged herself at once when her shame was revealed.

The blind Oidipus vanished from the eyes of Thebes. He wandered for many years, led by Antigone, the elder and stronger of his daughter-sisters, and his dreams were haunted by the pursuing Erinyes. His sons murdered each other, and the house of Laios was drowned in kindred blood as the oracle had prophesied. When he heard of the carnage that was left of his family, he cried:

> *O Destiny! You created me, beyond all men,*
> *For life-long wretchedness and pain. Before I came*
> *Forth from my mother's womb Apollo prophesied*
> *To Laios that his unborn son should murder him . . .*
> *I am not such a lost fool as to perpetrate*
> *That outrage on my eyes and on my own sons' lives*
> *Without being forced to it by divine malevolence.*
> *So be it; what should such a wretch as I do now?*[79]

Antigone, after long and desperate wandering, led her father on the road to Kolonos, Poseidon's rocky hill and one of the entrances to the underworld. There the Erinyes, the goddesses who avenge the Mother, had their inviolable grove. In this place

Oidipus was forgiven by the gods, and the earth opened to receive him at last.

This is, of course, a figment of Greek imagination, an untrue story without foundation. No archaeologist has ever found the bones of Oidipus. Yet we have already seen how mythic themes may be used to deepen our understanding of astrological symbols such as Pluto, and to help us to travel imaginative roads into experiences of inner life which are inaccessible to a more rational or empiric approach. The myth of Oidipus has come to be better known than almost any other, because it provided the foundation upon which Sigmund Freud built his great edifice of psychoanalytic theory. Jung, following after Freud into the hidden strata of man's archaic unconscious world, found that these 'untrue stories' are spontaneous and universal images of the typical development patterns of human life. Myths in other words, are a creative, imaginative self-portrait of the psyche describing its own evolution – its own fate. As Joseph Campbell puts it:

> It would not be too much to say that myth is the secret opening through which the inexhaustible energies of the cosmos pour into human cultural manifestation. Religions, philosophies, arts, the social forms of primitive and historic man, prime discoveries in science and technology, the very dreams that blister sleep, boil up from the basic, magic ring of myth.[80]

The Greek word *mythos* contains two nuances of meaning. In one sense, *mythos* is a story. In another, more profound sense, it implies a scheme or plan. It is this latter shading of the word which is most relevant both to psychology and astrology, because the universality of basic mythic motifs reveals a groundplan or purposeful pattern of development inherent in the human psyche as well as in the human body. The life of individuals and nations is therefore not random, nor shaped exclusively by environmental factors; it has *intent*, or teleology. Jung called the patterning factors in the psyche the archetypes, and we have seen how these archetypal 'designs' touch very closely on one of the possible meanings of fate. The birth horoscope too is a story, as well as a scheme or plan, and the two – horoscope and myth – form a dyad. Myth maps the universal human patterns, while the birth chart maps the individual one. These two also intersect, because the signs and planets of the zodiac are crowded round with mythic images and themes, and the development of life represented by the cycle of Aries through Pisces tells a mythic tale. This is a tale of fate, the pattern of growth from seed to mature plant to seed again, which has been written before the concrete story begins. But it is a different kind of fate from Moira, whom we have been exploring in the preceding pages. I am still in no position to know whether Chrysippos the Neoplatonist was right when he described dual fate as energy and substance. But I am prepared to give him the benefit of the doubt, and suggest that Moira represents the 'substance' aspect of fate (Madame Blavatsky, after all, equated karma with substance), while the destiny inherent in mythic themes is the 'energy' aspect. Perhaps the two are not really separate, but simply 'feel' different because they are experienced at different levels.

Socrates and Plato also distinguished between the goddess Necessity and her children, the Moirai, and another kind of deterministic force in human affairs. This latter they called the *daimon* (also spelled *daemon*).

> So, at last, we reach the notion of the individual *ker*, *daemon*, and *moira*. The *ker* is an *eidolon* [image], or winged sprite, which wears a sinister aspect – it is an object of fear. If it is angry and seeks vengeance, it is an *Erinyes*. Considered as allotted to the individual at his birth, it is his *moira* – the span or limit of his vital force, the negative and repressive aspect of his fate ... The *daemon* (*genius*) of a person, on the other hand, retains the element of beneficent power, of functional *mana*. When Heraclitus, for example, says that a man's character is his *daemon*, he means that it is the force which shapes his life from within, and makes or mars his fortunes, not a 'destiny' allotted him from without.[81]

There is a considerable although subtle difference between these two ways of viewing fate. This is reflected in our distinction, in English, between the word 'fate' and the word 'destiny'. The root of 'destiny' in Latin means 'to stand apart', thereby implying that, although destiny is fate in one sense, it is more concerned with the individual's development, that which makes him unique, that which makes him 'stand apart' from his fellows. Jung uses the word fate in both senses, sometimes more in one, sometimes more in the other. But the *daimon*, despite its more creative or 'beneficent' connotations, is no less deterministic than the boundaries of Moira. It is still 'that which I must do'. I am given the curious feeling that this doubleness of fate encompasses something with both a feminine and a masculine face, or, put another way, with a dark and a light face. Moira is unquestionably female. Her kingdom is that of instinct, inheritance and mortality. The *daimon*, when we meet it in the work of philosophers such as Plato, has a more active, ambitious quality. It tries to go somewhere; it contains the sense of a goal. Kerenyi also considers the meaning of the *daimon* in his work on *Zeus and Hera*:

> A 'dispenser' is the meaning of *daimon*, but not a human one. In
> the plural, in the language of Homer, *daimones* is completely
> equivalent to *theoi*, 'gods'. *Daimon* in the singular also is personal
> in sense. It appears in a personal occurrence, in a personal fate,
> we might say, although we must not understand 'fate' here as
> being existent on its own. The 'dispenser' occurred only in a
> personal case; it was a personal dispensation each time it
> happened.[82]

This forms a stark contrast to the collective impersonality of Moira
– and also the collective impersonality of the astrological Pluto.

When I attempt to grasp the essence of this mysterious *daimon*, I
am left with a sense of something that drives the individual from
within to fulfil a unique pattern. It is purposeful, teleological as
Jung would put it; it is trying to go somewhere, and the individual
in whom it is alive, or who, seen another way, is its embodiment,
therefore must himself go somewhere. The obvious expression of
such a driving force in the outer world is in the field of vocation.
Although the sense of a 'calling' is not experienced by everybody,
it is most unmistakable in those for whom it is a reality, and the
outer manifestation of that individual's 'character' in the form of a
sphere of creative endeavour is matched to the inner image of the
*daimon* which drives him. Socrates certainly had a *daimon*, and tried
to live in accord with its impetus. Jung might say that this is living
in harmony with, and in submission to, the Self. A conventionally
religious person might say it is living in accord with the will of God.
But the god is inside, and we are back to Novalis' equation of fate
and soul.

Other manifestations, less obvious in concrete terms than vocation, seem also to reflect the impetus of the *daimon*. One certainly
encounters it in love. Plato wrote that Eros was a great *daimon*, and
the commands of love override so many other considerations that
one might well say love can be one of the most profound experiences of fate that an individual can encounter. Love, too, 'goes
somewhere', for it changes the individual and can lead him into a
different phase of his development. Although Pluto figures
strongly in issues of compulsive attraction, the daimonic aspect of
love has a very different flavour. Plato puts it this way in the
*Phaedrus*:

> And so it is with the followers of the other gods. Each man in his
> life honours, and imitates as well as he can, that god to whose
> choir he belonged, while he is uncorrupted in his first incar-
> nation here; and in the fashion he has thus learned, he bears

himself to his beloved as well as to the rest. So, then, each
chooses from among the beautiful a love conforming to his kind;
and then, as if his chosen were his god, he sets him up and robes
him for worship . . . And this striving to discover the essence of
their proper god, by tracing him in themselves, is rewarded; for
they are forced to look on the god without flinching, and when
their memory holds him, his breath inspires them, and they
share his attributes and his life, as far as man can enter godhead.
And for these blessings they thank the loved one, loving him
even more deeply . . . He sees himself in his lover as if in a
mirror, not knowing whom he sees. And when they are
together, he too is released from pain, and when apart, he longs
as he himself is longed for; for reflected in his heart is love's
image, which is love's answer.[83]

Thus, one's love is one's destiny, because it reflects the god within
oneself. In fact, the entire pattern of a person's life bears the stamp
of his *daimon*, and when looked at with hindsight, or from a
distance, the pattern is clear. It is only while we live it that it is so
difficult, perhaps impossible, to see, except in those rare moments
of lucidity which can occur during great crisis or suffering, when
the purposefulness of experience leaves the awesome sense of a
mover other than the ego and different from the blind instinctual
boundaries which we considered in the first part of the book.

Although I have, all along, been dipping into the bottomless
reservoir of myth to illustrate some of the manifestations of Moira
in the individual life, I would like now to approach the body of
myth in a different way. My intention is to move through the signs
of the zodiac, gathering, if a florid metaphor may be excused,
mythic flowers as an enrichment of the ordinary definitions generally given to each sign. The signs of the zodiac which are
emphasised in an individual horoscope are more than markers of
behaviour. They are the soul of the person, the gods 'to whose
choir he belonged', and they are therefore his fate in the sense that
Novalis describes. A zodiacal sign is far more profound than
simply a list of qualities of behaviour. It is a *mythos*, a scheme or
plan which is imaged in a story – a pattern of development, an
archetypal theme. Several different mythic characters inhabit the
domain of one astrological sign, and a drama is enacted, sometimes tragic, sometimes comic, but always teleological. I am convinced that these stories, which form the bare bones of the
individual pattern of development, are something of what we
experience as fate – fate in the form of the *daimon* – because the
story is contained within us at birth, and merely awaits the telling
through being fleshed with the experiences and conscious choices

and perceptions of an individual life. Because, like Novalis, I feel that the *daimon* and the soul are two names for the same principle, the mythic stories which are suggested by the patterns within the horoscope are both outer and inner, and permeate not only the external life of the person but also the secret recesses of his dreams. Thus images appear in sleep which are characteristic of the horoscope and of the signs which are strongly tenanted; and these images are in turn the images of myth. They are different from, and more complex than, the traditional zodiacal animals. But they are part and parcel of the same *daimon*. We have already seen some of this in the dream examples I have given in earlier chapters. In turn, these mythic characters who embody the directives of the soul and unravel the individual fate or 'destiny' are also the ordinary people who inhabit one's outer life, whom one meets in parents, children, partners, co-workers, friends, enemies and in the larger collective.

Of all the mutiplicity of mythic tales, stretching from the sublime stories of the creation of the universe to the ridiculous and comic escapades of the trickster and the fool, one mythic theme is most relevant to the story of human development, and that is the tale of the hero. The heroic quest is what Joseph Campbell calls the 'monomyth', for it is universal and ubiquitous, ancient and modern, and is our most basic description of the processes of human growth from the darkness of the uterine waters to the darkness of the grave. The hero's journey is a map both of the development of culture and of the individual's psychic voyage through life. It applies to both men and women, to the primitive tribesman and the sophisticated Western city dweller, to the adult and to the child. It weaves its way through our dreams, our fantasies, our hopes, our fears, our aspirations, our loves and our ends. The stages of the hero's journey are found in every culture and at every epoch. The surface details may vary, but the skeletal structure remains the same.

> The two – the hero and his ultimate god, the seeker and the found – are thus understood as the outside and inside of a single, self-mirrored mystery, which is identical with the mystery of the manifest world. The great deed of the supreme hero is to come to the knowledge of this unity in multiplicity and then to make it known.[84]

Each sign of the zodiac portrays a mythic journey. It contains a hero, and also implies the nature of the hero's call to adventure. It contains, too, the helper who provides the magic clue, and the threshold of adventure; the battle with brother, dragon, sorcerer; the dismemberment, crucifixion, abduction, night-sea journey and whale's belly. The object of the quest is also contained: the beloved, the sacred marriage, the jewel, the atonement with the father, the elixir of life. And the *hubris* or flaw of the hero is also contained, and the nature of his inevitable end, within that apparently simple description of a single zodiacal sign.

Heroes (by which I mean both hero and heroine, for we are not here dealing with a sexist issue, but rather with the development of individual consciousness) differ a great deal. Herakles (or Hercules), for example, whose marvellous feat of the Twelve Labours is one of the best-known of heroic sagas, is not particularly intelligent. He has brawn rather than brains, possesses an immense reservoir of physical strength and courage, and has a tendency to club to death anything that opposes him. His stupid, robust, vital, dynamic and unquenchable character is beautifully portrayed in Robert Graves' novel of the quest for the Golden Fleece, called *Hercules, My Shipmate*. He is a universally human figure, but some of us are more like him than others; or, perhaps, it would be more accurate to say that parts of us behave more like him some of the time, and in certain situations. Odysseus, on the other hand, is called 'the wily one'. Guile, rather than brute force, carries him through; and his journey too is different, for he is the wanderer seeking his home rather than the warrior seeking fresh challenges. His path moves in a circle, rather than upward in an ascent or in linear fashion through a series of tasks. Jason is courageous but perfidious, and fails in the end through his treachery to the woman who has loved and helped him. Orpheus with his compassion and sweetness can wring tears from the very stones with the beauty of his music, and can even soften the heart of the stern lord of the underworld; but in the end he cannot retrieve his lost wife from the halls of Hades because he doubts the word of the Lord of the Great Place Below, and looks back. Siegfried is a complex Teutonic hero, fearless yet corruptible, naïve and godlike yet doomed. Parsifal is the Holy Fool, who redeems through the compassion born of his own blundering cruelty. Prometheus is a humanitarian thief, Oedipus – as we have seen – a noble and tragic pawn of fate whose uncontrollable anger and defiance turn prophecy into reality.

The heroines of myth vary too. Medea is proud, jealous and passionate, with occult powers; Phaedra too is jealous and passionate, but less honest, while Alkestis is meek and self-sacrificing, and Andromeda is simply a beautiful helpless pawn awaiting rescue. There are as many heroes and heroines, dragons and sorceresses, kings and gods as there are facets of human nature and variations on the single theme of human life. Different mythic themes are relevant at different times of life, for the major biological turning points of birth, puberty, childbirth, menopause, old age and death are accompanied by equally profound psychic changes which are reflected in the ever-changing panorama of myth. A man may at one point in his life be caught in the drama of Perseus confronting the terrible Gorgon as he attempts to leave his mother at adolescence and move out into life; at another point he may be caught in the ribald comedy of Zeus struggling with his nagging, jealous wife; he may meet the Gorgon again as he attempts to leave the stale stagnation of a mother–wife to pursue his own inner spirit; or he may reflect Pentheus, driven mad by the god Dionysos, or the victorious Theseus returning from Crete and his successful battle with the Minotaur only to find that his father has killed himself at the moment of the son's achievement. Astrology, with its twelve zodiacal signs and ten heavenly bodies encrusted with the dramas of many different myths, suggests, like Jung, that all myths move within us, some more dominant than others, some appearing in the guise of our 'outer world', all weaving the tapestry of the individual scheme of one's fate.

A few comments are appropriate on the relationship between myth and astrological symbolism. Myth is not a structured, orderly system of symbols like astrology or the kabala or the Tarot. It is a fluid, dynamic enactment of images, each of which has many different variations as the myth emerges spontaneously in different cultures and at different stages of one particular culture. Thus, the strange figure of Dionysos has several different fathers, several different kinds of deaths and resurrections, several different epithets added to his name, and several different spheres of human life over which he presides as *daimon*, traversing the spectrum from a god of death to a god of wine and drunkenness. But his core remains the same wherever, and in whatever guise, he is found. Robert Graves, in his work *The Greek Myths*, has laid out in impressive detail the enormous variations on each mythic figure. So has C. Kerenyi, whose writings on various of the Greek pantheon are always worth perusing. What I am hopefully *not* trying to do is to cram one symbolic system rigidly into another, by saying that only one particular myth has relevance for one particular sign. Mythic figures and stories are certainly imbued with different flavours and colours, and they tend to have affinity with some signs and not with others. Some myths are so universal that they are relevant to everybody: The quest of the hero is one of these. The great mythic sagas describe human development in general, and can be related to every sign and every life, and to the whole symbol of the zodiacal circle. Anyone who has ever tried to work out tight connections between mythic stories and figures has found himself in a hopeless soup where every myth blends with every other, and in the end one is left with what all great religions eventually promulgate as their unique and inviolable truth: There is only One. So I would suggest that myth be read as one would read a poem, with the feelings and the imagination rather than with the intellect, and with a sensitivity to the smell and taste and colour of the tale, rather than with a concrete determination to find out whether every Sagittarian one knows has, like Cheiron, a wound in the thigh.

There is, I feel, another important distinction between myth and astrological symbolism. The horoscope fixes life in time and space, and describes the incarnated individual in the temporal, three-dimensional 'real' world. It freezes the perpetually moving round of the heavens, and crystallises this into a pattern which describes the unfolding of a particular life. It is what has been written at birth for one person, living at one time. It is fate grounded in time and space, the *daimon* and the *ker* assigned to the individual for a little time. For this reason, anything can have a birth chart: a human being, a dog, a chicken, a book, a bumble-bee, an opera house, a bank. The moment something, some *thing*, appears in life, its beginning and its pattern of growth are mapped, fated, reflected, contained and circumscribed by its birth horoscope. Moira, as we have seen, means share or allotment, and *daimon* means dispenser; and the birth chart is the share and dispensation given of the heavenly round for one temporal moment.

Myth, on the other hand, is timeless and non-localised, as are the signs and planets in astrology before they are frozen into the posture of the birth horoscope. Myth does not exist as a thing in time and space. Achilles battling Hektor before the walls of Troy may be traced back to an historical event which occurred in pre-classical Greece in a certain century, because, as Schliemann discovered, there really was a Troy and a Trojan War. But the warrior–hero, of whom Achilles is one face, cannot be so pinned down, nor can the hero's battle with his brother–foe. This theme erupts spontaneously in every culture at every time; it is an image of an archetypal human situation. That it also enacts itself outwardly is therefore not surprising, for history reflects these archetypal patterns just as individual people do. Nor is it surprising that stories such as that of Achilles are remembered and retold century after century. They continue to resonate even in the apparently tamed and technological life of the modern Western man and woman. Myths are the shapers and denominators of culture as surely as they are of persons. They have no concrete form, no temporal or spatial reality, although the names and places in particular versions of a given myth bear these temporal and geographical stamps. They are tendencies, intents, ordering factors: images of instinctual patterns.

I am inclined to fantasise the gods, the heroes, the mythic protagonists, gathered in occluded shadow around the zodiacal wheel, behind the planets. Where a particular myth can find a congenial home within resonant patterns in an individual horoscope, then that myth will enter a person's life, and cling to him throughout his life as his *daimon*. It will appropriate that astrological configuration into its own story. Different gods are perhaps more or less at home in different horoscopes, and sometimes radically opposite characters attempt to live within one chart. They enter and exit at different stages of life, like actors on cue, according to the progressions and transits. And we may meet them in the form of 'other people' as well as in our own motives and character. I can think of no better parallel than the Greek theatre, where each actor wore a mask – called a *persona* (which is where Jung took the term from) – to announce the archetypal role he played. But the actor beneath the mask remained unseen and unknown except to his fellows. Thus, perhaps, we appear to the gods, playing out our parts, and believing ourselves to be 'different' and 'free', while all the time we dance the ancient dance that has been choreographed from the beginning of time. So perhaps it is as well to ask, in keeping with the spirit of the play, which god, or which pair or group of protagonists, combines with one's Venus in Aquarius opposite Pluto in Leo, or one's Sagittarian ascendant, or one's Mars conjunct Jupiter in Gemini in square to Saturn in Virgo in the tenth house. For until one has a feeling of the mythic drama at work, the statements of astrology are fragmented and incomplete and seem merely to describe static behaviour. And they do not reveal their story.

I have never found it to be very productive to play 'tell me what my myth is' games with the horoscope. There are so many myths, and the individual transforms or combines or cooks these myriad different themes into an individual broth that cannot really be delineated in a few sentences by even the wisest of astrologers. I also wonder whether it is truly possible to envision the course of the play while we are still on the stage. Perhaps on the other side of death the script may read complete, but the most we can glimpse at any given moment is the scene we are enacting, and the connections with past scenes, and the faintest intuitive flicker of what the next act of the drama might be.

Most of the myths to which I will be referring in the following pages are Greek, with the occasional smattering of Egyptian and Teutonic lore. This is not because other mythologies are irrelevant, but because I am not very well versed in them. It remains up to the reader to find out which mythic images are most resonant to him, or work best for him, and to amplify our astrological language further in accord with his own experience. I am personally drawn to the multiplicity and subtlety of the Greek pantheon, which, with the exception of the Hindu, is also the most ironic and filled with humour. Yet I have met people who have a deep love of the stark dignity and simplicity of Egyptian myth, or the romance and 'feyness' of Celtic fairy lore, or the moral honesty of North American Indian tales, or the passionate mysticism of Russian folk tales, or the grandiose cosmic sweep of the Hindu gods. I believe that the individual often feels a strong connection with the gods of his own heritage as well – family, national, and racial. One meets these 'hereditary' gods in dreams, although one might believe they were left behind by more cynical parents and grandparents long ago. The Bible, of course, abounds in some of the richest and most profound of mythic themes, and there are not many aspects of the human saga which it does not encompass; although there are some who might find this way of looking at it offensive, preferring to see it as a body of concrete and literal truth while the stories of other religions and cultures are 'merely' myth. On the other hand, it is salutary to remember that to the Greeks, Oidipus and Orpheus, Achilles and Zeus, the Erinyes, the Gorgons, Mother Dia and Moira were also 'true', and as factual and 'real' to that culture as the life of Jesus is to ours.

Even a single figure, such as Artemis the lunar goddess, or Hermes the trickster god, cannot be disinterred from the stories in which it is embedded. Myth contains motion, and is not static. It describes processes and movements, as well as qualities. A zodiacal sign, seen through mythic eyes, is also a dynamic story, rather than one set of character traits or one mode of behaviour. Each sign contains its own conflicts, ambivalences, dualities, motives, lacks, longings, collisions and resolutions between characters. It is my experience that when these dynamic figures move within a personality – and their movements can be seen most clearly in dreams and in astrological progressions and transits – they reflect movement between different parts of the psyche. If we exteriorise our myths, which all of us do at different times in life, then we draw others into our lives to take up one role or another, and we identify unconsciously with one or another figure in the story. In this way, the figures of myth are the active and dynamic aspect of our fate, the *daimones*, and we draw the outer world into our own myths at the points where the outer world's myths touch our own. Thus we, as the vessels for myth, create our fate.

# 8

# *Myth and the Zodiac*

## ARIES

*Have we not all one father? hath not one God created us?*

**Malachi ii.10**

We have already met the ferocious figure of Ares–Mars the war god, the ruler of the sign of Aries. We must now consider the Ram itself, for the constellations which are associated with the zodiacal signs are complex and very ancient, and contain many themes which add surprising dimensions to the traditional interpretations of astrology. We shall probably never know by what process a particular animal or figure came to be connected with a particular group of stars. But as with the names which have been bestowed upon the planets, there is a curious synchronous 'rightness' about these archaic associations. The Ram was known to the Egyptians as the primeval god Ammon, or Amun, whose name means 'the hidden one'. This antique ram-headed deity was said to be the force behind the invisible wind. He was also called 'he who abides in all things', and was imagined as the soul of all earthly phenomena. The Greeks associated Ammon the creator god with their own Father Zeus, for the phallic Ammon embodied the forces of generation and fertilisation, initiating and then maintaining the continuity of creative life.

The numinous procreative power of the ram-headed Egyptian god suggests that there is more to Aries than mere combat. This deity is an image of phallic power, whether this resides in a man or a woman; for Ammon is the original creative spirit which out of itself generates the manifest universe. There is no 'reason' for this dynamic impetus; it is simply an attribute of Aries, just as phallic power is an innate attribute of the Egyptian Ammon and the Greek Zeus, and of the Biblical Yahweh as well. Zeus or *Djeus* in the old Indo-European language means 'light of heaven', and Zeus is thus the illuminator, the *daimon* of lightning and lightening, of illumination and enlightenment. I have often wondered why traditional readings of Aries do not seem to touch on the intellectual power and vision which I have often met in this sign. I have seen far more Ariens (and by this I include Aries rising, moon in Aries, etc., rather than strictly sun in Aries) who are dedicated to mental and spiritual enlightenment than I have seen the traditional pugnacious sportsmen–Ariens who live for physical combat.

When the Greeks came to weave their magical mythic tales around the constellations which they inherited from Babylon and Egypt, they wove about the image of the Ram the story of the supernatural ram, sent by Zeus, which saved Phrixus and Helle from their wicked stepmother and carried them on its back toward Colchis. Helle fell off and drowned in the sea, which was named Hellespont after her, but Phrixus managed to arrive intact at Colchis and came under the protection of King Aeëtes, himself a magician and a son of the solar god Helios. Phrixus sacrificed the ram and hung up its fleece in a sacred grove guarded by a dragon, where it turned to gold; and it was this same golden fleece which Jason and his crew of Argonauts sought through many dangers. The fleece was sacred to Zeus, and once again we are presented with this unlooked-for connection between Aries and the fiery king of the gods. This golden fleece, and Jason's quest for it, seem to portray the theme of the slaying of the Old Father, and the quest for individual spiritual identity, which I feel to be at the core of the drama of Aries the Ram.

The story of Jason is relevant to our exploration into the pattern of development inherent in Aries. For the fleece came from Iolkos, Jason's birthplace, and is in some way a symbol of his 'true' father, his own inner spirit. Jason's tale is typical of the hero-myth. He was the rightful heir to the throne of Iolkos in Thessaly, but his wicked uncle usurped the power and the child's life was endangered. He was sent to the wise Centaur Cheiron in secrecy, where he was raised and taught the arts of war. The kingly inheritance usurped, and the endangered infancy, are, as Campbell points out in his work on the hero-myth, archetypal patterns which appear in every hero's story. He is not automatically born a hero, but must come to it through trials and suffering, in order to find what was always his had he but known it. Jason must contend, in his quest, with two destructive males, two kings, and here we are presented with the archetypal struggle with the Terrible Father. In Neumann's work, *The Origins and History of Consciousness*, he writes about 'the fathers' as the representatives of law and order, handing down the highest values of civilisation. They embody the world of collective values, which manifest themselves in the psychic structure as 'conscience'.

The hero must thus become a breaker of the old law, because he is the enemy of the old ruling system and the existing court of conscience. So he necessarily comes into conflict with the fathers and their personal spokesmen, who in the story of Jason are first the wicked uncle Pelias and second the sorcerer-king Aeëtes.

> The 'wicked king' or personal father figure, representing the old ruling system, sends the hero forth to fight the monster – Sphinx, witches, giants, wild beasts, etc. – hoping that it will prove his undoing ... With the help of his divine father, however, the hero succeeds in vanquishing the monster. His higher nature and noble birth are victorious, and are themselves proven in the victory. The ruin wished upon him by the negative father redounds to his glory and to the negative father's own ruin. Thus, the old king's expulsion of the son, the hero's fight, and the killing of the father hang together in a meaningful way. They form a necessary canon of events which, in symbol and in fact, are presupposed by the very existence of the hero, who, as the bringer of the new, has to destroy the old.[85]

When Jason came of fighting age, he returned to Iolkos, resolved to claim his inheritance. On his journey he lost a sandal while helping an old woman (who was really the goddess Hera in disguise) to cross a stream. Wicked Uncle Pelias, meanwhile, had received an oracle warning him to beware of a man with one sandal. When the two confronted each other, Pelias put on a bland face, acknowledged Jason as the rightful heir, and promptly sent him off to retrieve the Golden Fleece which his ancestor Phrixus had brought to Colchis, so that the disturbed ghost of Phrixus could be laid to rest. Thus the Terrible Father sends the son off into danger, hoping, as Neumann says, that it will prove his undoing. Jason, in response to this, gathered together the famous crew of Argonauts and made his voyage through many perils, helped by the gods Athene, Poseidon and Hera, to the court of King Aeëtes. Here he slew the dragon with the help of the King's daughter Medea, a priestess and sorceress, stole the fleece, returned to Iolkos where he rid himself of Uncle Pelias, and became King.

The impulse to launch oneself into dangerous situations in order to prove one's manhood is characteristic of Aries and, although it may sound strange at first, characteristic of the Aries woman as well as the Aries man. For this Terrible Father is not limited to men alone, nor is the quest for the 'true' creative Father within. The fleece itself, the emblem of this 'inner' and individual set of spiritual values, seems, as we have seen, to be the theriomorphic or animal representation of the 'hidden' god. King Aeëtes, who is its guardian, is a cut above Pelias in that he is semi-divine, and a sorcerer; he is the archetypal Terrible Father, where Pelias is the personal one. That this is a fate, rather than a mere imaginative exercise, is suggested to me by the number of Arien people I have met who have been driven out into life suffering from problems with a tyrannical or restrictive and destructive personal father. This father has often emasculated his son, or has been overly critical and suppressive of the son's natural 'inheritance', or has blocked the son from any independent creative expression. A similar situation often seems to occur in the lives of Arien women, where the father is no less dominant or restrictive, and the husband – who is unconsciously chosen because he is like the father and a necessary character in the myth – takes over the role of refusing permission for an independent life. The Terrible Father may reappear, long after childhood, in the form of institutions or superiors at work; or he may surface as masculine competition for a desired lover or a desired prize. This pattern is not 'pathological'; it is mythic, and is, on some level, the image of Aries' necessity. Here Father stands as both the obstacle and as the means of growth.

Jason managed to find his fleece and bring it home again through the agency of a woman. This is also characteristic of the hero-myth, for the 'woman' is the anima, the unconscious itself in the guise of 'helper' and 'bride', who finds solutions where the individual ego can find none. Were Jason a female character, no doubt he would have been helped by Aeëtes' son, for the animus in a woman's psyche seems to serve the same function in terms of development. In fact, more than one woman assisted Jason, for although the Argonauts comprised a boatload of male warriors, it was the goddess Hera, grateful for Jason's early service to her, who got him out of the nasty messes he encountered on his journey. And Medea with her witchcraft and occult powers helped him to escape the wrath of King Aeëtes, the guardian of the fleece. But Jason evidenced a typical Arien problem when he arrived back at Iolkos, for he tired of Medea and courted the daughter of the King of Corinth, giving up his connection with the inner 'witch-like' anima who had helped him and desiring instead a woman who could bring him collective power and recognition. He was not content with what he had got, but had to have more and yet more. This is the flaw, the *hubris* which is Aries' danger, and which if the individual is unconscious of it will lead him to a fall. Thus Jason angered Medea, who was not a woman to be taken lightly; and in revenge she slaughtered not only the new bride, but their own children as well, and escaped in a chariot drawn by winged dragons, leaving her former lover under a curse. After this, Jason plummeted steadily downhill, ageing and impotent, and was finally killed by a blow on the head from a fallen timber broken from his own rotting ship.

I am not suggesting that the ignominious end of Jason is necessarily the fate of Aries. But his problem certainly is. It is ironic, and
true to the subtle tragi-comic nuances of myth, that the young hero
who battles with the old Terrible Father to inaugurate a new order
should repudiate his own inner feminine self in order to court the
very collective power which he had previously undergone his
quest to fight. The mysterious identity between the hero and his
enemy is here implied, for Jason by the end of his story has become
himself the Terrible Father, and the *nemesis* which dogs him is that
his own children are killed. On an inner level, perhaps this sad
ending to a glorious tale is a necessary passage for Aries, before a
new cycle begins and a new quest arises for a new fleece. A great
deal may be destroyed before Aries rises out of his disintegration to
pursue another challenge. Aries as father or mother rather than as
son or daughter suffering at the hands of a domineering father may
discover that the myth is the same but the roles have changed, and
his own children rebel against his latter-day tyranny.

There are other mythic rams which have been associated with
the sign of Aries besides Zeus' golden phallic fleece. Lucian, the
Roman poet, identified the ram with the golden lamb which
figures in the tale of Atreus and Thyestes which we encountered
earlier. When these brothers were quarrelling over the throne of
Mykenai, according to one version of the tale, Zeus decided to
settle the dispute in favour of Atreus by sending him a golden
lamb, a symbol of sovereignty. But Thyestes seduced Atreus' wife
and persuaded her to steal the golden lamb for him. Zeus then sent
an even more impressive portent: the sun changed its course in the
heavens, and day turned into night. No one could quarrel with
that, and Atreus was duly made king, and Thyestes was banished.
We have already seen what happened next. But here once again
we encounter the image of the ram as sacred to Zeus, the symbol of
the god's potency and dominance, and the object of contention
between two brothers. This quarrel is another dispute about male
supremacy and potency, of which the ram is the emblem, and the
stealing of the woman as well as the golden lamb reflects another
dimension of Aries' fate: the love-triangle which is less about the
desired object and more about the competition involved. It is also
interesting to note that the ram is the primary sacrificial animal in
the Old Testament. It is the beast which is offered up to Yahveh,
who bears many similarities to both Zeus and Ammun – in
particular the latter, 'the hidden one'. The Yahveh of the Old
Testament is a highly ambiguous Father, and his relationship to his
good servant Job is as ambiguous as the relationship between
heroes like Jason and the Terrible Fathers with whom they must
struggle.

There are other myths which are relevant to Aries, but the one with which I would now like to conclude is the one which began this chapter: the story of Oidipus. This may seem surprising, for Oidipus, thanks to Freud, has become the emblem of the mother's son who must fight the father to obtain his incestuous and long-desired prize. For Freud, the problem of Oidipus is the problem of a man's fantasy-wish for union with his mother (or, under the label of 'Elektra-complex', a woman's fantasy-wish for union with her father). The killing of Laios thus represented for Freud the son's terror of castration by his father, and the murderous jealousy which springs from his desire to claim the mother. But evidently Freud did not read the complete myth, or chose to ignore salient aspects of it. Oidipus killed his father without having met his mother. It was his rage which overcame him; he was infuriated because the old King insisted on first passage down the narrow road. Oidipus in the story is fiery and red-haired, and his anger is notorious. From the beginning his conflict is with the Father: He refuses to accept Apollo's oracle, believing that his own will is capable of refuting the dictates of the god and of fate. Perhaps the ironic insight which this tale offers is that the violent battle between the males, arising from their own relationship and secret identity rather than from the contest over any woman or prize, leads in the end to the same source of life. Freud seems not to have placed much importance on the origin of the curse which came home to roost upon Oidipus, but I am inclined to feel it is exceedingly important. King Laios committed a sin, and the sin was perpetrated against a male and made another male its victim. Thus he violated the laws of host and guest, by raping Pelops' son, and violated also the laws of his own sex because of the violence of the assault. It is this infringement upon masculine 'rules' which eventually leads to the birth of Oidipus and the terrible fate which awaited him. Here the 'ancestral sin' is on the side of the father rather than the mother, and it must be expiated by the son. The father is not in 'right' relationship with the masculine principle; he has become truly terrible, and the son must fight him. As I understand the Oidipus myth, it is, from its beginning, a story of father and son.

The Oidipal battle within families seems to be a prime enactment of Aries' pattern, and I have seen it unfold in both men and women. But the point of the battle is not so much the possession of the parent of the opposite sex. It is the overthrowing of the old order and the assertion of the independent, individual spirit; and this enacts itself as the fierce competitiveness of the sign. Yahveh declares that His people must worship no other god; and so, too, does Aries, who often cannot abide any companion of his or her own sex unless that companion is so different as not to provide competition, or inferior enough not to pose a threat. Just as love-triangles are common with Libra for reasons which we shall explore in due course, so too are they common with Aries, for different reasons. The rescue of the damsel in distress (or the sensitive man in distress) is a favourite life-pattern of Aries, and so is the championing of the underdog and the lost cause. But the distressed lover is less relevant than the battle itself. If there were no battle, it is doubtful that Aries would bother with the damsel. Of course, it need not be a physical damsel; with some Ariens the thing which must be redeemed from the grip of the Terrible Father is an idea, or a philosophy, or a creative contribution which is not being valued by the 'fathers' in the world at large. It is Aries himself who feels the distress, and projects this upon an outer object, for the Terrible Father who castrates his son does so by not letting him achieve self-fulfilment and victory. As Neumann puts it:

> He [the Terrible Father] acts, as it were, like a spiritual system which, from beyond and above, captures and destroys the son's consciousness. This spiritual system appears as the binding force of the old law, the old religion, the old morality, the old order; as conscience, convention, tradition, or any other spiritual phenomenon that seizes hold of the son and obstructs his progress into the future. Any content that functions through its emotional dynamisms, such as the paralysing grip of inertia or an invasion by instinct, belongs to the sphere of the mother, to nature. But all contents capable of conscious realisation, a value, an idea, a moral canon, or some other spiritual force, are related to the father-, never to the mother-system.[86]

The father–son drama will appear again later in the zodiac, in particular in the signs Leo and Capricorn. The dimension which we are meeting here in the first sign is the initial battle for freedom, for there is room for only one god in heaven. The potency of Zeus, Ammon and Yahveh would be meaningless if there were several other deities all sharing the job, and for Aries there is and can never be any other than one deity, 'the hidden one' which manifests as his own phallic power. Because his battle is with God the Father, Aries must be fully conscious of what he is doing, and needs to reverence the deity against which he strives. In other words, he must be 'devout', rather than merely angry. If he acts in the arrogance of *hubris*, as Jason did when he threw Medea aside and scrabbled for the kingship of Corinth, then his deeds will infallibly come to naught. But his encounter with the Terrible Father creates personality and inner 'authority'; he can then handle the responsibility of the kingship he has fought for. Without this struggle, he remains the eternal son of his father, the eternal rebel who throws stones through windows from without, but can never enter the place where the fleece lies hidden which embodies his own manhood.

## TAURUS

*Mother of God! no lady thou:*
*Common woman of common earth!*
*Mary Elizabeth Coleridge*

Three different mythic bulls claim the honour of being associated with Taurus. One is the white bull that carried Europa from her home in Tyre to Crete; this bull was Zeus himself, transformed into animal form for the usual purpose of abducting or seducing the woman of his choice. The second is a cow rather than a bull, the animal form of Io, another of Zeus' paramours, whom Hera in her jealousy turned into bovine shape. The third and most famous is the Cretan bull with which Pasiphaë, the wife of King Minos of Crete, fell in love, and which fathered the monstrous Minotaur that the hero Theseus had to kill. We will consider the symbolism of the bull itself, and of 'cow-eyed' Aphrodite–Venus the planetary ruler of Taurus, in due course; but first let us begin with the story of the Cretan bull, which seems to have profound bearing on Taurus' fate.

King Minos was the son of Europa and Zeus, himself the child of the god turned bull. He was King of Crete, and wielded great power from his island seat over all the Greek islands and parts of the mainland. When young, he contended with his brothers Rhadamanthys and Sarpedon for the throne, and asserted his claim by divine right. He prayed to the god Poseidon, lord of the sea and of earthquakes, to send a bull out of the sea as a sign, sealing this prayer with a vow to sacrifice the animal immediately as an offering and a symbol of service. Poseidon, who is also portrayed in bull-shape, complied; the beast duly appeared; and Minos took the throne. But when he beheld the majesty of the beast, he thought what an advantage it would be to possess such a creature in his herd, and risked a merchant's substitution, which he supposed the god would not notice or mind. Offering on Poseidon's altar the finest white bull that he owned, he added the sacred sea-bull to his herd.

Poseidon, however, was not amused at the substitution. He retaliated at the blasphemy by enlisting Aphrodite to inspire in Minos' wife Pasiphaë an ungovernable passion for the bull. She prevailed upon Daedalus, the celebrated artist–craftsman, to make her a wooden cow in which she might receive the bull in sexual union. Daedalus performed the work, Pasiphaë entered the cow, and the bull in turn entered Pasiphaë. Of this union was born the Minotaur, a hideous monster with a human body and bull's head, which fed upon human flesh. Minos in his fear and shame hired Daedalus to construct a labyrinth in which the foul creature could be hidden, and into which groups of living youths and maidens were left for the Minotaur's meals.

The primary fault in this sorry tale lies not with Queen Pasiphaë, but with Minos himself, although the Queen acted out the fate he invoked. About Minos' flaw, Joseph Campbell writes:

> He had converted a public event to personal gain, whereas the whole sense of his investiture as king had been that he was no longer a mere private person. The return of the bull should have symbolised his absolutely selfless submission to the functions of his role. The retaining of it represented, on the other hand, an impulse to egocentric self-aggrandisement. And so the king 'by the grace of God' became the dangerous tyrant Holdfast – out for himself. Just as the traditional rites of passage used to teach the individual to die to the past and be reborn to the future, so the great ceremonials of investiture divested him of his private character and clothed him in the mantle of his vocation . . . By the sacrilege of the refusal of the rite, however, the individual cut himself as a unit off from the larger unit of the whole community, and so the One was broken into the many, and these then battled against each other – each out for himself – and could be governed only by force.[87]

Campbell goes on to describe this figure of the tyrant–monster who is so common in fairy tales (frequently a giant, like Fafner and Fasolt in Wagner's *Ring*); the hoarder of the general benefit, the monster avid for the greedy rights of 'my and mine'. It is interesting to note that Hitler was a Taurean, as were Lenin and Marx. So is Queen Elizabeth II, who seems to have understood to a remarkable degree the deeper meaning of her investiture as Queen, and remains a symbol of stability and moral firmness for the whole of the United Kingdom. But the tyrant–monster of which Campbell writes is the challenge of Taurus, its dark face which must at some point be met in life. The earthy power which allows the tyrant to accrue his wealth, as Minos gathered wealth and power over the seas, is the gift of Taurus; but the dilemma lies in his relationship with the god, and which god it is he serves, the deity or himself. The story of Minos ends in a stagnant situation, where a destructive monster lies at the heart of the apparently abundant realm. This situation of stagnation leads inevitably to the coming of Theseus, the hero who must release the deadlock. It is a characteristic irony of myth, which we have already met in Aries, that

Theseus – who, like Minos, is a king and divinely fathered – is the child of the bull god Poseidon. The creature which he must confront at the heart of the labyrinth is the dark, bestial form of his own spiritual father, as well as the symbol of Minos' sin. Thus Minos, his Minotaur, and the hero Theseus are bound by the same symbol of the bull, for they are aspects of the same archetypal core. And Minos and Theseus are in a sense doubles of each other, for one commits the sin against the god, while the other must redeem it.

But what is the bull, the symbol of power which must be dedicated to the god? We have seen, in the imagery of Aries, that the ram is connected with the hidden God, with phallic power and potency and the omnipotence of the Father. The bull is an altogether different animal. He is not fiery; he is earthy, and while he is connected with the fertility of the earth, this is not the same as the fertile creativity of heaven. In the Buddhist tale of the taming of the bull (which is sometimes portrayed as an ox), a man is shown in the various stages of development, where he must learn to tame the recalcitrant bull and where ultimately man and bull vanish and are revealed as part of the same divine unity. The bull is not evil, but if it is allowed to run the man, then it may lead him to destruction, for he is at the mercy of his desires. But repression likewise is not an answer. Man and bull must perform a dance where each comes to respect the other. In these Eastern images the problem of the relation between the ego and the instincts is portrayed, and this problem lies at the centre of Taurus' pattern of development.

Other mythic stories also portray the struggle with the bull. One of the most powerful is the Zoroastrian god–man Mithras, the Redeemer, who is always portrayed in his famous cap with his hands about the bull's throat. Herakles also must conquer a bull. These motifs of the conquering and sacrifice of the bull seem to deal with submission to a greater Self, and the realisation that the power of the bull is not 'mine' but must be directed towards a more transpersonal goal. Whether we consider bull or, as in the myth of Io, cow, we are faced with the same animal. The primary association with this creature is, not surprisingly, the goddess Aphrodite, who is called 'cow-eyed' and whose nature may tell us a good deal about the meaning of this beast which it is Taurus' fate to encounter and tame.

Aphrodite–Venus has more 'personality' and clearer outlines than virtually any other Greek goddess. She is not just an abstract concept meant to personify some dimly sensed order in the cosmos. She is terribly alive, and this quality transmits itself from the sculptures of her which we have inherited, dating back before the Greek era to the great goddess Ishtar of the Middle East. She is gifted with generous and carnal affection and a complete lack of ambivalence about sex. Paul Friedrich, in his book *On the Meaning of Aphrodite*, calls this 'sunlit sexuality', in comparison with female deities such as Artemis and Athene for whom the sexual act is equated with pollution. Where the body is a pollution to most of the Olympians, it is sacred to Aphrodite. This is in part why she is usually portrayed nude, where the other goddesses are almost always covered up. She seems to embody naked, unashamed nature. She also acts as a mediator between the world of the immortals and the world of men, just as Zeus does, for she is happy to mate with mortals. Generally a mortal man who has sexual relations with a goddess is punished by death or castration or worse. We have met an example of this in Ixion, who was punished by being bound forever to a fiery wheel for his attempt to seduce the goddess Hera. But Aphrodite is a potential lover for any god or hero who catches her fancy. In this sense she is prepared to come into incarnation, to relate to the world of living men and earthly things. She can be looked upon in her nudity by mortals; therefore she is accessible to human experience, unlike gods such as Apollo and Artemis who remain elusive and punish those who peer too closely.

Aphrodite is an active female: She takes the active role in wooing and seduction, love and love-making. She is never raped or assaulted by a male; she is so powerful sexually that this would be impossible. In no way does she resemble the victim-like women whom Zeus and the other male gods pursue, abduct, rape and humiliate. Aphrodite is an image of relative sexual equality, a rare being for a time in history when the prevailing collective view leaned in the opposite direction. She is also the patroness of courtesans, although she presides equally enthusiastically over passionate sex within marriage. While Hera, queen of the gods, stands for the structures and moral codes which bind the institution of marriage within the collective, Aphrodite embodies its conjugal joy and fertility. Procreation, desire and satisfaction, adornment and culture, beauty and erotic arts: all these belong to her. Her love-making is a civilised art, in contrast to the physical violence and rapacity of Ares–Mars. Paul Friedrich writes:

> The drives of sexuality are natural; on the other hand, sophisticated love-making is highly cultural. Aphrodite mediates between the two, 'puts them together'. Or, better, she does not make them *identical* but interrelates them and makes them overlap to a high degree. To put it yet another way, we can agree that she is a 'goddess of rapture' but ought to recognise that this rapture harmoniously blends natural and cultural ingredients.[88]

Aphrodite's gifts, however, have a double edge. The arts of love and the satisfaction of desire can unite man and woman in harmonious sexuality and a happy wedded life. But on the other hand they can generate rivalries, jealousies and passions that acutely threaten the relations between individuals, kinship groups and even nations. Thus Minos' passion for the sacred bull leads to his wife's overwhelming passion for the same bull, and the monster that results becomes the canker that rots the kingdom from within. Even the cow, which seems such a peaceable creature, can lead to chaos and destruction. In the early cosmogonies Aphrodite has no mother, but is born of the union between the sea and the severed genitals of Ouranos after he is castrated by his son Kronos. This suggests that whatever Aphrodite is, she is not maternal in the ordinary sense, although she is fertile. Perhaps it would be more appropriate to say that she is in no sense a wife, although she favours the physical joys of marriage. Friedrich suggests that she is the most 'solar' of the goddesses:

> Artemis and Hera are strongly lunar, the former typically moving in the moonlit midnight air, the latter often depicted with a lunar crescent. Their symbolism has rich antecedents in Old European civilisation, and there is of course the more general psychological association between the moon and menstruation, virginity, and the female principle in general . . . It is Aphrodite who more than any other goddess is unambiguously solar in many passages, and this solarity is naturally connected with her goldenness. Note that she seduces Anchises by daylight. There is a deep-lying opposition or contrast between her sunlit sexuality and Artemis' furtive and moonlit anxiety and hostility as regards carnal love.[89]

All this paints a vivid portrait of one aspect of our bull. One may well ask why Theseus, or Mithras, must then subdue it, for Aphrodite seems a benign goddess with qualities which our present culture badly needs. But it is due to her wiles that the Trojan War began, and the havoc she causes is always a threat to relationship, whether on an individual level or a collective one. She is a most ambiguous goddess. In Sparta, she was worshipped as a bloody battle goddess, and her Egyptian counterpart Hathor, the cow-headed goddess, likewise was said to thrive on blood and slaughter. Perhaps we need to look again at Hitler, who not only had the sun in Taurus but also Libra rising, and was therefore doubly ruled by Venus. The Buddhist formula seems to be a most appropriate one: Do not slay the bull, but learn to dance with it in a developing pattern of mutual respect, so that the bull becomes more human and the human more animal. I have met many

Taureans who have attempted to cope with the potential problems of the bull, its powerful passions and its single-minded covetousness, by 'splitting', i.e. withdrawing into the intellect in order to avoid the threat of the overwhelming senses. This is of course no solution; it is what Minos did by stuffing the Minotaur into the labyrinth. The body then usually rebels against the tyranny of the mind. Likewise I have met Taureans who are imprisoned in their senses, where the bull or cow runs the man or woman; and this too satisfies neither bull nor human partner, for then we are back with King Minos who repudiates the Self and attempts to possess for his own gratification what is not his, with tragic results.

We have so far dealt with the female aspects of the bull. But Aphrodite is part of a pair in myth, and although she is no wife in the conventional sense, nevertheless she is married: to the strange god Hephaistos, who is called Vulcan in Latin, and who was given to her as a husband by Zeus and Hera. Whenever gods are paired in this way in myth, I feel that something is implied about two halves of a single archetypal pattern. Although the marriage of Aphrodite and Hephaistos is an uncomfortable one, a marriage it is nonetheless; he is her 'right' spouse. We must therefore consider him, for he also can give us insights into the nature and fate of Taurus.

Hephaistos is the divine smith, and he is mirrored by the smith gods of many cultures, for he is ugly and lame. He has much in common with the Teutonic dwarfs, for he is a creature of earth and his skill lies in his artistry and his physical power. According to the tale, he was so weak and sickly at birth that his disgusted mother Hera dropped him from the heights of Olympus to rid herself of the embarrassment of such a pitiful son. I have met this sad pattern in the early lives of many Taureans, whose families had hoped for something more flamboyant, more brilliant, and more effervescent than the slow and earthy creature which the Taurean child so often is. Hephaistos survived this misadventure because he fell into the sea, where the sea goddess Thetis took care of him and helped him to set up his first smithy. He rewarded her kindness with many beautiful and useful objects. Eventually Hera saw Thetis wearing a lovely brooch which Hephaistos had made, and upon finding out that it was her lost son who was the creator, summoned him back to Olympus where she offered him a finer smithy, married him to Aphrodite, and made a great fuss of him. Eventually they patched up their quarrel, and he even went so far as to reproach Zeus for his treatment of Hera when the king of the gods hung his wife by her wrists from Heaven because she had rebelled against him. Zeus in anger heaved him down from Olympus a second time, and he was a whole day falling. On striking the earth he broke both legs, and became lame; afterward he could only walk with golden leg-supports. Graves says of him:

> Hephaistos is ugly and ill-tempered, but has great power in his arms and shoulders, and all his work is of matchless skill. He once made a set of golden mechanical women to help him in his smithy; they can even talk, and undertake the most difficult tasks he entrusts to them. And he owns a set of three-legged tables with golden wheels, ranged around his workshop, which can run by themselves to a meeting of the gods, and back again.[90]

This is a curious marriage, between the beautiful, indolent and mischievous Aphrodite and her ugly, ill-formed yet gifted spouse. She despises his ugliness and is forever unfaithful to him, yet she cannot be parted from him. I think that this pair of figures forms an uneasy core to the sign of Taurus, for there is that in the sign which possesses the marvellous skill, power and ingenuity of Hephaistos yet which is slow, clumsy and unglamorous, and there is also that which embodies beauty and which despises its own physical imperfection. Whether the Taurean acts this strange marriage out through an actual partner, or whether it forms an inner conflict between the idealism and the earthiness of the sign, nevertheless this marriage is a given, a kind of fate. The ego perhaps needs to come to terms with the bestial bull; but the bull itself is divided, between its coarseness and its grace, and all three comprise the *daimon* which infuses this deceptively simple sign.

## GEMINI

> *I fought with my twin,*
> *The enemy within,*
> *'Till both of us fell by the road . . .*
> Bob Dylan

Twins have always carried a numinous connotation. Despite our modern knowledge of the biological processes which lead to the birth of identical twins, nevertheless it is fascinating and disturbing to look at two people who look like one person, yet are not. Various sets of twins have been associated with the constellation of Gemini, and all of them carry this fascinating quality. One of the least known which is connected with Gemini is the pair called Zethus and Amphion, who were sons of Zeus by Antiope. Zethus was strong and energetic, and a true warrior; Amphion on the other hand received the gift of a lyre from Hermes, and played upon it with a master's skill. Zethus despised his brother's addiction to 'womanish' pursuits, while Amphion energetically defended the value of art and the intellectual life. With this myth we are already touching upon one of Gemini's fundamental conflicts: its inherent oppositeness.

The twins Castor and Polydeuces (Pollux in Latin) are much better known than Zethus and Amphion, and are the pair generally associated with the stars of the constellation of Gemini. They were the sons of Leda, the wife of King Tyndareos of Sparta. Zeus turned himself into a swan to court the lady, who laid two eggs as a result of their union. From one egg emerged Castor and Klytaemnestra, whom we have already met as the wife of Agamemnon in the *Oresteia*. These two were the mortal children, the offspring of King Tyndareos. From the other egg came Polydeuces and Helen, who were the children of Zeus. Thus there are two sets of twins in the story, one male and one female: Castor and Polydeuces, who are called the Dioscuri – which means sons of God – and Klytaemnestra and Helen. Half of each pair is mortal, half immortal. Here is embodied not only the motif of the hostile brothers (or sisters), but also of brother–sister twin-souls. In the story, Castor and Polydeuces quarrelled with another set of twins, called Idas and Lynceus. In the ensuing battle, Castor, who was mortal, was slain. Polydeuces' grief was so great at the loss of his beloved twin that he appealed to his father Zeus to restore his brother to life, or to accept his own life in ransom for Castor's. Zeus, rather out of character, displayed compassion for the twins, and the two brothers were allowed to enjoy alternatively the boon of life, passing one day beneath the earth in Hades' realm and the next in the heavenly abode of Olympus. Thus the twins reflect a cyclical experience of opposites, for when they are mortal, they must taste of death and darkness, but when they are divine they partake of the pleasures of the gods. It is traditionally given that Gemini is a moody sign, inclined to swing from elation to depression. This is not surprising when we consider this myth, which portrays vividly the conflicting experiences of bondage to a mortal body with its sense of loss and death, and exaltation to the realm of spirit and eternal life.

Myths relating to the birth of 'heavenly twins', one usually representing good and the other evil, occur in the epics of Greece, Rome, Egypt, India and China. They are one of the great archetypal motifs of myth. Sometimes both twins in an identical way have produced good for mankind or for their immediate society; thus the twin deities of Hindu tradition, the Asvins, the great charioteers of the sky, were rain-makers and givers of fertility. But more often one twin personifies the light and the other the dark. In Roman myth, the twins Romulus and Remus were sons of the war god Mars, and grew up suckled by a wolf; they founded the city of Rome. But the brothers quarrelled over the site, and Remus, in trying to kill Romulus, was himself slain. Remus is the 'dark' brother who seeks to destroy his 'light' brother Romulus, and comes to a bad end. This pairing of a dark force with a light touches on a profound human dilemma, the problem of what Jung calls the shadow, the inner enemy who is also a brother, born of the same womb, who cannot ever be wholly conquered yet who must be eternally fought. Another image of this problem may be found in the relationship between Jesus and Judas in the New Testament. In the Old Testament we meet the brothers Cain and Abel, who although they are not twins nevertheless represent a polarity. Cain is the dark brother, Abel the light. Satan and Christ are likewise both sons of God; so, too, are Esau and Jacob, another pair of quarrelling brothers. It would seem that the *daimon* which presides over Gemini brings the individual into inevitable conflict with this dark opposite. Frequently it is experienced through another, most often in the sibling relationship, where one brother or sister is the 'good' one whom the parents love, and the other is the 'bad' one who carries the projection of the shadow for the family. In these exteriorised situations it is much more difficult to discover the enemy within, and the warring of opposites which must ultimately meet at the centre.

Ivor Morrish has written an extremely interesting book called *The Dark Twin*, in which he explores the theme of the twins in relation to the problem of the shadow and of evil. About the twins, he writes:

> Whilst we have used the term 'twins' in relation to the opposition of Good and Evil, it should be noted at the outset that many of the 'doubles' in mythology relate simply to siblings, usually brothers, one of whom is 'good' or does acceptable things, and the other of whom is 'bad' or a performer of actions regarded as 'evil' or unacceptable in his society. Twins, however, have always been regarded as something special and, if not related directly to divinity, yet as possessing some unusual power or *mana* which works in opposition, rather like the positive or negative forces of electricity or the north and south poles of a magnet. There is, thus, in the concept of the twin a certain balance or equilibrium implied, a closeness and similarity without a complete identity; and ultimately, at least in mythology, a certain opposition is indicated which may lead through increasing hostility to an attempt by one twin to destroy the other.[91]

My experience with Gemini has taught me that in early life, either the 'good' or the 'bad' twin is separated off and projected outward onto someone or something else in the environment. Slowly the individual, by coming into collision with this opposite, begins to discover that it is himself, although this often does not occur until the second half of life. In the case of actual twins – and I have met many who are born under Gemini – this becomes even more difficult, for usually one twin is very obviously the extroverted and confident one and the other the inhibited and 'neurotic' one, and the pressure from family and society, not to mention their own needs, makes it difficult for a separation to occur. But sooner or later, the internal battle becomes apparent. Yet as Morrish points out, there is an equilibrium to these opposites. Each without the other is incomplete, and the whole personality is dependent upon them both. Neither would develop without the other. The opposites may vary. Like the first twins we met, Zethus and Amphion, the quarrel may be between masculine and feminine, or between intellectual and emotional values, or between spiritual and corporeal goals. Or it may fall between negative and positive qualities, of which both extremes are usually present in Gemini. As the rhyme goes, 'When she was good she was very very good, and when she was bad she was horrid.' If other people find this quirky or difficult, it is doubly difficult for the Gemini, who usually confuses himself thoroughly and who must find a way to reconcile these warring principles while at the same time accepting the fact that they may never wholly blend into some lovely harmonious idealised unit devoid of conflict. The danger is that if Gemini cannot face his own oppositeness and contrariness, the shadow (or the light) will inevitably land on siblings, friends, partners, or, most difficult of all, on a child of the same sex, who may then be doomed to act out the 'bad' side of the parent because this badness must exist somewhere outside if the parent is to retain his or her complacency.

The theme of dark and light extends even deeper into myth, and permeates the vision of the world's great religions. Hermes, whom we will explore in greater detail shortly, enters alchemy as Mercurius, the ambiguous and unpredictable, dark–light spirit that guides the *opus* yet threatens always to destroy it. He/she is volatile, androgynous, both base matter and elixir, the carrier of every conceivable opposite, and is portrayed as the dark twin to Christ. Thus Mercurius is the chthonic double of the Son of God, who is born to the darkness of Mother Earth. Dualistic religions such as Zoroastrianism also reflect this ambiguity of a double-faced universe. Ahura Mazda (Ormuzd) is the light principle, while Angra Mainyu (Ahriman) is the dark one. Ormuzd promotes life, happiness and eternal well-being; Ahriman seeks only death, misery and suffering. Through Gemini's eyes the cosmos falls into opposites, and just as Castor and Polydeuces spend half their time in Hades and half on Olympus, so too does Gemini, perceiving now only the good in life, now only the evil.

In Norse myth Baldur and Loge embody the quarrelling brothers. Baldur is beautiful, graceful and idyllic; in fact, he is too good to be true. Loge is dark and cunning – brilliantly portrayed in the Bayreuth centennial production of the *Ring* as an ugly hunchback, crooked in body as well as in thought – and is ultimately responsible for Baldur's death. Alberich and Wotan stand in this relationship in the *Ring*, where Wotan himself recognises their doubleness and calls himself 'white' Alberich while the dwarf is 'black' Alberich. On the human scale, Siegfried and Hagen confront each other as the golden hero and his black shadow. But the death of Siegfried at the hands of Hagen is, like the death of Baldur at the hands of Loge, in some way necessity, or fate. The bright hero is a little too bright, a little too invulnerable, and a little too far away from ordinary human suffering and ordinary human longing to perform his appointed task of redemption. He can be injured only from behind, implying that the bright heroic stance can deflect anything in life but the shadow, the unconscious. At the end of the *Ring*, all seems dark and depressing, because the hero has been destroyed and the world of the gods is coming to an end. But if I read Wagner's theme correctly, he seems to be saying that what is left after the destruction is humanity itself, after the gigantic world of the two-dimensional gods has fallen into twilight. Thus Judas must betray Jesus and Jesus must fulfil his appointed sacrifice, so that a symbol might be offered to man which unites the opposites in life. Cain must destroy Abel and be accordingly marked, and Satan must persuade God to punish Job and must plague Eve to eat the apple. Richard Donington in his book on the *Ring* cycle says:

> If Hagen is to some extent a shadow personal to Siegfried, Alberich is the very Prince of Darkness. If man takes to devilry, this scene reminds us, that is because the devil is always there to urge it. But the devil's provocation plays its part in the growth of character, which largely consists in learning how inseparable (but not irreconcilable) good and evil are. The diabolical is the underside of the divine.[92]

Wagner, who was himself a Gemini, was probably quite intimately acquainted with the problem. Certainly he has come down to us in biography as a thoroughly contradictory, insufferable and difficult man, yet also as one of the greatest artists history has ever produced. Less flamboyant Geminis have perhaps the same profound insight to gain, and it is my feeling that the turbulent changes that so often occur in Gemini's life and which are so frequently fostered by the individual's own tricksterish shadow-side are deeply necessary.

We may also find hostile sisters in myth, for as with all the signs the sex of the hero may as easily be replaced by its opposite. Inanna and Ereshkigal, whom we met earlier in the book, are two such inimical sisters, and once again the 'light' one has something to learn – nothing less than death and regeneration – at the hands of the 'dark' one. Artemis and Aphrodite are also enemies in Greek myth, as we saw when we explored some of the mythic themes of Taurus. Artemis' virginity and Aphrodite's carnality are thoroughly at odds. The theme of 'the other woman' (which also seems to be a recurrent theme in the lives of Geminis) appears in connection with Hera and all the numerous loves of her husband Zeus. Even in fairy tales we meet this theme of two jealous women, sometimes vying for the affection of a man, sometimes vying for power: Snow White with her Wicked Queen, and Cinderella and her ugly, jealous sisters. Psyche and Aphrodite battle with each other for the love of Eros, and even Dorothy must battle the Wicked Witch of the West in *The Wizard of Oz*. (Appropriately, the part of Dorothy was played in the classic film by Judy Garland, a Gemini.) Jealousy between siblings, envy between friends, conflicts with rivals – all these themes are the external enactments of the Gemini myth, which, sadly, is all too infrequently understood as a contest between two halves of oneself.

The character of Hermes embodies within itself this ambiguity and flickering of light and shade of which the twins are another emblem. Hermes is Zeus' cleverest son. He was born to Maia, which is both the name of a nymph and also the name by which Zeus addresses the great goddess Night when he seeks an oracle of her. Thus Hermes is not just the child of any ordinary woman; she is an older, more powerful deity, and the mating of Zeus and Maia becomes not just another of his usual rapes, but the union of the bright spirit with the dark unfathomable depths of the unconscious and of nature itself. Zeus, it is said in the story, courted her in a dark cave under cover of night, and she bore a son of great cunning: a deceitful flatterer, a robber and a cattle thief, a bringer of dreams and a nightly prowler (as Kerenyi puts it, 'as are those who lurk in the streets before the gates').

Hermes began his chequered career by inventing the lyre and stealing his brother Apollo's cattle. He later became the initiated Messenger on the path to the House of Hades in the underworld, thereby fulfilling the office of Psychopompos, the escort of souls. Thus he can traverse the worlds of above and below, and the mortal realm which lies in between. He is the only deity who is not assigned a 'place', for his place is the borderland, the roads and passageways and crossroads where suicides are buried and criminals hung. Human beings benefit from Hermes, but sometimes he wilfully leads them astray in the dark night. Interestingly, one version of the god's birth makes him the twin brother of Aphrodite; they are both children of the sky god Ouranos, and share the same birthday on the fourth day of the lunar month. Their son was Eros, the great *daimon* of love and discord. This curious tale of Hermes' birth offers us another dimension to his character, for he is far more than a mere trickster. His twin and soul-mate is the goddess of fertility, and their child is an image of the great binding force of life. Hermes fosters relationship even through quarrelling and separateness, and brings things together through their differences; and *vice versa*.

According to Walter Otto's description, Hermes 'lacks dignity'. His strength lies in his resourcefulness. He accomplishes his deeds through guile and enchantment; magic is more appropriate to him than heroism, which is perhaps why, in the Renaissance, the magical texts which we met earlier were assigned to Thrice-Greatest Hermes. He is an arch-wizard and patron of magicians. From him also comes gain, cleverly calculated or wholly unexpected – but mostly the latter. Otto writes:

> That is his true characterisation. If a man finds valuables on the road, if a man has a sudden stroke of luck, he thanks Hermes. The regular word for any windfall is *hermaion*, and the familiar expression for avidity is 'common Hermes' (*koinos Hermes*). To be sure, a man must often take a good deal of trouble before he receives the gift of this god, but in the end it is always a lucky find. The Hindu god Pushan is a parallel of Hermes, for this god also knows the way and leads the way, keeping a man from straying.[93]

Jung was fascinated by the sometimes brilliant, sometimes murky figure of the trickster, and in particular by the Mercurius of the alchemists. To him, this figure represented the mysterious momentum of the unconscious, sometimes destructive, sometimes humorous, sometimes terrifying; but always ambiguous, and always fertile. This ceaseless fertility that weaves the dreams and nightmares of our sleep was embodied by the pre-classical Greeks, who placed Herms – votary statues of the god – at every crossroads. The Herm was nothing more than a slyly smiling bearded head placed at the top of a rectangular pillar, with an erect phallus pointing the way. Jung writes in his essay on the trickster archetype:

> The trickster motif does not crop up only in its mythical form but

appears just as naïvely and authentically in the unsuspecting modern man – whenever, in fact, he feels himself at the mercy of annoying 'accidents' which thwart his will and his actions with apparently malicious intent.[94]

Jung connects this tricksterish figure with the shadow, and we have returned full circle to the hostile brothers of the Gemini myth.

The so-called civilised man has forgotten the trickster. He remembers him only figuratively and metaphorically, when, irritated by his own ineptitude, he speaks of fate playing tricks on him or of things being bewitched. He never suspects that his own hidden and apparently harmless shadow has qualities whose dangerousness exceeds his wildest dreams. As soon as people get together in masses and submerge the individual, the shadow is mobilised, and, as history shows, may even be personified and incarnated.[95]

Fate certainly plays tricks on Gemini, because this is an attribute of his own soul. The creative fertility of Hermes is reflected by the long list of Geminis who have left us a heritage of great art; Wagner, Dante and Thomas Mann are only three among them. But it is my feeling that the annoying 'accidents' of which Jung writes, and the conflicts with rivals which seem to be strewn across Gemini's path, can lead to a deep appreciation of the exquisite ambiguity of life and the mystery of a dark–light god. No doubt Gemini would be bored with anything less.

## CANCER

*Out of Water all life comes.*
*The Koran*

The constellation of Cancer, as one writer points out, is the most inconspicuous figure in the zodiac. The humble Crab was not even always a crab; for the Egyptians envisioned it as a beetle rolling a ball of dung. This was the *scarabaeus*, the symbol of immortality, with its nestball of earth in its claws. In Egyptian myth it is an image of self-creation, since it was believed to come into being of itself from its dung-ball. (In reality, if that is the right word, the ball of dung protects the eggs and larvae.) The scarab beetle was called Khephri, which means 'he who came forth from the earth', and it was equated with the creator god Atum, a form of the sun god because the beetle pushes its dung-ball before it as Atum pushes the solar ball across the sky. Humble though the constellation of Cancer may be, its symbolism is far from insignificant. To the Chaldeans and later the Neoplatonists, the Crab was called the

Gate of Men, through which the soul descended from the heavenly spheres into incarnation.

These numinous associations with Cancer suggest a dimension rather different from the good cook and mother with whom we are presented in popular astrological lore. Hugh Lloyd-Jones in his book *Myths of the Zodiac*[96] says that according to some early Greek writers, Cancer rather than Aries began the zodiac. This seems to accord with the idea that it represents the first emergence of life, the entry of the spirit into a corporeal body. The cusp of the fourth house in the horoscope, which is Cancer's natural house, has long been associated with the end of life; here it is also imaged as the beginning, for this is the point of the sun at midnight when the old day dies and the new day is born. In Egyptian myth the sun god traverses the heavens each day in his golden boat, and each night he descends into the caverns of the underworld; there he battles with the terrible Serpent, and emerges at each dawn victorious to begin a new day. This deeply mystical linking of Cancer with the very seed and source of life connects it not only with the primordial Mother, but with the Father as well, for this mythic language is concerned not only with emergence from the womb but also with the spiritual seed that fertilises and begins new life. I have seen this mystical element strongly at work in the lives of many Cancerian people; and it can sit paradoxically side by side with the more conventionally maternal and personal qualities of the sign.

The Greek myth of the Crab places it more firmly within the realm of the Mother. The Crab appears in the saga of the Labours of Herakles, in particular during that hero's battle with the Hydra, the nine-headed serpentine monster which had been destroying the Lernaean countryside. During the fight, all other living creatures favoured Herakles, but out of the marsh in which the Hydra lived crawled an immense crab, sent by the goddess Hera to defeat the hero who was her enemy. The crab snapped at Herakles with its pincers, biting him on the feet and ankles, and this rather characteristic Cancerian manoeuvre almost lost the hero his battle. But eventually Herakles stamped on the crab and crushed it. Hera honoured it for doing her bidding by promoting it to the heavens.

Hera's hatred of Herakles (whose name, with deep irony, means 'glory of Hera') is ostensibly because he was the son of one of Zeus' paramours. But it is really the anger of the matriarch against the upstart hero who threatens her rule. Certainly there is a darker face of Cancer which reflects this problem, and the battle to free oneself from the power of both mother and Mother is often a pronounced and difficult issue in the lives of Cancerian people. The crab is here the archaic Cancer for whom motherhood is all, and for whom the father is merely the provider of the seed. This more regressive

element in Cancer pits itself against the ego's claim to consciousness and freedom of choice, just as the archetypal Terrible Mother
prefers to battle with and even destroy her son rather than permit
him to escape her domination. The crab in the myth uses the classic
Cancerian wiles, snapping at the feet rather than confronting the
hero directly. In other words, it undermines the hero's stability
while he is struggling with the monster. Crab and Hydra are in
league, and one can see this rather unattractive pattern at work in
certain relationships where one partner will nominally give love
and support while secretly undermining the other during his or
her most difficult struggle. This is the dark side of the sign, which
must be met by whatever in the individual is heroic. The problem
of Hera's crab is not exclusively a feminine one either, for the crab
lurks in the swamps of both men and women in whom Cancer is
strongly tenanted in the birth chart. One can often see in Cancerian
men a great difficulty in relating to their own sex, because the
'heroic' aspects of the masculine seem merely brutal, aggressive
and violent.

Thus we are presented with two dimensions of Cancer: the
Terrible Mother who seeks to retain control over the nascent
individuality, and the Divine Father who is the source of life and
towards whom the individual aspires. Erich Neumann, in *The
Origins and History of Consciousness*, suggests that these two World
Parents are part and parcel of the same unity, which to the mind of
the primitive and the child appears androgynous and has been
imaged for millennia as the World Serpent or Uroboros, the snake
which eats its tail and devours itself only to give birth to itself once
again. This Uroboros is the most ancient symbol of man's origins,
arising from that depth of beginning where world and psyche are
still one, and where the original question about the origin of the
world is at the same time the question about the origin of man, the
origin of consciousness and the origin of oneself. In answer to the
query, 'Where did I come from?' this powerful image arises from
the depths, which is both mother and father at once. It is the
original perfection before opposites and conflict began, the egg out
of which the world was formed. Therefore the Uroboros is the
primal creative element – what Jung termed the ocean of the
collective unconscious – which slays, weds and impregnates itself
for all time. Cancer represents this maternal womb, but it is not
solely maternal. It is also a union of masculine and feminine
opposites, the World Parents joined in eternal cohabitation. I feel
that Cancer is driven to seek this divine source; that is its *daimon*,
which is imaged both as the beginning of life before physical
separation and birth, and the end of life when the soul is once
again joined in unity with the One. Thus it is both a regressive

longing for the womb, and a mystical longing for God. Understandably, the projection of this primal symbol falls first upon the personal mother, which is perhaps why she looms so powerfully in the lives of Cancerians regardless of whether she is really, in any objective sense, so potent. The classic 'mother-complex' of the Cancerian is not really about the personal mother. It is the first stage of a gradual unfolding towards an inner source, although usually Cancer during different periods of his or her life will seek this source embodied in a 'maternal' person, male or female, who can 'take care of' him and remove his fear of isolation and separateness. Cancer women too seek this Mother–Father in their relationships, or strive to become it themselves in the act of mothering. But it seems a sad if necessary fate that many Cancers are denied actual children, or must let those children go, so that the deeper meaning of the myth may enact itself in life and the divine Parent may become an inner container.

> Existence in the time before the beginning is supposedly connected with foreknowledge. The creature that still exists in the round participates in the knowledge of the unformed, is merged in the ocean of wisdom. The primal ocean, likewise an origination symbol – for as a ring-snake the uroboros is also the ocean – is the source not only of creation but of wisdom too.[97]

Along with the problem of what Neumann calls 'uroboric incest' – that overwhelming longing to retreat from life into the embrace of the World Parents – there is also an immensely creative power in Cancer. This is the realm of unformed images which the artist midwifes into birth, and for this reason I am more inclined to associate Cancer with the poet, the artist and the musician than I am with the good cook and housekeeper. The list is very long – Proust and Chagall are but two representatives – and it is an impressive one. This *daimon* that stands behind Cancer seems most concerned with bringing to birth the images of the oceanic realm, whether this is in the form of a corporeal child or an artistic creation. The latter is often more important to Cancer than the former; and it may be projected upon a 'creative individual' whose potential Cancer elects to nurture.

In Greek myth, the oceanic realm which is the source of life belongs to the sea goddess Thetis. She is both a beneficent life-giver and a monster; her predecessor in Babylonian myth is the great sea monster Tiamat, who was slain by the fire god Marduk and out of whose dismembered body the whole of creation was made. Thetis or Tethys is therefore the Creatrix. Her name comes from the word *tithenai*, which, like *daimon*, and also like *moira*, means 'to dispose' or 'to order'. At the beginning of Genesis the spirit of God moves over the face of the waters. But Thetis is not only God, she is the waters themselves, and she existed long before the Hebrew Yahveh came into being, containing within her depths both male and female, seed and womb combined. She is also called Nereis, whose name means 'the wet element'. From this name comes the strange mythic figure of Nereus or Proteus, the prophetic 'old man of the sea', who is pictured as fish-tailed with a lion, a stag and a viper emerging from his body. He is the sea-father just as Nereis or Thetis is the sea-mother, and he is a shape-changer and a prophet. If one wishes to receive answers from him, one must first bind him and wait while he transforms into various terrifying animal forms; until eventually he assumes his own curious shape and utters the voice of prophecy. Odysseus in his long wanderings sought advice from Proteus, and had to endure his shape-shifting until the old *daimon* eventually told him what he wished to hear. This act of binding the old man of the sea and waiting patiently while he mutates into every conceivable shape of beast and monster is suggestive of an important aspect of the creative process, where the artist must hold fast to something ineffable that wriggles and transforms until it emerges as a stable image. It is also suggestive of the analytic process, where the shape-shifting images of dreams and fantasies must be firmly held until they yield a meaning digestible by consciousness.

Thus Cancer has always had the reputation of being ambiguous and difficult to pin down, which, I feel, is a euphemism. It is in the nature of water and of the unconscious to slide fluidly from one shape to another; and it is in the nature of Cancer to live in a world where nothing is quite the same as it was five minutes ago. Perhaps the way in which Odysseus deals with Proteus is an image of something which it is important for Cancer to learn: to capture the magical old man of the depths and hold fast to him until he yields up his wisdom. Without Proteus, Odysseus could not have found his way home again, but would have wandered eternally over the waters, forever homeless.

Poseidon wanted to court Thetis, but it was prophesied that any son of Thetis would be greater than his father. This theme suggests that the children of the watery realm carry something numinous about them, and it also opens up another theme which is relevant to Cancer. This is the relationship of mother to son, and the relationship of Cancer to its children in general, biological or otherwise. Poseidon desisted from his courtship, and Zeus (who in some versions of the story wanted her himself) decreed that Thetis must marry a mortal, rather than endanger the gods by bearing a child who might threaten the greatest of the Olympians. Thus the sea goddess, who is also a prophetess in her male form of

Proteus, can mate only with men. In other words, her creative powers must be channelled through human consciousness and human expression. This seems to parallel something which Jung has said, that the transformations and developments of the psyche cannot occur as if by themselves, but depend upon the interaction with the ego, even though the relationship, like Thetis and her mortal lover, is that of something divine with something human. This curious paradox is also portrayed in alchemy, where the act of releasing the divine Mercurius, the philosophers' stone, from the womb of the earth depends upon the participation of the human alchemist, because the alchemical art 'makes perfect what nature leaves imperfect'. Jung quotes the seventeenth-century mystic Angelus Silesius:

> *I know that without me*
> *God can no moment live;*
> *Were I to die, then He*
> *No longer could survive.*
>
> *God cannot without me*
> *A single worm create;*
> *Did I not share with Him*
> *Destruction were its fate.*
>
> *I am as great as God,*
> *And He is small like me;*
> *He cannot be above,*
> *Nor I below Him be . . .*
>
> *. . . I am God's child, His son,*
> *And He too is my child;*
> *We are the two in one,*
> *Both son and father mild.*[98]

The result of the wranglings on Olympus about the fate of Thetis was that she married a man called Peleus. By him she bore the famous hero Achilles, who bears all the hallmarks of a Cancer. Graves calls his behaviour 'hysterical' when he sulks in his tent before the walls of Troy, and in childhood Thetis tried to protect him from involvement with the Trojan War by dressing him up as a woman. Thetis in fact bore seven sons to Peleus, and true to her matriarchal nature, she could not bear the idea that these would be mortal children who were doomed to die. She managed to steal six of them and burn off their mortal flesh so that they might ascend to Olympus and take their places among the gods. Peleus was outraged by this destruction of his sons, and managed to rescue Achilles just before all of the child was burned away; the father kept his hand firmly on the son's ankle bone, which remained mortal. This version of the tale seems to predate the story that Thetis dipped her son in the river Styx to render him immortal, forgetting the ankle she was holding. But the sentiment in both tales is the same. When I have encountered this myth at work in human lives, it often takes the form of a numinous projection upon a favoured and beloved child, who is expected to reach Olympian heights even if the child's humanity is destroyed in the process. Sometimes Cancer, if there are no actual children upon whom this vision of superhuman performance can be projected, will nurture this attitude towards his own creativity, finding anything that comes out of him flawed and distasteful unless it is divine. There seems to be an issue here of why Cancer will often not live out his creative potential himself, but will wait until a beloved partner or child can perform the task.

Achilles has a rather curious history. It was prophesied that he would either die young and gain great glory, or live a long but inglorious life at home. It seems that the Fates were undecided about him or else gave him more options than most people. Naturally his mother Thetis preferred the latter choice, but Achilles himself opted for the former. I do not think this needs to be taken literally, any more than any mythic motif demands literal enactment; but certainly the battle to free oneself from the goddess means risking one's mortality, and perhaps dying on other levels in order to become free. This monumental effort on the part of Cancer is often the act that releases the potential of the creative imagination. But there are as many, perhaps far more, Cancers who opt for the other path, and remain close to the comfort of the Mother all their lives, sacrificing whatever potential they might reach. Thetis took an active part in preventing Achilles from joining the warriors going to Troy, as we have seen; and it does seem that Cancer experiences the personal mother as holding him back from life. But Achilles was discovered hiding among the women by Odysseus, who fetched him to the war. Throughout the battles we see him being constantly interfered with by his goddess-mother, who rushes to his tent bringing new armour, proper clothes, clean linen and so on. One is surprised Homer does not mention chicken soup. If the *Iliad* were not such a great and tragic tale, it would be quite hilarious; and certainly this part of it is painfully funny. The only thing which has the power to draw the sulking Achilles from his tent to fight is the death of his dearest friend and lover Patroclus. Only then is his true courage and mettle revealed. This too seems to be a facet of Cancer: that nothing will goad the sign into open confrontation with life save deep emotional loss.

The theme of the Great Goddess is a thread which runs through many other signs of the zodiac in one aspect or another. Cancer seems to describe her as bringer-forth of life and ruler of the sea. She is the uterine waters from which the child emerges, and the unconscious waters from which the individual identity emerges; and this great image of Mother remains always the most powerful force in Cancer's life. It tends to shift, in later life, from the personal mother as the exclusive carrier to the creative unconscious, but in whichever form Cancer meets her, he is always bound to her for good or ill. The dark face of this *daimon* is the overpowering mother-bond which paralyses both man and woman, and binds them in such a way that individual potential drowns. The light face is the potential to midwife the images of the unconscious. The issue of separation from the mother is a monumental rite of passage in Cancer's life, and it must be done not once but many times, on many different levels. Like the actual crab, which must stay close to both water and land, Cancer is driven to anchor himself in the concrete world with one foot eternally in the water, so that he himself ultimately can become the womb through which the nascent children of the sea may be born.

## LEO

*Full fathom five thy father lies;*
*Of his bones are coral made:*
*Those are pearls that were his eyes:*
*Nothing of him that doth fade,*
*But doth suffer a sea-change,*
*Into something rich and strange.*
Shakespeare, The Tempest

The sign of the Lion, like that of the Bull, is a deceptively simple one. We have become accustomed to descriptions of the loud and kingly specimen of popular lore, and one could easily believe that this sign has no deeper meaning than an extroverted and exhibitionistic display of vigorous life. But there is an unexpectedly complex pattern at work in Leo, and the figure of the king in myth and fairy tale leads us very far away from the conventionally shallow and showy lion into much more mystical terrain. I have for a long time been convinced that Leo, ruled by the sun and connected therefore with the mystery of the individuality and the 'fated' path of individual maturation, is not really about 'creating' something that other people can applaud. More profoundly, it seems to describe the development of unique individual essence and its quest for its source. Although Leo is supposed to be the 'creative' sign and naturally rules the fifth house, a perusal of great names among painters, poets, novelists and musicians reveals a preponderance of Gemini, Cancer and Pisces; but Leo is sadly thin on the ground. Whatever creativity may be about, I feel that Leo's great creation is meant to be himself. Hence, like Capricorn which we will explore in due course, and like Aries which we have already met, the symbolism of Leo circles around the theme of the king and his son, or the hero and his father. And, as we shall see, although the lion has many female connotations in myth and is one of the Mother's accompanying beasts, the battle between man and lion, and the hero's quest for his spiritual father or the transpersonal value in his own life, are closely bound up together.

The Lion of the zodiac was known both to the Egyptians and the Babylonians, and was connected with the burning heat of the sun during the summer months. Sekhmet, the Egyptian solar goddess, is lion-headed, and scorches the earth with her rage. But the Greeks identified the lion with the creature that Herakles battled in one of his Labours, the Nemean Lion which was sent from the moon to earth by Hera to plague the hero who was her adversary. Why this lion should have come from the moon, and from the goddess, we shall see; but, as the story goes, the first of Herakles' tasks required that he slay the beast without weapons. An old man directed the hero to the lion's lair. Once he was within range he shot an arrow which struck the beast, but Hera had made it invulnerable, and the arrow bounced off. Then Herakles went after it with his club, thus violating the rules of the combat. The lion took refuge in its lair, a cave with two mouths. The hero blocked up one entrance with stones, and came upon the beast in the darkness. After a terrific struggle he managed to grasp it by the throat and choke it to death. Then he flayed it, and wore its hide ever afterwards as a garment.

The tale of man battling beast is the oldest of archetypal motifs. We have already met it in the myths connected with the first four signs. In the broadest sense, it is the battle between the developing ego and its instinctual roots, which must be tamed before the individual can become truly individual. But it is the particular sort of beast which is most relevant here, for this is a lion and not a ram, a bull, a dragon or sea-monster, or a hostile brother. Sekhmet, as we have seen, typifies the aggressive, fiery nature of the lion. Kybele, the Great Goddess of Asia Minor, rides on a chariot drawn by two lions, and Dionysos, whom we will meet later, also wears a lion skin like Herakles and is often portrayed with lions in his train. But the attributes of the lion, although often associated with the feminine, are very hot-blooded and fiery attributes, far from the cold-blooded snake-wisdom of the reptilian Mother. Jung has the following to say about the lion:

In alchemy, the lion, the 'royal beast', is a synonym for Mercurius, or, to be more accurate, for a stage in his transformation. He is the warm-blooded form of the devouring, predatory monster who first appears as the dragon ... This is precisely what the fiery lion is intended to express – the passionate emotionality that precedes the recognition of unconscious contents.[99]

The lion is also associated with concupiscence and pride. It has an unmistakable erotic aspect, hence the association with Dionysos and Kybele, but it is also a fighting animal and suggests healthy, as well as destructive, aggressive impulses. When we met the Crab, we met a cold-blooded creature from the underwater realm of the feminine. But the lion can be tamed and can respond to human care – lions were kept as pets by Egyptian and Persian royalty – and we are confronting something much closer to consciousness: the lordly passions of the heart. Herakles and the lion are certainly imaged according to the ancient pattern of man battling beast, but this hero dons the skin of the creature he has slain. He thus himself becomes lion-like, but the inflamed passions are now contained. One cannot imagine him donning the crab's shell, for it is too distant from human life. The emblem of kingship is in the most profound sense connected with this capacity to wrestle with the passions. The man who cannot contain his fiery impulses cannot govern others, nor serve as an example to them.

We shall probably not be wrong if we assume that the 'king of beasts', known even in Hellenistic times as a transformation stage of Helios, represents the old king ... At the same time he represents the king in his theriomorphic form, that is, as he appears in his unconscious state. The animal form emphasises that the king is overpowered or overlaid by his animal side and consequently expresses himself only in animal reactions, which are nothing but emotions. Emotionality in the sense of uncontrollable affects is essentially bestial, for which reason people in this state can be approached only with the circumspection proper to the jungle, or else with the methods of the animal trainer.[100]

No astrologer, I think, would argue that this quality of fiery passionateness is characteristic of Leo. But the lion is a stage in a process, as Jung suggests; and it is this process or pattern which brings us into the sphere of the 'fate' of Leo. It would seem, from what I have seen of the life histories of Leos with whom I have worked, that there is an alchemical work to be performed. The lion is not permitted to remain in his bestial form, but must give way to

something other. It seems a disturbing aspect of the pattern that
Leo is often treated, as Jung describes, with the cirumspection
'proper to the jungle', or with the 'methods of the animal trainer' –
the whip and the goad. This is a painful process for Leo, whose
childlike heart is deeply injured by the reactions of his fellows to
his own excesses. He 'meant it for the best', but somehow others
do not seem to be appreciative; they are more often angry. If Leo
himself does not glimpse the importance of the process, life tends
to teach him rather forcibly that a lion cannot roam loose among
men without some retaliation. More creatively, Leo chooses of his
own volition to undergo the quest, and for this reason the myth
which I associate most closely with the sign is the story of Parsifal,
or Perceval as he is known in French and English. This is a
medieval rather than a Greek myth, but its roots are much older;
and in virtually all its particulars I feel it portrays the life-pattern of
Leo.

The general outlines of the story of Parsifal's quest for the Grail
are well known, despite the many different versions. A mysterious, life-preserving and sustenance-dispensing object or vessel is
guarded by a king in a castle that is hidden or difficult to find. The
king is lame or sick, and the surrounding countryside is devastated
or wasted; this is the state of things in Eliot's poem *The Wasteland*,
which is based upon the myth of the quest for the Grail. The king
can only be restored to health if a knight of conspicuous excellence
finds the castle and at the first sight of what he sees there, asks a
certain question. Should he neglect to put this question, then
everything will remain as before, the castle will vanish, and the
knight will have to set out once more upon the search. Should he
finally succeed, after much wandering and many adventures,
particularly involving encounters of an erotic kind (for Leo will first
search for his treasure in love, before he discovers it may lie within
himself), and should he then ask the question, the king will be
restored to health, the land will begin to grow green again, and the
hero will inherit the kingdom and become the guardian of the
Grail.

This story describes, at its outset, a state of spiritual sickness.
The old king cannot help his land or his people, and it rests upon
the shoulders of a young man to pass the test. But the test is not a
feat of arms. It is a question, i.e. a capacity to become conscious of
the *meaning* of things, a quality of reflection. Parsifal begins his
story fatherless, brought up by his mother in an isolated wood.
This beginning which has no father (or no father-principle,
although there may be a physical father present) is something I
have seen in many Leos' lives. The father is either absent or
wounded on some more profound level, and he cannot provide

the sense of creative renewal of life which the son or daughter needs; and so the child must go out seeking this principle, in the form of his life's adventure.

Five knights in shining armour came riding through the forest, and when Parsifal saw them he was overwhelmed and decided he would become a knight. Naturally his mother, like Thetis with Achilles, tried to prevent his leaving, but Parsifal is no mother's son. He neither sulked nor dressed up as a woman to hide, but simply walked out without even a goodbye. His mother then immediately died of grief. This seems a necessary rite of passage for Leo, although at the beginning of his adventures Parsifal is clumsy and boorish. He is, indeed, the king in his theriomorphic or animal form, the unconscious ruler-to-be, overcome with emotional affect. Parsifal then battled with the Red Knight, who, by the colour of his armour, seems to be another image of the fiery emotionality of Leo, wearing the colour of blood, fire and life. Like Herakles, Parsifal donned the armour of his defeated enemy. He then encountered a lovely woman in distress, and received his initiation into the erotic arts; but he left his lady with the same clumsy callousness with which he abandoned his mother, once again necessarily blind.

At length Parsifal came to a deep river, over which there was no visible crossing; fate had brought him to the end of the road. He had been brought to the place of his potential task. He saw a fisherman, who told him the way to the Grail castle; and the castle suddenly appeared where previously there was nothing. The gate was open, for he was mysteriously expected, and the suffering Fisher-King awaited him. The king in the story was wounded in the groin or thigh: he cannot procreate, for his manhood is injured. This is a thinly veneered image of castration. A vision then appeared to Parsifal, of a sword, a lance which dripped blood, a maiden bearing a Grail of gold set with precious stones, and another maiden carrying a silver platter. Students of the Tarot will recognise these four sacred objects as the four suits of cups, swords, wands and pentacles, and students of Jung will recognise the quaternity which symbolises the wholeness of the Self. As these four holy objects passed, Parsifal did not dare to say anything. He retired to bed, and on waking found the castle deserted; upon leaving it, he was then told by another woman whom he met about the failure which he had just enacted. Had he asked the question – Whom does the Grail serve? – then the king would have been healed and the land renewed. Presented with his destiny for the first time, Parsifal has, as they say, blown it.

He could only find the castle again after he had achieved the necessary maturity, and the necessary compassion. At first none of it meant anything to him; it was merely a show put on for his entertainment. In their book, *The Grail Legend*, Emma Jung and Marie-Louise von Franz stress the lack of capability of suffering which is characteristic of the young Parsifal. Wagner, in his great opera of redemption, seized on this theme of Parsifal's lack of compassion. The hero first enters the stage having shot down an innocent swan for the sheer sport of it, and is harshly reprimanded by the Brothers of the Grail Castle for his callousness. Jung and von Franz say:

> His real offence actually lay in the primitive unambiguousness of his behaviour, which arose from an unawareness of the inner problem of the opposites. *It was not what he did but that he was not capable of assessing what he did.*[101]

Parsifal's insensitivity to his mother, to the Red Knight (whom he kills for no personal reason – it is not his quarrel – but simply because he wishes to show off), to Blancheflor (the woman whom he rescues and then abandons), and to the Grail King himself (for whom he does not yet experience compassion and the inevitable question which arises from that compassion) are embodied in the alchemical image of the lion, the animal form of the king-to-be. This naïve clumsiness is, I feel, an integral part of the young or immature Leo, just as is the state of fatherlessness; yet even with this clumsiness, fate chooses him for the vision of the Grail before he is ready to understand it. Whatever the Grail may be – a sense of personal destiny, an early success, a youthful spirituality – it seems to come early to Leo, not through labour but often through the natural gifts and intuition of the sign. But then it is lost, because the sense of its meaning has not been plumbed, and the ego claims the success for itself. Thus it must be refound in consciousness, and often through much hardship.

The king's wound is central to Wagner's *Parsifal*, and while admittedly the distortions of the Parsifal story according to Wagner reveal as much about the composer as they do about Parsifal, nevertheless Wagner has chosen an archetypal theme, only partly drawn from von Eschenbach's medieval poem *Parzival*. In the opera, the Grail King Amfortas received his wound from the evil magician Klingsor, at a moment when the king was rendered vulnerable in the arms of the seductive Kundry, that ambiguous feminine figure who serves both dark and light. Klingsor wanted to be a Grail Knight, but Amfortas refused him; so the magician castrated himself to make himself invulnerable to erotic temptation, and stole the spear from Amfortas in revenge. As a result of the wound and the loss of the spear, the Grail Kingdom lay in waste. Perhaps this gives us some insight into one of Leo's dilemmas; for in the brightness and nobility of his aspirations he will not permit the lowly shadow, his own flawed humanness, entry. That rejected shadow strikes back from the unconscious through the disintegrating effects of uncontrollable eroticism. Amfortas languishes unmanned in the arms of Kundry; he cannot retain his 'purity' of vision, and he is thus a mockery, a soiled king who is no longer fit to guard the Grail and is wounded by his own gnawing guilt. Leo is, of course, not only Parsifal, but the sick king as well, and also the evil magician; and he is, too, the woman who destroys the king yet who later serves to heal him.

After Parsifal left the Grail castle, he went through many adventures and much suffering. Through these experiences he accrued both wisdom and compassion. Then, at last, he was able to return once again to the castle, and look upon the Grail, and ask the fatal question. At his words the king sprang up healed, and revealed that he was Parsifal's grandfather; and the custodianship of the castle and the Grail now belonged to the young knight. So at last the fatherless son finds the father, but it is a higher father than the fleshly one. This is the grandfather, the Great Father, who is the benign source of creative life, and who begins the tale old, weary, and in need of redemption. I feel that Leo's deepest urge is this search for the Self, the central value in life – which is, in mythic terms, the same as the search for the father. It is not the same father whom we will meet in Capricorn, for Capricorn's father is the senex, the earthy law-giving principle which limits and structures worldly life. Nor is the father of the Aries confrontation, the fire god Yahveh with whom he must battle. Leo's father is the radiant life-giver, worshipped for millennia as the sun. He is the more merciful God of the New Testament, whose abundant flow of compassion is embodied in the image of the Grail. Yet this father–god needs renewal through the efforts of man to understand him. Hence Leo, usually represented as a showy extrovert, is motivated from within by a deeply spiritual urge. But the individual Leo may remain forever the young Parsifal, unconscious of the meaning of his existence and unable to ask the question.

Nor does redemption occur after the manner of the Indian doctrine of salvation, according to which everything has to be recognised as nothing but illusion. Here it happens in a different way, not through the action of a god (though naturally it is *Deo concedente*, since whosoever accomplishes it has to be destined thereto by God) and also not through nature, but solely by the unflinching exertions of a human being, Perceval; just as neither more nor less than this can be brought to the *opus* of alchemy or to the realisation of the Self. It must, however, be remarked that

Perceval's way to the Grail, the *opus* of alchemy, and the realisation of the Self all have this in common with the Christian way of salvation: they all signify an *opus contra naturam*, i.e. not of the least but of the greatest resistance.[102]

This quest for individual realisation is not, of course, solely the property of Leo. It is the basic path of the human soul, and we will have more to say about individuation and fate later. But the myth of Parsifal, although in a broader sense applicable to every man and woman, seems to foreshadow sometimes eerily the pattern of Leo's life. Perhaps the issue of discovering what it might mean to be an individual is of primary concern for Leo, the most relevant issue that can occur to him. It is therefore not surprising that Jung, who was himself a Leo, developed the concept of individuation which has proven to be of such importance to modern depth psychology. That this was the issue closest to his own heart is, from the point of view of an astrologer, predictable, if one knows something of the mythic backdrop of the sign; it was, of course, his fate. Thus the early success which he enjoyed as Freud's favoured disciple and chosen heir was not sufficient for him, where it might have (and did) satisfy others. He was compelled by his own myth to follow the lonely road into his own depths, so that the view of the psyche which he eventually developed came from his own experience, his own intuition, his own research and his own insight. And it was a peculiarly Leonine route, circling closer and closer to a centre which Jung felt to be as much a religious as an instinctual experience. His disappointment in his father, who was a churchman who had lost his faith, is also characteristic of the pattern. Jung attributed much of his own aspiration to this 'absent' father, namely, his quest for a different kind of father, a direct experience of the numinous. Leo, like Capricorn, often experiences this disappointment in the personal father, because he seems – and usually actually is – 'wounded', impotent in some way, spiritually 'lame', and cannot offer a sustaining vision of life as a meaningful and enriching experience.

We must now leave Parsifal behind, and consider one final mythic image in relation to Leo: Apollo the sun god. This deity, whose famous shrine at Delphi displayed carved in stone the injunction, 'Man, know thyself', is a superior and even a grandiose god. He is an image of loftiness of spirit, and is in himself a kind of Grail. As Walter Otto puts it in *The Homeric Gods*, Apollo is 'the manifestation of the divine amidst the desolation and confusion of the world', and he is the most sublime of the Greek pantheon. Phoebus, one of his epithets, means 'pure' or 'holy'. There is something mysterious and inapproachable about the god which commands an awed distance. Apollo is the great healer and purifier. He removes the pollution of corporeal reality and restores the unclean man or woman to a state of grace. It is something like this – the loss of the sense of inherent sin – which is bound up with the experience of the Self. The relation of Apollo to the suppliant is that of the Grail to Parsifal, and the question is the same; hence the injunction over the door to the temple. As Otto puts it:

> Life is to be freed of such uncanny barriers, of demonic entanglements over which even the purest human will has no power. Apollo therefore advises men in distress what is to be done and what left undone, where atonement and submission may be necessary.[103]

As I understand this psychologically, Apollo is an image of the power of consciousness, vested in it by the Self, which breaks the 'curse' and cleanses the unclean, freeing the individual of the 'uncanny barriers' which rise from the dark world of the unconscious. He is ego-power at its most glorious, the victor in the battle with the underworld serpent Python, the vessel of God as human realisation. It is to Apollo that people pray when they need clear sight, for his arrow penetrates even the murkiest of dilemmas, and his music stills the confused and turbulent heart.

Apollo is not a god of women. He has rather poor luck, in fact, with those women whom he courts, for he usually has a rival who is more successful than the god himself. This is often the pattern with Leo, who may have many adoring admirers, but often fails to obtain the chosen object. It is my feeling that Leo is not the easiest of signs for a woman, because its essence is so brightly and brilliantly allied with the realm of Logos. Perhaps for this reason many Leo women seem to evidence the lioness, the more emotive face of the sign, rather than engage in the long struggle to achieve the sense of inner meaning of which Parsifal is a symbol. Parsifal belongs exclusively neither to men nor to women, for individuality is not the prerogative of either; nor is the problem of redemption through compassion and an understanding of the deeper source which is the true creator of personality.

## VIRGO

*Truly, my Satan, thou art but a dunce,*
*And dost not know the garment from the man;*
*Every harlot was a virgin once.*
          *William Blake*, The Gates of Paradise

We have met already one of the myths which I feel to be intimately connected with Virgo: the abduction of Persephone. Although I mentioned this myth in relation to Pluto and Scorpio, the figure of

Persephone herself is a characteristic *kore* figure – a maiden – and her fate reflects something very relevant to Virgo. It is this image of the *kore* which I would now like to explore more fully.

The constellation of the maiden was identified by the Greeks with the goddess Astraea (or Dike), who represents the principle of justice. According to Hesiod, she was the daughter of Zeus. Once she lived on earth, during the Golden Age when there was no strife or bloodshed among men. She would sit in the company of ordinary folk, and gather together the elders in the market place and urge them to obey nature's laws. But with the gradual corruption of men, Astraea conceived a hatred for the human race because of its crimes, and left earth forever, flying up to heaven to join her father Zeus and becoming the constellation of Virgo. For Hesiod, the figure of Astraea is stern, and a punisher of crime; she has much in common with Nemesis, whom we have already met. But Astraea's justice is not about law courts and the niceties of social relationship. We will meet something more like that when we come to explore Libra. Astraea, who is generally shown carrying a sheaf of barley, is an earthier goddess. Jane Harrison, in *Themis*, her study of the social origins of Greek religion, writes:

> Dike [Astraea] is the way of life of each natural thing, each plant, each animal, each man. It is also the way, the usage, the regular course of that great animal the Universe, the way that is made manifest in the Seasons, in the life and death of vegetation; and when it comes to be seen that these depend on the heavenly bodies, Dike is manifest in the changes of the rising and setting of constellations, in the waxing and waning of the Moon and in the daily and yearly courses of the Sun.[104]

Here we have something not unlike the ancient figure of Moira, although Astraea is not such a primordial goddess, nor is she responsible for the apportionment of fate. She seems to be an image of the intrinsic orderliness of nature, and her disgust at humanity is a mythic image of the traditional Virgoan disgust at disorder, chaos and wastage of time and substance. Like Astraea, Virgo does not have a great deal of sympathy for those who have wantonly made a mess of it. All things have their time and place within the governance of the goddess Astraea; every natural form in the universe has its appropriate cycle and value. It is not surprising, with such a *daimon* presiding over the sign, that Virgo inclines to ritualism and to a vision of life where 'justice' ought to be restored.

Frances A. Yates has written a remarkable study of the theme of the Virgin Astraea in sixteenth-century politics (called, appropriately, *Astraea*) when Queen Elizabeth I, who was herself a

Virgo, was identified with this mythic figure. Yates has the following comments to make on the celestial Maiden:

> The parentage of the Virgin is obscure; some call her the daughter of Jove and Themis; others the daughter of Astraeus and Aurora; others call her Erigone, daughter of Icarus, a pious virgin whose little dog led her to her dead father's body. She has affiliations with several deities. The corn in her hand suggests that she must be Ceres [Demeter]. Sometimes she is affiliated with Venus. Others think that she is Fortune, because her head disappears amongst the stars. There is a hint of Isis in her nature . . . but the female deity whom she most resembles is Atargatis, the Syrian goddess, worshipped under the name of Virgo Caelestis at Carthage, and associated with Urania and, like Isis, with the moon. The just virgin is therefore a complex character, fertile and barren at the same time; orderly and righteous, yet tinged with oriental moon-ecstasies.[105]

Complex, indeed: Virgo seems to embody a deep paradox, a combination of upright and almost schoolmarmish Astraea set side by side with the orgiastic lunar harlot goddesses of Asia Minor. This paradox poses an enormous conflict for Virgo, and it is out of the conflict that Virgo's pattern of development arises. Whether this is enacted as a collision between personal and professional life, between marriage and independence (a common theme), between spirituality and materialism, between morality and abandonment, Virgo struggles with these opposites throughout life, trying to encompass them both. Often the Virgoan individual will try to embody one while sacrificing the other, and this generally provokes difficulties, for the fate of the sign does not seem to permit such splitting. I feel that Persephone as we meet her in the myth embodies only one half of Virgo's paradox; she has elected to remain the virgin rather than the harlot, and her secret unlived side – represented by Gaia or Aphrodite in the story – leads inevitably to her abduction and her enforced marriage to the lord of the dead.

The word 'virgin', like the sign, is complex. These days we are prone to understand it as referring to sexual intactness and inexperience, but this is far from the original sense of the word. Our astrological Virgo in her mythic context is scarcely a virgin. One need only look at figures like the black Artemis of Ephesus with her hundred breasts, at whose behest every young woman spent a night in the temple prostituting herself to a stranger as an offering to the goddess before marriage, in order to find a contradiction to our twentieth-century interpretation. Yet Artemis is called 'virgin'. As John Layard in his essay on the virgin archetype writes:

> In the first place, though we now think of the word 'virgin' as being synonymous with 'chaste', this was not the case either with the Greek word *parthenos* or with the Hebrew *almah* of which 'virgin' is the most usual biblical translation. For the Greek word was used of an unmarried girl whether she was chaste or not, and was in fact also applied to unmarried mothers. The Hebrew word means likewise 'unmarried' without reference to premarital chastity.[106]

This leads us, inevitably, to the problematic image of the whore, for the ancient virgin goddesses such as Atargatis and the Ephesian Artemis were themselves harlots, and their temples were served by prostitutes who embodied the deity and bestowed her divine favours upon devout men, thus raising them also to semi-divine status. In this sense, the prostitute is the same as the mythic virgin, for she is an archetypal image of the free woman who is wedded first of all to her inner being and only secondarily to a man. Layard writes:

> Thus in this sense the word 'virgin' does not mean chastity but the reverse, the pregnancy of nature, free and uncontrolled, corresponding on the human plane to unmarried love, in contrast to the controlled nature corresponding to married love, despite the fact that from the legal point of view sexual intercourse within the marriage bond is the only kind which is regarded as chaste.[107]

One can see why this internal paradox creates considerable tension in Virgo, which is known as a highly strung sign. Virgo's inner morality, when it is genuinely inner and not borrowed from the prevailing collective – as is the case with the more timid member of the sign – is not at odds with what might be considered rather unconventional sexual behaviour. Yet this inner morality of itself can be very strong, and no less based on a sense of 'rightness' than more conventional codes. I have met a number of professional prostitutes during the course of my work, and some of them have been Virgos, or Virgo ascendants, or moon or Venus in Virgo; and I have been compelled to acknowledge this curious dichotomy of a strong inner moral sense coupled with what society would consider grossly immoral, or amoral, behaviour. It has often made me wonder who are the real whores, in the sense that we generally use the word. I feel that the story of Persephone is a myth which becomes a fate in a literal way only if Persephone cannot align herself with her opposite – Aphrodite – and attempts to cling to virginity in the more literal sense, i.e. innocence and repudiation of life. Then life, like Hades, has a way of erupting from the depths and forcing experience on the maiden. But even when this mythic pattern is fulfilled – and there are many levels and kinds of rape – something fruitful emerges from the experience. Obviously this issue does not deal solely with sexual matters, but embodies an entire view of life. The harlotry of the virgin goddesses does not mean merely sexual availability to all callers any more than 'virgin' means merely sexual intactness. I would understand it more as an openness to the flow of life, a willingness to trust the natural order, an acceptance of penetration and change. Contrary to the popular descriptions of Virgo, I feel this paradoxical *daimon* to form the true core of the sign. But it is difficult to achieve, just as the quest for the Grail is difficult for Leo, and the reconciliation of opposites for Gemini, and the taming of the bull for Taurus, and so on. It is far easier, and more common, for Virgo to flee into ritualised or obsessional behaviour, where the sterner aspects of Astraea submerge the fecundity and joy of Atargatis. This is often the prelude to the arrival of psychosomatic symptoms, for Atargatis is a deity who demands entry through that most basic manifestation of life – the body.

The inherent paradox of Virgo is beautifully expressed in the gnostic text of the fourth century called *The Thunder, Perfect Mind*. This is a revelation discourse imparted by a female figure who seems to personify the idea of Sophia, or wisdom.

> . . . For I am the first and the last.
> I am the honoured one and the scorned one.
> I am the whore and the holy one.
> I am the wife and the virgin.
> I am the mother and the daughter.
> I am the members of my mother.
> I am the barren one
>    and many are her sons.
> I am she whose wedding is great,
>    and I have not taken a husband.
> I am the midwife and she who does not bear.
> I am the solace of my labour pains.
> I am the bride and the bridgroom
>    and it is my husband who begot me.
> I am the mother of my father
>    and the sister of my husband,
> And he is my offspring.[108]

For some months I had occasion to work with a highly intelligent woman whose sun and ascendant are both in Virgo. In her birth horoscope she also has a conjunction of moon, Saturn and Uranus in Gemini in the tenth house, which deals with the experience of mother. From this mother, my analysand, whom I shall call Susan, had learned that the great 'they' ruled in earth and in heaven, and that the codes of conventional morality could not be broken without severe retribution. The mother herself – as suggested by the powerful and contradictory tenth house conjunction – had considerable ambivalence about the issue of conformity, and, on a deeper level, about the 'role' of being a woman to begin with. Susan likewise felt this ambivalence, but was very unconscious of it, apparently wanting, when I first met her, nothing more than a husband, a home and children, and unchanging safety for the rest of her life. Unfortunately she kept falling in love with married or homosexual men who were ultimately unable to provide what she sought. Although she is an attractive and charming woman, she seemed to place no value on her own body, literally throwing herself into the arms of anyone who showed her a little affection; she was therefore a whore in the more negative sense, in that she derived no pleasure from these encounters, but felt they were 'expected' and the necessary price for 'catching' a husband. After several years of this sad and self-destructive behaviour, she had fallen in love once again with a married man, but this new lover showed signs of deep attachment and was preparing to leave his wife in order to offer her a more permanent relationship. This, far from delighting Susan, promptly filled her with feelings of great anxiety. She was also plagued by guilt, because breaking up a man's marriage seemed to her an unforgivable sin.

I will not elaborate on the parental implications of Susan's penchant for triangles, nor on the lack of reflection on her own contradictions which was so characteristic of her. She brought me the following dream after about two months of work:

> I am going to train as a prostitute. I arrive at the school where all the women are to learn sexual arts. The front of this place is a sort of shop, where a pleasant man is in charge. I feel strangely happy about this place, but I explain to the man that I am afraid of receiving a repulsive man as my first customer. He tells me I do not have to have sex with anyone I do not want. I must also choose a pair of earrings from a display in the window. Most of them are very ornate, but I select a pair of simple gold rings.

This dream seems to herald a kind of initiation. The guilt which Susan experienced was connected with her strong erotic attachment to her father, which was made intolerable not only because of the mother's jealous criticism but also because her identification with the mother – reflected by the tenth house moon – led her to assume the same collective morality. The new relationship had awakened these erotic feelings, which had remained completely suppressed despite a long chain of lovers. The fact that she had found a man she herself wanted, rather than a man whom she imagined might want her, had propelled her into a crisis. The dream foreshadowed the beginning of an increased awareness of her own body as possessing valid laws and desires of its own, rather than as an object which could be offered in exchange for love and security. Susan's initiation into the shop which is the modern symbol of the ancient temple leads her to the experience of the goddess, who claims the first lover as an affirmation of the feminine before the woman can become bound to a husband. Here the animus is the initiator, disguised as the shop proprietor, and he affirms her right to follow the commands of her own nature. She need only mate with those whom she herself desires. The gold earrings suggest not only wedding rings – once again implying a paradox – but also her own wholeness, her Self. The dream therefore suggests that this encounter with the mythic whore in herself, constellated by her new relationship, marks the beginning of Susan's individual development. This kind of dream is not uncommon in women of any sign who have faced the kind of maternal problems Susan has experienced. But I have quoted the dream here because it embodies so much of the 'fate' of Virgo.

The issue of bestowing one's gifts or one's bounty as one wishes, according to inner laws, rather than satisfying expectations to gain rewards, seems fundamental to the mythic figure of the Virgin. Esther Harding, in her book *Women's Mysteries*, writes about the virgin goddess:

> The chief characteristic of the goddess in her crescent phase is that she is virgin. Her instinct is not used to capture or possess the man whom she attracts. She does not reserve herself for the chosen man who must repay her by his devotion, nor is her instinct used to gain for herself the security of husband, home and family. She remains virgin, even while being the goddess of love. She is essentially one-in-herself . . . Her divine power does not depend on her relation to a husband-god, and thus her actions are not dependent on the need to conciliate such a one or to accord with his qualities and attitudes. For she bears her divinity in her own right.[109]

Human beings are not goddesses, and this description of a numinous mythic image is not likely to be attainable, save as an inner experience at rare moments of life. But I feel that Virgo strives towards this state, and external events often conspire to help create it. Sometimes the partner cannot provide the security that is hoped for, or a period of life must be spent alone. These apparently 'fated' happenings point towards an inner need to live from one's own values rather than from the values of others. The mythic virgin does not preclude relationship; but if Virgo tries to avoid the responsibility of her own nature, these relationships have a tendency to be at best dissatisfying, and at worst catastrophic.

It may well be asked how the powerful image of the virgin goddess who is also a harlot can apply to a man in whom the sign Virgo is prominent. But just as the masculine figures whom we have met are equally relevant to women, the female figure of Astraea can equally symbolise inner integrity for a man. The Virgoan man too may for a period of his life have to struggle with collective expectations and the serene security of doing what is acceptable, and his values may equally be those of society at the beginning of his adult life. Virgos of both sexes are often caught in the dilemma of having to choose between the safe, well-paid and ultimately barren path of external compliance and the fertile but often lonely path of inner loyalty. Virgo is a singular mythic figure; she rules, as Harding says, in her own right, and this leaves her essentially alone, for her truths must ultimately be her own. Greta Garbo, one of our more famous Virgoans, seems to have given voice to this in a very literal way. Sometimes this aloneness is forced upon Virgo for a time, so that in the silence of one's own company the inner voice can be heard. Loneliness and aloneness are, of course, not the same; for one may have deep companionship and remain in touch with one's essential differentness.

I would now like to focus more closely on the Demeter–Persephone pair, for these two figures, mother and daughter, are closely connected to Virgo. As Leo is a father–son tale, Virgo can also be a tale of mother and daughter. Although the Virgo man may experience these figures through the anima and the women in his life, the myth is no less relevant. Demeter and Persephone form a unity, the paradox of woman as maiden and mother. Jung says the following about this paradox:

> Demeter and Kore, mother and daughter, extend the feminine consciousness both upwards and downwards. They add an 'older and younger', 'stronger and weaker', dimension to it and widen out the narrowly limited conscious mind bound in space and time, giving it intimations of a greater and more comprehensive personality which has a share in the eternal course of things ... We could therefore say that every mother contains her daughter in herself and every daughter her mother, and that every woman extends backwards into her mother and forwards into her daughter ... The conscious experience of these ties

produces the feeling that her life is spread out over generations – the first step towards the immediate experience and conviction of being outside time, which brings with it a feeling of immortality.[110]

The sense of immortality of which Jung writes seems to me to belong to 'ordinary' life, rather than to the transcendant realm of the masculine spirit. It is the immortality of nature, the 'rightness' of daily routine. This mystery of mother and daughter offers another dimension to Virgo's ritualism, whose roots lie in the profound experience of each moment of life being a fresh beginning which emerges out of a preceding cycle and generates the next cycle.

Jung wrote in his essay on the *kore* that the maiden must always be sacrificed, so that she may become a mother. This is her 'fate'. We need not take this literally, for many women do not become literal mothers, and neither do men. But if mothering in the deeper sense is about the nurturing of potentials and the bringing to birth of the inner pattern in outer life, then this mythic theme does indeed apply to the Virgo of both sexes, who is generally compelled by his *daimon* to manifest his talents and gifts in an outwardly expressive and concrete way. But if these inner potentials are to be expressed in form, then the maiden must die, because the hope of perfection disappears with any physical creation. I suspect that the fascination which many men have with virginity (witness the number of films which deal with the seduction and deflowering of a young girl, not to mention the deep-rooted collective expectation that a woman must go to her bridal bed untouched by any save her spouse) has its roots in this myth. Soiled goods offend Virgo, yet the goods must be soiled if life is to be lived. The anima-figure which most closely approximates this fantasy of perfection in Western consciousness is that of Mary, who embodies the self-containment and sacredness of the unstained soul. Mary remains miraculously virgin even after the birth of Jesus, and this reflects the ever-renewing qualities of the virgin goddess who may be harlot and mother yet who retains her essential intactness within.

I have said nothing of Hermes–Mercury, who is the planetary ruler of Virgo, in part because we have already met him in Gemini and many of his attributes belong to Virgo as well. But I have never been comfortable with Mercury as the sole description of the complex web of character that lies in Virgo. Perhaps there is another planet waiting to be found which might be a co-ruler; or perhaps not. Hermes may sometimes be seen in feminine form in alchemical texts, where he/she is shown as a mermaid or melusine with a fish's tail. This fish-tailed lunar Hermes is the ancient image

of the Syrian goddess Atargatis, who is herself half fish and whom
Frances Yates felt had the closest affinity to Virgo. In his feminine
form, the Mercurius of the alchemists is the virgin mother, the
womb of matter which will bring forth the divine son – who is also
Mercurius, in his masculine form. If we are to be content with
Mercury as the planetary ruler of Virgo, then we must extend our
understanding of him into this paradoxical lunar dimension. For
lunar it is, and despite the expressiveness, cleverness, dexterity
and shrewdness which are Hermes' gifts to Virgo as well as to
Gemini, the figure of the virgin goddess looms behind all in her
unfathomable mystery.

## LIBRA

*His greatness weigh'd, his will is not his own,*
*For he himself is subject to his birth;*
*He may not, as unvalu'd persons do,*
*Carve for himself, for on his choice depends*
*The safety and the health of the whole state.*
                    Shakespeare, Hamlet

Libra is the only sign of the zodiac which is represented by an
inanimate object. This may sound insulting, but it suggests to me
that as we arrive at the point of equilibrium reflected in the
autumnal equinox, we meet something which is very far removed
from the instinctual kingdom. Libra has a highly confusing early
mythology, and this is perhaps fitting, because the faculties of
judgement, reflection and choice which seem to be so basic a
feature of the sign are the fruit of conscious effort and not 'natural'.
The name Libra itself, which means the Balance, does not seem to
have occurred before the second century BC. This has led some
writers to believe that the sign did not even exist as a separate
entity in early astrology. Instead, the Scorpion was double the size
of the present constellation, and encompassed two distinct facets
or aspects. The part of the heavens which is now called Libra was
originally known as *Chelae*, the Scorpion's Claws. This is very
suggestive: that the scales of balanced judgement should have
developed from what was originally the gripping organ of the dark
underworld creature which has always represented the chthonic
realm. It is as though our noble faculty of judgement emerged from
something much older, more archaic and more primitive, and
evolved over time into what we now understand as objective or
impartial assessment.

Although Libra the Balance is almost 'new', however, images of
judgement in myth are far older. The Egyptians used the scales as a
symbol of the judgement of the souls of the dead by Osiris in the

underworld, and the myth of this rite of passage is perhaps relevant to our understanding of Libra. It does seem that the Egyptians knew the Balance, although the Babylonians did not; and the Chelae was sometimes portrayed as a scale-beam. An even stranger image comes to us from Babylon: the claws of the scorpion are shown holding the Lamp of Illumination. Amidst these confusing images of what we now know as Libra, it seems that a single figure begins to emerge: a goddess of justice, a sort of civilised Moira, who has acquired something more refined than the dark and bloody instinct for vengeance. This goddess judges according to human law and morality, however, unlike Astraea who is more of a representation of the orderly pattern of nature. Judgement in the Libran sense rests upon careful assessment and reflection, before any sentence is given.

In Egyptian ritual, when the soul of the deceased had safely crossed the country between the land of the living and the kingdom of the dead, he was ushered into the presence of Osiris by Anubis, the Egyptian form of Hermes Psychopompos, guide of souls. In the centre of the hall of judgement was erected a vast scale, beside which stood Maat, the goddess of truth, ready to weigh the heart of the deceased. Meanwhile, the monster Amemait, whose name means 'the devourer' – a species of early Erinyes, part lion, part hippopotamus, part crocodile – crouched waiting to eat the hearts of the guilty. Forty-two personages sat around the hall in their winding-sheets; some had human heads, some the heads of animals. To each of these assessors the soul of the deceased had to proclaim his 'negative confession' – that is, a list of all the bad things he did not do. After this came the weighing of the soul. In one of the pans of the balance Anubis placed Maat herself, or else the feather of truth which was her symbol. In the other pan, he put the heart of the deceased. If the two pans were in equilibrium, and therefore if the man's sins did not outweigh the feather of Maat, then the divine judges passed a favourable verdict.

Maat, like the Greek Athene whom I also associate with Libra, seems to have personified law, truth and social order. She is definitely a thinking, civilised Moira, an emergence of something reflective out of the natural eye-for-an-eye vindictiveness of the Scorpion's Claws. Maat's law is not that of the Mother, but that of the ethical and moral codes of society. The forty-two judges in the hall of the dead represented the forty-two 'nomes' or provinces of Egypt, and the individual's sins were very much related to his conduct in society. We have met Athene in this role already, in the story of Orestes; her human court, which votes on the young prince's fate, is something 'new', something different from the bickering and angry gods. It is as though myth is here suggesting that in this eminently human although 'unnatural' faculty of rational judgement lies a potential resolution for, or point of equilibrium between, the collisions and conflicts within the unconscious psyche which the Greeks so loved to represent as quarrelling deities and family curses. The goddess Astraea also possesses something of this quality of discriminating judgement, although as we have seen it lies in a different sphere; but it is my experience that both Virgo and Libra share a similar sense of outrage at the breaking of the rules. But Libra seems to project this vision of justice out into life in a heightened way. It forms the basis of the sign's intense idealism and belief in the fairness of life. I have never felt that Libra was concerned, as some popular descriptions would tell us, with romantic love, flowers and candlelight, except as an abstract concern with the appropriate rituals of courtship according to an ideal conception. Romantic 'feeling' is not a property of Libra. The sign is much more connected with questions of ethics and morality, judgement and apportionment. This theme of morality is one which I have encountered many times in the lives of Librans, for there is that within the sign which longs for the verification of this deity who holds the perfectly balanced scales of judgement; and in order to achieve such an experience, imbalance and extremes and the violation of the law are necessary happenings from which Libra does not readily escape.

The mythic image of Osiris judging the souls of the dead is a portrayal of the gods' judgement on man, and implies the existence of universal principles of right and wrong by which human life must be lived. These principles are not 'natural' in that they are not the laws of the kingdom of nature. But they belong to the realm of the human spirit and its vision of perfection. There are two mythic tales I would now like to explore where it is man's judgement of the gods which is the primary theme, and these myths have, I feel, bearing on the patterns which shape Libra's development. In these stories, a human being is called upon to decide an issue about which the gods are quarrelling, much as the human jury of Athens must pronounce judgement between Apollo and the Erinyes. The trouble which ensues after such a judgement is also a relevant theme in the myths, and implies that judging the gods is not a simple issue, nor one without its consequences. In the figure of Osiris and the scales of Maat we can see a vision which is dear to the heart of Libra: The cosmos is ultimately just and fair, and good is rewarded and evil punished. There is no sign so oriented towards the 'good, true and beautiful' as Plato puts it, although how that good is defined depends, in the end, upon the individual's definition of it. Libra, however, does not see it as an individual issue, but rather one of finding the universal ethics which transcend mere human choice.

But in the stories of Paris and Teiresias we find two humans who, because of their superior experience and perception, are called upon to do something which the gods themselves cannot do. Thus the vision of a just cosmos is something that the human spirit can contribute to life, and to the gods, rather than the other way around. Both Paris and Teiresias suffer consequences which strike me as typical of the kind of entanglements into which Librans have a tendency to stumble. For the business of judging, as these stories suggest, is a hazardous occupation because the gods themselves will not play by the rules.

Paris was the son of King Priam and Queen Hekabe of Troy. An oracle or dream had warned his mother that he would grow up to be the ruin of his country. Therefore the infant was exposed on Mount Ida, where he was saved and suckled by a she-bear. But his royal birth was eventually recognised by the outstanding beauty, intelligence and strength of the young prince. Because of his prowess with women and his superior powers of judgement, Zeus chose him to arbitrate between three quarrelling Olympian goddesses. The young man was herding his cattle one day when Hermes, accompanied by Hera, Athene and Aphrodite, appeared before him. Hermes handed him a golden apple, and delivered Zeus' message: 'Paris, since you are as handsome as you are wise in affairs of the heart, Zeus commands you to judge which of these goddesses is the fairest, and to award to the winner the golden apple.'

Since Paris was no fool, he understandably baulked at this request, knowing full well that whatever he did he would incur the anger of two of the deities. So, like a good Libran, he offered gallantly to divide the apple equally among the three. Zeus, however, would have none of this evasion, and demanded that the young man choose. Paris then begged all the goddesses not to be vexed with him should they lose; for the task had been foisted upon him against his wishes, and was none of his choosing. All three promised not to seek revenge should they lose the contest. The goddesses were then asked to disrobe. Athene insisted that Aphrodite remove her famous girdle, which made everyone fall in love with her and gave her an unfair advantage. Aphrodite insisted that Athene remove her battle helmet, which made her look more noble and distinguished. Hera did not stoop to such tactics, but merely removed her clothes with the dignity befitting a Queen of the gods.

Hera then offered Paris the rulership of all Asia, and promised to make him the richest man alive if he chose her. Paris, being a typical Libran, was not especially attracted by the responsibilities of such enormous wealth and power. Athene then promised that she would make him victorious in all his battles, but since this is a Libran myth and not an Arien one, that too held no appeal for him. Aphrodite, being herself by far the best judge of what motivated Paris, promised him the most beautiful woman in the world to be his wife. This was Helen, the daughter of Zeus by Leda and the wife of King Menelaos of Mykenai. Paris objected that Helen was already married; how then could she be his wife? Leave it to me, said Aphrodite, and Paris awarded her the golden apple without a second thought. By this judgement he incurred the hatred of both Hera and Athene, who, reneging on their own promises to be good losers, went off arm in arm to plot the destruction of Troy. When Paris eventually met Helen at her husband's court, the two fell instantly in love, and during the King's absence eloped together and fled to Troy. This incident provoked the Greeks to avenge the insult, and provided them with the excuse to do what they had always wanted to do: burn Troy to the ground. During this war, not only Paris but his three sons by Helen were slaughtered, but Helen, being semi-divine and blameless as Aphrodite's pawn, was returned repentant to her husband.

Thus Paris, one of the most Libran of mythic heroes, was confronted with the necessity of making a judgement – one of personal values and ethical choice – to which he responded in a characteristic way. That he came to a bad end does not imply that this is the concrete fate of Libra, although sometimes Libra's choices in love do lead to considerable confusion and difficulty. I have seen enough of the typical love-triangles of Libra, where such choices are thrust upon the individual to draw him into some fairly strenuous emotional dilemmas (and sometimes financial ones as well), to be convinced that in this myth lies a typical development pattern for the sign.

Teiresias, on the other hand, is a rather different kind of character. When we meet him in the tale of Oidipus, he is a blind seer, renowned for his insight and judgement. It is he who warns Oidipus that the accursed thing which has polluted Thebes is the king himself. But the story of Teiresias' blindness is an interesting one. There are several versions of this tale, and in one of them, Teiresias, like Paris, was called upon to judge who was the most beautiful among four goddesses: Aphrodite and the three Graces. By awarding the prize to one of the Graces, he incurred the wrath of the goddess of love, who turned him into an old woman. But the best known version of the Teiresias myth begins when he was once wandering on Mount Kyllene. There he saw two serpents in the act of coupling. When both attacked him, he struck them with his staff, killing the female. Immediately he was turned into a woman, and spent several years as a celebrated harlot. Seven years later he hapened to see the same scene at the same spot, and this time regained his manhood by killing the male serpent. Because of his unusual experience of both sexes, Zeus then called upon him to decide a judgement between himself and Hera. These two had been quarrelling, as was their wont, about Zeus' infidelities to his wife, and the god had defended himself by arguing that when he did share his wife's bed she had the better time because women derived more pleasure from the sexual act. Hera denied this, insisting that the truth was to the contrary, for why else should her husband be so flagrantly promiscuous? Teiresias, summoned to settle the dispute, replied:

> *If the parts of love-pleasure be counted as ten,*
> *Thrice three go to women, one only to men.*[111]

Hera was so exasperated by this response that she struck Teiresias blind. But Zeus took pity on him since he had, after all, taken the side of the god; so he was granted inner sight and the ability to understand the prophetic language of the birds. He was also given a life-span which lasted for seven generations and was permitted to keep his gift of insight even in the dark fields of the underworld.

Both Paris and Teiresias have forced upon them the necessity of making a judgement. This necessity springs from the gods themselves, who are, apparently, in dispute. In the case of Paris, the nature of the choice is not difficult to discern, for this is not really a beauty contest but rather a decision about what is ultimately of most value to him. Jane Harrison writes about the judgement of Paris:

> It is an anguish of hesitancy ending in a choice which precipitates the greatest tragedy of Greek legend. But before Paris was there the Choice was there. The exact elements of the Choice vary in different versions. Athene is sometimes Wisdom and sometimes War. But in general Hera is Royalty or Grandeur; Athene is Prowess; Aphrodite of course is Love. And what exactly has the 'young man' to decide? Which of the three is fairest? Or whose gifts he desires the most? It matters not at all, for both are different ways of saying the same thing.[112]

It would seem that, by the fiat of Zeus, Paris may not have all three, and that too suggests something about the 'fate' of Libra. He cannot have his cake and eat it too. We could as easily substitute a woman for Paris, and three male deities as the contestants. One might speculate fruitfully on what then would be the elements of Choice. Might one favour Zeus with his gift of power, or Dionysos with his gift of ecstasy, or Apollo with his gift of long sight? Or perhaps Ares for his courage, or Hermes for his cleverness, or Hephaistos for his artistic skills? This myth does not describe an exclusively masculine problem. It is perhaps relevant that it is among the attributes of the goddesses – the anima or soul – that Paris must choose; he is not called upon to select masculine goals which he favours, but those which pertain to his deepest inner values. But the choosing of one thing over another, which life seems to force upon Libra, not only contradicts the sign's innate desire for having everything in proportion rather than one thing at the expense of another. Such a judgement also involves psychological consequences, for any decision of an ethical kind made by the ego means the exclusion or repression of some other content of the psyche, which produces enormous ambivalence and sometimes great suffering. I believe that Libra's famous 'indecisiveness' does not stem from any congenital inability to make choices, but from the fear of the consequences those choices will entail. It might be argued that Paris made the wrong choice. But whichever goddess he had selected, the other two would have been angry; and had he refused to choose at all, then Zeus would have struck him down.

It is not surprising that Libra perpetually complains about the unfairness of life. So it is; poor Paris did not ask for his fate, and tried his best to avoid it by an equal division of the apple. But he is chosen from the beginning because of his superior experience and insight, and this implies that we must pay for our gifts and accomplishments. Perhaps life is just after all. It would seem that the development of Libra encompasses a curious paradox: that the sign is in love with the orderly laws of life and places great faith in their fairness, yet is perpetually confronted by the disorderly and immoral aspects of life, which fragment and divide Libra's cherished unity. Yet in these apparently unfair vicissitudes the footprints of a deeper and more ironic order may be tracked. Libra's propensity to get stuck in a choice between two women, or two men, or two vocations, or two philosophies, suggests that while the sign cannot bear division or disharmony in the universe, something within the Libran himself forever drives him to divide himself, so that he can discover himself through the deepening knowledge of the processes of choice.

Teiresias came to a better end than Paris, although he too had to suffer for his judgement. But there are compensations. His story is a strange one. Its beginning, with the vision of the two serpents coupling, suggests a kind of archetypal perception of the origins of life. We met the uroboros, the serpent which devours, slays and begets itself, in the sign Cancer, and the uroboros in alchemy is often imaged as a pair of serpents or dragons forming the circle of unity. Teiresias has evidently spied upon a deep mystery, for these snakes are the World Serpent, male and female together. Thus they attack him, for he has no business seeing what he has seen. It is like the mythic attack of Artemis upon Actaeon, who accidentally stumbled upon her bathing: Nature is jealous of her secrets. Libra's cool intellect undoubtedly spies where it is not 'permitted' to go, especially in the sphere of love, and love often turns and attacks the Libran for his disinterested judgement. In defence, Teiresias kills the female serpent – thus perhaps attempting to protect himself from the instinctual side of life. In doing so, he sacrifices his own manhood. That is perhaps an image of the price paid for this stage of the journey, for the distinctive repression of and distaste for the body and the fleshly odours of life which is so characteristic of Libra can result in a loss of self and a selling of the soul. But eventually the future prophet experiences once again his vision of the origins of life, and on this second occasion defends himself against the overriding patriarchal principle which has previously made him an enemy of his own sexuality. Thus he is restored to himself. This seesaw between male and female, spirit and body, seems typical of both the Libran man and the Libran woman. So, too, does the symbolic experience of the opposite sex, where one is estranged from one's own biology and is possessed by the trans-sexual unconscious. Libran men are traditionally known for their affinity with the 'feminine' sphere of adornment, ornamentation and beautification, while Libran women are known for their clear rational thinking and organising capacities. This myth of Teiresias suggests that the often ambivalent sexuality of Libra has archetypal roots.

It is as a result of the wisdom which Teiresias gained that he was honoured by Zeus to solve the Olympian marital squabble. This is like the judgement of Paris: a mortal is asked to provide what the gods themselves do not possess, the capacity to reflect upon the opposites with unbiased judgement. Teiresias suffers for his judgement, but had he sided with Hera, no doubt Zeus would have punished him instead. Like Paris, and strangely like Job in the Old Testament, Teiresias was made to pay for his too great insight into the nature of the gods themselves. But the old prophet was given a gift in exchange, and the image of blindness in myth is often a portrayal of the eyes turned inward towards the Self. Thus he can no longer be seduced by worldly beauty, as Paris was. Wotan in Teutonic myth also offered up one of his eyes in exchange for knowledge. The prophet's long life and position of honour in the underworld suggest that something eternal remains beyond the mortal span of the wisdom for which he had to pay such a high price.

I am inclined to feel that Paris is an image for the youthful Libran, Teiresias for the mature one. Somehow this issue of choice progresses from the necessity of deciding where one's values lie, and the ensuing conflicts, into glimpses of the deeper dilemmas where the gods themselves are revealed as double-faced and needing the help of man's consciousness. Through this insight both man and gods are changed. This is the theme to which Jung addressed *Answer to Job*, and I believe it is one of the underlying themes in Libra's fate. Not least of all the possible lessons inherent in the stories of Paris, Teiresias and even Job is the realisation that the gods may not be as just as man. If Libra can ultimately accept this, then his role as a bringer of civilisation and reflection becomes a genuine one, and dignifies the nobility of the human spirit.

## SCORPIO

*Here we may reign secure, and in my choice*
*To reign is worth ambition though in hell:*
*Better to reign in hell, than serve in heav'n.*
                    Milton, Paradise Lost

We have met in preceding chapters the realm of the archaic Mother whose theriomorphic images are the spider, the snake and the dragon. These cold-blooded creatures, far distant from the warm mammalian kingdoms of which man is a part, are images of the autonomous unconscious functions of the body: the snake as intestinal process, the whale and sea monster as womb, the root chakra at the base of the spine which is the seat of life. All the myths which we have explored in relation to Pluto are relevant to Scorpio, for in the grim figures of the Lord or Lady of the Great Place Below are imaged the presiding *daimones* of this zodiacal sign. We have also looked at the constellation of the Scorpion in relation to Orion the hunter, who offended the goddess Artemis–Hekate and was destroyed by her giant scorpion sent from the depths.

There are other mythic images which I feel are relevant to this sign, and these circle around the archetypal theme of the hero and the dragon. Just as the ram, the lion, the crab and the hostile sibling are differing aspects of the hero's quest, the dragon is a distinct entity, a relative of the World Serpent, and a representation of the daemonic forces of the unconscious experienced as Terrible Mother. Creatures such as the Erinyes are aspects of her, but one of her most common faces is the serpentine monster. The dragon fight is a universal motif, but it is particularly relevant to Scorpio, who must confront in perhaps greater depth and more frequently this reptilian face of instinctual life with its terrifying and destructive power. One classic myth of this kind is that of Herakles' battle with the Hydra. Another example is Siegfried's confrontation with the dragon Fafner who guards the Niebelung hoard. Perhaps we must all deal with this dragon at some time in our lives; but for Scorpio, there is a kind of cyclical collision, a permament and increasingly profound confrontation with the dragon's realm.

Another vivid image of the battle with the dark forces is portrayed in the story of Perseus and the Gorgon. Like all proper heroes, Perseus had a magical birth. His father was Zeus, he was endangered in infancy by a wicked male relative, and he grew up ignorant of his true parentage. He had many adventures, not all of which concern us here, but his confrontation with Medusa is an archetypal Scorpio motif. Medusa herself is part of Scorpio's journey, for as with all myths, hero and monster form a unity, two aspects of a whole. As the story goes, Medusa was once a beautiful woman, who happened to offend the goddess Athene:

> The Gorgons were named Stheino, Euryale, and Medusa, all once beautiful. But one night Medusa lay with Poseidon, and Athene, enraged that they had bedded in one of her own temples, changed her into a winged monster with glaring eyes, huge teeth, protruding tongue, brazen claws and serpent locks, whose gaze turned men to stone.[113]

Another version of this story tells that Medusa was raped by Poseidon, and that the terrifying visage which froze on her face was the expression of her horror and outrage. Either way, we are back to the familiar Scorpionic themes of rape and offended sexuality. Whether Medusa's horrific ugliness was the result of an outraged Athene or an outraged feminine spirit, they are in many ways the same thing, for Athene, the virgin goddess who is Zeus' wisdom, is an image of judgement against uncivilised behaviour. Medusa's face is a portrait of feminine anger and hatred, and her effect upon anyone who happens to look her way is paralysis. As a psychological picture, this is an exceedingly pointed one, for this enduring hatred towards life and the bitterness which leads to inner apathy are both problems which many Scorpios must sooner or later face.

Perseus was given the task of slaying Medusa in order to prevent his mother being forcibly married to King Polydectes. Here is the motif of redeeming one feminine figure by conquering another, darker one; but both, in essence, are Mother. The personal mother can only be redeemed if the archetypal one is confronted. Often, in a man, the inheritance of the mother's unconscious rage and bitterness taints his own inner soul, so that he carries her hatred for her; then the issue of redeeming not only the personal mother but his own anima from the grip of the Gorgon becomes a critical one.

This battle to free the feminine from the blacker face of nature is an integral part of the journey for both Scorpio men and women.

Perseus was helped on his quest by several deities. Athene warned him never to look at Medusa directly, but only at her mirrored reflection, and presented him with a brightly polished shield. As a symbolic image this is fairly self-explanatory; the capacity for reflection, for symbolic thinking, is fundamental in coping with the overwhelming rage of a Medusa. Hermes also helped Perseus, giving him an adamantine sickle with which to cut off the Gorgon's head. He also acquired a pair of winged sandals, a magic wallet to contain the decapitated head, and a dark helmet of invisibility contributed by Hades. All these magical implements could only be obtained through a visit to the three old Graiai, who had a single eye and tooth between them, and who knew the secret path to the Gorgon's lair. They are really another form of the three Fates, the Moirai. Thus, fate must be with him – as the alchemists would have said, *Deo concedente*. Naturally the hero succeeded in his quest, with all those divine powers on his side. He released, as a sort of by-product, the magical steed Pegasus, which sprang full grown from Medusa's body. This horse was fathered on her by Poseidon, but she was unable to give birth to it because of her hatred. Thus Perseus released her, as well as himself. The winged horse is a bridge between opposites, an earthy creature which has the power to ascend into the spiritual realm. Perseus was then able to use the Gorgon's head against his enemies, for having conquered the creature himself, he was in a position to utilise its powerful properties on behalf of more consciousness-directed goals.

The Gorgon, and the Hydra which Herakles must meet, are, it seems to me, characteristic images of the destructiveness which it is Scorpio's task to deal with. Medusa can only be beheaded through the power of the reflected image, for to stare directly at her is to be overwhelmed by one's own darkness. This is a psychotic state, and the blind terror and paralysis which one meets in certain forms of psychosis can find no better symbol than the Gorgon's head. The Hydra too has a particular formula by which it can be conquered, for like Medusa it is a semi-divine being, and like her when she brings forth the winged horse, the object is a transformation rather than a riddance or a repression.

The Hydra, according to Graves' description, had a prodigious dog-like body, and nine snaky heads, one of them immortal. It was so venomous that its very breath, or the smell of its tracks, could destroy life. This attractive creature is one known to many Scorpios. Herakles first had to force it to emerge from its dark cave with burning arrows, and then held his breath when he caught hold of it. But the monster almost overcame him, because no sooner was one head crushed than two or three more grew in its place. The hero shouted to his charioteer Iolaus to set one corner of the grove alight. Then, to prevent the Hydra from sprouting new heads, he seared the roots with blazing branches. Thus the flow of blood was checked – cauterised – and Herakles used a sword to sever the immortal head, part of which was gold, and buried it, still hissing, under a heavy rock.

These two dragon fights – Perseus with the Gorgon and Herakles with the Hydra – embody a wisdom about the preparation and handling of the reptilian poison which one finds if one digs deep enough. Neither monster can be conquered by brute force alone. Reflection is necessary, and fire – whether we take this as the burning of intense emotion held within, or as the light of insight and consciousness. Both creatures are divine, and cannot ultimately be destroyed, although they may transform. Whether these monsters describe the emotional darkness with which so many Scorpios must contend, or whether they are projected outwards into the world and are seen as the world's evil and suffering which must be purged, Scorpio's *daimon* drives him into collision with all that is terrifying, dark and destructive in life. Many Scorpios have contributed their resources to battling with the monster in society: Martin Luther (sun in Scorpio), Gandhi (Scorpio rising) and Freud (Scorpio rising) are but a few who have taken the dragon fight to a level which has generated changes in society and culture. But the most profound expression of this battle is within the individual, for Medusa and the Hydra are met in the dirty alleyways and swamps of one's own soul. They do not remain buried, but rise up and challenge the individual not once but many times during the course of life; and each occurence potentially yields new fruit.

There is a subtler form of dragon than these which Scorpio may meet, and this is embodied in the myth of Faust. Here, as with Parsifal, we enter the world of medieval legend, but the figure of the magician and his struggle with his dark double, the serpentine Mephistopheles, is an ancient tale. Mephistopheles himself is a true son of the Mother, 'that power that wills forever evil yet does forever good'. The story of Faust's lust for power and pleasure, his corruption and his eventual redemption, has spawned operas, novels, plays and dreams over the ages, for although we have more difficulty these days in believing in such creatures as Gorgons and Hydras, Mephistopheles is only just around the corner. The myth of the magus is a tale about the man or woman who, from bitterness, loneliness and isolation from his fellows, is willing to barter his soul for power over all those things in life which have injured him. Thus he acquires magical powers, but his soul is no longer his own, and he is doomed to eternal damnation. His devilish double now dogs him everywhere, and destroys any pleasure the power might have granted. In the end, everything he touches is blighted. Yet he is heroic, like Lucifer in *Paradise Lost* (Milton also had Scorpio rising), for he has dared to traffic in realms where the ordinary 'good' person would not have the strength to enter. And he still retains something worth saving which God wants. Hence, at the end of Goethe's great poem, he is redeemed.

> 'Mass here, mass there,' said Dr Faust. 'My pledge binds me absolutely. I have wantonly despised God and become perjured and faithless toward Him, and believed and trusted more in the devil than in Him. Therefore I can neither come to Him again nor obtain any comfort from His grace which I have forfeited. Besides, it would not be honest nor would it redound to my honour to have it said that I had violated my bond and seal, which I have made with my own blood. The devil has honestly kept the promise that he made to me, therefore I will honestly keep the pledge that I made and contracted with him.'[114]

Thus, according to medieval biography (which is more like biographical fiction) spoke the real Dr Faust, a shadowy and unimpressive figure who lost his life in a demonstration of flying and who harks back to the tradition of the sorcerer Simon Magus of *Acts* viii. Marlowe stayed close to the legend of the corrupt and foolish Dr Faustus in his drama, but Goethe, who had Scorpio rising and saw into it more deeply, turned it into a statement of the soul's journey through darkness to God. Goethe focused upon Faust's egotism and restless groping for power as his great flaw, but he infused into his character all the tarnished greatness of the fallen angel Lucifer. This egotism opens the door to Mephisto-pheles, the spirit of negation. Rather than being too hot and inflamed with passion, this reptilian devil is cold, so cold that he withers all that is youthful and innocent. In the introduction to his translation of *Faust*, Philip Wayne writes:

> It is perhaps an easy saying, but it has its depth, that cynicism is the only sin. This devil of Goethe's must be known to be appreciated. He is the world's most convincing portrait of Satan, and cynicism, scoffing, negation, is the keynote of his intellec-tuality ... He is more modern than yesterday. Today's typist encounters him if she finds, to her secret resentment, that in the office any word of aspiration is at once twisted with a grin into smut. It seems that Satan has present activity with an ancient title; for the old word *diabolos* turns out to have, before our

history, the same root as ballistics, and means, roughly, 'mud-slinger'.[115]

The attitude of cynical negation is a plague to many Scorpios. Often it lies beneath a more optimistic surface, and the individual does not know his own destructive negativity except in its inadvertent effects in life. It is a kind of depression or apathy, a conviction that nothing will ultimately work; and it often springs from the despair of childhood, and the peculiar sensitivity to the dark side of the psyche which the Scorpio individual possesses when very young. Faust ultimately makes a bargain with Mephistopheles, that the Devil can have his soul if he ever attempts to stop life and cling to the present moment rather than permitting change and flow. This is perhaps connected with the fixity of Scorpio, which because of the bitterness and negativity can often try to possess something happy or pleasurable rather than letting life flow through him; and at the moment of possession, the happiness is lost. Scorpio's reputation for jealousy and possessiveness, which often works as a bad fate within his relationships, thus is revealed to have more complex roots. This is how Faust puts it to Mephistopheles:

> *If to the fleeting hour I say*
> *'Remain, so fair thou art, remain!'*
> *Then bind me with your fatal chain,*
> *For I will perish in that day.*[116]

At the end of the poem, Faust almost pronounces those fatal words. But the restless striving spirit in him rescues him from falling into this trap. Although he dirties his hands with corruption and darkness, this is a necessary aspect of his quest not only for power, but for illumination and love. Therefore much is forgiven him. The Angels at the climax, hovering in the higher atmosphere and bearing all that is immortal of Faust upwards towards heaven, proclaim:

> *Saved is our spirit-peer, in peace,*
> *Preserved from evil scheming;*
> *'For he whose strivings never cease*
> *Is ours for his redeeming'.*
> *If, touched by celestial love,*
> *His soul has sacred leaven,*
> *There comes to greet him, from above,*
> *The company of Heaven.*[117]

The dyad of Faust and Mephistopheles seems to me a vivid portrait of a conflict inherent in Scorpio, who, despite his susceptibility to pride and egotism, cynicism and power-lust, nevertheless does not cease to aspire towards an experience of love which is ultimately his redemption. Whatever we may feel about Faust, he is one of the most complex and the greatest of literary creations, for he embodies an archetypal human dilemma. In Part Two of Goethe's poem he moves through an alchemical opus, through air, water, fire and earth, descending into the mysterious world of the Mothers and ultimately ascending again to heaven; and throughout this journey of burning and purification he never abandons his soulful striving.

Jung was fascinated by the figure of Faust. He saw in him the embodiment of a problem inherent in Western culture, the difficult and thorny path of walking the narrow tightrope between a renunciation of life sprung from bitter cynicism about the world's possibilities, and a too great identification with and indulgence in the realm of material gratification. Because Faust is both a spiritual and a sensual man, he falls prey to the traps of both: distaste for humanity on the one hand, and the rejection of God on the other. Jung describes his complex character as follows:

> Faust's longing became his ruin. His longing for the other world brought in its train a loathing of life, so that he was on the brink of self-destruction. And his equally importunate longing for the beauties of the world plunged him into renewed ruin, doubt and wretchedness, which culminated in the tragedy of Gretchen's death. His mistake was that he made the worst of both worlds by blindly following the urge of his libido, like a man overcome by strong and violent passions.[118]

In this portrait I imagine I can see a great deal of Scorpio's *daimon*, which pulls violently both upwards and downwards yet which, like the more primitive image of the dragon fight, must confront and ultimately learn to live with that vital and terrifying image of instinctual life of which the Gorgon and the Hydra are negative faces. The lofty aspirations of Scorpio, which as Jung points out can lead to a loathing for life, and its powerful sensuality, which wishes to drown in the world, are extremely uncomfortable bedfellows. Yet they spring from the same mysterious core, half sexuality and half spirituality, which leads Faust on his long journey. The difficult combination of spiritualised eroticism and eroticised spirituality is a handful for Scorpio. It is not surprising that so many Scorpios seem to repress or sublimate one or the other in despair that no reconciliation is possible. Faust thoroughly embraces both, although he 'made the worst of both worlds', and remains a figure of potential dignity and redemption.

## SAGITTARIUS

> *Nothing more certain than incertainties;*
> *Fortune is full of fresh variety:*
> *Constant in nothing but inconstancy.*
> Richard Barnfield, The Shepherd's Content

Before we explore the figure of the Centaur who represents the constellation of Sagittarius, we must first consider Jupiter, the planetary ruler of the sign, whose Greek name is Zeus. We have met him several times already, in particular in connection with the sign of Aries, but Zeus has a remarkably well-documented 'life history' and, like Aphrodite, is one of the most vital and vibrant of the gods.

Certain features which belong to Zeus–Jupiter will already be apparent in Robert Graves' amusing retelling of the story of the Creation of the World. Chief among these features is the intensely competitive, conquering, bombastic nature of this ultra-male deity. Although these qualities are traditionally associated with Aries, I have seen them no less in Sagittarius, who is not nearly so easy-going and good-natured as he is usually described in popular astrological lore. Although Zeus is created by Rhea and permitted to hold power only by her consent, he is determined to efface all signs of his dependency on the feminine. He never quite succeeds, however, for his marriage to Hera, queen of the gods, binds him once again to his feminine side. But he does not fail for lack of trying. The tales of Zeus and his paramours, and his turbulent marriage to his sister–mother–bride, reveal a highly individualistic personality to this powerful god which is not so 'macho' as it seems.

> Zeus did not come to power simply by means of his victory over the Titans; a victory which he owed, indeed, to Mother Gaia (Rhea) and some of her children. His dominion was founded much more upon marriages, upon allegiances with Gaia's daughters and granddaughters.[119]

Zeus is the father of gods and men. We have already seen that his name, *djeus*, means 'the light of heaven', so that he is the *daimon* of lightning and enlightenment. When he emerges as the victorious king of the gods, overthrowing the rule of the earthy Titans and establishing his own heavenly domain, he reflects the emergence into collective consciousness of a spiritual principle which is greater than Moira. It is therefore appropriate that Sagittarius should follow Scorpio, for Zeus embodies that which belongs to the eternal spirit rather than the mortal flesh. He is called Rain god,

Descender, Downpourer, Father, King and Saviour. He offers the light of the spirit, in contrast to the doomed and fated life of the body, held in the vicelike grip of Necessity. This is, as I understand it, the primary vision of Sagittarius – this ceaseless quest for a spirit which will transcend fate and death.

> In view of the mystery which envelops 'doom' and its con-summation – that is, where the circles of the gods and of fate intersect – it is conceivable that the greater the deity is the more easily it can be placed on a par with dark Necessity or even supplant it. When Agamemnon speaks of his fateful blindness he names Zeus ahead of Moira. But with thoughts of 'a decree of Zeus' or of 'the gods' the imagination turns from murky destiny to intelligent plan and counsel.[120]

As Sagittarius arises from the fumes of 'murky destiny' and the collision with the underworld which is embodied in Scorpio, so Zeus arises from the dominance of the chthonic Mother and assumes rulership over gods and men. Out of the gloom of Faust's realm of 'the Mothers', where man's powerlessness and mortality, his allotment of family fate and his share of collective evil have been recognised and accepted, rises that bright aspiration which forms the core of all religious rituals: the promise of the immortal spirit with its benign care, waiting in the embrace of the Good Father.

> The gods who now rule life as guides and as ideas no longer belong to the earth but to ether; and hence of the three realms and their gods ... only one remains as the place of divine perfection, and that is Zeus' realm of light.[121]

Thus Walter Otto describes Zeus, who is a far more comfortable deity than Moira – albeit unpredictable – and far closer to the God of our Judaeo-Christian dispensation.

But Zeus is not wholly free, nor is he wholly in command. He may have superseded Moira, or so Aeschylos believed, but his marriage to Hera is the eternal thorn in his divine side. This marriage contract – emphasised always as a *contract*, a binding and permanent tie like the runes of contract carved into Wotan's spear in Wagner's *Ring* – links him eternally to the feminine world of form. Unlike the Judaeo-Christian deity, Zeus cannot escape his wife. Hera is both spouse and sister, and Kerenyi stresses the importance of her status: she and Zeus represent a marriage of exact equals. They engage in perpetual matrimonial quarrels such as the one we met in connection with the prophet Teiresias, and this wrangling is a theme which seems to run true to type in the life-pattern of Sagittarius. Zeus forever pursues other women. The list of his lovers and his illicit progeny fills volumes. Hera forever thwarts him, spies on him, persecutes her rivals, spoils his romantic idylls, and attempts to destroy or drive mad his bastard children. These two remain eternally locked in battle and eternally wedded, an image of the fiery creator-spirit bound to the world of form, the world of human ties and human commitments, the world of morality and 'decency' and worldly responsibility which is as much part of Sagittarius' nature as the wild promiscuity of which Zeus is an emblem.

It is therefore not surprising that so many Sagittarians run headlong into the fate of a marriage like that of Zeus and Hera. The textbook Sagittarian avoids marriage because he feels trapped by too many rules and rigid expectations. He dislikes being 'tied', and prefers to be 'spontaneous' which means that he finds the consequences of his actions unpleasing and prefers to avoid them. But it is my experience that there is some kind of fate at work for those late-marrying Centaurs, male or female. They tend to find their Heras sooner or later. Of course, it may not be a spouse; it may be a job, or a cause to which the individual is bound, or a house, or some other object in the outer world. In one version of the Zeus–Hera saga, Hera, whose name simply means 'the mistress', seduced him with a love charm, a magic girdle. Brother and sister went to the marriage bed in secret, beneath the ocean, to avoid the vengeance of their father Kronos. This seduction through the magic girdle which seems so alluring, tends to trap Sagittarius, who despite his apparent worldliness and his freedom-loving nature tends to remain remarkably naïve about other people's motives. Frequently it is an actual pregnancy which traps him (or her). Yet without Hera, Zeus would be nothing. As Kerenyi points out, he owes most of his power to her and to her female relatives, and the friction and tension caused by the inviolable marriage bond does more than drive him into constant illicit love affairs. It also keeps him vital and alive. Without that friction he would fall slack and lazy, qualities which he displays in many stories, and it is doubtful that he would pursue his loves with such enthusiasm were they not forbidden to him.

'I do not heed your anger; what though you were to flee to the utmost end of the earth and sea, where Iapetos and Cronos abide, without sunshine or breath of wind; what though you were to travel even so far in your wandering, I would not heed your anger,'[122]

says Zeus to Hera in Homer, because one of her ways of retaliating against his infidelities is, much like her human counterparts, to leave him and go off on repeated journeys which always end with her return and their reconciliation. Yet despite Homer's brave portrayal of him, he does in fact heed her anger; he must chronically reassert his manhood.

Zeus mated with Eurynome, daughter of Okeanos, and begat on her the three *Charites* or Graces. *Charis*, according to Kerenyi, is the word from which *chairein*, 'to rejoice', is derived; so, too, is our word 'charity'. It is the opposite of *erinus* and the Erinyes, who personify hate and vengeance and the anger of the Mother. Here Zeus' progeny provides a counterpoint to the Mother-dominated underworld, for 'to rejoice' means to be beyond the confines of Moira's gloom. Zeus also mated with Themis, a Titan, and she bore him the Horai. Their names are Eunomia ('lawful order'), Dike ('just retribution') and Eirene ('peace'). Thus his struggle to be free of Hera generates many of the qualities which we traditionally associate with Sagittarius; and, perhaps more importantly, a realm of justice is born which is an alternative to the merciless vengeance of Nature and Necessity, Nemesis and Moira.

Another of Zeus' paramours was Mnemosyne, which means 'memory', and their children were the nine Muses, the culture-bringers. Strangest of his loves was the goddess Necessity herself. Here Zeus unites with Moira. Wotan does this, too, with the prophetic earth goddess Erda, and fathers the Valkyries on her. Zeus, according to the tale, pursued Necessity over earth and through the sea. She transformed herself into many shapes to escape him, eventually choosing that of a goose. He in turn transformed into a swan, and coupled with her. She laid an egg, and the child born of this egg was the famous Helen whom we have already encountered, who helped to start the Trojan War. (In the more common version of the story the mother of Helen is Leda, Queen of Sparta.) Thus, in conquering Moira, Zeus unleashed upon mankind another kind of fate: fatal beauty, fatal attraction. Moira's death-fate may be broken by the illumination of the spirit, but she takes her revenge in the fateful power of sexual attraction.

The list of mortal women whom Zeus seduced or pursued is endless. By Danaë he fathered the hero Perseus; by Semele, the god Dionysos; by Europa, King Minos of Crete; by Demeter, his sister-goddess, the maiden Persephone; and on and on. What I understand to be the chief point in all this is his endless fertility, his boundless creativity, his restlessness and inconstancy, and his Protean inventiveness. These are his characteristics; but Hera is his fate.

We may move now to the curious figure of Cheiron, or Chiron, the Centaur whose image forms the constellation of Sagittarius. There are two stories about his parenting. In one, Ixion, a mortal man, beheld the goddess Hera and coveted her. Being a dutiful wife, and also desirous of making her husband jealous, she reported this to Zeus, who, in order to discover the truth, fashioned an image of his wife from a cloud and called her Nephele. Ixion, fooled by the deception, embraced the cloud, and begat on it a child that was half-man, half-horse. Sometimes this child is called Kentauros, and he mated with the mares on Mount Pelion and bred a race of Centaurs, those wild forest-dwellers on whose four-legged body of a horse was set the upper body of a man. Cheiron was one of these. Sometimes the horse-child is represented as Cheiron himself.

The second story of the Centaur's birth makes him the son of Kronos–Saturn, and therefore half-brother to Zeus. Kronos once lay with Philyra, daughter of Okeanos, and was surprised by his wife Rhea in the act. Whereupon he turned himself into a stallion and galloped off, leaving Philyra to bear her child as half-man and half-horse, the Centaur Cherion. Loathing the monster she had to suckle, Philyra prayed to the gods to be freed, and was turned into a linden tree.

Whichever story we consider, Cheiron is a son of earth, by mortal or Titan, and not an Olympian. He was known as the wisest and most righteous of the Centaurs. His fame as healer, scholar and prophet spread everywhere. But he is a chthonic deity, and belongs to that group of phallic or half-animal tutors of the gods who symbolise the wisdom of nature and of the body itself. Cheiron became King of the Centaurs, and in a cave beneath the summit of Mount Pelion he brought up the heroes and sons of the gods. Outstanding among these was Asklepios, the semi-divine healer, to whom the Centaur taught the physician's arts.

> In an old vase-painting he appears in a robe covered with stars, with an uprooted tree over his shoulder carrying his spoils of the chase, and with his dog beside him: a savage hunter and dark god.[123]

This 'hunter and dark god' has a tragic fate. Like Zeus, he is trapped, and it is his body which ensnares him. While entertaining Herakles on Mount Pelion during that hero's efforts to capture the Erymanthian Boar, he was accidentally wounded by one of Herakles' arrows – in the knee, foot, or thigh, depending upon the version of the myth, but in any event in the horse part of him. These arrows were dipped in the blood of the Hydra which the hero had killed and whom we met a few pages ago; and they were deadly poison. Distressed at the accident to his old friend, Herakles drew out the arrow, and Cheiron himself supplied the medicines for dressing the wound. But they were of no avail, and the Centaur retired howling in agony to his cave. He could not die, for he was immortal; but he could not live, because the Hydra's poison had no antidote and his anguish could not be alleviated. Much later, when Prometheus committed his theft of fire and was punished by Zeus and then freed by Herakles, Zeus demanded a substitute for Prometheus, an immortal who went down into the underworld and suffered death in his stead. This immortal was Cheiron, and the inventor of the art of healing took upon himself the death of the beneficent Titan Prometheus who brought fire to man.

This is a sad tale with an even sadder end. The noble and kindly figure of the wise Centaur scarcely deserves such a fate. Yet the image of the suffering Cheiron with his incurable wound somehow fits, like shadow to light, the imperious and unquenchable figure of Zeus, the king of gods and men. Perhaps where there is so much light, there must be darkness. The wound lies in the animal aspect of the Centaur, and is in the leg – that which we must stand on, or take our stand, in the material world. Cheiron is one of a long list of lamed gods who have been injured in the foot, or, in other words, in their relationship with physical reality. All his wisdom cannot help him, because the poison of the Hydra is the incurable poison of life's shadow side. My feeling is that this sadness and woundedness are an integral part of Sagittarius, and form a kind of depression or despair beneath the bright optimistic surface of the sign. I believe this is why Sagittarians can be so manic in their strenuous efforts to be happy and entertaining. Zeus creates thunder and lightning in heaven, and there is no sign more positive or resilient. But hidden in his cave is the suffering Centaur, who can heal and give wise prophetic advice to every man's ills save his own, and who is poisoned by the collision of his benign nature with the darkness and poison of the world.

Perhaps because of this wound, Sagittarius is able to offer hope and optimism to himself and others, rather than despite it. This is not a sign which is at home in the body; nor is it comfortable with the limitations and mundane requirements of life. The character of Sagittarius is truly that of Zeus. Its direction is upwards, following the flight of the archer's arrow, and the sense of life's meaningfulness and the benignity of the spirit is what is most readily recognised, and appreciated, by others. But there is sometimes a fanaticism in Sagittarius' enthusiastic preaching of the gospel, and fanaticism is generally closely linked with deep inner doubts. I have found that there is sometimes a profound bitterness and hurt which lurks underneath, and it is, in a sense, incurable: that is, it is a psychic fact which generates much of Sagittarius' aspiration, and provides the impetus for his upward flight. It is incurable because man cannot be a god. So it cannot be said that this depression or woundedness is 'bad', because it is in many ways the most creative aspect of the sign. Put another way, it is the suffering of the animal in man, which cannot fly so high, which is mute, and which is bound to the laws of nature. This is the part left over from the battle in Scorpio, the poison which remains. If Sagittarius can bear to face such a wound, then it strengthens him immeasurably, because he does not aspire quite so high and can therefore produce with his gifts in a more practical and relevant way. Cheiron's self-sacrifice is also important, for he offers up his life on behalf of Prometheus and takes his place in the underworld with Zeus' consent. His own gifts, those of earth-magic, are thereby lost to men, while the gift of fire which Prometheus has given is now acceptable and no longer a sin. What this might mean I am not sure; but it suggests the theme of a sacrifice of the magical intuition and 'luck' which so often accompanies Sagittarius in the early part of his life, and which may need to give way to a more conscious adaptation to the world.

Zeus is the *daimon* who presides over Sagittarius, but the myth of Cheiron hangs in the background, forming the shadowy underworld of the sign. I once met a Sagittarian man who told me that he had an actual wound: he had had an accident just after his marriage, when he was in his twenties, when he fell down a flight of stairs. A splinter entered his hip, and the wound had never healed. Despite the best medical attention and courses of various antibiotics, it remained septic and continued to suppurate slightly, and caused him some considerable pain. The constant presence of this physical problem, although not serious enough to impair either his working or personal life, was sufficient to quiet him down and make him thoughtful, because such a problem in the body conveys a strange and autonomous feeling – as though it comes from 'somewhere else' and has a mind of its own. He happened to hear me speaking about the myth of Cheiron at a workshop, and found it both disturbing and startling that his own life fitted the myth so exactly. I likewise found it disturbing, but not startling, because I have encountered literal enactments of myths before. It is always a little frightening when the world of the archetypal images clothes itself in flesh in such an obvious way. Usually we are more covert in the ways in which we live out the ancient tales. One must ask oneself what such a thing might mean. Perhaps for this man only something as tangible and awkward as a physical disability could suffice to turn his usually outgoing and fiery spirit inwards to contemplate such profound issues as the point of his life, or the deeper meaning of marriage, which coincided with the injury.

But this is precisely where Cheiron's wound leads. Like all else in myth, it can be understood teleologically. The wound points upwards to Zeus and the eternal life of the spirit; and it also points down to the equally divine life of the body which must bear such a fiery soul and suffers accordingly. Like the *magnum miraculum* of the *Corpus Hermeticum*, Sagittarius is a creature worthy of dignity and honour, part *daimon* and part god, part beast and part immortal, who turns his eyes to the immortal half of himself, and must then pay the necessary price of caring for the suffering body he has so long ignored.

## CAPRICORN

*Wist ye not that I must be about my Father's business?*
St Luke ii.49

We have seen through the preceding signs how myths are not only images of life-patterns, but are also modes of perception which colour the individual's way of seeing and experiencing his life. Therefore they appear, both inside and outside, as qualities of soul and as worldly events. For Scorpio, life is focused upon the battle with the serpent-monster, or with the devil; for Sagittarius, on the flight upwards from the suffering flesh to the arms of the eternal spirit. For Capricorn, whose familiar goat is one of the oldest symbols of lechery, lust and fertility, the *daimon* circles downwards again, and the spirit, refreshed by its revelation of the 'light of heaven', now prepares for its initiation into bondage in the name of the Father.

In both Homer and Hesiod, the planet Saturn is given two Titans who preside over its powers: Kronos and Rhea. These were earth gods, fathered on Gaia by Ouranos the sky-father. He, repelled by their ugliness, banished them to Tartaros. Gaia persuaded her sons to attack their father, and armed Kronos, the youngest of the seven, with a flint sickle, the signature of the moon and of the goddess' power. Kronos grasped his father's genitals in the left hand and hacked them off, and threw the organs into the sea. The drops of blood flowing from the wound fell upon Gaia the earth, and she bore the Erinyes. Encapsulated in this story is a conflict very different from the bickerings of Zeus and Hera, although we have met facets of it already in Aries: the confrontation between father and son.

The theme of the sacrifice of the old king to ensure the fertility of the crops is an ancient motif which I relate particularly to the sign Capricorn. The king must die, the new king must be born, and the two must fight and, in death, be revealed as one. In Aries, son meets father as a fire god, whose jealous wrath challenges nascent manhood. In Leo, son meets father as a sick spirit, whose wound must be redeemed through consciousness. In Capricorn, the father is the earth itself, the reality principle. Alchemy took up this motif of the old king and portrayed him descending into the depths of the sea, where he mates with his mother or sister, is dismembered, and is reborn as the young king from his consort's womb. Old King Kronos eats his children to protect himself from their threat, knowing full well that he may face the same fate as his own father; the hidden son rises in rebellion, just as he himself did, a story as inevitable as fate itself. Kronos' earthy nature, as a Titan, immediately relates him to the Earth Mother. Gaia and Rhea are the same goddess, both representing the fertility of the earth. Kronos is not an independent masculine principle, but rather the masculine side of the generative principle over which the Mother presides. His cousins, Pan and Priapus, are phallic images of nature's fertility. Kronos and his sickle are, according to Graves, symbols associated with ritual king-sacrifice: the bill-hook carried by Saturn, Kronos' Roman counterpart, was shaped like a crow's bill (the word Kronos not only means 'time' but also 'crow'), and the crow was believed to house the soul of a sacred king after the sacrifice. This ritual sickle gave the signal for the death which would fertilise the earth and renew the crops. Kronos was worshipped at Athens as the barley god Sabazius, and was annually cut down in the cornfield and bewailed like Osiris. He is himself both the young king and the old, for what he does to his father is later done to him. This duality and unity of father and son, *senex* and *puer*, is one of the dominant mythic motifs of Capricorn.

The ancient symbol of king-sacrifice is also newer than we might think, for it is present in the figure of Christ, the son of God and the King of the Jews. He was born (like all sacrificial king-redeemers) at the winter solstice, a birthday he shares with Mithras, Tammuz, Adonis and even King Arthur. This is the time of year when the sun is weakest and the world is darkest. The earth lies in waste and the people long for redemption; barrenness and death lie everywhere, not least within the souls of men. T. S. Eliot in *The Wasteland* puts this most beautifully:

> *What are the roots that clutch, what branches grow*
> *Out of this stony rubbish? Son of man,*
> *You cannot say, or guess, for you know only*
> *A heap of broken images, where the sun beats,*
> *And the dead tree gives no shelter, the cricket no relief,*
> *And the dry stone no sound of water.*[124]

We have met this waste land in the story of Parsifal and the Grail; but where Parsifal is Leo's version, Capricorn's is that of the sick Grail King himself. Like Attis, Christ the son of God is nailed to a cross: the tree of matter, mother, material life. It is an image which bears similarity, as Fraser knew in *The Golden Bough*, to the annually sacrificed king dismembered and ploughed into the earth to renew the crops. But the ritual dismemberment of the Eucharist renews the spirit, and has left behind long ago that prototype which was meant to renew nature. The theme of the waste land and the long wait for the redeemer in depression, despair and deadness is all too often a pattern in the lives of those born under Capricorn, not least the ones who have achieved the worldly success for which the sign reputedly strives so hard.

One may see the enactment of the myth in apparently ordinary ways. The burdensome shouldering of unwelcome responsibility, so characteristic of Capricorn's rite of passage, seems to reflect this crucifixion in matter. Imprisonment, limitation and bondage belong to the early part of Capricorn's life, whether this means going to work in father's business or marrying the woman one has made pregnant, or any one of a myriad obligations which bind with no hope of release. Often Capricorn walks willingly into this bondage, although other alternatives may be open to him. It is as though he seeks and welcomes this fate, for obscure and often unconscious motives. I have also met many Capricorns who put off this day of reckoning as long as possible, living almost wholly in the *puer* or *puella*, fearing the suffering of the bondage, and no less dominated by it in rebellion as in compliance. But the fate of Capricorn is not that of Sagittarius. The Father's arms are not open to receive such a prodigal son unless he has paid in good solid coin, for this Father does not live in heaven, but in the earth itself. Back and down the prodigal must go, to be nailed upon the cross of worldly experience. The crisis of despair and lost faith also belongs to Capricorn, the cry of Christ on the cross: Father, why hast thou forsaken me?

The mythic theme of atonement with the father is one about which Joseph Campbell writes eloquently in *The Hero With a Thousand Faces*. Capricorn almost always seems to find the personal father a disappointment, just as Leo does, for the Father he seeks is nothing less than divine. But the wrath of this father is a deeply significant issue for Capricorn. Saturn is the Terrible Earth-Father, and his devouring and destroying face, his jealousy and paranoia and power-lust provoke the experience of guilt and sin which seem to be so embedded in Capricorn's psychology.

The ogre aspect of the father is a reflex of the victim's own ego – derived from the sensational nursery scene that has been left behind, but projected before; and the fixating idolatry of that pedagogical non-thing is itself the fault that keeps one steeped in a sense of sin, sealing the potentially adult spirit from a better balanced, more realistic view of the father, and therewith of the world. Atonement (at-one-ment) consists in no more than the abandonment of that self-generated double-monster – the dragon thought to be God (superego) and the dragon thought to be Sin (repressed Id) . . . One must have a faith that the father is merciful, and then a reliance on that mercy.[125]

I understand Campbell to be saying by this that the father–son polarity, the avenging Lawgiver whose strict and structured rules of life collide with the lusty, libidinous goat-like desires of the son, exists within the one individual. Morality and shame, law and lawlessness, seem to comprise some of the polar opposites of Capricorn. The son must face the father's punishment, only to find that the father is within himself; and the father, the old king, must face the son's rebellion, only to find that it is his own youthful spirit that he thought he had outgrown long ago. The initiation of the son by the father is an inner experience which, it seems as though by fate, Capricorn is often denied in the actual parental relationship, and he must therefore seek it within himself on a deeper level. By this description I am, as usual, not talking about men only, for this father–son constellation belongs as much to woman and her capacity for effectiveness and self-sufficiency in the world as it does to man.

When the child outgrows the popular idyl of the mother's breast and turns to face the world of specialised adult action, it passes, spiritually, into the sphere of the father – who becomes, for his son [or daughter] the sign of the future task . . . Whether he knows it or not, and no matter what his position in society, the father is the initiating priest through whom the young being passes on into the larger world.[126]

This rite of initiation, with its revelation of father first as ogre and persecutor, its requirement of acceptance of the 'rules' and conditions of the world, and its ultimate vision of a merciful Father and an immortal soul, seems to be the archetypal Saturanian path. The young man or woman does not wish to observe the conditions or the necessary preparations; it must be done now, it must happen now, why should one wait? This is the quality of the *puer*, for whom all things must be instantaneous and spontaneous. But Capricorn's initiation is not won by boyishness or girlishness. For anyone undergoing a transit or progression involving Saturn, this ritual is offered at the deepest level; for Capricorn, it recurs over and over in life, for each thing that is worth having must be approached by the route that winds past the throne of the Father.

*Come, O Dithyrambos,*
*Enter this, my male womb,*

cries Zeus to Dionysos his son in Euripides' *Bacchae*, and this entry
into the world of the Father and the separation from the Mother
forms the leit-motif of Capricorn's passage through life. Often the
manifestation of this movement occurs in the field of work: the
commitment to a vocation and to worldly life. Acceptance of
earthly responsibility and limitation is also the process of passage
from being the son to being the father, from boy to man, from
ungrounded spirit to active contribution in incarnation. Incarnation also involves a sense of community, a species of service,
and one of the more difficult aspects of the descent is the participation in the community life – which for the *puer* is an irritant and a
threat because it seems to spoil his specialness and uniqueness,
and offends his narcissistic focus. Paradoxically, the 'imprisonment' which is entailed in such a commitment is also a freeing. It is
the atonement with the Father, without which no genuine living-
ness of faith can enter life. Otherwise, spirit remains an ideal 'up
there' somewhere, and falls to bits when put to the test of challenge, conflict and failure. Failure is a necessary aspect of Capricorn's journey, for his faith is meaningless unless it is tried against
his despair.

Following is the dream of a Capricornian client, a man who came
to have his horoscope interpreted during the period when Saturn,
his sun sign ruler, was transiting in conjunction with Pluto across
his ascendant at the end of Libra. This long transit had taxed him in
many ways. My description of the themes of imprisonment and
limitation provoked him to tell me the dream.

> I am with my wife in a prison. It is a peculiar place because the
> doors are open, and we are free to leave. But there is a feeling of
> having voluntarily accepted this imprisonment. A female guard
> stands outside the door, an older dark woman. She watches
> impersonally but does not interfere. My wife is uncomfortable
> about shutting the door, which I feel is necessary to show that
> we have freely consented. I reassure her, telling her that the
> imprisonment will not last forever, but for reasons which in the
> dream are obscure, we must endure it.

At the outset of the transit, my client had been experiencing great
dissatisfaction with his job, his marriage, his children, and his own
physical body. Everything in his life seemed a trap. He had
achieved considerable success in the field of law, but had never felt
it was really 'him'; there was always something else that might
have been better. This is characteristic of the *puer*, who lives in a

perpetually provisional state where the 'real thing' is always later, but never now. Now is only a trial run, and therefore not worthy of full commitment. My client had always carried a sense of 'one day when I grow up', a feeling of discontent and a fantasy of greater fame and achievement and a more satisfactory relationship 'one day'. The youth is not yet prepared to become father, because he fears the loss of creative possibilities and the destruction of the fantasy that he can be anything. So he remains a youth, although my client was a father in fact and well into middle age. Although he was getting on in terms of age, he had only just begun to experience the inner initiation of father to son, and the paradoxical freedom of the voluntary imprisonment.

This dream suggests to me that my client was gradually changing through the course of the Saturn–Pluto transit over the ascendant, and that he was on the verge of understanding that the 'real thing' was whatever was in his life. This is, at its most profound, a religious attitude, for it is an acceptance of what one has been given and a voluntary decision to treat what has been given with respect and with the whole of one's care. The theme of this dream, which seems to me to be about an ultimate coming to terms with one's life *as it is*, is echoed in Mary Renault's novel, *The King Must Die*, where old King Pittheus of Troiezen says to the young Theseus:

> Listen, and do not forget, and I will show you a mystery. It is not the sacrifice, whether it comes in youth or age, or the god remits it; it is not the blood-letting that calls down power. It is the consenting, Theseus. The readiness is all. It washes heart and mind from things of no account, and leaves them open to the god. But one washing does not last a lifetime; we must renew it, or the dust returns to cover us.[127]

The motif of voluntary imprisonment and crucifixion runs like a red thread through the dream- and fantasy-life of Capricorn. This seems true regardless of the religious persuasion of the individual, or his sex; for the relationship between *puer* and *senex*, youth and old man, can be equally relevant for the woman whose creative spirit seeks expression in external life. The birth in flesh, the sense of sin before the wrathful father, the despair and bondage and dark night, the cynicism and loss of faith, and the dawning sense of a firm spiritual principle or ethical code by which one can at last commit oneself – all these are, in human form, the enactment of the myth of the redeemer who must die in order to renew the old king. If life does not provide experiences ready at hand for Capricorn to make his rite of passage, then he will create his problems for himself. It is no wonder that, given the choice of the easy way or the hard, the Goat will almost always take the hard one. Nor is it surprising that it is only later in life that the jubilant boy, at last contained by the Father, looks out of the eyes of the middle-aged man, or the young girl, full of the joy of a youth she probably missed in actual youth, smiles from the face of the experienced woman. This faith fought hard for, doubted, lost and found again in darkness is the sustenance of the mature Capricorn, who – man or woman – can then father the next generation with grace.

> Through the Christian church (in the mythology of the Fall and Redemption, Crucifixion and Resurrection, the 'second birth' of baptism, the initiatory blow on the cheek at confirmation, the symbolical eating of the Flesh and drinking of the Blood) solemnly, and sometimes effectively, we are united to those immortal images of initiatory might, through the sacramental operation of which, man, since the beginning of his day on earth, has dispelled the terrors of his phenomenality and won through to the all-transfiguring vision of immortal being.[128]

In psychological terms, the *puer* and the *senex* are embodied in the myth of Saturn-Kronos first overthrowing his father, then becoming father, then devouring his own sons to prevent them from doing the same to him, and at last being himself overthrown by the young Zeus. Whether the *senex* is the personal father, a set of rigid 'superego' ethics within the person, or the external institutions and authorities of the outer world, Capricorn's *daimon* seems to drive him into this cycle so that he can experience its duality within himself. James Hillman in his book *Puer Papers* quotes from the tenth century *Picatrix* a prayer to Saturn:

> O Master of sublime name and great power, supreme Master; O Master Saturn: Thou, the Cold, the Sterile, the Mournful, the Pernicious; Thou, whose life is sincere and whose word sure; Thou, the Sage and Solitary, the Impenetrable; Thou, whose promises are kept; Thou who art weak and weary; Thou who hast cares greater than any other, who knowest neither pleasure, nor joy; Thou, the old and cunning, master of all artifice, deceitful, wise and judicious; Thou who bringest prosperity or ruin and makest men to be happy or unhappy! I conjure Thee, O Supreme Father, by Thy great benevolence, and Thy generous bounty, to do for me what I ask.[129]

Needless to say, this prayer is a mass of paradoxes and contradictions. Hillman points out that in the figure of Saturn, the dual aspect is more vividly real than in any other Greek god-figure – even more than in Hermes. Father Saturn is both pernicious and truthful, bounteous and stingy, terrible and merciful. What he is not, in this prayer, is youthful; for the youth in himself is experienced in the suppliant, and is projected outside. Hillman feels that astrology itself is a Saturnian art, because it concerns the limits and boundaries within which the individual must develop:

> Thus personality descriptions of the senex given by astrology will be statements of the senex by the senex. It is a description from the inside, a self-description of the bound and fettered condition of human nature set within the privation of its characterological limits and whose wisdom comes through suffering those limits.[130]

To accept these limits is, in a sense, for father and son to become one.

I would now like to explore the strange Capricornian goat–fish which is the astral emblem of the sign. The mythic tale associated with this constellation seems at first disconnected from the theme of the crucifixion and resurrection of the king. According to Graves, the fish–goat or goat–fish (depending upon where one wishes to put the emphasis) is Amaltheia, the goat–nymph who suckled the young Zeus on Mount Dicte when his mother, Rhea, hid him from the devouring wrath of his father, Kronos. This is a paradox, and we have met it already in several myths. Kronos himself is the Old Goat, and god of fertility; in Teutonic myth as well as in Greek, the goat is associated with the harvesting of the grain, and with the abundant Cornucopia full of the fruits of early winter. Amaltheia is the succouring goat, the one who gives life to the young and helpless son; Kronos is the destroying goat, who will eat his own young. Thus, as in the case of Theseus with his bull-father, a single symbol unites all the characters.

Zeus was grateful to Amaltheia for her kindness, and when he became lord of the universe he set her image among the stars as Capricorn. He also borrowed one of her horns, and it became the Cornucopia or Horn of Plenty which is always filled with whatever food or drink its owner may desire – a kind of Grail. This bounteous side of Saturn was worshipped by the Romans at their Saturnalia, which coincided with our Christmas; in other words, in Saturn's month. The strange pairing of the positive and negative sides of the goat embedded in this myth seems to suggest, as with Theseus, that there is a profound collusion between the dark and light aspects of the same deity. The Terrible Father, who seeks to destroy his son secretly and unconsciously, also offers him salvation through the feminine aspect of the same emblem which he himself wears. It is this secret collusion which is quite awesome to meet in analytic work. One becomes aware that despite the individual's fears, resistances, symptoms and problems, there is something, whatever word one chooses to give it, which has a secret purpose to those very symptoms and problems, as though divided against itself, yet on some very hidden level undivided and working towards the greater wholeness of the individual. That principle which causes Capricorn his greatest suffering – the rigid, guilt-ridden, narrow, fearful, paranoid old king – is also the same principle which gives him the endurance, determination and foresight to struggle through that which blocks him, just as in the myth where one face of the *daimon*, Kronos, attempts to destroy while the other face, Amaltheia, succours and preserves.

It is interesting, in context of the symbolism of the goat–fish, to discover that there is a myth connected with it even older than that of Kronos and Amaltheia. This is the ancient figure of the Sumerian water god Ea, whose symbol is the fish-tailed goat. This god Ea later translated into Oannes in Greek, and the name Oannes in turn became John; and we arrive at the mythic figure of John the Baptist, who has older theriomorphic forerunners, and who prophesies the coming of the redeemer. This is the paradox of that strange father–god to whom Capricorn is bound, the *daimon* of his fate. It is in many ways akin to Yahveh, although it is more God's law than God's fire that we meet in Capricorn. This is the perverse and antinomian God who both afflicts and succours Job, and paradoxically, according to Christian doctrine, brings His only son into the world and then crucifies him, thereby Himself suffering the fate of mortals, in order to redeem both them and, secretly, Himself.

## AQUARIUS

*For Mercy has a human heart,*
*Pity a human face,*
*And Love, the human form divine,*
*And Peace, the human dress.*
        Blake, Songs of Innocence

We arrive now at the sign of the 'New Age', which in the 1960s was proclaimed to be the age of love and brotherhood but which, it is increasingly apparent, may be a little more complex than that. Aquarius is a complex sign, with two planetary rulers, Saturn and Uranus; but its rulers, unlike those of Scorpio, have little in common. In fact they are enemies in Greek myth, as we have seen, and the struggle between them seems to portray an inherent duality or ambiguity within Aquarius itself. We have seen quite a lot of Kronos–Saturn already, and there is little mythic material on the sky god Ouranos save the fate he suffers at the hands of his son. In fact the only salient piece of information we have about this ancient and elusive deity is that he was repelled by the children he begat on his mother–wife–sister Gaia, the earthy Titans and the grotesque hundred-handed Giants, and imprisoned the whole brood in Tartaros, the bowels of the underworld, so that they would not offend his aesthetic eye. This tells us a good deal about Aquarius, in fact, more than the paucity of material might suggest. I have seen this process of repression of the earthy and the bestial so often in Aquarians that it seems a fundamental necessity of the sign. The offensiveness that the crude and the chthonic hold for Aquarius accounts, perhaps, for its ceaseless efforts to reform and redeem mankind, and its almost ferocious civilising instinct which is forever worrrying at the baser aspects of the human personality like a dog at a bone. Like Ouranos, the 'heavenly' *daimon* of perfectionism suffers eventually at the hands of that which it has cast out, but is redeemed in other, more ambiguous forms. The severed genitals which Kronos throws into the sea breed the goddess Aphrodite, who combines in herself both the sensuality of the earth-born Titans and the aestheticism of the sky god who is her father. The Erinyes, as we have seen, are also his progeny, born of his suffering and his blood, and are a kind of permanent law against the shedding of the blood of kin.

But we must look further afield than Ouranos if we are to grasp the mythic pattern of Aquarius. My feeling is that an equally important figure who embodies much of the meaning of the sign is the beneficent Titan Prometheus, who comes of the same race as Kronos yet who sides with Zeus in his battle against his father, and who ultimately takes the side of man against the gods. Prometheus is the great cosmic social worker, whose theft of fire from Zeus to give to man embodies a spirit which is not content with merely instinctual life, but must forever grow better and more enlightened.

There is some disagreement about Prometheus' birth in the stories. All agree that he was a Titan, but he is sometimes Hera's illegitimate child, and sometimes the son of Iapetus the Titan. His name means 'the one who foresees' or 'the provident'. He had a brother, Epimetheus, whose name means 'he who learns only from the event' or 'the heedless'. Together these two Titans seem to describe opposite qualities of the human spirit. Because Prometheus was gifted with foresight, he knew the outcome of the rebellion of Zeus against his father Kronos, and although he was himself a Titan he wisely preferred to fight on Zeus' side. He assisted at the birth of the goddess Athene from Zeus' head, and she in turn taught him architecture, astronomy, mathematics, navigation, medicine, metallurgy and other useful arts. These in turn he passed on to man. In fact, the oldest version of the

Prometheus myth tells that it was the Titan himself who made men, with the consent of Athene, out of clay and water in the likeness of gods; and Athene breathed life into them. This is similar to the Talmudic account of Creation, where the archangel Michael (Prometheus' counterpart) formed Adam from dust at the command of Yahveh.

The arts which Prometheus taught man mark him as the *daimon* of the cultural impulse. He is an image of that instinct which strives to raise man beyond his animal origins – i.e. to become godlike. There is a long passage in Aeschylos' *Prometheus Bound* which expresses eloquently the gifts which the Titan, against the wishes of Zeus, has bestowed on man:

> *Of wretched humans he [Zeus] took no account, resolved*
> *To annihilate them and create another race.*
> *This purpose there was no one to oppose but I:*
> *I dared. I saved the human race from being ground*
> *To dust, from total death.*[131]

Prometheus goes on to speak of how men could not understand nor see things properly, nor comprehend the world around them; how they could not build houses, possessing no carpentry; how they could not make sense of the orderly cycle of the changing seasons and the growing of crops. He tells of how he introduced them to astronomy and mathematics, the training and care of animals, and shipbuilding. He also taught them medicine and healing and prophecy and the reading of omens, and the working of gold, silver and iron.

> *So, here's the whole truth in one word:*
> *All human skill and science was Prometheus' gift.*[132]

This benign impulse of good will toward mankind I feel to be one of the dominant themes in Aquarius, and it is certainly the one which most descriptions of the sign portray. But the myth of Prometheus is not so simple, for there is another character in the story who also belongs to Aquarius, with whom the Titan is involved in kinship and enmity: Zeus, king of the gods. Zeus wanted to destroy man, and spared him only at the Titan's plea; and he grew gradually angrier and angrier at the increasing powers and talents which Prometheus' human protegées began to display. This is the jealous God of Genesis, who does not wish His creation to partake of the fruit of the Trees of Knowledge and Life, lest man become as God. Zeus here is more like his own father Kronos, and seems to embody that aspect of the psyche which does not wish to become conscious, but attempts to thwart and hold back the development of the individual ego, threatening dire punishments and instilling a sense of sin in the renegade. Prometheus is incessantly at odds with Zeus over the issue of how much or how little mankind should be permitted in its development. It is as though these two deities represent some profound truth about the nature of ourselves. I feel that Aquarius, whose powerful impulse towards the development of the civilised and conscious aspects of man is well known, has likewise an equally powerful antithetical aspect within him, which forms the drama of his own mythic pattern.

Prometheus evidenced his contempt for Zeus' tyranny in numerous ways. According to the tale, one day the Titan was invited to act as arbiter in a dispute about which portions of a sacrificial bull should be offered to the gods and which given to men to eat. He flayed and jointed the animal and sewed its hide to form two open-mouthed bags. Into one he put the delicious flesh, concealed beneath the untempting stomach. Into the other, he put the bare bones, covered with a rich layer of fat. Then he offered Zeus the choice. The god, easily deceived, chose the bag with the bones and fat, and in fury at the deception punished Prometheus by denying man the gift of fire. 'Let them eat their flesh raw!' he cried. Prometheus then went to Athene, his patroness, who let him into Olympus by the back stairs. He lit a torch at the fiery chariot of the sun and broke from it a fragment of glowing charcoal. This he thrust into the pithy hollow of a giant fennel stalk. Then, extinguishing his torch, he stole away and delivered the sacred flame to man.

Zeus swore revenge. He ordered Hephaistos, the divine smith, to make a clay woman. The four Winds breathed life into her and all the Olympian goddesses adorned her. This woman, called Pandora, Zeus sent as a gift to Epimetheus, Prometheus' brother. But Epimetheus had been warned by his foresighted sibling to accept no gifts from Zeus, so he refused the woman. Zeus then had Prometheus chained naked to a pillar high in the Caucasian mountains where a greedy vulture (or eagle) tore at his liver all day, year in and year out. Every night the liver grew whole again. Epimetheus, alarmed by his brother's fate, married Pandora. She opened a jar which Prometheus had warned him to keep closed, and in which he had been at pains to imprison all the Spites that might plague mankind: Old Age, Labour, Sickness, Insanity, Vice and Passion. These flew out in a cloud, and attacked the race of mortals. Delusive Hope, however, which Prometheus had also shut in the jar, discouraged men by her lies from a general suicide.

The suffering of Prometheus, intended by Zeus to be eternal, was, however, finite, for the hero Herakles pleaded for his release, and it was granted. We have already seen how the Centaur

Cheiron offered to exchange mortality with the Titan, so that Hades should not be cheated of a soul. Having once condemned Prometheus to everlasting punishment, Zeus stipulated that, in order to appear still a prisoner, the Titan must wear a ring made from his chains and set with Caucasian stone. Mankind now began to wear rings and wreaths in honour of their benefactor, and Zeus set the arrow which Herakles used to shoot the vulture which tormented the Titan in the stars as the constellation Sagitta.

Prometheus is the redeemer of mankind from darkness. As he himself says in Aeschylos' tragedy, all arts and sciences which the human race has developed stem from him. This beneficent aspect of the mythic figure is recognisable enough in the Aquarian concern for human welfare and development. But the problem of Zeus is less simple, and likewise the image of his torment. Here is the parodoxical problem of the urge towards consciousness colliding with the urge towards unconsciousness. Prometheus is not 'man' in the sense of the ego; he is the *daimon* who seeks to help man develop. This perpetual tension on an archetypal level creates inevitable suffering, because the collision is inevitable. We can look upon Prometheus as a hero, because he has offered man the divine creative fire. But from the point of view of the gods' world, he has committed a crime, a sin, and this situation is one which Jung was particularly concerned with: the sense of sin which arises when any effort is made at individual realisation.

Jung had Aquarius on the ascendant, and therefore his preoccupation with this problem must have had something to do with him as well as something he observed in his patients. By opening up the Pandora's box of the unconscious, he was, paradoxically, playing both the role of Prometheus and that of Zeus. His constant doubt in the validity of his own work is, I think, some indication of what that vulture or eagle attacking the liver might mean; for the liver, in ancient astrological–physiological correlation, is the organ of Zeus–Jupiter and therefore Zeus' vulture destroys that part of the mortal body which is also the god himself. We are back yet again to that peculiar doubling of symbols which we have already met several times. The god punishes Prometheus through the very aspect of the Titan which reflects the god. Perhaps this might be described as his faith, or his belief in himself. I have found that, side by side with the genuine altruism of Aquarius, there also lies a profound self-doubt, and I have rarely seen people quite so adept at self-punishment and self-denigration as those Aquarians who have managed to express something of the Promethean spirit and have contributed something, however small, to individual or collective evolution. In traditional astrology the sun is in 'detriment' in the sign of Aquarius, and this is said to indicate that the principle of self-expression and self-confidence is hampered by Aquarius' perpetual concern with the power and viewpoint of the group. Aquarius is often tormented with the horror of being 'selfish', and is the most riddled of all the signs with 'shoulds' and 'oughts'. The myth suggests a deeper ground for this fear of self-fulfilment. It implies the problem of the sense of sin which accompanies any real effort at development.

> Genesis represents the act of becoming conscious as a taboo infringement, as though knowledge meant that a sacrosanct barrier had been impiously overstepped. I think that Genesis is right in so far as every step toward a greater consciousness is a kind of Promethean guilt: through knowledge, the gods are as it were robbed of their fire, that is, something that was the property of the unconscious powers is torn out of its natural context and subordinated to the whims of the conscious mind. The man who has usurped the new knowledge suffers, however, a transformation or enlargement of consciousness, which no longer resembles that of his fellow men. He has raised himself above the human level of his age ('ye shall become like unto God'), but in so doing has alienated himself from humanity. The pain of this loneliness is the vengeance of the gods, for never again can he return to mankind. He is, as the myth says, chained to the lonely cliffs of the Causcasus, forsaken of God and man.[133]

I could not put this better than Jung has, and no doubt he knew all too well the 'pain of this loneliness', because he stole a considerable amount of fire. Needless to say, isolation from fellows is a profoundly painful dilemma for the socially minded Aquarian. We are Jung's beneficiaries; but no doubt the man himself had, despite the remission of punishment which occurs in the myth, to continue to wear the ring forged from his chain, the reminder of the offence against the gods. All the traditional Aquarian fields of endeavour – science, invention, social welfare, psychology, even astrology – are tainted with this loneliness which is the price of offending Zeus. It forms the secret shadow-impetus behind the one who 'must' help others, for it is through these helping relationships that some little portion of the intense loneliness of insight is alleviated. It is well to remember that Lucifer, that rebellious angel who opposed the wishes of God, means 'light-bearer' in Latin, and that in Aquarius we have met another form of the dialogue between rebellious son and jealous father. In Capricorn, this dialogue occurs between the father who has crystallised into old rigid forms, and the son who rebels against these worldly restrictions to the detriment of his own productivity. In Aquarius, we are confronting that jealous god whose creation has illicitly spied out the secrets of his origin.

It is probably relevant that in one version of the Prometheus myth, Zeus remits the punishment not out of compassion or favour to Herakles, but because Prometheus the foresighted knows the future fate that awaits the king of the gods. Zeus, reluctant to have this information withheld from him, allows himself to be blackmailed. Once again we encounter that mysterious left-handed handshake which is the secret collusion between conscious and unconscious. Zeus, although he could have blasted Prometheus into atoms for his sin, permitted him to continue to exist and even to go free, because the Titan had something the king of the gods himself needed. He required knowledge of the future from Prometheus, and guidance in how to meet it. This is the old alchemical heresy once again, that God needs man to achieve the work of perfection. It is also one of the major themes which runs through Jung's work, and which infuses it with such a deeply mystical feeling. The struggle towards individuation is not just a 'cure' for neurotic discomfort, but a sacred work done both for man and God. Ego and unconscious thus possess a strangely ambivalent relationship. They are enemies, yet they are dependent upon one another. Zeus and Prometheus sprang from the same seed: Ouranos the sky god, who is the image of the eternal heavens. But they are of different stock: Zeus is an Olympian, and therefore 'airy', while Prometheus is a Titan and therefore 'earthy'. One is allied to spirit, the other to the world. Their delicately balanced relationship is full of dangers, yet it is a partnership of equals, in value if not in nature.

We may now consider the actual constellation of Aquarius, and those myths which are connected with it. The Waterbearer in Egyptian lore was the god who presided over the river Nile. He was called Hapi, and was portrayed as a vigorous fat man with woman's breasts, dressed as a boatman or fisherman, who resided near the First Cataract in a cavern where he poured water to heaven and earth from his urns. Because the whole of Egyptian civilisation depended upon the yearly flooding of the Nile, Hapi was an important deity. But he did not do anything else besides pour his water. The Greeks put an altogether different myth upon the constellation: that of Ganymedes the beautiful son of King Tros of Troy. According to this story, he was the loveliest youth alive, and Zeus desired him and chose him to be cupbearer to the gods. The Olympian disguised himself as an eagle and abducted the boy to heaven. Afterwards, on Zeus' behalf, Hermes presented King Tros with a golden vine and two fine horses in compensation. Ganymedes was made immortal and dispensed nectar to the gods, while Zeus set his image among the stars as the Water-bearer.

What relevance this pretty little myth might have to the complex psychology and fate of Aquarius is not immediately apparent. Robert Graves has the following comments to make about it:

> The Zeus–Ganymedes myth gained immense popularity in Greece and Rome because it afforded religious justification for grown men's passionate love of a boy ... With the spread of Platonic philosophy the hitherto intellectually dominant Greek woman degenerated into an unpaid worker and breeder of children wherever Zeus and Apollo were the ruling gods.[134]

Now I am inclined, since not all Aquarians are homosexual, to take symbolically, rather than literally, this charming story of gay Greek gods. Graves connects the myth with a repudiation of the feminine, and a reduction in its power. This is certainly a relevant theme for Aquarius. There is a noticeable horror of the base and the biological inherent in the sign – we have seen this already in the story of Ouranos rejecting his Titan children – and there is likewise a deep fear of the irrational. The image of homosexuality in myth might, among other things, suggest an exclusively masculine world, a place where women and the instinctual plane of life cannot enter – a union which produces no offspring other than those of the mind and spirit. This applies no less to the Aquarian woman than to the Aquarian man, for she is often more at home with masculine company and masculine ideals. The tribal custom of taking pubescent boys away from their mothers and setting them up in exclusively masculine 'clubs' or groups in order to counteract the power of the feminine, matriarchal realm is an anthropological parallel which suggests how archetypal is the quest for male strength in the exclusion of the feminine. Zeus and Ganymedes together reject Hera the Mistress. When the king of the gods takes a female paramour, Hera can at least compete. With Ganymedes, she cannot even get near it. I feel this is an Aquarian pattern, although it generally occurs in spheres other than the sexual one. This sign is most definitely the champion of light and spirit, and the only feminine deity with whom Prometheus himself had any dealings at all was Athene, herself hardly a friend of the Great Mother as she is a father's virgin daughter. Thus the Promethean world is a masculine world, in which the drama of the struggle for evolution and its inevitable repercussions are imaged.

## PISCES

*Teach me half the gladness*
*That thy brain must know,*

*Such harmonious madness*
*From my lips would flow*
*The world should listen then – as I am listening now.*
　　　　　　　　　Shelley, To a Skylark

The sign of the Fishes is steeped in myth, for unlike many of the other zodiacal creatures, the lineage of this last of the signs clearly precedes the Greeks by many centuries. Pisces is also one of the most surprising of signs, for an exploration of its myths yields insights which are not normally associated with the traditional 'sensitive soul' who may become a drunkard, a musician or a nurse. The last sign is also the first, because it forms the background from which the new cycle will spring; and when seen in this way, it is not strange that the symbolism of the Fishes connects us not with the god Neptune, nor with any other male deity, but with the primal Mother whom we have already met in the sign Cancer, whose manifestation is water.

The fish has a very old and varied symbolism. It is one of those theriomorphic images which spans the spectrum from the orgiastic watery depths of the fertility goddess to the transcendant flesh of Christ. Like the dove, which traverses the same spectrum and is Ishtar's and Aphrodite's bird as well as the symbol of the Holy Ghost, the fish is both pagan and Christian, and ultimately feminine in nature. If we pick our way through the tangle of interconnected tales and deities, we will eventually arrive at a common theme. The earliest Egyptian and Babylonian stories about the two heavenly Fishes associate them with the Syro-Phoenician fish cult of the great goddess Atargatis, whom we met in connection with Virgo. Her temples had pools with sacred fishes in them which no one was allowed to touch. Meals of fish were ritually eaten in these temples, for the goddess herself was sometimes portrayed in the form of a fish, and her priests wore fish skins. This fish goddess had a son, called Ichthys, and he too was a fish. Later he evolved into the Babylonian fish god Ea, who is also associated with Capricorn, the goat–fish. Atargatis and Ichthys are also Ishtar and Tammuz, Kybele and Attis, Aphrodite and Adonis. According to the Babylonian story, two fishes found a giant egg in the Euphrates, which they propelled to land. There a dove settled on it. After a few days there emerged from the egg the goddess Atargatis. At her request, the fishes were honoured by being placed in the heavens. In the Greek version of this tale, Aphrodite and her son Eros fled from the monster Typhon, disguising themselves as fishes; or, in another version, they were rescued by fishes, who were repaid for their kindness with a place in the sky. So that they should not be separated, their tails were tied together.

That the Great Mother and her seasonal, ritually sacrificed son–lover are fishes is not so strange if we understand the way in which the fish was symbolised in myth. Jung describes this nicely:

The mythological Great Mothers are usually a danger to their sons. Jeremias mentions a fish representation on an early Christian lamp, showing one fish devouring the other. The name of the largest star in the constellation known as the Southern Fish – Fomalhaut, 'the fish's mouth' – might be interpreted in this sense, just as in fish symbolism every conceivable form of devouring *concupiscentia* is attributed to fishes, which are said to be 'ambitious, libidinous, voracious, avaricious, lascivious' – in short, an emblem of the vanity of the world and of earthly pleasures ('voluptas terrena'). They owe these bad qualities most of all to their relationship with the mother- and love-goddess Ishtar, Astarte, Atargatis, or Aphrodite. As the planet Venus, she has her 'exaltatio' in the zodiacal sign of the Fishes.[135]

So one of these fishes is the great fertility goddess, and the other her son. She is devouring, destructive and lascivious: the primordial world of instinct. He is the redeemer, Ichthys, the Christ. They are bound forever by the cord which ties their tails; they cannot escape one another. The ambivalent attitude towards the fish in ancient religious symbolism reflects this pairing, for on the one hand it is unclean and an emblem of hatred and damnation, and on the other it is an object of veneration. Ironically, the fish was also sacred to Typhon, that monster from whom the goddess and her son fled disguised as fishes; so yet again we meet that repetition of a single image in myth, where both pursued and pursuer wear the same form, and that which redeems bears the same countenance as that which is damned. Perhaps we are here confronting an image of the transient yet sacred life of the individual soul, born out of the Mother and doomed to return to her, forever bound to her, yet for a brief season the fertiliser of the earth and the creative spark which renews life.

The Piscean myth is therefore closely connected with the Mother and her lover–son, and in particular with the mythic tragedy of the son's early death and resurrection. The seasonal redeemer god is dismembered by the Mother herself, or by one of her totem animals – boar, snake, stag, wolf. We met this redeemer son in Leo and in Capricorn, but in those signs he is the son of his father. In Pisces we meet the Mother's child, the bittersweet tale of the son who is 'on loan' only for a season, and whose poignant story has come down to us only thinly disguised in Christian doctrine. The connections of the astrological age of the Fishes and Christianity are obvious, particularly in the references provided by the Gospels themselves – 'fishers of men', fishermen as the first disciples, miracle of loaves and fishes. The symbolism shows Christ and those who believe in him as fishes, fish as the food eaten at the religious meal, baptism as an immersion in a fish-pond, and so on. The dismembered Christ is ritually eaten, his blood ritually drunk; in this sense he is the direct descendant of Attis, Tammuz and Adonis, and his early death on the cross of wood, the tree-symbol of the Mother, is a fated death not because Roman or Jew has pronounced it, but because the Mother has called him home again.

The theme of redeemer and victim is very close to the heart of Pisces. Whether the individual Piscean identifies more with the victim and becomes the one whom life has dismembered, or with the redeemer who is the saviour of suffering, there is not much to choose between them, for they are two facets of the same thing. So too is the voracious fish, the goddess, from whom the victim must be rescued; or to whom the redeemer must be sacrificed to absolve others of sin. These three images – saviour, victim and devouring monster of sin and damnation – are part and parcel of the same mythic motif. It has speciously been said that Pisces people incarnate either to suffer or to save. As a generalisation, it is truer than most, and it is usually both, for only the injured has compassion. No sign is so inclined to present itself as life's victim, nor is any sign so inclined to genuine empathy for suffering. Nor have I seen any sign so quick to flip into the chaos and orgiastic licence and dissolution which is embodied in the image of the wild goddess Atargatis, the watery element out of which, as the Koran tells us, all life comes.

What does this tell us of the developmental pattern of Pisces? I think first of all that it implies that the two fishes cannot be separated. For Pisces, the chaotic world of the Mother is always uncomfortably close. From those depths Pisces, like Cancer, may create; there is a long list of musical, artistic and literary 'great names' who have manifested the sweet and tragic longings of that watery world with its boundless depths. Most of these people suffered greatly in their personal lives. This bondage to the world of the unconscious is no easy task for a man in our culture. It is often terrifying for masculine psychology to find itself a Son of the Mother, because dismemberment always looms so close; and even in artistic creation the experience of death and dismemberment, for Pisces, is an integral part. I have met many Pisceans who have tried to become super-rational, intellectual creatures, yet it always rings a little false, because just beneath the surface lies the irrational world. Often these Pisceans will become fatally involved with people who act out the goddess' chaotic world for them; thus they touch the depths vicariously, and become the 'nurses' of the mad. Einstein, a Piscean who made his greatest contribution in the world of science and mathematics, was an unashamed mystic. He knew very well whose gift his intuitive insights were. Yet to live in such proximity to the depths, to be bound to the Mother with such a cord, is not an easy life. Easier by far is the woman who identifies with the Mother, and succours the victim—husband, the lover who has been hurt by life, the sick patient who needs her care.The frightening shadowy side of this scenario is that she (or he) may have a great unconscious investment in the loved one *remaining* sick. And even if such an identification is partly successful, there also looms the orgiastic darkness of the goddess, and her propensity to devour her lover–sons. In our modern show-business world, we might consider a film star such as Elizabeth Taylor, herself a Piscean, for the twentieth-century's enactment of such a role, seeking her redeemer in an absurdly lengthy list of husband–candidates.

The planet Neptune, which is the astrological ruler of Pisces, is not, to my mind, a very good mythic description of the depths of this sign. Neptune's antecedents lie in the Greek god Poseidon, Earthshaker and Lord of Bulls. He is an earthy rather than a watery deity, although he nominally rules the sea; but this latter domain is taken from the sea goddess Thetis. The oceanic depths have always belonged to the goddess, as have the depths of the underworld, and Neptune is a very late arrival. The Babylonian Ea is a more suitable image, but he cannot be separated from his mother. If I must choose a single mythic figure who embodies what I understand to be the curious androgynous complexity of Pisces, I would look to the god Dionysos, whom Walter Otto in his study of the deity believes to be an image of 'creative madness', and whom Kerenyi, in *his* study, calls 'the irrational ground of the world'. In the birth, life and attributes of Dionysos we shall find a vivid description of the *daimon* who presides over Pisces, and spans the spiritually sublime world of his father Zeus (Jupiter is the co-ruler of Pisces) and the mad, ecstatic depths of the Mother.

Kerenyi begins his *Dionysos* by distinguishing between two Greek words for life, *zoë* and *bios*. *Bios* carries the ring of characterised life; it is attributed to animals when their mode of existence is to be distinguished from that of plants. We, of course, derive our word biology from this root. *Zoë*, on the other hand, is life in general, without further characterisation. Animals and plants each have their season and die; but life as *zoë* is infinite, and does not encompass death. It is the life-force which sustains through the cyclical changes of forms. Kerenyi quotes Karl Otfried

Muller, a classical philologist and mythologist of the nineteenth century:

> Nature overpowering the mind and hurrying it out of a clear self-consciousness (whose most perfect symbol is wine) lies at the basis of all Dionysian creations. The cycle of Dionysian forms, which constitutes as it were a peculiar and distinct Olympus, represents this nature-life with its effects on the human mind, conceived in different stages, sometimes in nobler, sometimes in less noble shapes; in Dionysos himself the purest blossom is unfolded, combined with an *afflatus* which arouses the soul without destroying the tranquil play of feelings.[136]

If we can pick our way through the nineteenth-century mannerism of this description, what seems to be implied is a sense of unity on the instinctual as well as the spiritual level. It is the state of *participation mystique* with nature, with animals, plants and wine, all of which appear in material identity with the god. This ecstatic unity with natural, undying life – best known in individual dream-image as the orgy – is combined in the personality of the god with an experience of acute suffering. Dionysos is a sort of shadow-Christ, a Christ with a phallus, for he himself, like Christ, is both victim and redeemer.

The mother of Dionysos is variously named in myth. Sometimes she is Demeter, whom Zeus raped; sometimes Persephone, her daughter. More usually she is Semele, daughter of King Cadmos of Thebes, with whom Zeus had a secret love affair. Hera, jealous as usual, disguised herself as an old neighbour and convinced the girl to demand that Zeus appear before her in his true form. Semele, not recognising that this would destroy her, coaxed a promise from the king of the gods to give her whatever thing she desired, and then asked him to reveal his godhead. She was already six months pregnant. Condemned by his own promise, Zeus was forced to appear as thunder and lightning, and Semele was burned to ashes. But Hermes saved her unborn son, and sewed him up inside Zeus' thigh and in due course delivered him. Thus Dionysos was called 'twice-born', or 'the child of the double door'. He is a male born of a male, yet he is a womanish god and a god of women, usually portrayed as an effeminate soft-featured youth. At birth he was a horned child, crowned with serpents. One of his totem animals is the goat, symbol of fertility and lustfulness. At Hera's orders the Titans seized him, and despite his transformations into animal shapes, tore him into shreds. They boiled the pieces in a cauldron, while a pomegranate tree sprouted from the soil where his blood had fallen.

But his grandmother Rhea rescued him and brought him to life again. He was raised in secret, disguised as a girl (like Achilles, who suffered a similar indignity). But Hera found him again, when he reached manhood, and drove him mad. He went wandering all over the world, accompanied by his tutor Silenos (a satyr) and a company of wild Maenads. He taught the art of the vine to Egypt and India, and then returned to wander around Greece. Eventually he arrived at Thebes, the place of his mother's birth. There King Pentheus, whose name means 'the one who suffers' (like Dionysos himself), disliked the god's dissolute appearance, and arrested him and his shabby train. But Dionysos drove the King mad, and Pentheus found that he had shackled a bull instead of the god. The Maenads escaped and went raging out upon the mountains, where they tore wild animals in pieces. King Pentheus attempted to stop them but, inflamed with wine and religious ecstasy, the Maenads, led by the King's mother Agave, rent him limb from limb and wrenched off his head. Thus he met the same fate as the god whom he had rejected.

The story of Dionysos is a cruel one, and the god himself displays a savagery unparalleled by any mythic figure save the one to whom he is the closest: the Dark Mother as Kali, Bast or Sekhmet. That I should associate this quality of savage cruelty with the gentle and inoffensive Pisces may seem strange; but it is as well to remember historical Pisceans such as Kemal Ataturk, who in 1915 saw fit to massacre nearly a million Armenians in an act of genocide nearly comparable to Nazi Germany. Such Pisceans embody the devouring fish of the sign, the monster Typhon, who is the perpetual companion of the redeemer. It is the innate savagery of nature, the crowd which kills Christ, the boar which rends Adonis, the Death Mother who requires the flesh of children and the hearts torn out of the breasts of her sacrificial victims. But nature can also be loving and benign, and so too can Dionysos. The sweetness and ecstasy of his rites, which included both the brutality of dismembered animals and the poignant unity with the godhead, embodied this ambivalent spirit of nature, the *daimon* which is both vicariously destructive yet promises eternal life.

Kerenyi quotes Bernhard Schweitzer:

> It is a form of world-experience, one of those great fundamental forms of man's confrontation with the things that we call 'mystical' and whose specific nature can only be characterised by the catch-word 'Dionysian'.[137]

The strange link between mysticism, the seeking of union with the divine, and the bloody cruelties embodied in Dionysos' revenge upon Pentheus his human double, is one of those paradoxes which consciousness finds difficult to digest. It is inherent in virtually all the stories about the saints, which combine the holy with the vicious and sadistic; somehow these figures belong with the fates they attract. I believe that in Pisces these two opposites live side by side. It might even be possible to suggest that each generates the other. It is therefore not surprising that many Pisceans flee into the safety of the intellect to offset this dilemma. The enmity between Hera and Dionysos, son of Zeus – the youthful god is sometimes called the 'subterranean Zeus', suggesting an identity between the two – is the enmity (and love) between mother and son, where the boundaries between love and hate, possession and destruction, blur and the erotic becomes the devouring. Dionysos is a Zeus of women, whereas the Olympian is a Zeus of men. When worshipping Dionysos, the women kept to themselves; no man might be present at the rites. Our word mania is the same as the Greek *mania*, which means both raging love and raging hate or anger. The word Maenad, the female worshipper of the god, comes from the same root. The god himself is called *mainomenos*, which means raging in the sense of passionate. Redemption from the savagery of the passions is the task of the son, the redeemer; the passions themselves are the Mother. Yet in a strange way this god towards whom the aspirant longs, with whom he seeks unity, is not really a male deity, and certainly not the patriarchal Yahveh of the Old Testament or the Zeus of the Greeks. He is an androgyne, as female as he is male. Both the horror and the longing begin and end in the same sea. Kerenyi, writing about the ivy and the grape which are both associated with Dionysos, says:

> The growth of the ivy presents only soothing, comforting features. A special aspect of life is here disclosed: its least warm, almost uncanny aspect, also presented by the snake. Such is *zoë* reduced to itself, yet forever reproducing itself. In the ivy, it is present not as meaning but as reality: not as the meaning of a symbol or as an allegory for abstract ideas, but concrete and reassuring despite its inedible bitter fruit. The sweet fruits are borne by the vine, which with its slow, spreading growth is capable of imparting the greatest restfulness, and with its rapidly fermenting juice of arousing the greatest unrest, a life so warm and intense that one living thing inflicts upon another that which is the irreconcilable opposite of life: death.[138]

Whichever part Pisces plays in this mythic drama, he is in reality all the actors; or, to put it more appropriately, all the actors live within him. Dionysos the god and Pentheus the scoffing ego who rejects the dissolute *daimon* are really the same figure, for both suffer the same fate: madness and dismemberment. It is the Titans who destroy the god, and they are of the earth. Perhaps this is an image of the suffering which the Piscean spirit endures being incarnated in dense flesh. The flesh can be a prison and a devourer of the spirit; but the spirit likewise is not only a redeemer but a devourer of the flesh. Certainly, in Pisces, the two do not get on. The classic Piscean alcoholic or drug addict, in search of spirit, dismembers his bodily prison. Yet the invocation of Alcoholics Anonymous, which has helped so many suffering from this problem, is to place faith in a power greater than oneself.

Perhaps it is the fate of the Piscean to live with this extraordinary *daimon*, because repudiation of him, as the myth of Pentheus suggests, can be dangerous. Life itself can dismember, if he is not welcomed. Identification with the figure of the Messiah is also a Piscean theme. So too is identification with the victim, for as we have seen they are one and the same. Yet the profound compassion of which Pisces is capable, and its creative access to the depths of the boundless watery world, are the gifts of enduring the proximity of such a god.

In the preceding pages we have encountered a number of mythic stories and figures, each of which personifies a different facet of the complex dance of life. There are obviously a multitude of tales which I have left out, but I hope that some flavour has been imparted of the way in which myth, which seems to express the meaning and purposefulness of experience, and the astrological signs, meld together. Although I have, for the sake of coherence, described each astrological sign's patterns as though it applied specifically to the sun sign, in actuality this does not seem to be the case. Although both the sun and ascendant dominate the natal chart, and the patterns of both these placements are very relevant to the development of the individual, anything in the chart may be viewed through mythic eyes. This includes aspects between the planets, as well as house placements, and it is the very complicated pattern thus woven which communicates the individual quality of a particular horoscope. It has been pointed out in various astrological texts that a few themes will usually be found to repeat themselves when one examines a natal chart closely. The same statement might be said by, for example, Venus in Scorpio, Pluto in the seventh house, several planets in the eighth, and so on; and the primary themes which emerge in this way form the spinal column of the chart and the main story-line of the individual life.

The same thing occurs when we use myth as an amplification of astrology. If we look at particular astrological placements from the point of view of the story as well as from the point of view of characteristics, then we will usually find within an individual horoscope that particular mythic figures and stories repeat themselves. In examining the chart of Ruth, for example, the story of Hades and Persephone is suggested not only by the strong aspects to Pluto, which opposes the sun and Mercury (the chart ruler), squares Mars and also squares Jupiter, but also by the Virgo ascendant, and by the sun in the sixth house, which is Virgo's natural house. The chart ruler too, which is Mercury, is involved in the grand cross, and is in exact opposition to Pluto. Thus, although Ruth is a Piscean, the Plutonian theme is a dominant one in her horoscope and in her life. This is emphasised by the particular time at which she came to see me, for the grand cross was being activated, and thus the mythic themes which pertain to it were particularly relevant in her life.

One cannot, as I have emphasised, be too literal with myth. But there are times and situations where the archetypal background to events and emotions helps the individual to 'see into' what is happening in a way which lifts the experience out of a cause-and-effect framework and gives it a deep and timeless dimension. It is not merely comforting, but sometimes transformative, to sense and know that we as individuals are part of a pageant, and that our little personal problems and dilemmas and sufferings are lent dignity by the ancient story. In the sense that I have equated myth with fate and character, the 'story' or 'scheme' is the bridge between the cherished idea of 'potential' and the concrete reality of those things we cannot change. The archaic theme of the *daimon* which is given to us at birth and shapes our lives from within offers dignity both to fate and to individual choice, and permits the possibility of doing 'gladly that which I must do'. I do not know whether the *daimon* is really an aspect of Moira, or whether they are separate things; but although they seem so disparate, my suspicion is that retributive fate and destiny are not so very different after all. It may be that there is a unity behind them, a central pattern, which we have yet to explore and contemplate.

# PART THREE

---

## *Pronoia*

# 9

# Fate and Synchronicity

---

*A certain M. Deschamps, when a boy in Orléans, was once given
a piece of plum-pudding by a M. de Fortgibu. Ten years later he
discovered another plum-pudding in a Paris restaurant, and
asked if he could have a piece. It turned out, however, that the
plum-pudding was already ordered – by M. de Fortgibu. Many
years afterwards M. Deschamps was invited to partake of a
plum-pudding as a special rarity. While he was eating it he
remarked that the only thing lacking was M. de Fortgibu. At that
moment the door opened and an old, old man in the last stages of
disorientation walked in: M. de Fortgibu, who had got hold of the
wrong address and burst in on the party by mistake.*[139]

We have travelled a considerable distance in our exploration of
fate, and have left the ancient world behind – or so it would seem.
In the writings of Jung we shall find a new word for fate, and a new
concept of the mysterious orderedness of psyche and world; and
this new concept is perhaps more appropriate for an age in which
our increased rational consciousness craves scientific hypotheses
rather than myth. Nevertheless, the experience of fatedness is still
with us, as the edifying story above suggests, and we must therefore now consider the difficult concept of synchronicity in order to
understand what depth psychology makes of this issue of fate.

I would like to begin with two stories. The first is from Dr
Gerhard Adler's paper, 'Reflections on "Chance", "Fate", and
Synchronicity'. In this paper, Dr Adler writes about the mysterious
occurrence which led to his meeting with Jung and his subsequent
training and life work as an analyst.

> As a young man I was very fond of dancing and especially of
> fancy-dress balls, which were in vogue in the Berlin of the
> twenties and early thirties. I think it was in 1928 that I had danced

through two nights with hardly any sleep. On the following morning, a Sunday, I was pretty fagged out. So I was not at all pleased when the telephone call of a friend . . . woke me up, inviting me to a party he was going to throw that afternoon. I refused, but, in the end, the persuasive power of my friend won the day and I went. As I entered the room, my then very susceptible eye was immediately caught by the sight of a beautiful girl. When my friend introduced me to her, the introduction went like this: 'Dr Adler – Mrs Adler.' This kind of thing hits one; at least it hit me . . . We talked quite a bit and were both quite curious about each other. So we decided to continue our talk on another occasion. We met again, several times after that. In short, this first meeting, if not yet of common souls but only of common names, led to a close and most fruitful friendship. But – and now comes the crunch – as it turned out, my namesake had seen Jung and was deeply steeped in his ideas. In true anima fashion, she kindled a considerable curiosity in me about this strange man and his Analytical Psychology; until then, I had been much more interested in Freud . . .

'*This* is how it started' – but what is 'this'? . . . Here the fate of two people was deeply intertwined in a complex pattern because of what, in ordinary language, one can only call a chance meeting. Chance, fate, nurturing an inner preparedness for change and direction – how can one disentangle them? At any rate, here we can discern a 'meaningful coincidence' of inner fate and external events.[140]

Dr Adler cites other personal examples of this apparent emergence of a secret pattern into ordinary life, where one is given the feeling that 'something' is at work shaping the direction in which the individual develops. One can often only see the importance of such occurrences with hindsight; and these occurrences are not always as peculiarly striking as the one given above. But the 'chance' meetings which, like the *deus ex machina* of the Greek theatre, suddenly appear in one's path and herald a crisis or change of major import for the future can come in ways other than meetings with significant people. Sometimes the right book, virtually 'fallen' from a library shelf, or the right film, which one has been reluctantly taken by friends to see, or the 'random' occurrence witnessed in the street, or an impeccably timed accident or illness, or even an apparently 'bad' event such as theft, can cast an eerily meaningful aura because it coincides with a time when inner changes are occurring. At such times the individual is in some way more receptive to the symbolic significance of what he has seen or met. The event may mean nothing to others, but to the individual in whom it resonates, it provokes a strong sense that something important is happening, and this feeling is most difficult to ignore. I have heard it described most often as a feeling of 'fate', as if some nodal point had been reached, some hunch or intuition surfaced that a crossroads has arrived. Although some people are perhaps more sensitive to such occurrences than others – perhaps related to the intuitive function which tends to draw meaningful connections quite readily – they are by no means limited to those interested in esoteric arts or depth psychology. They happen to everybody, and even the most prosaic soul, given a chance, will have a strange story to tell. These 'meaningful coincidences' invoke a conviction that another world lies somewhere beneath the apparent one, and intrudes, on suitable occasions, with an experience of fated orderedness.

Dr Adler raises the question of the relationship between the inner and the outer, and whether these two might not be so disparate as they at first seem.

> Is there some destiny within us that preforms the pattern of our life, or is it the actual experiences which shape it? Are the experiences we encounter predestined, or do we feel them so intensely and remember them so well because of an inner need? Or is there a coincidence of inner needs and outer events, an interconnectedness of within and without, which makes this division into two spheres irrelevant and even misleading?[141]

This connection between 'soul' and 'fate' is what I feel to be embodied in the mythic images which we have been exploring in the preceding pages. Myths, as we have seen, cross the boundaries between 'inner' and 'outer', and manifest on both levels. But if myths reflect a basic pattern, what then is it which fills the pattern in with such peculiar events as Dr Adler's meeting with Mrs Adler? Every astrologer meets the 'intermediate place' of myth in every horoscope, for the astrological pattern seems to describe both character and destiny, as though they were the same thing. The mythic patterns of the zodiacal signs are a particularly clear illustration of how an inner mode of perception and experience coincides with an outer life pattern. But something 'other' is at work to provoke the 'meaningful coincidences' which remind us of the unity of ourselves with our world. Jung thought that synchronous experiences which united inner and outer seemed to rest on an archetypal foundation. In other words, something is at work that transcends the artificial division between psyche and 'outer' physical environment – an inherent ordering pattern which unites the individual with his concrete life experiences in a common meaning. I think that most astrologers have experience of this 'archetypal foundation' as a general theory to understand why a planetary placement or transit or progressed aspect correlates an inner quality or trend with a particular type of experience. What is harder to grasp is the specificity of experience, such as the meeting described by Dr Adler. However causal and mechanistic the astrologer might become – and some, understandably, seek a physical 'effect' that the planets might have upon human life – it is difficult to explain away the awesome and sometimes deeply ironic occurrences of these 'meaningful coincidences' which Jung calls synchronicity.

The second story with which I would like to illustrate this experience of 'fatedness' or meaningful order is one about my own introduction to astrology. Like the fateful encounter of the two Adlers, my experience rested upon an apparently 'chance' meeting, although not with someone bearing my own name. During the winter break of my third year at university I happened to be in Boston, Massachusetts, where I made the acquaintance of someone who was interested in astrology and esoteric philosophy. At the time I had neither experience nor interest in such things, but was preoccupied with confusion about my own direction – whether to pursue psychology or a career in scenic and costume design for the theatre. I was 'persuaded', unwillingly and with a certain resentment, to make a visit to my acquaintance's astrologer – who turned out to be Isabel Hickey, then resident in Boston but as yet unknown in the larger astrological world. At this time, nearly twenty years ago, there was no 'larger' astrological world, in fact, but only individual people studying the subject in a relative vacuum. Mrs Hickey had a small but devoted circle of students around her, and an appointment was made to have my horoscope read.

Naturally the reading interested me, although it was very brief – only half an hour – and I was perplexed by its insight and accuracy: a familiar enough experience for any layman first encountering the uncanny revelations of the birth chart. I was certainly deeply impressed, and forced to consider alternative ways of looking at things from the behavioural psychological viewpoint which I had been learning. But the chart reading alone would not have been sufficient to lead me to study the subject in any depth. Mrs Hickey, however, seemed to take a pointed interest in me, suggested that I might do well as an astrological student, and offered to include me in her classes and provide some private tuition. This idea was met with enthusiasm on my part, but before I was able to take advantage of her offer, she, for reasons which still remain obscure to me, reversed her initial interest and took a passionate dislike to me, insulted me, and barred me from her classes. I was not, and am not now, astonished that she might have disliked me; after all, I am probably as dislikeable as the next person. But the intensity and overt aggressiveness of her attack amazed me. I could think of no earthly reason for it, nor could my friend, and it seemed very unlike the wise and compassionate woman whom I had first met and of whom everyone spoke with respect and fondness. I had hardly exchanged more than a few sentences with her, and had certainly not knowingly offended her in any way. I tried to obtain a copy of my birth chart from her, which was normal procedure for her students, but was curtly refused. My friend then tried to find the chart in her office files, to which he had access, but to my bewilderment he told me that the chart had vanished; everyone else's was there but my own.

My initial reaction to this rather sore experience, which had begun so promisingly and ended so embarrassingly, was to detach myself from the whole thing. I left Boston, and lost contact with the friend who had first introduced me to Mrs Hickey. But the thing gnawed at me, and raised rather paranoid fears that she had seen some horrible thing about me in my horoscope which had made her recoil, or had foreseen some dreadful fate about which I could not be warned. I was also quite hurt and, consequently, very angry. The result of this was that I resolved to learn to set up my own chart, so that I could face whatever nightmare she might have discerned. As I knew no one who was even remotely interested in astrology among my fellow psychological students, I was reduced to having to struggle through what few books were then available on the subject, most of them rather theosophically oriented and not very edifying for a psychologist. Thus I educated myself, through a process of trial and error and experimentation through discussion with friends whose charts I had set up. By the time I had realised that no monstrous configuration or hideous fate was reflected in my birth chart, I had become addicted. As Dr Adler writes in his article, '"This is how it started" – but what is "this"?'

As I look back on this experience, it is apparent now, with hindsight, that my own confusion about direction and my inner receptivity to something new entering my life coincided with the external events just described, in a synchronous way. I stood at a crossroads, and my fate came to meet me. If I am honest with myself, I must recognise that the hostile reaction I received was precisely the right trigger to set me moving along my own path. Had I been accepted and nurtured as one of Mrs Hickey's students, it is entirely possible that I would now still be one of Mrs Hickey's students, continuing to perpetrate, despite her recent death, *her* very individual astrological method with its particular blend of theosophical thought and traditional astrological wisdom. Instead, I was condemned to find my own way and develop my own insights; and whatever relevance my exploration of psychological astrology might have for the broader field of the study, it is unquestionably forged from my own direct experience and observation, and is not the product of a teacher or a school. I am deeply grateful for that, and for the strange encounter I had, unpleasant though it was at the time and incomprehensible though it still is to me.

Naturally I was quick to inspect the transits and progressions in operation at the time of my meeting with Mrs Hickey and its subsequent repercussions. The most striking transit at work was Jupiter passing through Gemini and making a direct station on my natal Uranus in the seventh house. This is a classic representation of a 'fated' (or synchronous) encounter, which brought opportunities in its wake but left my life as quickly as it had come. I have learned since to pay close attention to the transits of Jupiter, for although they often pass quickly and without any noticeable concrete benefits for the person who sits waiting for heaven to shower *manna* on him, they often coincide with opportunities which can greatly expand one's vision and understanding. But one must act on such openings which appear in the curtain that masks the inner world. We might do well to remember Zeus, who with lightning quickness pursues and mates with his chosen paramours, and then vanishes as quickly, leaving them fertilised with a semi-divine child to bear.

Another relevant aspect in force at the time was the conjunction of progressed Mercury to natal Neptune in Libra in the tenth house. This also speaks for itself, for the involvement of the tenth house suggests a new direction in terms of goal and vocation, or, at a more profound level, in terms of one's eventual contribution to the collective. The appearance of Mercury is classically associated with new interests and spheres of learning, and Neptune, of course, is associated with all kinds of occult and otherworldly things. Reading this particular configuration, I would say that it reflected a 'right moment' in my development when I was ready, inwardly although unwittingly, to encounter the imaginal world of the unconscious and its ancient symbols which would eventually become my vocation in life. As they say in Buddhist teaching, when the pupil is ready the teacher appears; although in my case the teacher disappeared as rapidly, leaving me to find my way alone.

These two configurations – the transit of Jupiter over Uranus and the progressed conjunction of Mercury to Neptune – are the primary indicators of 'something happening' at the time of my

encounter with Mrs Hickey. They are not immediately recognisable as monumentally significant aspects such as one might feel
about progressions of the sun, or transits of the outer planets. I
would be surprised if any astrologer, without hindsight, could
have looked at these configurations and said, 'Ah, this is one of the
great turning points of your life'. This raises an important question, which is about the relationship between the 'significance' in
subjective terms of an experience and the apparent strength of the
aspects which reflect that experience in the chart. I have found that
these two things do not necessarily coincide. Something *other*
seems to be involved in how important a particular experience is to
the person, besides the astrological significators; but whatever this
'something' is, it seems to depend upon or to be reflected by an
appropriate planetary movement which provides a channel or a
'timer' for its expression. What this 'something' might be we will
explore in due course, when we come to the issue of fate and the
Self. But as I understand it, the constellation of archetypal contents
and synchronous events occurs in co-ordination with planetary
transits and progressions, and the meaning of the experience, and
its essential qualities, are reflected by the planets involved. The
importance of the experience for the individual, however, is not
necessarily in proportion to the 'power' of the transit or progression according to the conventional astrological rules.

In Jung's writings on the subject, he comes to the conclusion that
synchronous happenings tend to occur when the individual is
overcome by emotional affect. He describes this process as follows:

> The archetypes are formal factors responsible for the organi-
> sation of unconscious psychic processes; they are 'patterns of
> behaviour'. At the same time they have a 'specific charge' and
> develop numinous effects which express themselves as *affects*.
> The affect produces a partial *abaissement du niveau mental*, for
> although it raises a particular content to a supernormal degree
> of luminosity, it does so by withdrawing so much energy from
> other possible contents of consciousness that they become dark-
> ened and eventually unconscious. Owing to the restriction of
> consciousness produced by the affect so long as it lasts, there is a
> corresponding lowering of orientation which in its turn gives
> the unconscious a favourable opportunity to slip into the space
> vacated. Thus we regularly find that unexpected or otherwise
> inhibited unconscious contents break through and find expres-
> sion in the affect. Such contents are very often of an inferior or
> primitive nature and thus betray their archetypal origin.[142]

One of the more obvious situations where we may see this process
of affect breaking through and disorienting the individual's

consciousness, thereby allowing unknown unconscious contents to rise to the surface, is in the experience of falling in love. This is extremely fertile soil for synchronous events, as Jung found when he mounted his famous astrological experiment with married couples. The – to the layman – astonishing correlation of a deep emotional experience with a highly precise and statistically outrageous correspondence of astrological factors between two birth charts, is familiar to any astrologer who deals with synastry. There are no particular astrological factors, so far as I can see, that indicate with any assurance that one is going to fall in love, although the constellation of marriage in Jung's survey seems related to sun–moon conjunctions, trines and sextiles across the charts. But the state of 'in-love-ness' is not a legalised fact like marriage, and is experienced differently by different people. Frequently Venus and Neptune and the moon are involved whenever any strong affective state is present, although it may not necessarily be 'love'. But I have seen people declare that they are in love under such stringent configurations as sun to Saturn, or Mars to Uranus. It would seem that the internal constellation reflected by a transit or progression over some sensitive point in the birth chart, and the outer encounter with the 'other' who provokes such overwhelming emotion, are together a prime example of synchronicity. I have sometimes been awestruck at the mysterious and incomprehensible way in which people find each other from opposite ends of the earth whose complexes are so beautifully matched, whose parental backgrounds are so eerily similar, and whose charts fit together with such hand-in-glove tailoring. The beloved object in such circumstances, who is 'responsible' for invoking such an uprush of archetypal imagery, is rarely human, but more often something semi-divine, because of the mythic nature of the projection and the numinosity which accompanies such experiences of the deep inner world. Such encounters are usually called 'fated' because that is how they feel. It is difficult to refute this, because there is certainly a sense of 'rightness' about such meetings not only in terms of their effects in the immediate present, but also in terms of their influence upon the course of both people's development.

As I understand this process in relation to astrology, a particular placement in the birth chart reflects a particular 'pattern' or 'psychic organisation' within the individual. Such patterns, which I understand to be both the core of mythic stories and also the core of what Jung calls complexes, are, in a sense, fate, because they are written from birth. Neptune placed in my tenth house, moreover, is different from Neptune in someone else's ninth house, so this is a highly individualised fate. I am 'destined' to encounter Neptunian experiences, and to make Neptunian themes manifest, in the sphere of vocation and contact with the public, as well as, earlier in life, meeting the planet through the inheritance from the mother. Neptune in the ninth house, on the other hand, would be 'destined' to encounter such experiences in the sphere of spiritual and religious matters, and in the realm of moral and ethical choices. Thus individuals express universal motifs in highly individual ways, and the ancient archetypal imagery manifests in highly personal ways in dreams, as I have shown by numerous examples.

To follow on from this, a transit or progression triggers, or, more accurately, coincides with the emergence of this archetypal potential, and an affect develops. In my case, the sense of confusion and indecision as to which direction to follow constituted the *abaissement* which allowed the unconscious to 'slip in' with its peculiar synchronistic properties. The unconscious was activated because it was the 'right time'. I am convinced that such timing is inherent from the birth of the organism, just as the timing for a tomato plant to flower and produce a fruit is inherent in its nature. So, as if by chance, I encountered someone who led me into the next phase of my life, through a 'meaningful coincidence' of an inner discovery and an outer event. The inner experience, the readiness to explore the Neptunian world, was reflected outwardly by the meeting with Mrs Hickey, and the meaning inherent in both inner and outer happenings was in turn reflected, in astrological terms, by progressed Mercury conjunct Neptune and transiting Jupiter stationary on Uranus.

Jung felt that 'stuck' situations tended to breed synchronous phenomena, for the situation of an impasse in life constellates the compensatory nature of the unconscious, and archetypal dreams and images tend to arise as a kind of 'way through'. From the point of view of astrology, however, it is the other way around. It is the archetype which precipitates the sense of being stuck, for the appearance of an important transit or progression heralds a profound change in the inner patterning of the individual. Something new thus tries to enter the life of the ego, something which has previously been locked in a fairy-tale sleep of unconscious potential. I feel that it is the collision between this new development and the static situation of the environment, which was previously perfectly satisfactory, that results in the feeling of being stuck. I have heard so many people use this word at a time when the chart reflects impending changes of great magnitude that I have come to the conclusion that 'stuckness' is the preliminary stage of any important movement in the chart – and in the individual. One is not stuck unless something moving has encountered an obstacle. Sometimes the obstacle is a pre-existent attitude towards life, reflected by an external situation, which suddenly begins to feel too tight. At such times one often finds people seeking help from psychotherapy, or paying a visit to an astrologer, because life has become 'meaningless', or one cannot find the sense of which way to go. This latter was also the situation Dr Adler found himself in when he encountered Mrs Adler. He was 'stuck' in terms of confusion about his direction. Such, too, was my own situation when I encountered Mrs Hickey. But a look at the horoscope at such apparently sluggish times usually reveals that things are far from being stuck or stagnant; they are, in fact, moving to ripening, and it is the ego which is still tied to its old outlook yet which feels the buffeting of new winds.

One of the queerest things about synchronous phenomena is the overriding sense of some kind of *a priori* knowledge in the unconscious. 'Something' – we are back again to that strange unknown – knew that in order for Dr Adler to fulfil the requirements of his pattern he had to get to Jung, so 'it' evidently arranged for Mrs Adler to arrive at the same party, and 'it' also evidently convinced his friend to throw the party in the first place. This sounds absurd, but subjectively, it feels that way. 'Something' likewise knew that in order for me to fulfil the requirements of my own pattern, I had to encounter astrology, so 'it' made sure I was in Boston, brought me together with the friend who introduced me to Mrs Hickey, and also caused Mrs Hickey to behave in a fashion guaranteed to engender a stubborn determination in me to learn something about the subject which had been dangled and then snatched away in such a bizarre manner. Likewise 'it' made sure that these arrangements coincided with a transit and a progression which precisely fit the meaning of the time.

Now, I realise that this attributes some fairly awesome powers to 'it', and it is not surprising that this 'it', when one runs headlong into its workings, is generally experienced as God. The sense of the omniscience of the unconscious, without any conceivable causal basis, gives rise to a peculiar feeling of fatedness when we encounter synchronous events. 'Something' knows enough not only to move the psyche, but to move the world of matter as well, or, as it is put in the film 'E. T.', to 'manipulate the environment'. 'It' seems to have fingers, if that is the appropriate word, in both the inner and outer worlds, in the realms of both spirit and matter, as though there were really no distinction between these opposites. This is what I understand by Jung's term 'psychoid', which he uses to describe the nature of the archetype: It is a unity which encompasses, and transcends the opposition of, psychic and physical, inner and outer, personal and collective, individual and world. Jung quotes Lao-tzu:

*There is something formless yet complete*
*That existed before heaven and earth.*
  *How still! how empty!*
*Dependent upon nothing, unchanging,*
*All-pervading, unfailing.*
*One may think of it as the mother of all things under heaven.*
*I do not know its name.*
*But I call it 'Meaning'.*
*If I had to give it a name, I should call it 'The Great'.*[143]

This is the Tao of Eastern philosophy, which in the West was known to the alchemists as the *unus mundus*, the one world, the interrelated and interconnected single organism of life. The Greeks knew it too, as they moved away from Moira's omnipotence, as the *pronoia* or *nous*, the mind of Zeus or God's Providence. Christianity adopted this concept of God's Providence, and set it against the old pagan view of fate, for although at bottom it is difficult to distinguish between the two in terms of 'fatedness', yet the subjective sense of them is very different. Moira, the feminine face of fate, was associated with a sense of doom and death, for no 'plan' in a teleological sense was ever equated with her power; she merely represented the boundaries of nature. God's Providence, which has a distinctly masculine feel, has on the other hand the quality of 'order' and 'intent', a movement towards the 'good' (although how subjective that is may be a matter for some debate), and is associated with loving care and an omniscient, beneficent Will.

When early religious writers attempted to describe the 'something' which they envisioned as the unknowable Will of God, or Providence which arranges the affairs of life, they had a difficult time articulating the warping of time, space and causality which any intrusion of this Providence seems to entail. For this reason God's Providence is referred to as being beyond space and time: The future, and the past, are all present simultaneously within the Mind of God, and the whole of creation occurs spontaneously within the same moment. It is only the ego, in psychological terms, which experiences life through a linear space–time continuum, and when the unconscious erupts into the field of consciousness with its accompanying synchronous phenomena and its quality of 'absolute knowledge', the experience is one of timelessness and of preordained fate. Jung puts this as follows:

> The 'absolute knowledge' which is characteristic of synchronous phenomena, a knowledge not mediated by the sense organs, supports the hypothesis of a self-subsistent meaning, or even expresses its existence. Such a form of existence can only be transcendental, since, as the knowledge of future or spatially

distant events shows, it is contained in a psychically relative space and time, that is to say in an irrepresentable space–time continuum.[144]

This problem of what the religious person understands as God's foreknowledge led to some rather fiery confrontations in the course of the development of Christian theology. It was inconceivable to the early churchmen that God could be anything but omniscient; but if He was omniscient, then He knew what sins a man would commit in the future, which meant that sin, salvation and damnation were already predestined. But that smacked too much of the old pagan concept of fate and the problem of astrology; and moreover, if a man's sins and salvation were already written, then there was not a great deal of point either in making the moral effort not to sin, or even bothering with the Church's guidance to begin with. Thus something more subtle had to be thought of, which acknowledged God's Providence while repudiating fate and the compulsion of the stars. Bertrand Russell paraphrases St Augustine on this matter:

> Astrology is not only wicked, but false; this may be proved from the different fortunes of twins, who have the same horoscope. The Stoic conception of Fate (which was connected with astrology) is mistaken, since angels and men have free will. It is true that God has foreknowledge of our sins, but we do not sin *because* of His foreknowledge.[145]

Augustine was profoundly convinced that all men share the sin of Adam and therefore deserve judgement. Of His great mercy, however, God predestined some men to salvation; others He predestined to the punishment which their sin deserved. All men, being stained by sin, deserve damnation, but God of His free choice selects some to be saved. Augustine held that God had predetermined the precise number of those who were to receive His grace, and not one soul could be added nor taken away from that elect number. Yet despite this, he declares, angels and men have free will. This illustrates, I think, some of the difficulties which arose around the problem of accommodating human freedom of choice with God's omniscience.

The doctrine of Providence and predestination was also held by Thomas Aquinas, who like Augustine rejected astrology for the usual reasons. In answer to the question, 'Is there such a thing as fate?' Aquinas suggests that we *might* give the name fate to the order impressed by Providence, but it is wiser to find some other term, since fate is a pagan word. This leads inevitably to the argument that prayer is useful, but Providence is unchangeable. God sometimes works miracles, but no one else can.

It seems to me, when initially confronted with this complex theological vision of a fate which is not fate but behaves like it and really is it if a different word could be used, that a number of very eminent Church Fathers were trying extremely hard to reconcile the experience of fatedness in life with a religious outlook which had, of necessity, to exclude fate because such a belief eroded the interest in and dependence upon the Church as a means of salvation. Just this problem erupted during the Reformation, when Calvin's belief in the predestination of elect souls removed the necessity of a priesthood who stood as intermediaries between men's souls and God. One can understand the theological dilemma, and can even admire the subtlety of the argument. But the more I have thought about this issue, the more I feel that the theological answer to Moira goes somewhat deeper than mere intellectual juggling to preserve the power of the holy edifice. That, no doubt, is part of it. But Providence is perhaps not exactly the same as Moira after all, for Moira's laws, as they are expressed in Greek myth, are causal. That is, Oidipus is destined from birth to murder his father and wed his mother, and *because* this is written by the hand of fate, he must, out of necessity, fulfil the oracle. Augustine is at pains to point out that God's foreknowledge does not cause men to sin. It is more like the 'absolute knowledge' of the unconscious of which Jung speaks, which, because it exists in an 'irrepresentable space–time continuum', perceives past, present and future simultaneously and creates the external and internal coincidences of life perpetually afresh in every moment because every moment is one eternal moment. Now Jung was exceedingly careful to insist that what he was describing was the unconscious, not God; one could not possibly, as a psychologist, presume to know the Unknowable. But the ways in which human beings experience God, as opposed to the nature of God, is certainly the province of psychology, and this human experience posits a God who manifests through synchronicity and appears to possess 'absolute knowledge' yet does not make men sin in the sense that Moira makes men fulfil a particular fate.

Thus *pronoia* or Providence became a kind of counterpoint to the old Stoic concept of *heimarmenê*, the fate written in the heavens. Although everything, including salvation, may be predetermined from the beginning in the Mind of God, it is not the same as planetary compulsion, because the will of God, in the Christian sense, does not preordain people to sin; it foreknows their sins, which is different. Thus the famous Prayer of Cleanthes, which Russell quotes as an example of pagan belief in Providence, could as easily be a Christian prayer with a slight change of names:

*Lead me, O Zeus and thou, O Destiny,*
*Lead thou me on,*
*To whatsoever task thou sendest me,*
*Lead thou me on.*
*I will follow fearless, or, if in mistrust*
*I lag and will not, follow still I must.*[146]

This echoes Jung when he declared that free will is the ability to do gladly that which one must do.

There seems to be a kind of progression or evolution expressed in the transition from the causal and concrete fate of Moira to the synchronous fate of God's Providence. Moira, although less palatable to twentieth-century consciousness, is easier to understand. Jung's definition of synchronicity is that it is the simultaneous occurrence of a certain psychic state with an external event (or events) which appears as a meaningful parallel to the subjective state. This is, in essence, what we encounter when we interpret any placement in the birth chart, and in particular when we consider prognosticative factors such as progressions and transits, horary charts and solar returns. Like the problem of the young man who saw Death in the market-place in Isfahan, the problem of whether a particular situation might be avoided or changed becomes, in a sense, irrelevant. One might well ask whether, if Dr Adler had refused his friend's party invitation, some other 'arrangement' might have occurred which sent him off to Zurich. I have certainly wondered, had I not met Mrs Hickey, what would have been 'arranged' to introduce me to astrology. But these are impossible questions, because, as with the peculiarly precise and 'right' images which arise in dreams, the situations which actually did happen were absolutely and unerringly appropriate for both person and time.

There are innumerable examples of synchronicity which arise in astrological work, which any practitioner sooner or later experiences. They are part of the awesome fascination of the study. All the examples of dreams coinciding with critical transits which I have cited are set pieces of a synchronous kind. So, too, are the 'ordinary' phenomena which many astrologers and also psychotherapists experience which are so difficult to explain to the layman yet which happen so often that one ceases to question them but merely laughs instead. For instance, one always seems to attract clients whose problems reflect or constellate one's own, even if those clients enter one's life through something as impersonal as an ad in the newspaper. Every analyst has experience of this sort of thing, as well as the almost magical way in which, if the analyst succeeds in making some kind of breakthrough or has some further insight into his own issues, so do his analysands, without any word passing between them about it. Here we encounter the peculiar *unus mundus* of the unconscious, which connects analyst and analysand with a left-handed and secret handshake, so that it becomes difficult, at times, to distinguish whose psyche is doing what to whom. I have also heard many colleagues complain of those 'bad weeks' when one's analysands, one's clients, one's husband or wife, one's mother and even the teller at the bank become rude, intractable and difficult for no visible reason; but where, if the horoscope is inspected, a situation is revealed where the individual is himself undergoing some important change or crisis and the outer world enacts for him the nature of his own conflict. These are the times when the 'accidents' occur, the tax bill comes in the post, the burglar breaks into the house, the water main bursts and the cellar floods, and one begins to feel that 'something' is definitely on the hunt.

Common, too, are the 'runs' of clients of a particular sign who turn up to see the astrologer when a certain movement is occurring in the astrologer's own horoscope. I have noticed that, from time to time, I will get a series of clients, usually about a dozen, who all have the sun, moon or ascendant in the same sign, and even the same degree, one after another; and this happens although the appointments were made at different times and in no particular astrological order. When I have examined my own internal issues, I have usually found that whatever is represented by that particular zodiacal symbol has some relevance to me at that particular time. This often coincides with some transit in my own chart, although not necessarily with anything in my clients'. I could go on endlessly about these synchronous situations, for they seem to flock like crows around astrological and analytic work. Perhaps this is because these fields require a constant encountering of and relationship with archetypal material, and once one enters this archetypal 'field' one rapidly becomes exposed to the strange way in which it seems to 'order' both outer and inner events.

I believe that the phenomena of clairvoyance also belong to the category of synchronous events. Methods of divination such as the Tarot, clairvoyance, the *I Ching* and so on, tend to provoke fear and ambivalence in the layman because of the implication that the future is fated. Of course, I do not know the answer to this, even with such a nice term as synchronicity at my disposal. But if we consider these things from the point of view of depth psychology, we are not dealing with a 'causal' fate which has written everything from the beginning, but rather with a meaningful connection between an inner state and an outer happening which becomes perceptible to the seer because he or she has penetrated into the

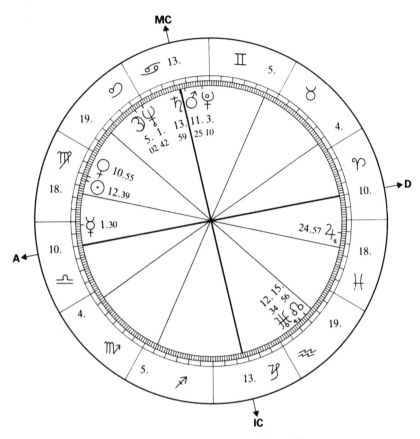

DIAGRAM 14. Birth horoscope of David Bates

b. 6 September 1915
8.00 a.m.
Birmingham

Progressions for date of death

| ☉ 15 ♍ 01 | ♄ 16 ♋ 25 ℞ |
|---|---|
| ☷ 1 ♐ 31 | ♅ 11 ♒ 52 ℞ |
| ☽ 12 ♒ 35 | ♆ 2 ♌ 40 ℞ |
| ☿ 26 ♎ 15 | ♇ 3 ♋ 06 ℞ |
| ♀ 29 ♍ 42 | |
| ♂ 15 ♌ 56 | A 22 ♏ |
| ♃ 18 ♓ 41 ℞ | MC 15 ♍ |

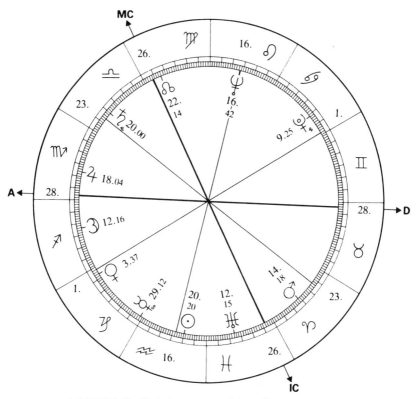

DIAGRAM 15. Birth horoscope of Jean Bates

b. 10 February 1923
2.30 a.m.
Hemel Hempstead

Progressions for date of David Bates' death

| ☉ | 11 | ♈ | 14 | | ♄ | 16 | ♎ | 49 ℞ |
|---|----|----|----|---|---|----|----|------|
| ☽ | 27 | ♐ | 27 | | ♅ | 15 | ♓ | 22 |
| ☊ | 19 | ♍ | 32 | | ♆ | 15 | ♌ | 29 ℞ |
| ☿ | 14 | ♈ | 17 | | ♇ | 9 | ♋ | 07 |
| ♀ | 6 | ♓ | 48 | | | | | |
| ♂ | 23 | ♉ | 45 | | **A** | 15 | ♑ | |
| ♃ | 17 | ♏ | 22 ℞ | | **MC** | 24 | ♏ | |

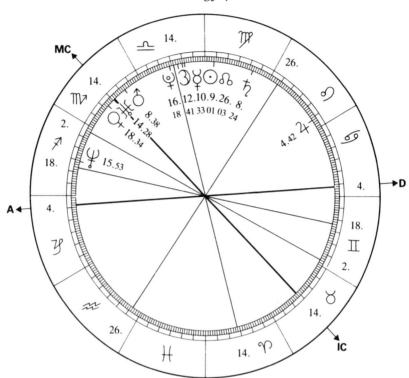

DIAGRAM 16. Death horoscope of David Bates

d. 2 October 1978
3.00 p.m.
Wimbledon

archetypal realm. The clairvoyant has therefore by-passed the
ordinary space–time continuum and reached that 'intermediate
place' where past, present and future are occurring at once. Since
this seems to be a sphere of spontaneous creation, it would appear
that the intrusion of consciousness has some effect on that creation, in the same way that the scientific observer has an effect on
the experiment which he is observing. Thus we have seen how
working on dream material, which is also an intrusion into the
world of the unconscious, affects both observer and observed –
although it is not always clear just who is really the observer or
subject, and who the observed object. If there is any such thing as a
transformation of fate, then herein lies some possibility of it: the
relationship with the archetypal realm. The same thing might be

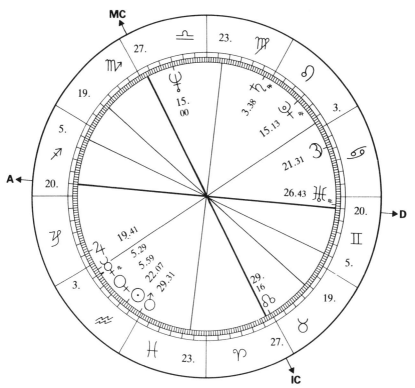

DIAGRAM 17. Birth horoscope of Trevor Bates

b. 11 February 1949
4.20 a.m.
London

Progressions for date of David Bates' death

| ☉ | 22 ♓ 06 | | ♄ | 1 ♍ 17ᵣ |
| ☽ | 26 ♌ 36 | | ♅ | 26 ♊ 32ᵣ |
| ☊ | 27 ♈ 41 | | ♆ | 14 ♎ 23ᵣ |
| ☿ | 28 ♒ 00 | | ♇ | 14 ♌ 34ᵣ |
| ♀ | 13 ♓ 13 | | | |
| ♂ | 23 ♓ 03 | | A | 20 ♑ |
| ♃ | 25 ♑ 32 | | MC | 27 ♍ |

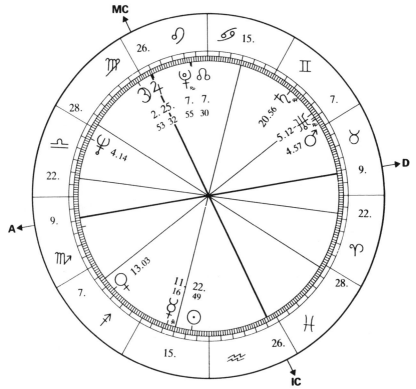

DIAGRAM 18. Birth horoscope of Brian Bates

b. 14 January 1944
3.30 a.m.
London

Progressions for date of David Bates' death

| | | | | |
|---|---|---|---|---|
| ☉ 28 ♒ 13 | | ♄ 19 ♊ 41 ℞ |
| ☽ 4 ♐ 16 | | ♅ 4 ♊ 50 |
| ☊ 5 ♌ 39 | | ♆ 3 ♎ 46 ℞ |
| ☿ 7 ♒ 40 | | ♇ 7 ♌ 08 |
| ♀ 25 ♑ 29 | | A 2 ♐ |
| ♂ 12 ♊ 42 | | MC 3 ♎ |
| ♃ 21 ♌ 17 ℞ | | |

said of an astrological prediction: As long as the individual remains unconscious, and retains his old viewpoint, then any new inner development will take a predictable expression, since it can only manifest itself according to the channels which are available. But if the movements of the unconscious are able to be received by the ego in a spirit of genuine openness, then both partners in the equation are affected, and it becomes increasingly difficult to determine in any concretistic way the precise outer expression of the inner dynamic. I assume this is what the 'blueprint' school of astrology is trying to express, but what it does not stress is the long struggle and effort required to make that relationship with the unconscious psyche. Thus we are back once again to Marsilio Ficino and his 'natural' magic, and back also to poor King Henri II, whose death, synchronous with certain planetary transits, was so eminently predictable.

Above is given a group of family charts: a man and his wife and their two sons. I have chosen these horoscopes to illustrate a case of fate and synchronicity because of the death of the man, whom I will call David Bates, in a sudden and unexpected fashion. This event is reflected not only in his own chart, but in the charts of the rest of the family. We shall see later that it is reflected even in the charts of the four grandchildren, although they were too young to fully appreciate their loss and did not know him well. Death, like birth, is the most archetypal of events. It is experienced by everything living, and its meaning penetrates many dimensions of inner and outer life. The occurrence of death in a family is not an isolated event happening to one person in a vacuum. It is reflected synchronously in the horoscopes of every family member, although its expression varies in each case because the experiences mean different things to different people. Other circumstances were also occurring within this family at the time of David Bates' death which were not causally related but, as we shall see, were connected in meaning. David died of a heart attack while enjoying a game of tennis, and prior to this he had suffered no ill health or symptom which might have suggested such a thing happening to him at a relatively young age. Yet we shall see that the shadow of some crisis was cast long before, although perhaps not predictable in any specific or concrete way. David's physical death was one event in an interconnected web of experiences, inner and outer, all of which bear the same archetypal stamp of death on one level or another. I have been fortunate enough, through the offices of Jean Bates – who provided the birth data for her husband and their sons – to obtain the time of David's death, so that we may also examine the 'death chart' shown above. This is essentially a horary chart for the specific time of an event; and this 'death chart' is in itself an expression of synchronicity, displaying no less than four planets plus the moon's north node in the eighth house, and Uranus, fitting for the suddenness of the demise, placed precisely in the midheaven.

The connections between the charts of the members of this family are fascinating, and reflect what we have already seen in the case of the family of Renee, the autistic child: a repeated occurrence of particular signs, aspects and house placements. That in itself is a strange piece of synchronicity, for there is no causal basis for such recurrences, yet they happen anyway. For the moment, however, I would like to focus on the transits and progressions active in David Bates' chart at the time of his heart attack. The first and perhaps most striking progressed aspect in effect was the progressed sun in 15 Scorpio almost exactly in square to the moon's ascending node in the fourth house. We have already met the rather strange medieval reputation of the nodes of the moon, where the transit of Saturn over the ascending node in King Henri's chart was a signal to Luc Gauricus of His Most Christian Majesty's imminent death. I am not Luc Gauricus, and would be hesitant to be so literal about planetary movements over the nodes, but this progressed aspect certainly gives me an uncomfortable feeling that some inevitable crisis or event is reflected. I do not have to dwell on the traditional meaning of the fourth house as the 'end of life'. It has other meanings as well, including the beginning of life, the relationship with the father, and the relationship with roots and the inner world. Possibly David Bates had the option of expressing his progression through any of these levels which might have been open to him; or possibly not. In addition to the solar progression, progressed Mars had also moved into 15 Leo, making an opposition to the node, so that progressed sun and progressed Mars were also in square. Finally, the progressed node itself had moved into exact conjunction with natal Uranus, also in the fourth house.

No doubt Gauricus would have written off David Bates just as he wrote off the French King, but I am for the moment more concerned with the meaning of these aspects. There is certainly a smell of anger and great conflict about these astrological contacts. Whatever was happening inside David at the time of his heart attack, I think he must have been extremely frustrated and dissatisfied, perhaps with the whole edifice of his life and the meaning (or lack thereof) which he found in it. Some necessity for change seems to have been pressing upon him, with which, due to the intense reluctance he felt towards all 'inner' things, he apparently could not deal. This change had begun three years before his death, when the progressed sun moved into square with natal Uranus, the ruler of the fifth house. The sun rules the eleventh and is also placed in the eleventh; thus a conflict is reflected between David's goals and activities in society, and his individual development. This suggests that something was required of him, in the sphere of individual expression; but because David was not a person who inclined to 'selfish' introspection, this change or movement into a new dimension of experience was thwarted. All that he did, at the time of the progression, was retire; but this retirement was not in any way reflected by any expansion. It was simply a cessation of work, while everything else remained exactly the same.

By profession David Bates had been the headmaster of a boys' school, a vocation which seems to have suited him admirably with his Virgo sun and Cancer midheaven. He liked his work and was in turn respected and well liked by both his students and his peers. For a Virgo who has worked all his life at one job in one place, an event such as retirement is a major crisis, because Virgo tends to identify with its work and something deeper than a change in schedule is required to counterbalance what has been lost. This three-year period in David's life, between the sun–Uranus progression and the sun–node progression, was a period of complete reorientation, and an opportunity to find out who one is when the outer persona has been stripped away. That the persona was rather obsessively important to David we may deduce from the placement of Saturn exactly at the midheaven. This suggests, first of all, an extremely dominant and powerful experience of the personal mother, emphasised by the presence of the moon–Neptune conjunction in Leo also in the tenth house. Later in life, it reflects a certain anxiety or insecurity about one's position in the outside world, and a tendency to always try to do the 'right' thing in the eyes of others. David's feelings about his work are complicated; he found it emotionally fulfilling and gave a great deal of himself to it, which I understand the moon–Neptune conjunction to express, but at the same time he clung like the proverbial crab to 'the rules', and could not find it in himself to do or think anything that was not 'respectable'.

Thus he was unable to take the opportunity offered to him by the progressed sun–Uranus square. Although he was no longer holding the same position in society, he tried to retain the same personality and the same code of ethics. In short, he attempted to remain exactly the same individual as he was before the sun–Uranus aspect. My feeling is that a planet such as Uranus demands the utmost of us, because it attempts to shatter crystallised attitudes and release libido for other purposes. If the individual cannot accommodate this kind of change, then there is usually a price to be paid later, and in my experience this price is often

physical illness. To put it baldly, because death in David Bates'
chart is reflected as a conflict rather than as a harmonious development, I feel he may have died because something in him refused
the new life that was being offered. Now, it can be argued that
death is a 'new life', and that it is not a negative event but merely a
passage. This is the viewpoint held both by reincarnation and by
orthodox Christianity, although the other end of the passage
differs. I am inclined to agree with this philosophical viewpoint in
essentials, and I have no idea whether David was 'fated' to die. But
from what I have gleaned of his history, he was a kind and gentle
man who was too timid to live his life, and he carried with him a
perpetual sense of dissatisfaction and failure. In this case, death
was perhaps less the fulfilment of a life than the timely escape from
it. One can sometimes see progressions at the time of death which
reflect a sense of serenity and fulfilment; death is then shown as a
gift, the flowering of a full life. In the case of David Bates, the
progressions are turbulent, and reflect death as a conflict.

The transits across David's chart at the time of death further
increase my sense of some unresolved conflict finding the only
possible outlet. These transits are, in fact, the 'death chart' illustrated. It will be apparent if this chart is examined that a solar
eclipse occurred earlier in the day of David's demise. This eclipse,
which conjuncted transiting Mercury and transiting Pluto, landed
with the accuracy of a Sidewinder missile on David's natal
ascendant. The eclipse also fell in square to the Mars–Saturn–Pluto
conjunction at the midheaven. Now, we have had some dealings
already with Mars–Saturn–Pluto, in the examples of Timothy S.
and Angela. I do not need to elaborate here on the suppressed
intensity and passion reflected by the configuration. Whatever else
solar eclipses might mean, they are, in essence, a new moon, and
therefore reflect a new beginning, the end of one cycle and the start
of another. As the ascendant is the most intimate point in the
horoscope, reflecting the birth of the individual and the myth and
mirror of his essential outlook on life, this eclipse seems to have
synchronised with a time when David's old attitudes, represented
by the planets at the midheaven, were being challenged. Mars–
Saturn–Pluto in Cancer is a good deal more frustrated and circumscribed than Mars–Saturn–Pluto in Leo, which can at least vent its
anger through eruptions of temper. But the sensitive and retiring
nature of Cancer virtually guarantees that the dominant planet in
this conjunction will be Saturn, holding all the passions and
ambitions in check lest ripples be made in worldly standing. David
Bates was an excellent headmaster in the opinion of everyone who
knew him; but he himself felt that he had never been able to
achieve the recognition or power he craved. I would guess,

although Jean Bates would not discuss it and I did not probe, that David felt impotent in a good many senses of the word, not least in terms of his effect upon the world and in terms of his essential masculinity. In his marriage, he appears to have been the more flexible and submissive partner. David's will and passion and self-assertiveness had always been tightly bound by the voice of collective authority represented by Saturn; and it was this voice which was being challenged. Another and perhaps more Plutonian view of this would be that David's bondage to his mother and the codes of behaviour which she set for him had extended throughout his life, in both profesional and personal spheres; and that bondage now had an opportunity of loosening, with all the attendant consequences.

Four months before his death, Pluto had been stationary in 13 Libra, in exact square to Saturn at the midheaven. This was the fourth time that Pluto had passed this point, the culmination of a long and subterranean process of change. During the three years between the retirement and the death, or, astrologically considered, between the sun–Uranus and sun–node squares, Pluto crossed the natal ascendant several times as well, making two stations on it. As Pluto is placed in the ninth house in the birth chart, this transit carries with it the implication of questioning one's philosophical and moral outlook, and gradually becoming aware of the more ambivalent aspects of a God which, to David Bates, had always been *summum bonum*, nothing but good. Once again, I am left with the sense that David, in the time subsequent to his retirement, had begun to glimpse a few things about himself and his life, and did not like what he saw. Perhaps he had begun to experience anger at the lack of real freedom or individuality in his life, or at the way in which he had so often trapped himself in the name of collective morality. As we shall see, the cross-aspects between David's chart and Jean's are by no means easy, and the conflicts between them were being stirred up during this three-year period of reorientation. But far from coming out into the open, these conflicts were stringently suppressed by both parties. Perhaps David needed his heart attack because the only alternative to it was a different kind of death, which he could not countenance.

It is also interesting to note that transiting Saturn had entered David's birth sign and was approaching the conjunction of his sun and Venus in Virgo in the eleventh house. As Venus is the ascendant ruler, and as the eleventh house concerns, among other things, one's vision of the future and one's contribution to group goals, it would seem that a period of necessary depression and re-evaluation was occurring. David's lifestyle and persona, however, would not have permitted him to undergo a 'good' depression in order to find out what he was about when he was no longer a headmaster with a job which provided him with his life's meaning. He may also have begun to experience a sense of difficulty in his marriage, which is typical of Saturn over Venus, but was atypical of David, who colluded with his wife to present to the world's eyes a 'perfect' marriage. Saturn generally presents to Venus insights into relationship and the limitations of love – another's and one's own – and requires a certain 'separateness' to occur, so that the realities of both people can be accommodated within the relationship. This couple, however, tended to live as one amorphous unit, with no visible separatene ss either of a physical or a psychic kind.

I realise that what I have said about David Bates sounds as though I feel his death was in some way a failure, an inability to resolve a conflict. That is not in accord with Moira, whose laws require that all mortal things die; nor is it in accord with any more pragmatic view which sees death as a physical event occurring, in this case, 'by chance'. But this particular death has a strange feeling about it; it seems to have provided the way out of an impasse. I do not think it was a 'failure', for things could not really have been any different. Given the tenor of the birth horoscope, it is not surprising, with the gentleness and refinement of the temperament, that any overt or aggressive changes would have frightened David, and would not have been allowed to enter consciousness. If character is fate, then David's character fated David's death, which was the inevitable result of character colliding with its own enforced growth. The sun conjunct Venus and the moon conjunct Neptune combine with the Libran ascendant and Cancer midheaven, all conspiring to make David a thoroughly decent person who disliked quarrels, hated hurting people, avoided conflicts whenever possible through mediation and discussion, and refrained from opposing the general trend. Thus, his death is not a 'failure', but a psychic necessity. But I feel I can be excused for probing what other possible kinds of death might have been available, had David brought more consciousness to bear on his situation. Perhaps he would still have had to die; one simply cannot know.

One further transit needs to be mentioned before we turn to the 'death chart' and the horoscopes of the rest of the family. This is the conjunction of transiting Jupiter to the natal moon in Leo. This conjunction was almost exact at the time of death, and, with ironic predictability, occurred in the sign which for millennia has been associated with the physical heart. Here we meet another evidence of synchronicity: the relationship between a psychic predisposition reflected by a zodiacal sign, and an organ in the physical body. To say that Leo 'rules' the heart implies a causal situation. But it would seem that whatever archetypal principle Leo represents, the physical heart and the symbolic sphere of the heart are united in the same image. We have already explored the myth of Leo, with its yearning for spiritual redemption and its energetic pursuit of the source of individuality. At the moment of death, what seems to have been constellated in David Bates was an intense longing for renewal of love and life. Ordinarily, Jupiter over the moon would seem a 'good' aspect, because it 'opens the heart'. But the sudden uprush of vital life reflected by the transit could evidently find no outlet of expression; it proved 'too much' for David, and, at the risk of sounding both florid and simplistic, it would seem that, on some inner level, his heart broke.

The 'death chart' illustrated is no different from the birth chart, in that it reflects the qualities of the moment. But the birth chart describes the patterns and internal meaning of David Bates' life, whereas this other horoscope describes the quality of his death. A chart such as this one can help us gain insight into the meaning of an event, not only from the point of view of how the planets affect the individual's birth horoscope, but also as a description of the inherent flavour and meaning of the moment of death. It would seem that the heavens here conspired with David Bates to reflect a map whose emphasis lies in the realm of death, for four planets, including the sun, moon and chart ruler (Saturn) all lie in the eighth house. This is traditionally the house that concerns death, destruction, regeneration, and the meeting with the 'other' in the depths of oneself. It is largely a harmonious map, with no oppositions and only two squares. But there is something extremely uncomfortable about that clustering in the eighth house. Taken merely as a moment in a day, this chart, to put it crudely, suggests that it was a good moment for someone to die.

Marc Edmund Jones, in his book *Horary Astrology*, makes the following comment about the principles by which such maps of an event operate:

> The question often raised by a non-astrologer is the practical proposition: how can this patterning of some trivial life situation have its reflection in the heavens? The answer is found in the general concordance of events in an orderly universe or integral energy system.[147]

Thus the principle of synchronicity in the quality of the moment is as relevant as synchronous phenomena in relation to an individual. Some moments are more 'death-filled' than others, and this is one of them. The presence of death is not linked with David's horoscope specifically, but is a property of the particular point in time when he died. That this 'death-filled' moment also affects his own horoscope very precisely (with aspects such as Jupiter exactly conjunct moon) makes it even more awesome. I can no more explain the reason for such coincidences than I can explain why chickens come from eggs.

David's 'death chart' is the chart not of a person but of a moment, and therefore we cannot interpret it according to the patterns of human psychology. In many ways, such a chart is barer, more stark, because it is not filled out with human flesh. The peacefulness of this horoscope, with its many sextiles and lack of oppositions, reflects with eerie precision the peacefulness of David's demise. As far as types of death are concerned, the sudden fatal coronary is probably one of the least unpleasant; thus the sun, moon, Mercury and Pluto all in conjunction in Libra are in sextile to Neptune, suggesting a tranquil slipping away. The jarring note in the chart is the exact conjunction of Uranus with the midheaven. But this is appropriate for the suddenness of the event, and appropriate, too, for the separation from loved ones through death suggested by the conjunction of Uranus and Venus in Scorpio. Thus the 'death chart' tells us very literally what kinds of patterns or archetypal influences are at work in the moment. I have felt for some time that the midheaven, as one of the four angles of the chart, was concerned not only with vocation and with mother, but with the process of physical manifestation, perhaps even more so than the ascendant – which is usually taken to be the point of birth. Some years ago I collected data on the times of several severe earthquakes, and found that Uranus appeared consistently in the midheaven. This led me to think about the midheaven in connection with manifest events. Further research with composite horoscopes led me to discover that at the time that a potential relationship concretises, there is often a powerful transit over the midheaven of the composite chart. As a result of these and other observations, I am convinced that this angle of the horoscope is related to things coming to birth in concrete reality. Thus the midheaven represents not only mother, but mother as body, and the physical characteristics of the individual are often reflected by the sign and planets at the midheaven more strongly than by the ascendant. In other words, the midheaven is the place of outward manifestation, and the Mars–Uranus–Venus conjunction at the midheaven of David's 'death chart' suggests a sudden, violent, separative event occurring in the outer world at that precise moment. The event of physical death, reflected by the placement of Uranus at the midheaven, could only 'happen' in a literal sense at the precise moment when that planet reached the midheaven – which in turn 'happened' to coincide with the precise moment of David's coronary.

There is certainly something very strange and unsettling about the testimony of this 'death chart'. The implication is, of course, that every moment carries its own pattern, and some moments are more fraught or powerful than others. Perhaps we are in some way 'sensitive' to the eternally moving round of the heavens so that what we do is always appropriate for the moment; or else, because we ourselves are part of that unified life which also includes the heavens, we and they coincide. Thus, if some archetypal configuration such as death is reflected in the heavens – as it obviously was at the time of David's demise – then those individuals in whom the same archetypal configuration is also constellated will respond with an experience of death on some level at that moment. We may toss about that word synchronicity because it sounds so much more rational, but what it feels like is simply fate.

I would like to look now at the horoscope of Jean Bates, whose own experience of her husband's death is reflected in very different ways. Oddly, the transits and progressions active at the time do not involve the seventh house, as might be expected with an event such as the death of the partner. Rather, they emphasise the fourth house, through the conjunction of progressed Mercury to natal Mars in 14 Aries in that house. Now I do not think even Luc Gauricus would have read 'husband's death' out of that one, but what I read, although it may initially sound strange, is a crisis involving father and roots. I can only deduce from this that for Jean, her husband was a father figure more than he was a husband, and his primary significance was the providing of home, roots and security. We shall see as we go along if this surmise is in any way supported by other aspects. What the progression in Jean Bates' chart states is: a father figure, rather than a husband, is in crisis or trouble. As Mrs Bates adored her own father and despised her mother, it is not surprising that such an element would have become an integral part of her married life.

If one wished to be literal, one could interpret David's fourth house Uranus as a fate of sudden death, a sudden ending to life. I have met some very old people with Uranus in the fourth, although that does not rule out the possibility that when they go, they will go suddenly rather than lingeringly. Likewise one could look with literal eyes at Jean Bates' Venus, the ruler of the seventh house, in opposition to Pluto in the eighth, and read a fate of the death of the partner. Certainly Jean did not give me the impression of being a person who would have permitted Pluto into her marriage in any other way. It was a 'perfect' marriage, and any darkness or destructiveness was entirely unconscious and covert.

This natal oppositon of Venus and Pluto was triggered by the eclipse in 9 Libra which fell on David's ascendant and which also fell in Jean's tenth house. This eclipse, along with transiting Pluto, also collided with the natal Mars and progressed Mercury. As Jean's Venus–Pluto is mixed up, in cross-aspect, with David's Saturn–Mars–Pluto conjunction by square, we may surmise that there might have been some less than perfect elements at work in this relationship; a rather turbulent emotional and sexual situation is suggested between them through David's Saturn exactly square to Jean's Mars and Jean's Saturn widely square David's Mars. This is a basic 'marriage problem', each partner being inclined to frustrate and anger the other one. What is curious is that the entire web of aspects between the two charts was being constellated by the transiting sun–moon–Mercury–Pluto configuration at the time of the death. I am not sure how to read this, but I suspect that, mixed up with whatever other fate and motives might have been at work in this death, David Bates left his wife in the only way he knew how.

Another interesting feature in Jean's horoscope is that, at precisely the same time that the progressed sun squared Uranus in David's chart and he retired, Jean was experiencing the progressed sun in square to Pluto. She, too, was undergoing profound changes; a death of some kind loomed on her horizon too, three years before the event. She told me that during this period she was quite 'ill', suffering from swoons and fainting fits which produced no medical diagnosis. We cynical analytic folk would tend to look at the emotional side of such symptoms, particularly as they were occurring during a time which Jean described as 'wonderful', when she and her husband were especially close and were never out of each other's sight. The progressed sun in square to Pluto describes the death of the partner more accurately than the aspects in force at the time of the actual death, and this is very mysterious. It is as though something died, for her, earlier and coincident with the time of David's retirement. This is what I meant by the shadow of this death being cast long before. Perhaps, now that her husband was no longer swathed in his collective garments, she was faced with the challenge of getting to know him, and confronting darker elements in her own feelings towards him. The progressed sun in square to Pluto suggests a period when an individual is confronted with all that is dark, primitive and unknown about his own nature. My feeling is that Jean Bates could not, or would not, look at these things; hence the 'blacking out' symptoms which she manifested at the time, which, taken as a symbolic picture, could not be a better description of 'going unconscious'.

A crisis seems to have loomed for both these people, who certainly, in their fashion, loved each other deeply, but who were ill-equipped to cope with the more convoluted unconscious aspects of themselves and their relationship. For this they can scarcely be 'blamed', since the values and standards with which both had been brought up had hardly prepared them for the seamier side of marriage as personified by Pluto, which aspects both Venus and Mars in both charts. Without spending a further fifty pages on the particular psychological complexions of the couple, suffice it to say that David's experience of mother and therefore of women is reflected in his horoscope as extremely powerful and very manipulative; while his experience of father and therefore of the possibilities of his own manhood is reflected as frustrated and disappointing. Jean, on the other hand, has an image of the mother similar to her husband's, for both have Saturn in the tenth house; and her image of the father also is not dissimilar to her husband's, for her sun is in opposition to Neptune, suggesting idealisation and adoration masking a sense of loss and disillusionment; while Mars in the fourth opposite Saturn and in square to Pluto suggests a covert violence and powerful unexpressed sexuality connected with the father. Thus both people have the same pattern: a repressive and powerful mother, and a frustrated and angry father who appeared 'weak'. Perhaps, for each of them, the other was experienced as a surrogate parent, a not unusual situation in many more conventional young marriages. This incestuous and deeply unconscious tie did not break until David 'retired' in both senses of the word under his sun–Uranus progression, and began to break free. The atmosphere in a house where two people are never out of each other's sight and are simultaneously undergoing major solar progressions to outer planets cannot have been peaceful. But Jean Bates could remember nothing wrong at all, save that she kept inexplicably fainting.

The transit of Pluto which had been crossing David's ascendant and squaring his Saturn at the midheaven had also, as I mentioned, been opposing Jean's natal Mars and triggering both the Mars–Saturn conjunction in the birth chart and the Mercury–Mars progression. This once again implies a situation of frustration and deep anger, and a need for change and release. I would guess that David and Jean were beginning to discover all kinds of deep grievances towards each other, although neither party was able to deal with such emotions. Jean is a very characteristic Aquarian, who would never dream of saying a hurtful or selfish thing to anyone. Her outlook is positive and benign, and there is little sign of the Scorpio ascendant, or of the Venus–Mars–Pluto T-cross which is present in her chart. But this strong Plutonian component in her suggests that she must have made her feelings known through the atmosphere and in all kinds of covert ways, and those feelings must have been very potent indeed. The swooning fits usually accomplished their purpose on the surface, for her husband was always extremely attentive, caring and devoted when she felt 'ill'. On some other level, however, he was no doubt exceedingly angry. I can only surmise what this death meant to Jean on levels other than the conscious one. Of course, she was plunged into a period of grief and disorientation afterwards, for he was the most important thing in her life. But my sense is that this death was also the loss of a battle, for her husband had succeeded in slipping out of her grasp; and thus it was a final breaking free from her increasingly urgent and angry need to possess and, in consequence, a rejection on the deepest level.

There are other transits which are no doubt relevant in these two charts, and I have not touched at all on the midpoints which might be involved, nor on other methods of prognostication such as primary and tertiary progressions, or solar and lunar returns. But the aspects which I have mentioned tell a remarkably vivid story of death on many levels, occurring – or trying to occur – over a considerable period of time. When one considers that the timing of these aspects was inherent at the birth of both people, it is even more striking to observe the enmeshed cross-aspects occurring at the time of the death. I am not suggesting that marital problems were the 'cause' of David's coronary. But I am suggesting that the rising to the surface of these problems, and the psychic necessity of change, were synchronous with the death.

I would now like to consider the experience of the father's death in the horoscopes of the two sons, beginning first with the younger son, whom I will call Trevor. Oddly, no major progressed aspects are in evidence in Trevor's chart at the time of his father's demise. Both sons had removed themselves from the family in a rather telling fashion – although not telling to Mrs Bates. Trevor had emigrated to Australia and his brother Brian to America some years before the event. Thus, at the time of death, Trevor was not embroiled in the family's problems, although certain aspects in the birth chart, such as the moon in square to Neptune and the sun in opposition to Pluto, suggest that the dilemmas which his parents could not themselves solve have passed down to the next generation. Trevor also has the telltale Mars–Saturn contact, which he shares with both parents, and which is a kind of 'family signature'. But there was one major progressed aspect in effect the year before the death: the sun had moved into 21 Pisces and was making a trine to the natal moon in 21 Cancer in the seventh house. This aspect, which is generally considered to be a harmonious and stabilising one, suggests that Trevor's life was actually moving in very constructive directions, and that he was experiencing a period of personal happiness both professionally and in his marriage. This is interesting in light of the difficulties which his parents were experiencing, as though his own 'inner marriage' of sun and moon represents a kind of separation from the family web and a healing of his own internal split between mother and father – suggested by the quincunx between sun and moon. I have often found that the death of a parent coincides with a time in the child's life when a separation internally from that parent has occurred. Thus the cord which binds parent and child on an unconscious level has broken, and both are left free to pursue their own fates. I have had occasion to watch this process at work in my analysands, where the unconscious begins to throw up symbols which seem to concern the internal separation from a parent months before the actual death occurs. Only with hindsight does it become apparent that some inner knowledge of the approaching death is already at work; or, looked at another way, that the internal freeing from parental bonds synchronises with the external experience of the loss of the parent.

Trevor's relationship with his father, as reflected by the birth chart, was not a close one. The fourth house ruler, Mars, is in opposition to Saturn in Virgo in the eighth house, suggesting that the more structured and earthy side of his father (who was a Virgo) was the facet most in evidence for this younger son, and that it was not entirely well received. When we come to examine the chart of Brian, the elder brother, we shall also find an eighth house Saturn; thus both sons reflect a certain distance or loss surrounding the experience of the father. The aspects between Trevor's and David's charts are also rather difficult, and suggest an opposite-ness and great difference in outlook. For example, David's moon–Neptune conjunction in Leo falls opposite Trevor's Venus–Mercury conjunction in Aquarius, suggesting an emotionality and self-centredness in the father which collided with the rationality and detachment of the son. Trevor's natal sun in opposition to Pluto also suggests a difficult experience of fathering, because of the element of power and struggle for dominance which is implied; it seems as though Trevor has inherited what his father David Bates could not express of his own Plutonian forcefulness. I would guess that the wilfulness and passion and dominance of the Mars–Saturn–Pluto conjunction at David's midheaven, although unexpressed in ordinary life, was very apparent to his son, and contributed to Trevor's unprecedented move to Australia.

The transits are more revealing than the progressions, when we examine what was effective in Trevor's chart at the time of the death. One of the aspects which is most striking is the coincidence of David's demise with the tail end of Trevor's Saturn return. Although the exact conjunction had already occurred two months preceding the death, Saturn was still within orb, and the entire period for several months previous and several months following a Saturn return carries the essential meaning of the transit. One feature of this cycle, which affects everyone at roughly the same age, is that it signifies a kind of 'growing up', a movement away from the values and standards of the family and an affirmation of one's own standpoint and outlook. It is a psychological hardening, a maturation which enables the individual to leave some of his parental dependencies behind, to cope better with the external world and its demands and limitations, and to accept one's own nature, flaws as well as strengths, in a better spirit. Thus, David Bates' death is shown as a deeply symbolic as well as a literal event, because on an inner level the father was already dying – the old standards and values were dropping away – and this internal change was accompanied by the toughening and isolation of a son growing from boyhood to manhood. Trevor was at this time already a father himself, and was beginning to become successful in his chosen field of chemical research. In some way David's death seems to have represented for him a freeing from the old Saturnian Terrible Father who held him back, and a simultaneous birth of a more positive Saturnian principle within himself which enabled him to move forward in the world.

Thus Trevor was already in a process of separation from the father during the months preceding the actual death. One of the motifs in this theme of separation is the motif of worldly failure or success. David Bates, as I have mentioned, seems to have been burdened with an acute sense of not having lived his potential in the world. He died feeling that he had been weak and ineffectual. How much of an objective truth this is, and how much a subjective feeling, I cannot tell; but it is apparent that within the family system, he was certainly the weaker partner in the marriage. Trevor was, until the time of the Saturn return, burdened with a similar feeling, for he had shared these sentiments with his mother from time to time. This sense of impotence is characteristic of Mars–Saturn, which both son and father have in the birth horoscope. After the Saturn return, although the inner implications of this aspect are by no means solved and present a lifetime's challenge, it became easier for Trevor to become successful and to feel 'potent' in worldly terms, for he was no longer so identified with his father.

Other transits are in evidence in Trevor's chart, although I feel that the return of Saturn to its own place in the eighth house is the most telling in terms of David's death. Jupiter, which had approached the exact conjunction of the moon in David's chart, was coming into exact opposition to Trevor's Venus–Mercury conjunction from the eighth house cusp. This transit has a rather literal feeling about it: an experience of death disturbs the stability and security of the second house Venus. Transiting Uranus was also approaching the exact square to natal Pluto in 15 Leo in the eighth house; once again, there is the connotation of a sudden experience of death, a collision with an irrevocable fate of some kind. There was also a conjunction of transiting Pluto with Trevor's Neptune in 15 Libra in the ninth house. The involvement of the ninth house, which also occurs in Jean Bates' chart, carries the implication of some deep change in world views occurring, which had been in process for some time before the death. Neptune in the ninth house is an extremely idealistic placement; Trevor shares this attribute with his mother, who also has Neptune in the ninth in 16 Leo. Thus both begin life with a vision of the cosmos which is blissful and loving; God is *summum bonum* and sacrifice and submission are the requirements of the soul. At the time of David's death, Uranus by transit was in square to Jean's ninth house Neptune; and transiting Pluto was conjuncting Trevor's Neptune in the same house. Thus both seem to have been undergoing some deep change in their religious and philosophical attitudes around the time of David Bates' death. Jean's childlike vision of a loving and caring deity was shattered by the unexpectedness and 'unfairness' of the death; Trevor's was undermined and subtly deepened during the months before it. The death did not cause these changes, but it was synchronous with them; for any sudden and 'undeserved' tragic event has a tendency to coincide with a time of questioning one's essential religious beliefs. Once again the archetype of death is at work, although in a different sphere.

The elder son, Brian Bates, seems to have registered his father's death much more strongly than did his brother, for the progressions and transits at the time are extremely strongly marked. Perhaps the event meant much more to him, and coincided with more turbulent changes in his own life. The first progressed aspect we must explore is the opposition of progressed Mercury to natal Pluto in the ninth house. This aspect, like Jean's Mercury–Mars progression, could not be construed as a 'death' progression in the ordinary sense. What it does suggest, however, is a period in Brian's life when he began, perhaps unwillingly (squares and oppositions usually reflect reluctance to deal with a problem), to encounter an entirely different dimension of reality. Mercury–Pluto exposes the individual to the underworld in such a way that

his outlook and attitudes are changed; his opinions about himself
and about life are forced to deepen, and nothing is ever as simple
again. Mercury is placed in the second house in the birth chart, and
rules the eighth; thus the implication is that this profound change
in outlook springs from an experience of loss and disrupted
stability.

Another progressed aspect noticeable at the time is that of
progressed Mars in opposition to natal Venus, also placed in the
second house. This progression coincided with the beginning of
the breakup of Brian's marriage, an event which at first seems
unconnected with the death of the father, but which, as we shall
see, is more closely allied than one might think. Once again a death
is in evidence, but here it is the death of a relationship, and
Mars–Venus contacts are typical reflections of turbulence and
difficulty in this sphere of life. The individual needs are colliding
with the need for security, reflected by Venus, ruling the seventh,
in the second. Brian's marriage was a second-house situation, a
'background' of stability for him. At the time that his father 'left'
his mother, he was in process of leaving his wife. Mars was
progressing through the eighth house, thus underlining the theme
of death, although the death of the father – on a symbolic level in
Brian's case – seems more concerned with an encounter with a
deeper and more mysterious facet of life and with the eruption of
emotional elements that had previously been unconscious. Like
his father, Brian had made a 'perfect' marriage. Also like his father,
the archetype of death, constellated so powerfully in this family,
seems to have activated in him a bitter realisation that something
was less than perfect in his life. Both, on some level, 'died',
although Brian's death concerned the demise of a persona, a
particular lifestyle and a veneer of social normality beneath which
a great deal had been quietly festering. Jean Bates, in relating this
difficult period in her elder son's life, was visibly upset and baffled
by it, for, as with her own marriage, 'everything had seemed so
lovely'. When I consider all these lives together – Trevor undergoing his worldly initiation, Brian undergoing the death of his old
life, David leaving life behind, and Jean suffering from fainting fits,
I am given the strong sense that some essential glue or binding
substance, that previously held this family in an enmeshed and
paralysing grip, had begun to dissolve. This dissolution released
both the sons into different lives, released the mother into
widowhood and a great many disturbing questions, and released
David into death.

One final progression is worth noting in Brian's chart: the
progressed moon had come into exact opposition to the Mars–
Uranus conjunction in 5 Gemini in the seventh house. This aspect

is classically connected with disruption and separation, and it is interesting to note that Uranus is the ruler of Brian's fourth house – the house which concerns the relationship with the father. Brian, like Trevor, did not experience his father as a sweet-natured, loving man; here the fourth house ruler is conjunct Mars and in square to the moon in the tenth (ruling the mother). Thus Brian seems not to have been oblivious to the undercurrents of battle which existed between his parents but which everyone was so careful to ignore. This synchronicity between the loss of a father and the loss of a marriage reveals that in some fashion the nature of Brian's marriage was bound up with his parents' marriage – as though he had tried to eradicate the deep anxiety of Mars–Uranus–moon by plastering it over with a 'nice' exterior modelled after the 'nice' exterior he observed at home. Thus, with the severing of one relationship through death, the cord that bound the other was broken as well. Neither caused the other; but they happened together. This progressed lunar aspect is the only lunar progression which shows up in the four charts so far considered. Jean Bates had no lunar progressed aspects in force at the time of the death, nor did Trevor, nor did David Bates himself, although his progressed moon, had he lived for another month, would have arrived at the trine to natal Neptune and sextile to natal Mercury. I am not sure what to make of this absence of lunar progressed aspects, since the progressed moon is usually an excellent marker of the ebb and flow of life experience. The only conclusion I can come to is that Brian was the only immediate family member who actually *felt* the impact of the loss of his father at the time it happened. The others registered it, but perhaps only experienced it on an emotional level afterwards. This is not uncommon, since we do not all feel things in the same way at the same time. Often there is a delay between the time of a concrete experience and the time that one digests it. The moon is the receptacle of experience on a feeling level, a 'gut' level as it were, for it digests life's happenings and makes them personally our own. The lack of lunar aspects in all the charts save Brian's suggests to me that although Jean Bates had registered the *idea* that her husband had died, she did not *feel* it or its implications; and indeed, I was given the distinct impression, when speaking to her, that on some level she has still not wholly digested this death although several years have passed. When I asked her about the funeral, and her feelings about it, she explained that she had given instructions for her husband's body to be cremated. None of the family actually went to see the body before cremation save Brian, which the rest of them all thought rather odd. It would appear that this death was not wholly a reality for any family member save him.

Finally, to conclude this exploration of the family charts, one transit in Brian's horoscope seems relevant. This is the transit of Saturn over the natal moon and in square to the Mars–Uranus conjunction, which occurred before the death. Brian's moon in Virgo links him with his brother, who has Saturn in Virgo very near it, and in turn with his father, although the orb of conjunction between Brian's moon and David's sun is technically too wide. But this transit of Saturn in Brian's chart, like the Saturn return which was occurring in Trevor's, seems to suggest that Brian had matured in a rather embittered way in the months before his father's death. The squares to the seventh house planets reflect the painful separation which was occurring in his marriage, revealing conflict between a sense of responsibility and an urgent need for freedom. But the transit of Saturn over the moon suggests an issue in relation to the mother. As well as leaving father behind, Brian was also leaving his mother, for in some sense it appears he had married her, or her surrogate. A movement away from childhood and maternal bonds had begun to occur just before David's demise, combined with an increased need to ground himself in the world. Brian's chosen profession is that of a solicitor, and it would appear that the break-up of the marriage and the death of the father were also synchronous with an increased commitment to his professional life. Thus both sons were undergoing their own passage from childhood in the months prior to the death. I am left with the impression that Jean Bates, who is an extremely needful and possessive woman and very frightened of letting go of anyone she loves, had 'lost' both her sons during this time. Although both had physically separated and put great distances between themselves and the family, they had not yet 'left' emotionally; but the year preceding David's death saw the cutting of these cords. On some level this must have registered on Jean, albeit unconsciously, and provoked a certain increase of anxiety and a tendency to unleash upon her husband the whole battery of her emotional needs. As he himself was also undergoing a kind of separation, he was forced into the position of having to confront her, which the sons, by moving to opposite ends of the earth, had to some extent avoided doing. Given the choice between this confrontation, which on an archetypal level is represented by the mythic dragon fight, and a quick exit, he seems to have chosen the latter, although I do not mean that he 'chose' in any conscious sense.

I would like to make it clear that the above analysis is not an indictment of Jean Bates as the 'cause' of her husband's death. Whatever that death meant, it was reflected in his own chart, in an uncomfortably 'fated' way, and was therefore his own necessity. But this brief and in many ways incomplete examination of some of the dominant influences operating within the charts suggests that a family complex was beginning to break up, leaving each member to cope with his or her own emotional issues. Each one responded according to the individual temperament. Jean Bates informed me, as a kind of afterthought, that when Brian had returned to America after the funeral he had written to his mother and related a strange dream. She had remembered the dream because it was a connection, albeit tenuous, with the dead man, and made her feel comforted in some curious way. Brian dreamed that he had been washed up on a rocky shore from the depths of the sea, and as he climbed onto dry land he saw his father walking jauntily into the water. David Bates turned with a smile and said goodbye, with a gesture that implied it was now Brian's turn to tackle life; and then he disappeared into the same depths from which the son had just emerged. This is a deep and moving dream, although its implications were lost on Jean; for it portrays the cycle of life and the passing on of responsibility from father to son. The mythic theme behind it is the passing of the old king and the birth of the new one; and here it is portrayed as a willing acceptance, rather than as a struggle. I feel that this dream reflects something about this father and son too in the idea that Brian, in breaking the maternal cords which bound him both to his mother and his wife, had accomplished a task which the father could not do. It is rather Parsifal-like, for the young man succeeds where the old, sick one cannot. The dream is a fitting image of the mythic or archetypal patterns at work within this family at deep and unknown levels, of which the physical death of the father was only one manifestation.

I would like to close this summary with a brief mention of some of the synchronous reflections of the event in the charts of the four grandchildren. I have reproduced these charts below, although we will only deal with them in a very cursory fashion; but it is of interest to note the recurrence of signs, aspects and house placements, the reflection of family inheritance and family fate.

Bruce and Sally Bates are the children of Trevor Bates, while Rupert and Henry are the children of Brian. In Bruce's horoscope, it will be seen that Jupiter is placed exactly at the IC in Aquarius; and transiting Jupiter was approaching the exact opposition to this point at the time of his grandfather's death. As the fourth house concerns the father and the inheritance from the father's line, this aspect seems appropriate, although Bruce was not personally much affected by the death, being only, at the time, five years old. Sally, who was two at the time of her grandfather's death, also shows this movement across the meridian in her horoscope, but in her case it is transiting Neptune which was approaching the exact conjunction with the midheaven and applying to the opposition of

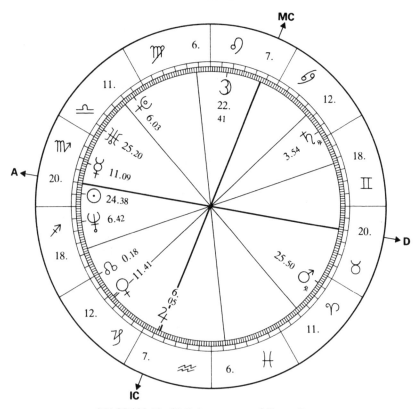

DIAGRAM 19. Birth horoscope of Bruce Bates

b. 17 November 1973
5.00 a.m.
Sydney, Australia

the moon at the IC. Thus in both these children's charts, some
change or crisis is suggested in the sphere of the family, although
they can hardly have been conscious of the deeper implications of
the death. Also, Saturn by transit, which was in 8 Virgo at the time
of David's death, was making an exact square to Sally's natal sun in
8 Gemini. This aspect likewise has traditional associations with the
relationship with the father and with the masculine line, and with
some experience of loss or disappointment.

Rupert and Henry were older and knew their grandfather better;
at the time of his death Rupert was eleven years old and Henry
seven. Saturn, transiting in 8 Virgo, was approaching the exact
conjunction to Rupert's natal Venus; this aspect no doubt reflects

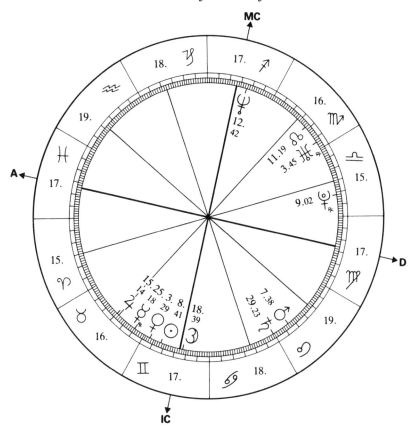

DIAGRAM 20. Birth horoscope of Sally Bates

b. 30 May 1976
12.40 a.m.
Sydney, Australia

the emotional hurt and sense of loss at the dissolution of his
father's marriage, for Venus rules the fourth house in Rupert's
chart. But once again the synchronicity of events is shown, for the
aspect coincides with the death of Rupert's grandfather. In
Henry's chart, the powerful opposition of transiting Uranus to the
ascendant is shown, and this too may be taken as a reflection of the
break-up of the parental marriage; but it is also synchronous with
the grandfather's death, for 14 Scorpio is the degree which appears
at the midheaven of David Bates' 'death chart'. Henry's ascending
node is placed in precisely the same degree of the same sign as his

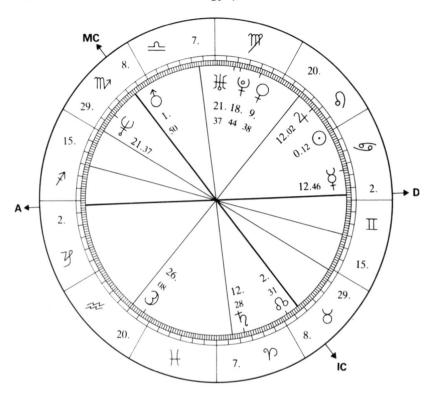

DIAGRAM 21. Birth horoscope of Rupert Bates

b. 23 July 1967
7.20 a.m.
New York City

grandfather's – 15 Aquarius – and it falls in Henry's tenth house,
squared by the transiting Uranus. And once again we find Jupiter
applying to the conjunction of the IC in 7 Leo. Thus, however we
wish to interpret these transits in the charts of the four grandchildren, one point emerges most clearly: the fourth house is affected
in all four charts, either by a planet approaching the cusp or by a
transit affecting the ruler. This synchronous link-up in all four
charts, showing some crisis or change in the sphere of the father
and the father's line, is rather impressive.

   The story of three years in the life of the Bates family, astrologically considered, is a good reflection of the way in which synchronicity can display itself. But such tie-ups are by no means
exceptional or uncommon. They may be met with in every family

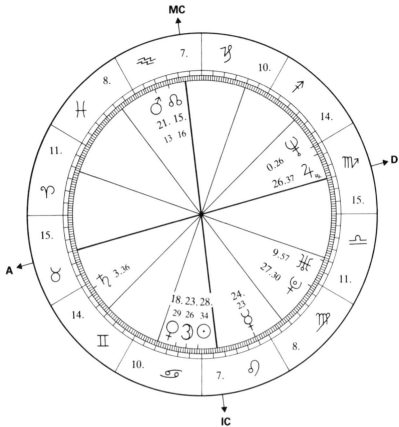

DIAGRAM 22. Birth horoscope of Henry Bates

b. 22 July 1971
1.10 a.m.
New York City

whenever an event is of significance to that family as a unit, and they may be met with in relationships as well where the developments in the life of one partner synchronise with changes in the life of the other. Through this great interconnected chain separate lives are brought together in common meaning, and that strange unity of substance is revealed which alchemy called the *unus mundus* and which Jung called the collective unconscious. The operation of synchronicity is awesome, not least because of that quality of absolute knowledge which seems to be displayed. As Aniela Jaffe puts it in *The Myth of Meaning*:

The synchronistic phenomena arranged by the archetype often arouse wonder and awe, or an intuition of unfathomable powers which assign meaning. In Goethe's view there exists an ordering power outside man, which resembles chance as much as providence, and which contracts time and expands space. He called it the 'daemonic', and spoke of it as others speak of God.[148]

Whether it is God, 'daemon' as Goethe puts it, or fate, I do not know. But the experience of 'unfathomable powers' is unmistakable, and so is the feeling of a web of some kind with filaments that radiate out into unknowable distances. Unsurprisingly, the spider is one of the most ancient symbols of fate. This web is what the Stoics meant by *heimarmenê*, and it upset the early Church to such an extent that it was forced to develop the concept of God's Providence to counteract the sense of fatality which any encounter with the web provoked. It is exceedingly difficult to penetrate the apparent paradox here, wherein events 'synchronise' with astrological configurations and internal psychic states because the 'archetype' has been constellated. Yet at the same time those astrological configurations which are synchronous with events and inner experiences have been 'ordained' from the moment of the individual's birth because of the orderly clockwork of the heavens. In other words, both the causal fate (Moira) and the acausal (the unconscious) are equally valid ways of interpreting experience. The line between Moira and the *unus mundus* of the collective unconscious in which the archetypes play is a very thin one indeed, for it would seem that fate is both causal and acausal at once, already written yet being written in each moment, irrevocable yet subject to human tampering. We have explored the intricate web which those 'unfathomable powers' weave, the arrangements 'they' or 'it' make, in some detail. It is now time to consider those 'powers' themselves, or itself, which Jung, during the course of his life, came to describe as the Self.

# 10

## Fate and the Self

*What will you do, God, should I die?*
*Should your cup break? That cup am I.*
*Your drink go bad? That drink am I.*
*I am the trade you carry on,*
*With me is all your meaning gone.*

**Rainer Maria Rilke**

A single theme connects each example of the characteristically
human dilemmas described in previous chapters of this book.
Whether we are considering the difficult inner and outer life of
Ruth, or the impenetrable autism of Renee R., or the melancholy
suicide of Timothy S., or the apparently preordained end of the
French King, Henri II, or the sudden death of David Bates, there is
a sense of order or teleology or necessity surrounding these
examples. Sometimes this order was apparent to the individual
involved in the experience; this was the case with Ruth, who –
although she and I did not discuss her horoscope in our sessions
together – came increasingly to feel that the apparently 'chance'
misfortune of her imprisoning relationship was not so chancy after
all, but was the outward expression of an intelligent 'something'
within her which not only caused her considerable suffering and
conflict, but was also moving somewhere, towards some goal. In
other cases, such as the suicide of Timothy S. or the death of David
Bates, no such sense of meaningfulness was apparent to the
individual. But it becomes apparent to the astrologer, when the life
pattern is connected with the horoscope and the synchronicity is
seen between planetary placements and the individual's inner and
outer life. An event isolated from its context seems to be chance,
but when it is placed within the fabric of a total life with its family
background, its particular bias of character, its inner unfolding
reflected in dreams, and its horoscope, then chance becomes a
quite inappropriate word and qualities such as 'inevitable',

'orderly', 'right',' meaningful' and 'necessary' suggest themselves. As Jung puts it,

> What happens to a person is characteristic of him. He represents
> a pattern and all the pieces fit. One by one, as his life proceeds,
> they fall into place according to some predestined design.[149]

When life deals a harsh and unexpected blow, then we experience the dark face of fate, which the Greeks called Moira. When life
seems to be guiding us towards a goal and fills us with a feeling of
destiny, then we experience the bright face of fate, which Christianity calls Providence. The former, faithfully reflected by its
primordial female image, seems stern, pitiless, and without reason
or design related to the individual. Moira, after all, draws her
boundaries without favourites, for they are collective or universal
boundaries, not personal ones in any individualistic sense. The
latter, even if it involves pain, seems ultimately benevolent, full of
wisdom, and caring especially of the individual. Often both these
facets of fate are experienced at once, and the sense of the two
coming together – or being part of the same whole – is a not
infrequent occurrence in analytic work, where the 'unfair' limitations and hurts and losses of life are gradually related to an inner
pattern which moves towards a goal and slowly enlarges and
enriches the personality. Aniela Jaffe phrases this coincidence as
follows:

> Basically, individuation consists of constantly renewed, con-
> stantly needed attempts to amalgamate the inner images with
> outer experience. Or to put it differently, it is the endeavour to
> 'make what fate intends to do with us entirely our own
> intention'.[150]

Thus fate, as Chrysippos suggested, seems to embody a duality or
a paradox, because it manifests at one time as a doom and at
another as an act of grace. The problem of this paradox preoccupied Jung, who saw in it the reflection of a morally ambiguous
godhead, a deity whose ambivalent face was revealed to the
perplexed Job as both God and the Devil. In Jung's formulation of
the concepts of individuation and the archetype of the Self, these
two disparate threads which weave that dual fate of which Chrysippos wrote have been joined together. 'Self' is a marvellous term
to use to unite all the opposites within the complex and paradoxical
human being, and that is precisely, in Jung's view, what the Self
does. Ultimately elusive though it may eventually prove to be, it is
worth attempting to explore what he meant by this term in context
of the horoscope. For it is the closest, psychologically speaking,
that we may be able to come towards making sense of those

contradictory expressions of fate, and of the equally paradoxical relationship of fate and free will with which life perpetually confronts us.

I will first quote one of Jung's varied definitions of the Self, which is rather lengthy but which will help us to grasp what he means by the term.

> As an empirical concept, the self designates the whole range of psychic phenomena in man. It expresses the unity of the personality as a whole. But in so far as the total personality, on account of its unconscious component, can be only in part conscious, the concept of the self is, in part, only *potentially* empirical and is to that extent a *postulate* . . .

> Just as conscious as well as unconscious phenomena are to be met with in practice, the self as psychic totality also has a conscious as well as an unconscious aspect. Empirically, the self appears in dreams, myths, and fairytales in the figure of the 'supraordinate personality', such as king, hero, prophet, saviour, etc., or in the form of a totality symbol, such as the circle, square, *quadratura circuli*, cross, etc . . . Empirically, therefore, the self appears as a play of light and shadow, although conceived as a totality and unity in which the opposites are united . . .

> The self is not a philosophical idea, since it does not predicate its own existence, i.e. does not hypostasize itself. From the intellectual point of view it is only a working hypothesis. Its empirical symbols, on the other hand, very often possess a distinct *numinosity*, i.e. an *a priori* emotional value, as in the case of the mandala . . . It thus proves to be an *archetypal idea*, which differs from other ideas of the kind in that it occupies a central position befitting the significance of its content and its numinosity.[151]

Sometimes Jung writes about the Self as 'an' archetype – that is, one of the various ordering or patterning factors in the unconscious. Thus, just as Moira is a self-portrait of that primordial instinct within nature which allots boundaries to material life and avenges transgression of those boundaries, the Self, with its impressive range of symbolic representations – diamond, circle, mandala, philosopher's stone, flower, treasure, androgyne, golden ring, etc. – is an image of that instinct within the individual to evolve into himself, to become the unique and single and meaningful whole that was always there in potential but which takes the entirety of a lifetime – or many lifetimes – even to partially unfold. Put another way, the Self is an image of the religious instinct, that aspect of the psyche which aspires to an experience of unity or divinity. When Jung writes about it in this way, the Self is 'the' archetype, the Great Round which encompasses all aspects of the psyche and welds them into a unique whole. Aniela Jaffe phrases it as follows:

> The archetype of the self is 'nameless, ineffable', a hidden X whose concretisations are indistinguishable from God-images ... Individuation has to be understood as the realisation of the 'divine' in man.[152]

In formulating this concept of the Self as the centre of individual development (and collective development as well, for its images are 'indistinguishable from God-images'), Jung parted ways irrevocably with Freud and the Freudians, who have tended to be unsympathetic to the idea of a 'religious' instinct as basic and as innate as those biological drives with which psychoanalysis in the orthodox sense is primarily concerned. Religious aspiration, to the more reductive-minded psychotherapist, is a 'sublimation'. For Jung, it is no such thing; it is rather an *a priori* urge within the psyche, existent from the beginning, to develop in accord with a unique pattern towards a unique goal (according to the 'will of God'), and that pattern and goal fulfil not only the urges of the body but also the urges of the spirit. Thus Moira and Providence unite within a single centre, which is both corporeal and spiritual, personal and collective. The following passage from *The Development of Personality* reflects what has been called Jung's 'mystical' view of the psyche:

> What is it, in the end, that induces a man to go his own way and to rise out of unconscious identity with the mass as out of a swathing mist? Not necessity, for necessity comes to many, and they all take refuge in convention. Not moral decision, for nine times out of ten we decide for convention likewise. What is it, then, that inexorably tips the scales in favour of the *extraordinary*? It is what is commonly called *vocation*: an irrational factor that destines a man to emancipate himself from the herd and from its well-worn paths. True personality is always a vocation and puts its trust in it as in God ... But vocation acts like a law of God from which there is no escape ... He *must* obey his own law, as if it were a daemon whispering to him of new and wonderful paths. Anyone with a vocation hears the voice of the inner man: he is *called*.[153]

Now, there are a number of problems posed to the astrologer by this thing Jung calls the 'vocation' of 'true personality'. When the Self is described as 'the unity of the personality as a whole', we can look to the total horoscope as its blueprint, including not only

signs, planets and houses but also aspects and balances (or imba-
lances) of elements and qualities, lunar phases, every detail, in
fact, that comprises the art of horoscopic interpretation. The Self is
therefore the entire chart, natal and progressed. But there is a
difficulty in that whatever it is that 'induces a man to go his own
way' does not appear to be in the horoscope. Any experienced
astrologer will have come across those people who, far from
manifesting the highly individual story of the birth chart, do not in
any way resemble it, but are rather like cardboard figures cut out of
a popular magazine or television series with ideas, beliefs and
responses that are wholly collective. There is, to put it baldly,
nobody at home; that is, no individual is at home, but rather a
collective mouthpiece out of whose mouth emerges the family
system of beliefs and values and, on a broader level, the beliefs and
values of the prevailing culture in which the person lives and
works. There is nothing in the horoscope which can tell us why
that person is not expressing his horoscope; but it stares one in the
face from the opposite chair. Thus there is something about the
Self which is not only the totality of the horoscope, but is also more
than the horoscope.

There are also many people at varying stages of individual
expression; one can see the moon active, or the sun square Uranus,
or the Venus at the midheaven, but the Mercury–Pluto conjunction is nowhere in evidence, nothing has yet been met of the eighth
house Saturn except in its most superficial form, and the fourth
house Mars–Uranus conjunction has completely disappeared.
This is generally where most of us live: in a state of gradual
encounter with more and more of that total personality which first
meets us as 'fate' in the outside world and only latterly, sometimes
with considerable effort, as aspects of ourselves – although no less
'fate'. One of the more interesting features of analytic work to the
astrological eye is the manner in which people become more like,
rather than less like, their horoscopes as consciousness of self
increases. Far from 'transcending' the birth chart, the individual
seems to become more at home in it; he and it begin to fit each
other; and, concurrently, he is more at home in himself as what he
is. This, of course, can occur without any discussion of astrological
themes, so I can hardly be accused of 'making' my analysands fit
their charts when I have often not seen their charts until years of
work have elapsed. Most particularly, it is the sun sign which
seems to 'shine' increasingly out of the person, as though this
point in the horoscope is above all the individual as 'vessel' of the
Self. But we are no closer to the answer of why one person elects to
make the individual journey and another not.

Another problem which is raised in relation to the Self and the horoscope is that issue which we have already confronted many times: Why does a particular astrological configuration manifest in one person on one level and in another person on an altogether different level? Some things in the psyche can undoubtedly be tampered with, but others cannot; the case history which follows shortly is an illustration of the latter. But it would seem, when one views a life from a broader perspective, that the boundaries which are given – whether by Moira, Providence or the Self – are precisely the right boundaries to facilitate the development of that individual. It is difficult to describe this unless one has experienced a feeling of it; but the phrase I have often heard (and myself felt) is that one would not change any aspect of one's past life, because somehow it has all 'fit' and led to the present and, beyond the present, into the future; and that includes the 'bad' or 'unhappy' pieces, the 'mistakes', the 'wrong choices' as well as the 'happy' pieces and 'right choices'. This profound subjective experience of a 'fit' does not seem to be bound up with the horoscope; rather, one feels it *about* the horoscope, as if that is the chart one would have chosen, if such a selection were possible. But the chart does not describe such precise mundane details as the kinds of synchronous happenings we have seen in the preceding chapter. The 'arrangements' which life offers are reflected in meaning by the horoscope, but not in detail in terms of their actuality. Once again, we meet with some aspect of the Self which lies beyond the birth chart.

What looks like the grim face of Moira from one point of view becomes a meaningful design from another, and it does not appear to be given to everyone to be able to see it from the latter point of view. Perhaps not everyone needs to; or perhaps everyone could, but opportunity is lacking, or refused. The same feeling of a 'fit' emerges when one works deeply with dreams, for a person's dreams fit that person, and while they seem at first to wind about in a random and senseless course, they eventually reveal a remarkable order and design, where motifs are met again and again and themes which appear to have vanished months before resurface in perfect juxtaposition, reflecting the changes in consciousness which have occurred in the interim. It is a running commentary of life, reported by 'something' inside. There is an inescapable sense of a superhuman artistry in this weaving. Writing about the spontaneous fantasy products of the psyche – dreams and 'active imagination' – Jung says:

> A dark impulse is the ultimate arbiter of the pattern, an unconscious *a priori* precipitates itself into plastic form ... Over the whole procedure there seems to reign a dim foreknowledge not only of the pattern but of its meaning.[154]

This same sense of artistry emerges when the pattern of a life is considered, as though it were a dream the contents of which are symbolic as well as literal. But when we look at the horoscope as an assembly of planetary placements, it does not at first convey such a sense of weaving. Rather, its components are the differently coloured threads that 'something' uses to make its tapestry. The events of 'real' life and the flow of inner images are both regulated in some mysterious fashion by the Self, and the 'stuff' of which both inner and outer experiences are fashioned is symbolised by the horoscope. Sometimes the manifestation is as an outer event, sometimes as an inner image; and even in considering the world of concrete happenings, two apparently opposite happenings can be described by the same astrological configuration. Thus, one man may experience marriage under the transit of Saturn over Venus, while another may find himself divorcing. The intrinsic meaning is the same: it is a coming to terms with the reality of the other person, and a collision between the ideals of love and the different-ness of the partner. But these two disparate circumstances, one often 'happy' and the other often 'unhappy', are individually tailored for a perfect fit depending on the individual. It would seem that this thing Jung calls the Self makes its arrangements using the astrological chart as a weaver uses his threads.

I sometimes feel that it is towards this end that the astrologer's, as well as the analyst's, work is directed: that the individual might gradually discover, come to terms with, and give his utmost to that totality of which the horoscope is the tool, the individual the vessel, and the Self the creator. This is a highly subjective issue and it will be obvious that it is a realm where statistics, although useful elsewhere, have no place.

> Every life is the realization of a whole, that is, of a self, for which reason this realization can also be called 'individuation'. All life is bound to individual carriers who realize it, and it is simply inconceivable without them. But every carrier is charged with an individual destiny and destination, and the realization of these alone makes sense of life. True, the 'sense' is often something that could just as well be called 'nonsense', for there is a certain incommensurability between the mystery of existence and human understanding. 'Sense' and 'nonsense' are merely man-made labels which serve to give us a reasonably valid sense of direction.[155]

The feeling of 'sense' as opposed to 'nonsense' is the closest I can come to describing any experience of the Self at work in life. It is when something makes meaningful sense to *me* in terms of *my* life, not anybody else's, that a glimpse is captured of that 'something' which is both fate and individual Self. Perhaps the 'sense' is relative and subjective rather than being an inherent property of objective life. But that makes it no less a psychic reality; and what exactly is 'objective' life anyway? This point cannot really be argued to a conclusion; it is like the issue of God, phrased in the rather florid statement at the beginning of the film *The Song of Bernadette*: 'For those who believe in God, no explanation is necessary; for those who do not, no explanation is possible.' Thus any position in a birth chart may empirically describe character or an event, but it may be 'nonsense' in that it is merely those things, a statement of impersonal fate, with which the individual himself feels no real relationship. He is not a 'co-creator' in his own universe. Or it may resonate as something deeply meaningful because it is recognised as part of oneself, rather than something imposed from 'outside' by those flying pieces of rock we call planets. This is where Jung's concept of the Self, and the kinds of inner experiences that individuals have when encountering their own psychic substance, differ from the old *heimarmenê*, the universal 'planetary compulsion' which vented itself upon the sinful body but could not touch the soul. Put the Self at the centre and we are suddenly involved with something deeply individual. This is no planetary compulsion; the planets merely reflect, or are symbols of, a pattern which exists in the inner man or woman, and which is orchestrated through life experience by that archetype which stands as the essence of his individuality. The planets do not 'compel' contrary to the soul, but rather are the vessels for it.

The chart which follows is that of a woman whom I will call Alison. She is an astrological client rather than an analysand, although the inner world of the psyche is not unfamiliar to her since she works with it herself. Alison is both a singer and a counsellor with a wide variety of therapeutic skills which she uses in conjunction with the voice in workshops and individual work. She is also blind but her blindness is not total and she is sometimes able to discern light and shadow, movement and colour. The condition of her blindness began at birth although it took years to manifest. As she is an exceptionally vital and creative woman, I felt it would be of value not only to explore her horoscope but also to include her own description of her visual loss and the gradual process of coming to terms with it, for this story reveals not only a good deal of Alison's character – which will be apparent from her horoscope – but also that elusive feeling of 'sense' that her life pattern seems to hold for her. I have therefore transcribed a conversation with her about the issue of her blindness, because her own words are much more expressive than my paraphrasing could be.

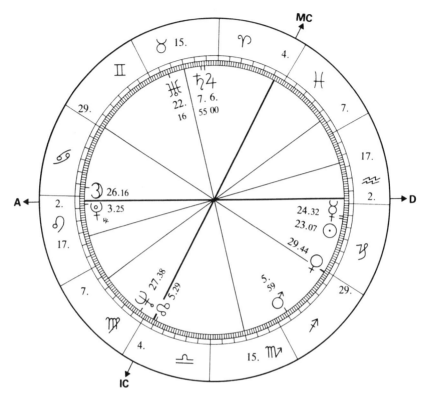

DIAGRAM 23. Birth horoscope of Alison J.

b. 13 January 1941
6.00 p.m.
Workington, Cumberland

My first question to Alison was about the physical aspect of her blindness: what is its medical definition, when did it start, what were her initial reactions to it.

**Alison:** It's chronic uveitis, which is inflammation of the uvea – the front wall of the eye. I also have glaucoma now in both eyes although originally, before 1971, it was only in the left eye. And there are cataracts in both eyes. There are other minor complications as well but those three are the main ones. The glaucoma in the left eye was there from the time I was a baby. That eye was always slightly larger than the right. Glaucoma is raised interocular pressure.

**Liz:** *Were you actually born with it?*

**Alison:** They don't know. I may have been. As a very small child it was obvious in photographs that one eye was slightly larger than the other. Quite likely I was born with it; nobody knows. I was also very myopic which was what was noticed first. I went to an ophthalmic specialist because I couldn't see the blackboard at school, when I was five. I was given glasses then, in 1946. I probably also had the uveitis then but it was undiagnosed. Not until my early teens did it actually start making a difference to me, because I began to have blurring patches. But they always cleared up. I told my specialist about them. But he just kept changing my glasses. When I was sixteen I was doing my mock GCE and found I couldn't read the papers. So I went to my GP and asked for a second opinion. The GP sent me back to the specialist. He gave me tests and came up with nothing.

**Liz:** *I find that very strange, that both glaucoma and uveitis should be entirely overlooked in that way.*

**Alison:** I still don't know how all this could have happened, how they could have missed what was going on. But they did. They patted me on the head and said, 'It's your age, you'll grow out of it.' They changed my glasses yet again, so that by now they were really thick and unpleasant. Then I left school on my specialist's advice. That was fine with me because I hated school.

**Liz:** *What did you prefer doing?*

**Alison:** All through my childhood I painted and drew. That was what my mother did, and that was what I wanted to do myself. But fate intervened there too by giving me the most hideous art mistress imaginable. I was so dedicated to painting and drawing. But this art mistress was the epitome of a tight-lipped, tight-faced ... Everything had to be drawn realistically and she really put me off it. So, in a funny way, it was right. Rather than going on to art college, which had always been my ambition, when I came to sixteen and my specialist said it would actually be better to leave school, I said, 'Whoopee!' and went off to Liberty's to train as a fashion buyer. That seemed a good idea, it gave my artistic side some outlet. But my sight rapidly went downhill then. I was getting up at half past six in the morning and travelling to London and tiring myself out, so it really began to show for the first time. My vision blurred and didn't clear up again. I went back to my specialist. He still misdiagnosed me. He told my mother, but not me, that I had retinal detachment in the left eye which was the one so badly damaged by the glaucoma  He sent me off to Moorfields for a contact lens.

**Liz:** *That sounds like a bit of fate at work, the constant misdiagnoses.*

**Alison:** He was the consultant for the whole of Hertfordshire. I think it was a kind of fate. So that was how I first went to Moorfields. Talk about fate again! In fact, my first visit to Moorfields was to sing at a nurses' party. This was about a month before I was sent there as a patient. They took one look at me and shook their heads. I was put on medication, which I've been on ever since. This was in 1957. I was given cortisone drops as well as a variety of other drops. They weren't meant to be curative, it isn't open for cure. But they've kept the inflammation stable for over twenty years. Then I was in and out of hospital while they operated on the left eye several times. When I was seventeen I was in for four months.

**Liz:** *Would you say that this was the first time you had to face the fact that the condition was incurable?*

**Alison:** It's funny, but I have no clear sense of when that actually dawned on me. There must have been a time, I'm sure. But I feel it much more as a gradual realisation, because I remember that my expectation at first was that in six months I'd be able to read again. I had to give up my job at Liberty's during that time. I looked at doing teachers' training and applied to a couple of colleges. But they turned me down without even meeting me because of the poor eyesight. They wouldn't do that now, actually. They would have at least given me a chance. So there I was, in and out of hospital, one operation after another, wondering what my prospects were. I suppose for the first year of that, I did assume that with enough time and treatment I would get enough sight back to be able to go to teachers' training college.

**Liz:** *How did your family react to all this?*

**Alison:** Luckily, my parents were very accepting and supportive to me. I spent days at home, drawing and listening to music. Mum was at home, and my grandfather. We did a lot of swimming and walking and cycling through the woods during the summer. Mum read to me a lot. I did some voluntary work for people at the hospital. Somehow I never felt at a loss for what to do. But I did feel very unsure about what the future would hold. At seventeen, I thought I would marry my boyfriend and that would solve it all. But that didn't last very long. There was a gradual realisation that I would probably never be able to read again or do a normal sort of job where sight was required.

**Liz:** *How did you cope with that gradual realisation? Did you go through any extremes of emotion about it? Or were you able to accept it more easily?*

**Alison:** I've gone through very occasional feelings of 'Why me?' But very rarely. I guess with my kind of Capricornian practicality in facing the realities of the world, I feel self-pity to be such an eroding thing. It doesn't do anybody any good. Although I do go into that periodically, the sense of what a useless emotion it is to regret or resent or be bitter or self-pitying really does catapult me out of it pretty quickly. I hate being in that state. So I find resources inside myself to get away from it. People have said to me, 'Aren't you angry with your specialist?' or 'Why don't you sue him?' Well, he certainly did his job badly.

**Liz:** *How does your attitude towards your visual loss mesh with whatever religious or philosophical views you might hold? Has it made you think about that side of things at all?*

**Alison:** Oh, yes, but it's gone through many different phases. When all this happened in my teens, I was a church-going Christian, which I had been consciously since the age of thirteen. By the time I was sixteen I was already, in a very unscholarly way, interested in Paul Tillich and was moving into that less orthodox realm of Christianity, although I remained a Sunday School teacher until I was twenty-one because I happened to like the kids. I went into the Methodist Church for a while and became very friendly with a woman who had quite severe multiple sclerosis. I find the 'Thank you, God, for giving me an infirmity to rise above' attitude pretty sickening. But certainly my beliefs were a support to me. By the time I gave up orthodox Christianity I had got myself a combination of self-resource and other philosophic props.

**Liz:** *What about your work, once the teachers' training colleges were closed to you?*

**Alison:** I heard about a social work training course, which I couldn't do until I was twenty-one. But I got a job as a receptionist at a local factory. For a couple of years that gave me a bit of money and an identity as someone with a job. I drew and I wrote, and it was quite a useful transition. Then I applied for the social work course and moved to London. It gave me something which was a response to my own dilemma and also work which used my experience. It gave me the chance to do something challenging. The whole experience of being four months in hospital, and in and out of hospital, and being with people when they lost their sight, made a great impression on me. I used to visit a woman who was deaf and blind, an old woman, until she died. Spending a lot of time with someone totally deaf and totally blind started making me think about very deep issues. I went into social work with elderly blind people. They had such awful lives, in North Paddington and

Kensal Rise . . . appalling housing conditions, atrocious landlords . . . I remember the day the pension went up to £4. I questioned my own role in it, and also where God was in all of it. I went through a period of being quite depressed, although I've never been prone to depression of the classical sort. Temperamentally that isn't my style. But the realities I encountered daily were very depressing. But I sang throughout it all.

*Liz: How did your singing fit in?*

**Alison:** I had already started singing when I was sixteen, and I very consciously used that as a channel. I get tremendous pleasure from it and I love the positive feedback I get. The necessity to sing was and is a counterbalance to facing the issue of my own visual loss, other people's visual loss, death, all those depressing issues. In 1965 I took to a kind of unorthodox Marxism. But it never sat very comfortably on me. That lasted for about five years. It was a very strange period. I was involved with an artistic group of whom the leader was a singing and theatrical genius. He was also a Marxist. I got an immense amount out of it. We did recording projects and radio projects and theatrical projects. That absorbed me creatively and philosophically for a time. When the Women's Movement came along, it made much more sense to me than the Marxist view of the world. Now I've come back to a more holistic understanding of the world which has helped me to accept things. Once you can do that, then somehow you find resources in yourself, and you stop demanding answers and justice. Those questions become irrelevant. There are no solutions. Taoism attracts me. The more separate we feel from other people, animals, whatever, the more we're capable of persecuting and destroying. I suppose Jung's view of things appeals to me. My loss of sight has been very much part of the thread which has led me to all that.

*Liz: Then you feel it's given you something, as well as taken something away.*

**Alison:** Well, without that problem I certainly would not have had to face certain kinds of things. It took me into working not only with blind people but with drug addicts as well. You really have to look death in the face in that work. I went to more funerals in the four years I worked with them than I have at any time during the rest of my life. I don't really think I came to any genuine freeing up or acceptance of my blindness though until only about two years ago. I had the first operation on my right eye then. Any surgical procedure on an eye as damaged as mine creates a potential for complete deterioration. It's very risky. I always knew that if I continued as I was, without any surgery, then eventually the cataract would thicken so that all vision would be lost. Then they could operate to remove it. I could get a considerable amount of sight back, no one knows how much, or it might pack up altogether. That was the dilemma I always knew I would reach. I actually had a dream about it. I dreamed I went down to the operating table and talked to the surgeon about what would happen when I came out of the anaesthetic. Either it would be sight or blindness. But the dream showed no outcome. The eye survived the actual operation, although I was told later it was very much touch and go. The pressure went down considerably. But then it went up again. After the relief it was an awful letdown. For three days it sat on me like a cloud. During all that time before the operation there was always the uncertainty of the outcome and it kept me from being completely present. But going through the operation, being relieved and then disappointed again, I let go of something. That's given me a kind of freedom. Of course I don't want to lose what sight I have left. But I've stopped worrying about it. I've also stopped looking for cures.

*Liz: Did you try the alternative medicine field?*

**Alison:** Yes, that was a phase I went through. I met a woman in California who was in the first stages of glaucoma. She had just been diagnosed with hardly any visual loss as yet. She had started seeing various healers, which was also what I had been doing, and she asked me what my experience of them was like. I had tried spiritual healers, acupuncture, macrobiotics, Bates method, all sorts of things. I told her that it had taken up so much time and energy I just couldn't be bothered any more. Given the diagnosis that I'd had this condition from birth, to reverse forty years' worth of that kind of damage just took up too much time and energy. I told the woman I had come to the point where I just wanted to get on with living. She was immensely relieved. She was frightened that her life would become a vendetta against visual loss. It's difficult to be around the alternative medicine and therapy scene in California, or in London for that matter, because they're so absorbed in healing you. I've met people who have been keener on healing me than I've been myself. It made me wonder who was the sick person?

*Liz: You find a similar thing in psychotherapy, the determination to cure the patient. It's hard to avoid.*

**Alison:** Yes, but being on the receiving end of it was interesting. I've been a social worker and a counsellor and a therapist myself, apart from my own therapy. So it was quite interesting to meet that need to cure me. I realised that I myself wasn't that bothered any more. Some of the most difficult times I've ever had in relation to my sight came when I was involved with alternative medicine. But it's got to the point where it's not that important. The visual loss gives me as much as it takes away.

*Liz: Where do you see yourself going now?*

**Alison:** I did something new recently, at a workshop with Pat Watts on enacting myths. I actually sang a myth. I read the story the day before and improvised singing it. It was a wonderful experience being part of that history from Homer, who was also blind. It was a different way of seeing the world. I do have a sense of that now. Mostly through the voice, singing and telling songs that have mythic qualities. The visual loss has made me acutely aware of sound and the voice. I'm doing voice workshops now. I suppose I'm a bizarre combination, someone who's lost her sight and a therapist and an unaccompanied singer. But there I am.

Alison's resilience and realism speak for themselves. I would now like to explore her horoscope, both the birth chart and the progressed planets and transits that were operative between the ages of sixteen and eighteen. Alison did not profess to have experienced any momentous transpersonal insights, nor did she espouse any particular religious theory to explain or justify her life pattern. She is a strong and optimistic person who has dealt constructively with a difficult limitation, knitting it together with the overall fabric of her life so that her visual loss is not the dominant thing about her, but rather her individual personality itself. This is often not the case where fate has struck in a person's life, for in many instances it is the condition which is apparent before the person. I would not care to offer any theory about whether Alison is 'individuated' or has 'experienced the Self'. Such phrases, although I have been using them throughout this chapter, are somehow not appropriate. But she is an extraordinarily whole person, who has managed to put together extremes of both a positive and a negative kind. Her life makes sense to her, and therefore her effect on others is very marked. She has given up seeking answers, and has therefore herself become a kind of answer; thus whatever she gives carries an inner authority with it. As Aniela Jaffe puts it:

> As with all questions bordering on the transcendental, the only answer psychology can give is an antinomian one: man is free and is not free. He is not free to choose his destiny, but his consciousness makes him free to accept it as a task laid upon him by nature. If he takes responsibility for individuation he voluntarily submits to the self – in religious language, he submits to the will of God.[156]

Dominating Alison's birth horoscope is the planet Pluto which conjuncts the ascendant in Leo, conjuncts the twelfth house moon in Cancer, opposes the sun–Mercury conjunction in Capricorn in the sixth house, squares the Jupiter–Saturn conjunction in Taurus in the tenth, trines Mars in Sagittarius in the fifth, and sextiles Neptune at the end of Virgo in the third. Pluto thus aspects every planet in the chart save Uranus and Venus, and trines the mid-heaven as well. I do not need to elaborate on the quality of fatedness which I feel this powerful Pluto conveys; we have seen quite a lot of Moira in the first part of the book. Suffice it to say that nature's allotment here has some very strong and clearly defined boundaries, focused particularly in the physical body, as reflected by the conjunction of Pluto with the ascendant. The birth of the individual is also reflected by the ascendant, and often when Pluto conjuncts it the experience of birth has been difficult, or there is an illness of some kind, or something very wrong in the environment into which the baby emerges. Something fated – either physical or psychological – is shown presiding over the birth itself, which would wield irrevocable influence over the whole of the rest of life. As the ascendant is also concerned with the capacity of the· individual to express himself outwards into the world, this expression would be profoundly affected, hampered and altered by Pluto's position. Although obviously not everyone with a rising Pluto has a physical limitation such as Alison's, there is usually a deep and irrevocable limitation of some kind – a birth trauma, a near death, an ill mother who cannot nurse – which leaves its mark on the individual, blocking or thwarting ordinary expression, turning him in upon himself in some way, and forcing him into a transformed vision of life. Thus there seems to be a hereditary or biological fate at work in Alison's chart, and this is also suggested by the conjunction of Pluto with the moon in the twelfth. 'Family karma' of some kind may be in evidence here although its nature remains a mystery both to me and to Alison. The oppositions of Pluto to the pair of Capricorn planets in the sixth house also suggest that Pluto's fate will work itself out through the body; this house is concerned, among other things, with the individual's relationship to his physical vehicle and his daily life. My first reaction to Alison's horoscope, at the time she originally came to see me, was to consider this dominant Pluto, and to be left with a sense that her blindness was a kind of fate; that it would probably not be affected very much by treatment, orthodox or unorthodox, and that it was the springboard from which her inner development would take place. One might look at it as Moira; or one might suggest that this Pluto is one of the chief tools of the Self in helping Alison to pursue the 'vocation' of 'true personality'.

Much of Alison's character as it is expressed through her comments is also evident from the dominant Pluto. Her sunny, expressive and forthright nature, characteristically reflected by Leo on the ascendant (Apollo the sun god was the god of music), has been deepened and introverted by the experience of her blindness, so that her own limitations have become a means by which she can enter the imprisoned lives of others. The kind of work to which she has been attracted – dealing with the handicapped, the damaged and the disturbed – is typically Plutonian. It would seem that she has accepted willingly the burden and 'task' which this planet has placed upon her, rather than running away from it or seeking to 'transcend' it. Perhaps she is too earthy to be inclined to blot out the implications of human suffering which her own suffering has led her to face. But I am brought back to the same question here that I have voiced earlier: What is it that has allowed Alison to deal with such a formidable placement of Pluto in almost invariably constructive and creative, rather than life-denying, ways? I cannot answer this question, at least not from an astrological perspective, because 'it' is not, in my estimation, to be found in her horoscope. The dogged persistence and fortitude she has displayed are typically Capricornian; but dogged persistence is not really enough. Even her experiences with the doctors, who displayed a far greater degree of blindness than she herself is afflicted with, seem to slot into the design; as Jung says, 'all the pieces fit'. Presumably, if Alison's condition had been discovered earlier, there might not have been quite so much damage to both eyes. But it would seem from the placement of Pluto that although some people are able – or are 'permitted' – to find help, orthodox or unorthodox, Alison was not fated to be one of them. Something else has been required of her and she has risen to meet its challenge; but what then has proferred this requirement?

As an earthy sign, Capricorn is more inclined to work out its issues in practical ways, and is less likely to brood about them and make an internal Byronic meal out of life. The strongly Saturnian side of Alison's nature seems to speak loudly when she talks of self-pity as an 'eroding thing' with which she has little patience. Thus, whatever blackness and suffering that might have waited to overwhelm her in connection with the rising Pluto and the moon–Pluto conjunction has been translated into service to the blackness and suffering she has found in the world around her. This is also in keeping with the sixth house emphasis. Alison's dedication to her work, and her determination to get on with things in as normal a way as possible, reflect this earthy quality in her, which is by far the most dominant element in the horoscope. There is a no-nonsense quality about earth when it is faced with real emergency;

it tends to simply become too busy to brood. The deep concern for social problems, and the voyage into Marxism as a potential solution for them, is also a characteristically earthy approach to life, for earth does not have much time for grand visions and theories. Capricorn, in particular, offers its lasting respect to those who achieve something, who actually help in a recognisable way and contribute to the community; and it is often through this kind of work that Capricorn learns to respect himself. That Alison did not stop with the element of earth, but probed more deeply beneath the surface of things, is perhaps reflected by Pluto in opposition to the sun and Mercury. Also, her fiery ascendant would eventually lead her into a more mythic or symbolic world, which appears to be the direction in which her life is now moving in her forties. And the sun in a grand trine with Neptune and Uranus also suggests that her vision is considerably greater than the often circumscribed world of earth. But the core of her is unmistakably Capricornian and this communicates itself very strongly in conversation. The myths associated with Capricorn, which I have described earlier, concern the symbolism of crucifixion and imprisonment, despair and the finding of unshakable faith in the waste land of material life. Alison has not only experienced her own waste land but has voluntarily entered it in terms of the kinds of people she has chosen to help, submitting to the depression and despair which such encounters inevitably bring. I would be inclined to mistrust many people who speak of 'acceptance' of a limitation such as blindness, for often there is a festering beneath which drives them into a kind of frenzied optimism and programme of concerted dissociation. But I am inclined to believe Alison, who has, as a good child of Saturn, paid her dues. She has few illusions about life and does not seem to need the fluffy clouds of esotericism to prop her up. She has found out how to prop herself up, and the combination of Saturn and Pluto has produced a formidable survivor who also possesses the genuine warmth and sense of fun that Leo on the ascendant represents.

I did not probe Alison about the conditions of her family background, because she has probed them enough herself in her own therapy to feel she sees them with reasonable clarity. She experienced her childhood as supportive and does not seem to 'blame' anybody for her own circumstances. But I am struck by the Jupiter–Saturn conjunction in the tenth house which concerns the mother, and also by the moon–Pluto conjunction which likewise concerns the mother. I am given the feeling that some difficult issue lies here in the maternal background, something with which Alison's mother perhaps could not cope, but which Alison herself has been required to contend with. This may possibly be connected with those very primitive or passionate emotions of which Pluto is the astrological significator, and of which Alison herself has her share. This, along with the condition of blindness, may have also contributed to her choice of working with individuals in a state of inner despair. I find it extremely interesting that Alison's disability has forced her away from the artist's life embodied by her mother, so that her own considerable creative talents have had to be conjoined with practical service to life. Painting, the mother's vocation, was not 'permitted'.

Thus, both in character and in the pattern of her life, Alison reflects her birth horoscope. That in itself is not strange; from the point of view of astrology, it is what people are supposed to do. What I am struck by, however, is the quality of consciousness which Alison has brought to bear on her life, so that it is all 'of a piece' and 'makes sense'. The placement of the sun gives us a key to *how* this 'knitting together' might occur, for it is a symbol of the ego which is in many ways the vessel or material expression of the Self. Thus the individual who works to develop the sun is also moving away from the collective so that he becomes himself and experiences himself as a separate and unique entity. Placed in the sixth, the sun in Alison's chart suggests that her unfolding individuality would take place within the sphere of the physical body and the conditions imposed on it; the working life and the round of daily tasks; the ordinary affairs which are to be met with in material living. In short, this is the realm of the goddess Astraea who governs the orderly patterns of nature. Alison's visual loss has been a catalyst for increased consciousness of this sixth house sphere, because material life becomes full of obstacles and challenges and mysteries rather than being taken for granted. A person with no visual loss does not think about what his eyes do for him, but without eyes that apparently banal sphere becomes a profound dilemma and potentially a place of deep revelation. Thus the Self, if we consider it from this point of view, makes itself known to Alison through a striving to cope with the difficulties of the sixth house realm.

Aniela Jaffe writes about the process of individuation:

Individuation does not consist solely of successions of images from the unconscious. These are only part of the process, representing its inner or spiritual quality. Its necessary complement is outer reality, the development of individuality and its attendant fate. Both aspects of the process are regulated by the powerful archetype of the self. In other words, in the course of individuation the self emerges into the world of consciousness, while at the same time its originally psychoid nature splits apart, so that it manifests itself as much in inner images as in the events of real life.[157]

Thus the Self here manifests both as the blindness, which has forced Alison into a particular path of development, and as the inner response to that blindness which has led her to find meaning and creative potential in it.

Among the planetary progressions for 1957, the only aspect in force during the difficult period when Alison first went to Moor-fields and underwent her series of operations was progressed Venus coming into trine with Uranus and then arriving at the conjunction with the sun. Looked at from an orthodox point of view, that is hardly the sort of picture which would describe the difficulties to which she was subject. That she had a boyfriend whom at the time she thought she might marry is much more in keeping with these aspects. But viewed from a more unorthodox point of view, the conjunction of Venus to the sun in the sixth, which is also the ruler of the chart, suggests a time when Alison's individuality was just beginning to flower. In short, it marks the onset of her true development. That this onset was accompanied by a considerable degree of discomfort and hardship is not told us by this sole progressed aspect. But I have become convinced that progressed aspects do not necessarily tell us how something will feel; rather, they tell us what that something means.

The picture shown by the transiting planets is more edifying from a literal point of view. As we are looking at a two-year period, it is the heavy planets which we must consider, since the others move too quickly to suggest the kind of profound change which this time in Alison's life portended. The most striking transit is that of Uranus, which had entered Leo the preceding year and was hovering about Alison's ascendant. In April of 1957 Uranus was stationary exactly on the ascendant and conjuncting natal Pluto; it remained there through June. Uranus, as we have found in other case histories, has a propensity to drag things out into the light; it suggests a time of realisation and breakthrough. During this period the true nature of Alison's condition was discovered; or, put another way, it was the time when she came to realise the nature of her fate. Her sight had begun to truly fail during the period of the transit, and I cannot help but associate the closing in of the boundaries with the contact of Uranus to Pluto. It is as though Moira has at last made herself known. Uranus continued its transit through the first decanate of Leo through the first half of 1958, during which time it also squared the natal Jupiter–Saturn conjunction, placed in the tenth. Thus Alison was plagued with the question of what she would do with herself; teachers' training college, her initial choice, was an impossibility. Along with the realisation of the physical condition came conflicts of a tenth house kind, pertaining to future vocation.

Neptune was also active by transit during this time. It had entered Scorpio at the end of 1956 and was thus squaring the ascendant, natal Pluto, and transiting Uranus during the first half of 1957. It remained in the first decanate of Scorpio, also opposing Alison's natal Jupiter–Saturn, for a full three years. Along with the traditionally confusing and bewildering feelings which Neptune so often throws up during its transits, there is also the implication of a sacrifice having to be made on many levels. Among other things, hope of a trouble-free prognosis had to be sacrificed; and all the profound implications that the giving up of sight involves were beginning to be faced. Transiting Pluto was also involved, leaving the last few degrees of Leo at the beginning of 1957 and entering Virgo in the summer, and beginning its long square to Alison's natal Mars in Sagittarius which was to last for several years. Pluto–Mars contacts, as we have seen, raise the issue of frustration and thwarting of the will and of personal freedom; I would guess that Alison experienced greater anger and despair during this time than she is perhaps able to recall. Pluto also transited in trine to the Jupiter–Saturn conjunction, so that, along with the obstruction to Mars with its fierce Sagittarian independence, there was also the gradual formation of a sense of purpose or vocation, beginning with Alison's decision to train as a social worker and her involvement with other blind people. Finally, transiting Saturn was in the first decanate of Sagittarius during the early months of 1957, within orb of conjunction with natal Mars; so the picture of limitation, curtailment, and a complete rechannelling of energy is complete.

The involvement of the three outer planets during this time is quite striking, although not surprising, since I have found that the outer planets do tend to gather around at particularly 'fated' times in life. I do not associate them with any special 'spirituality', nor do I feel that they represent the Self, any more than any other planet does; but I am convinced that they 'release' fate, in the sense that they activate the birth chart at a very deep level and reveal its most profound underlying design. Under the transits of the outer planets our myths are revealed to us, and the shape of our Moira; and if anything has been avoided, or remained unseen, or been disguised, then the outer planets will rip away the veil and expose the stark outlines of the pattern which we have been given and within which we must find a way to live.

The question of one's response to one's total life-pattern is really the issue of how consciousness responds to the dictates of the Self, the psychic totality. That is in many ways a moral problem, and inevitably any solutions which are to be found are not going to be found in collective formulae. The quality which I have been trying to convey which I feel Alison possesses is a quality of free and individual response to her fate. There are many ways in which she might have reacted, but ultimately her morality is her own. As I understand it, this encompasses the 'free will' of which Jung writes, the 'ability to do gladly that which I must do'. This kind of free will does not come cheap; it is not a 'given'. It has to be fought for, and the process of that fight is also the process of individuation. Ego and Self are part of a totality, but they are not the same; they eye each other across the court sometimes as lovers, sometimes as enemies, but they cannot be separated. Jung describes this relationship as follows:

> The intrinsically goal-like quality of the self and the urge to realize this goal are not dependent on the participation of consciousness. They cannot be denied any more than one can deny one's ego–consciousness. It, too, puts forward its claims peremptorily, and very often in overt or covert opposition to the needs of the evolving self. In reality, i.e. with few exceptions, the entelechy of the self consists in a succession of endless compromises, ego and self laboriously keeping the scales balanced if all is to go well.[158]

Consciousness may identify with its transcendant partner, in which case there is an inflation, and even a psychosis, wherein the individual believes he *is* God, rather than being an individual. Consciousness may negate the reality of the Self altogether, although that does not in any way alter the pattern of the psyche, and then there is an experience of meaninglessness and a feeling of black fatality when life does not show the proper willingness to submit to the will of the ego. One may traverse the entire spectrum in a lifetime. I do not have now, any more than I did at the beginning, any real answer as to whether we are fated or free, or what fate is, or whether it can be transformed. But I find that Jung's mysterious postulate of the Self describes a great many of fate's paradoxes, and also contains them in a fashion which does not split us assunder between fatalistic passivity and arrogant ego-aggrandisement. That inner authority which may be experienced in so many ways is difficult for the astrologer to refute as he has a map of planetary positions which describe its intentions; but equally it denies the smooth escape into the language of 'potentials', since any encounter with this inner authority does not feel like tasting a potential, but rather more like colliding with the will of the gods, or God.

I feel it is fitting to end, as I begin, with a fairy tale. This one is a well-known story, and it contains a deep irony. Whether or not it is really about fate, or about the Self, I leave the reader to decide. But it is certainly about human nature, which contains a good deal of both.

## THE FISHERMAN AND HIS WIFE[159]

Once upon a time there was a Fisherman who lived with his wife in a pigsty close to the sea, and every day he went out fishing; and he fished, and he fished. And once he was sitting with his rod, looking at the clear water, and he sat and he sat. Then his line suddenly went down, far down below, and when he drew it up again he brought out a large Flounder. Then the Flounder said to him: 'Hark, you Fisherman, I pray you, let me live, I am no Flounder really but an enchanted prince. What good will it do you to kill me? I should not be good to eat, put me in the water again, and let me go.' 'Come,' said the Fisherman, 'there is no need for so many words about it – a fish that can talk I should certainly let go anyhow.' And with that he put him back again into the clear water, and the Flounder went to the bottom leaving a long streak of blood behind him. Then the Fisherman got up and went home to his wife in the pigsty.

'Husband,' said the woman, 'have you caught nothing today?' 'No,' said the man, 'I did catch a Flounder, who said he was an enchanted prince, so I let him go again.' 'Did you not wish for anything first?' said the woman. 'No,' said the man; 'what should I wish for?' 'Ah,' said the woman, 'it is surely hard to have to live always in this pigsty which stinks and is so disgusting; you might have wished for a little hut for us. Go back and call him. Tell him we want to have a little hut, he will certainly give us that.' 'Ah,' said the man, 'why should I go there again?' 'Why,' said the woman, 'you did catch him, and you let him go again; he is sure to do it. Go at once.' The man still did not quite like to go, but did not like to oppose his wife either, and went to the sea.

When he got there the sea was all green and yellow, and no longer so smooth; so he stood and said:

> Flounder, flounder in the sea,
> Come, I pray thee, here to me;
> For my wife, good Ilsabil,
> Wills not as I'd have her will.

Then the Flounder came swimming to him and said: 'Well, what does she want, then?' 'Ah,' said the man, 'I did catch you, and my wife says I really ought to have wished for something. She does not like to live in a pigsty any longer; she would like to have a hut.' 'Go, then,' said the Flounder, 'she has it already.'

When the man went home his wife was no longer in the sty, but instead of it there stood a hut and she was sitting on a bench before the door. Then she took him by the hand and said to him: 'Just come inside. Look, now isn't this a great deal better?' So they went in, and there was a small porch, and a pretty little parlour and bedroom, and a kitchen and pantry, with the best of furniture, and fitted up with the most beautiful things made of tin and brass, whatsoever was wanted. And behind the hut there was a small yard with hens and ducks and a little garden with flowers and fruit. 'Look,' said the wife, 'is not that nice!' 'Yes,' said the husband, 'and so it shall remain – now we will live quite contented.' 'We will think about that,' said the wife. With that they ate something and went to bed.

Everything went well for a fortnight, and then the woman said: 'Hark you, husband, this hut is far too small for us, and the garden and yard are little; the Flounder might just as well have given us a larger house. I should like to live in a great stone castle; go to the Flounder, and tell him to give us a castle.' 'Ah, wife,' said the man, 'the hut is quite good enough; why should we live in a castle?' 'What!' said the woman, 'Just go there, the Flounder can always do that. 'No, wife,' said the man, 'the Flounder has just given us the hut, I do not like to go back so soon, it might make him angry.' 'Go,' said the woman, 'he can do it quite easily, and will be glad to do it; just you go to him.'

The man's heart grew heavy, and he would not go. He said to himself: 'It is not right,' and yet he went. And when he came to the sea the water was quite purple and dark blue, and grey and thick, and no longer so green and yellow, but it was still quiet. And he stood there and said:

> *Flounder, flounder in the sea,*
> *Come, I pray thee, here to me;*
> *For my wife, good Ilsabil,*
> *Wills not as I'd have her will.*

'Well, what does she want now?' said the Flounder. 'Alas,' said the man, half scared, 'she wants to live in a great stone castle.' 'Go to it then, she is standing before the door,' said the Flounder.

Then the man went away, intending to go home, but when he got there he found a great stone palace, and his wife was standing on the steps about to go in, and she took him by the hand and said: 'Come in.' So he went in with her, and in the castle was a great hall paved with marble, and many servants, who flung wide the doors; and the walls were all bright with beautiful hangings, and in the rooms were chairs and tables of pure gold, and crystal chandeliers hung from the ceiling, and all the rooms and bedrooms had carpets, and food and wine of the very best stood on all the tables so that they nearly broke down beneath it. Behind the house too there was a great courtyard, with stables for horses and cows, and the very best of carriages; there was also a magnificent large garden with the most beautiful flowers and fruit trees, and a park quite half a mile long, in which were stags, deer and hares, and everything that could be desired. 'Come,' said the woman, 'isn't that beautiful?' 'Yes, indeed,' said the man, 'now let it be; and we will live in this beautiful castle and be content.' 'We will consider about that,' said the woman, 'and sleep upon it.' Thereupon they went to bed.

Next morning the wife woke first, and it was just daybreak, and from her bed she saw the beautiful country lying before her. Her husband was still stretching himself, so she poked him in the side with her elbow and said, 'Get up, husband, and just peep out of the window. Look, couldn't we be the King over all that land? Go to the Flounder, we will be the King.' 'Ah, wife,' said the man, 'why should we be King? I do not want to be King.' 'Well,' said the wife, 'if you won't be King, I will; go to the Flounder, for I will be King.' 'Ah, wife,' said the man, 'why do you want to be King? I do not like to say that to him.' 'Why not?' said the woman. 'Go to him this instant; I must be King!' So the man went, and was quite unhappy because his wife wished to be King. 'It is not right; it is not right,' thought he. He did not wish to go, but yet he went.

And when he came to the sea, it was quite dark grey, and the water heaved up from below, and smelt putrid. Then he went and stood by it, and said:

> *Flounder, flounder in the sea,*
> *Come, I pray thee, here to me;*
> *For my wife, good Ilsabil,*
> *Wills not as I'd have her will.*

'Well, what does she want now?' said the Flounder. 'Alas,' said the man, 'she wants to be King.' 'Go to her; she is King already.'

So the man went, and when he came to the palace, the castle had become much larger, and had a great tower and magnificent ornaments, and the sentinel was standing before the door, and there were numbers of soldiers with kettle-drums and trumpets. And when he went inside the house, everything was of real marble and gold with velvet covers and great golden tassels. Then the doors of the hall were opened, and there was the court in all its splendour, and his wife was sitting on a high throne of gold and diamonds with a great crown of gold on her head, and a sceptre of pure gold and jewels in her hand, and on both sides of her stood her maids-in-waiting in a row, each of them always one head shorter than the last.

Then he went and stood before her, and said: 'Ah, wife, and now you are King.' 'Yes,' said the woman, 'now I am King.' So he stood and looked at her, and when he had looked at her thus for some time, he said: 'And now that you are King, let all else be, now we will wish for nothing more.' 'No, husband,' said the woman, quite anxiously, 'I find the time passes very heavily, I can bear it no longer; go to the Flounder – I am King, but I must be Emperor, too.' 'Oh, wife, why do you wish to be Emperor?' 'Husband,' said she, 'go to the Flounder. I will be Emperor.' 'Alas, wife,' said the man, 'he cannot make you Emperor; I may not say that to the fish. There is only one Emperor in the land. An Emperor the Flounder cannot make you! I assure you he cannot.'

'What!' said the woman, 'I am the King, and you are nothing but my husband; will you go this moment? Go at once! If he can make a king he can make an emperor. I will be Emperor; go instantly.' So he was forced to go. As the man went, however, he was troubled in mind, and thought to himself: 'It will not end well; it will not end well! Emperor is too shameless! The Flounder will at last be tired out.'

With that he reached the sea, and the sea was quite black and thick, and began to boil up from below so that it threw up bubbles, and such a sharp wind blew over it that it curdled, and the man was afraid. Then he went and stood by it, and said:

> *Flounder, flounder in the sea,*
> *Come, I pray thee, here to me;*
> *For my wife, good Ilsabil,*
> *Wills not as I'd have her will.*

'Well, what does she want now?' said the Flounder. 'Alas, Flounder,' said he, 'my wife wants to be Emperor.' 'Go to her,' said the Flounder; 'she is Emperor already.'

So the man went, and when he got there the whole palace was made of polished marble with alabaster figures and golden ornaments, and soldiers were marching before the door blowing trumpets, and beating cymbals and drums; and in the house, barons, and counts, and dukes were going about as servants. Then they opened the doors to him, which were of pure gold. And when he entered, there sat his wife on a throne, which was made of one piece of gold, and was quite two miles high; and she wore a great golden crown that was three yards high, and set with diamonds and carbuncles, and in one hand she had the sceptre, and in the other the imperial orb; and on both sides of her stood the yeomen of the guard in two rows, each being smaller than the one before him, from the biggest giant, who was two miles high, to the very smallest dwarf, just as big as my little finger. And before it stood a number of princes and dukes.

Then the man went and stood among them, and said: 'Wife, are you Emperor now?' 'Yes,' said she, 'now I am Emperor.' Then he stood and looked at her well, and when he had looked at her thus for some time, he said: 'Ah, wife, be content, now that you are Emperor.' 'Husband,' said she, 'why are you standing there? Now, I am Emperor, but I will be Pope too; go to the Flounder.' 'Oh, wife,' said the man, 'what will you not wish for? You cannot be Pope; there is but one in Christendom; he cannot make you Pope.' 'Husband,' said she, 'I will be Pope; go immediately, I must be Pope this very day.' 'No, wife,' said the man, 'I do not like to say that to him; that would not do, it is too much; the Flounder can't make you Pope.' 'Husband,' said she, 'what nonsense! If he can make an emperor he can make a pope. Go to him directly. I am Emperor, and you are nothing but my husband; will you go at once?'

Then he was afraid and went; but he was quite faint, and shivered and shook, and his knees and legs trembled. And a high wind blew over the land, and the clouds flew, and towards evening all grew dark, and the leaves fell from the trees, and the water rose and roared as if it were boiling, and splashed upon the shore; and in the distance he saw ships which were firing guns in their sore need, pitching and tossing on the waves. And yet in the midst of the sky there was still a small patch of blue, though on every side it was as red as in the heavy storm. So, full of despair, he went and stood in much fear, and said:

> *Flounder, flounder in the sea,*
> *Come, I pray thee, here to me;*
> *For my wife, good Ilsabil,*
> *Wills not as I'd have her will.*

'Well, what does she want now?' said the Flounder. 'Alas,' said the man, 'she wants to be Pope.' 'Go to her, then,' said the Flounder; 'she is Pope already.'

So he went, and when he got there he saw what seemed to be a large church surrounded by palaces. He pushed his way through the crowd. Inside, however, everything was lit up with thousands and thousands of candles, and his wife was clad in gold, and she was sitting on a much higher throne, and had three great golden crowns on her head, and round about her there was much ecclesiastical splendour; and on both sides of her was a row of candles the largest of which was as tall as the very tallest tower, down to the very smallest kitchen candle, and all the emperors and kings were on their knees before her, kissing her shoe. 'Wife,' said the man, and looked attentively at her, 'are you now Pope?' 'Yes,' said she, 'I am Pope.' So he stood and looked at her, and it was just as if he was looking at the bright sun. When he had stood looking at her thus for a short time, he said: 'Ah, wife, if you are Pope, do let well alone!' But she looked as stiff as a post, and did not move or show any signs of life. Then said he: 'Wife, now that you are Pope, be satisfied, you cannot become any greater now.' 'I will consider about that,' said the woman. Thereupon they both went to bed, but she was not satisfied, and greediness let her have no sleep, for she was continually thinking what there was left for her to be.

The man slept well and soundly, for he had run about a great deal during the day; but the woman could not fall asleep at all, and flung herself from one side to the other the whole night through, thinking always what more was left for her to be, but unable to call to mind anything else. At length the sun began to rise, and when the woman saw the red of dawn she sat up in bed and looked at it. And when, through the window, she saw the sun thus rising, she said: 'Cannot I, too, order the sun and moon to rise? Husband,' she said, poking him in the ribs with her elbows, 'wake up! Go to the Flounder, for I wish to be even as God is.' The man was still half asleep, but he was so horrified that he fell out of bed. He thought he must have heard amiss, and rubbed his eyes, and said: 'Wife, what are you saying?' 'Husband,' said she, 'if I can't order the sun and moon to rise, and have to look on and see the sun and moon rising, I can't bear it. I shall not know what it is to have another happy hour unless I can make them rise myself.' Then she looked at him so terribly that a shudder ran over him, and said: 'Go at once; I wish to be like unto God.' 'Alas, wife,' said the man, falling on his knees before her, 'the Flounder cannot do that; he can make and emperor and a pope; I beseech you, go on as you are, and be Pope.' Then she fell into a rage, kicked him with her foot, and screamed; 'I can't stand it, I can't stand it any longer! Will you go this instant?' Then he put on his trousers and ran away like a madman. But outside a great storm was raging, and blowing so hard that he could scarcely keep his feet; houses and trees toppled over, the mountains trembled, rocks rolled into the sea, the sky was pitch black, and there was thunder and lightning, and the sea came in with black waves as high as church towers and mountains, and all with crests of white foam at the top. Then he cried, but could not hear his own words:

*Flounder, flounder in the sea,*
*Come, I pray thee, here to me;*

*For my wife, good Ilsabil,*
*Wills not as I'd have her will.*

'Well, what does she want now?' said the Flounder. 'Alas,' said he, 'she wants to be like unto God.' 'Go to her, and you will find her back again in the pigsty.' And there they are still living to this day.

# *Notes*

## Introduction

1 Bertrand Russell, *History of Western Philosophy*, George Allen & Unwin, London, 1946, p. 237.
2 F. M. Cornford, *From Religion to Philosophy*, Harvester Press, London, 1980, p. 20.
3 Gilbert Murray, *Four Stages of Greek Religion*, Oxford University Press, London, 1912, p. 115
4 Margaret Hone, *The Modern Textbook of Astrology*, L. N. Fowler & Co. Ltd, London, 1951, p. 17.
5 Jeff Mayo, *Astrology*, Teach Yourself Books, London, 1964, p. 6.
6 Mary Renault, *The King Must Die*, Longmans, Green & Co. Ltd, London, 1958, p. 16.
7 Russell, p. 32.

## 1 Fate and the Feminine

8 Plato, *The Republic*, translated by Benjamin Jowett, Penguin Books, London, 1979, p. 690.
9 Aeschylos, *Prometheus Bound*, translated by E. H. Plumptre, David McKay, New York, p. 111.
10 Heraclitus, *The Cosmic Fragments*, translated by G. S. Kirk, Cambridge University Press, 1954, p. 284.
11 *Thrice Greatest Hermes* (*Corpus Hermeticum*), translated by G. R. S. Mead, Hermes Press, Detroit, 1978, Vol. 2, p. 202.
12 Cornford, p. 40.
13 Russell, p. 130.
14 'Little Briar-Rose', from *The Complete Grimm's Fairy Tales*, Pantheon Books, 1944.
15 H. R. Ellis Davidson, *Gods and Myths of Northern Europe*, Penguin Books, 1964.
16 Idries Shah, *World Tales*, Penguin Books, 1979.
17 See the works by Marie-Louise von Franz on fairy tales: *An Introduction to Fairy Tales*, *Shadow and Evil in Fairy Tales*, *The Feminine in Fairy Tales*, *Individuation in Fairytales* and *Redemption Motifs in Fairy Tales*.
18 C. G. Jung, *The Archetypes and the Collective Unconscious*, CW9 Part 1, para. 91.
19 C. G. Jung, *The Symbolic Life*, CW18, para. 1228.
20 C. G. Jung, *Psychology and Alchemy*, CW12, n. 17, p. 30.
21 C. G. Jung, *Symbols of Transformation*, CW5, para. 371.
22 Jung, CW9, para. 158.
23 J. J. Bachofen, *Myth, Religion and Mother Right*, translated by Ralph Manheim, Bollingen Foundation/Princeton University Press, 1967, p. 18.
24 Bachofen, p. 165.
25 Aeschylos, *The Oresteia*, translated by Tony Harrison, Collings, London, 1981.
26 Erich Neumann, *The Great Mother*, Bollingen Foundation/Princeton University Press, 1955, p. 30.
27 Neumann, p. 303.
28 Neumann, p. 230.

29  James Hillman, *The Dream and the Underworld*, Harper & Row, New York, 1979, p. 27.

## 2 Fate and Pluto

30  Hillman, p. 20.
31  Walter F. Otto, *The Homeric Gods*, Thames & Hudson, London, 1979, p. 264.
32  Sylvia Brinton Perera, *Descent to the Goddess*, Inner City Books, Toronto, 1981, p. 24.
33  Perera, p. 21.
34  Robert Graves, *The Greek Myths*, Penguin Books, 1955, Vol. 1.
35  J. R. R. Tolkien, *The Lord of the Rings*, Guild Publishing, London, 1980, p. 145.
36  Sigmund Freud, *The Interpretation of Dreams*, Penguin Books, 1976, p. 332.
37  Hillman, p. 161.
38  Hillman, p. 162.
39  Luigi Aurigemma, 'Transformation Symbols in the Astrological Tradition', in *The Analytic Process*, ed. Joseph Wheelwright, C. G. Jung Foundation, New York, 1971.

## 3 The Astrological Pluto

40  James Hillman, 'On the Necessity of Abnormal Psychology: Ananke and Athene', in *Facing the Gods*, ed. James Hillman, Spring Publications, Dallas, 1980.
41  Aeschylos, *Prometheus Bound*, translated by David Grene, quoted in the above essay by Hillman.
42  Paracelsus, *Selected Writings*, translated by Norbert Guterman, Bollingen Foundation/Pantheon Books, 1958, p. 203.
43  Otto, p. 47.
44  Erich Neumann, *The Origins and History of Consciousness*, Bollingen Foundation/Princeton University Press, 1973, p. 186.
45  Sigmund Freud, *Three Essays on the Theory of Sexuality*, Penguin Books, 1981, p. 25.
46  Hillman, *The Dream and the Underworld*, p. 145.
47  Bradley Te Paske, *Rape and Ritual: A Psychological Study*, Inner City Books, Toronto, 1982, p. 44.
48  Te Paske, p. 62.
49  Te Paske, p. 73.
50  Te Paske, p. 73.
51  'Mother Hölle' from *The Complete Grimm's Fairy Tales*.

## 4 Fate and the Family

52  Salvador Minuchin, *Families and Family Therapy*, Tavistock Publications, London, 1974, p. 9.
53  Frances Wickes, *The Inner World of Childhood*, Appleton-Century, New York, 1966, p. 17.
54  C. G. Jung, *The Development of Personality*, CW17, para 217a.
55  Jung, CW9, Vol. 1, para. 159.
56  Peter Hill, 'Child Psychiatry', in *Essentials of Postgraduate Psychiatry*, Academic Press, London, 1979, p. 128.
57  Wickes, p. 70.
58  C. G. Jung, *The Psychogenesis of Mental Disease*, CW3, para. 429.
59  Michael Fordham, *The Self and Autism*, William Heinemann, London, 1976, p. 85.
60  Fordham, p. 88.

### 5 Fate and Transformation

61 Marsilio Ficino, *Letters*, translated by the School of Economic Science, London, Shepheard-Walwyn Ltd, 1975, Vol. 1, p. 94.
62 See Jung, CW12, 13 and 14 (*Psychology and Alchemy, Alchemical Studies*, and *Mysterium Coniunctionis*).
63 *The Divine Pymander and Other Writings of Hermes Trismegistus* (extracts from the *Corpus Hermeticum*), translated by John D. Chambers, Samuel Weiser, New York, 1982, p. 78.
64 Marie-Louise von Franz, *Alchemy*, Inner City Books, Toronto, 1980, p. 44.
65 *Thrice Greatest Hermes*, Vol. 3, p. 245.
66 *Thrice Greatest Hermes*, Vol. 2, p. 315.
67 Ficino, Vol. 3, p. 75.
68 Frances A. Yates, *Giordano Bruno and the Hermetic Tradition*, Routledge & Kegan Paul, London, 1964, p. 65.
69 Ptolemy, *Tetrabiblos*, translated by F. E. Robbins, Harvard University Press & William Heinemann Ltd, 1971, p. 23.
70 Gauricus, *Opera Omnia*, Vol. 2, p. 1612.
71 Julius Firmicus Maternus, *Mathesis: Ancient Astrology, Theory and Practise*, translated by Jean Rhys Bram, Noyes Press, N.J., 1975, p. 27.
72 Firmicus, p. 50.
73 Firmicus, p. 256.
74 Firmicus, p. 56.

### 6 The Creation of the World

75 Quoted from Robert Graves, *The Golden Fleece*, Hutchinson & Co., London, 1983, pp. 150–3.

### 7 Fate and Myth

76 Euripides, *The Phoenician Women*, translated by Philip Vellacott, Penguin Books, 1972, p. 237.
77 C. Kerenyi, *The Heroes of the Greeks*, Thames & Hudson, London, 1974, p. 98.
77 Kerenyi, p. 98.
78 Kerenyi, p. 98.
79 Euripides, pp. 289–90
80 Joseph Campbell, *The Hero With a Thousand Faces*, Sphere Books Ltd, London, 1975, p. 13.
81 Cornford, p. 110.
82 C. Kerenyi, *Zeus and Hera*, Routledge & Kegan Paul, London, 1975, p. 16.
83 Quoted from Mary Renault, *The Charioteer*, New English Library, 1983, p. 98.
84 Campbell, p. 38.

### 8 Myth and the Zodiac

85 Neumann, *The Origins and History of Consciousness*, p. 176.
86 Neumann, p. 187.
87 Campbell, p. 21.
88 Paul Friedrich, *The Meaning of Aphrodite*, University of Chicago Press, 1978, p. 145.
89 Friedrich, p. 79.
90 Graves, *The Greek Myths*, Vol. 1, p. 87.
91 Ivor Morrish, *The Dark Twin*, Fowler & Co. Ltd, London, 1980, p. 37.
92 Richard Donington, *Wagner's Ring and Its Symbols*, Faber, London, 1963, p. 232.
93 Otto, *The Homeric Gods*, p. 108.
94 Jung, CW9 Part 1, para. 469.

95    Jung, CW9 Part 1, para. 478.
96    Hugh Lloyd-Jones, *Myths of the Zodiac*, Duckworth, London, 1978, p. 27.
97    Neumann, *The Origins and History of Consciousness*, p. 23.
98    Jung, CW6, para. 432.
99    C. G. Jung, *Mysterium Coniunctionis*, CW14, para. 404.
100   Jung, CW14, para. 405.
101   Emma Jung and Marie-Louise von Franz, *The Grail Legend*, Hodder & Stoughton, London, 1971, p. 183.
102   Jung & von Franz, p. 294.
103   Otto, *The Homeric Gods*, p. 70.
104   Jane Harrison, *Themis*, Merlin Press, London, 1977, p. 517.
105   Frances A. Yates, *Astraea*, Peregrine Books, London, 1977, p. 32.
106   John Layard, 'The Virgin Archetype', in *Images of the Untouched*, Spring Publications, Dallas, 1982, p. 170.
107   Layard, p. 171.
108   *The Thunder, Perfect Mind*, from *The Nag Hammadi Library*, translated by George W. MacCrae, E. J. Brill, Leiden, 1977.
109   Esther Harding, *Women's Mysteries*, Rider & Co., London, 1971, p. 124.
110   Jung, CW9 Part 1, para. 316.
111   Graves, *The Greek Myths*, Vol. 2, p. 11.
112   Jane Harrison, *Prologomena*, Merlin Press, London, 1962, p. 298.
113   Graves, *The Greek Myths*, Vol. 1, p. 127.
114   E. M. Butler, *The Myth of the Magus*, Cambridge University Press, 1979, p. 128.
115   Goethe, *Faust*, Part 1, translated with introduction by Philip Wayne, Penguin Books, 1949, p. 22.
116   Goethe, *Faust*, Part 1, p. 87.
117   Goethe, *Faust*, Part 2, p. 282.
118   Jung, CW5, para. 119.
119   Kerenyi, *The Gods of the Greeks*, p. 91.
120   Otto, *The Homeric Gods*, p. 283.
121   Otto, *The Homeric Gods*, p. 158.
122   Kerenyi, *The Gods of the Greeks*, p. 98.
123   Kerenyi, *The Gods of the Greeks*, p. 160.
124   T. S. Eliot, *The Waste Land*, in *The Complete Poems and Plays of T. S. Eliot*, Faber, London, 1969, p. 61.
125   Campbell, *The Hero With a Thousand Faces*, p. 113.
126   Campbell, *The Hero With a Thousand Faces*, p. 117.
127   Mary Renault, *The King Must Die*, p. 17.
128   Campbell, *The Hero With a Thousand Faces*, p. 123.
129   James Hillman, *Puer Papers*, Spring Publications, Dallas, 1979, p. 15.
130   Hillman, *Puer Papers*, p. 17.
131   Aeschylos, *Prometheus Bound*, translated by Philip Vellacott, Penguin Books, 1961, p. 27.
132   Aeschylos, *Prometheus Bound*, p. 35.
133   C. G. Jung, *Two Essays on Analytical Psychology*, CW7, para. 243.
134   Graves, *The Greek Myths*, Vol. 1, p. 117.
135   C. G. Jung, *Aion*, CW9 Part 2, para. 174.
136   C. Kerenyi, *Dionysos*, Routledge & Kegan Paul, London, 1976, p. 27.
137   Kerenyi, *Dionysos*, p. 28.
138   Kerenyi, *Dionysos*, p. 64.

**9 Fate and Synchronicity**

139   C. G. Jung, *The Structure and Dynamics of the Psyche*, CW8, para. 431.
140   Gerhard Adler, 'Reflections on "Chance", "Fate", and Synchronicity', in *The*

*Shaman from Elko*, C. G. Jung Institute of San Francisco, 1978, p. 90.
141 Adler, p. 90.
142 Jung, CW8, para. 841.
143 Jung, CW8, para. 918.
144 Jung, CW8, para. 938.
145 Russell, p. 355.
146 Russell, p. 264.
147 Marc Edmund Jones, *Horary Astrology*, Shambhala, London, 1975, p. 58.
148 Aniela Jaffe, *The Myth of Meaning*, Penguin Books, 1975, p. 153.

### 10 Fate and the Self

149 C. G. Jung, *Psychological Reflections*, edited by Jolande Jacobi, Routledge & Kegan Paul, 1971, p. 322.
150 Jaffe, p. 79.
151 C. G. Jung, *Psychological Types*, CW6, para. 789–91.
152 Jaffe, p. 79.
153 Jung, CW17, para. 299.
154 Jung, CW8, para. 402.
155 Jung, CW12, para. 330.
156 Jaffe, p. 91.
157 Jaffe, p. 78.
158 Jung, CW11, para. 960.
159 'The Fisherman and His Wife', from *The Complete Grimm's Fairytales*.

# Glossary of Mythological Names Referred to in the Text

**Acheron** [Greek]. One of the rivers of the underworld. The name means 'stream of woe'.

**Achilles** [Greek]. One of the heroes of the Trojan War, Achilles was the son of the sea goddess Thetis by Peleus, a mortal. When he was a baby his mother dipped him in the river Styx to ensure his immortality, but forgot to immerse the heel by which she held him. He met his death through this vulnerable part during one of the battles with the Trojans.

**Adonis** [Phoenician]. Son and lover of the goddess Ishtar or Aphrodite, he was a youthful vegetation god, of an extraordinary beauty. He was killed by a wild boar while hunting. An agricultural divinity, his death and resurrection were celebrated in connection with the sowing and harvesting of crops. He is related to Tammuz, Attis and Osiris, as well as Dionysos – all youthful gods who were destroyed and resurrected.

**Aeëtes** [Greek]. King of Colchis, he was the son of the sun god Helios. He became guardian of the Golden Fleece, and held it until his daughter Medea fell in love with the hero Jason and ran away with her lover and the Fleece. See *Jason* and *Medea*.

**Aegisthos** [Greek]. The lover of Queen Klytaemnestra of Argos, he plotted with her to murder her husband Agamemnon when the King returned from the Trojan War. Aegisthos himself was murdered by Orestes, the son of Klytaemnestra and Agamemnon. See *Orestes*. (For the complete story of Orestes. see p. 89.)

**Agamemnon** [Greek]. King of Argos, he was a member of the house of Atreus, upon which a curse had been laid. He was one of the war-leaders of the Greek ships sailing to the Trojan War. He was murdered, upon his return, by his wife Klytaemnestra and her lover Aegisthos. See **Orestes**. (Also see p. 89.)

**Ahriman** [Persian]. God of evil and darkness, he is roughly equivalent to the Devil in Christian myth; however, Ahriman was an equal power to the god of light, Ormuzd, perpetually striving with him for mastery.

**Alberich** [Teutonic]. One of the race of dwarfs, Alberich in Wagner's *Ring* steals the Rhine maidens' gold and forges it into a ring of power by abjuring love. He is represented as a dark, greedy, malevolent figure whose realm of Niebelheim is a kind of underworld.

**Amaltheia** [Greek]. The she-goat who suckled the infant Zeus while he was hidden from his tyrannical father Kronos. In gratitude for saving his life, Zeus, when he eventually became king of the gods, placed her in heaven as the constellation of Capricorn, and turned one of her horns into the Cornucopia or Horn of Plenty.

**Ammon** [Egyptian]. The primal creator god, portrayed with a ram's head. Ammon is roughly equivalent to the Greek Zeus and the Biblical Yahveh. His name means 'the hidden one' and he is the original generative force which creates the universe.

**Amphion** [Greek]. One of a pair of mythic twins, Amphion was the more poetic and musical of the two, while his brother Zethus was warlike and quarrelsome. Each despised the other for these differences.

**Ananke** [Greek]. Her name means 'necessity', and she is another form of Moira, the great goddess of fate.

**Andromeda** [Greek]. Daughter of King Cepheus and Queen Cassiopeia of Ethiopia, she was offered in sacrifice to a sea monster sent by Poseidon to punish the boastful vanity of her parents. However, the hero Perseus fell in love with her and rescued her from the rock to which she was chained. He destroyed the monster and married her.

**Anubis** [Egyptian]. An underworld deity, he is portrayed with a jackal's head. He is the psychopomp or guide of souls into the underworld. He is roughly equivalent to the Greek Hermes in his role of psychopomp.

**Aornis** [Greek]. One of the rivers of the underworld. The name means 'birdless'.

**Aphrodite** [Greek]. The goddess of sensual love and beauty, she was born from the union of the sea with the severed genitals of the god Ouranos after his son Kronos had castrated him. She is equivalent to Inanna in Sumerian myth and Ishtar in Babylonian, and presides over fertility and all the arts and wiles of love. She is also a battle goddess, inciting men to bloody fighting. She is generally vain, jealous and vindictive, but always irresistible.

**Apollo** [Greek]. God of the sun, music and prophecy, he is the son of Zeus and twin brother to Artemis the moon goddess. His oracle at Delphi foretold the future to the suppliant, but in terms so ambiguous that he was called 'double-tongued'. He is also the patron of young boys, and is the most gentlemanly and rational of the Olympian gods.

**Ares** [Greek]. The god of war and battle-lust, he was born of Hera, the queen of the gods, without a father. He is described in myth as vicious, violent and treacherous. His Roman equivalent is Mars.

**Artemis**, Diana [Greek]. Twin sister of Apollo the sun god, she is a deity of the moon and is portrayed as a wild virgin huntress and mistress of untamed beasts. In Asia Minor she is represented also as a harlot and a fertility goddess, although paradoxically also virginal, and a protectress of pregnancy and childbirth. She is also associated with Hekate, another lunar goddess and underworld ruler.

**Asklepios**, Aesculapius [Greek]. The son of Apollo the sun god, he was raised by the centaur Cheiron and taught the arts of healing and medicine. He was the patron of healers, and could also raise the dead. He is sometimes shown in the form of a serpent, and was himself resurrected from the dead, having been killed by one of Zeus' thunderbolts. He is also portrayed as lame.

**Astraea** [Greek]. The goddess of justice. A daughter of Zeus, she once lived on earth and mingled with men, but became increasingly disgusted at their baseness and eventually retreated to the heavens as the constellation of Virgo.

**Asvins** [Hindu]. A pair of divine twins who were rain-makers and givers of fertility, they were called the Heavenly Charioteers.

**Atargatis** [Syro-Phoenician]. One of the great fertility goddesses of Asia Minor, she is also a lunar deity. Like Ishtar and Inanna, she is both virgin and harlot, worshipped with orgiastic rites. She is portrayed as a fish or with a fish's tail, and is accompanied by her son–lover Ichthys, also portrayed as a fish.

**Athene** [Greek]. Goddess of wisdom and the strategy of war, she is a champion of heroes. She is the daughter of Zeus, sprung from his head without a mother, and is perpetually virgin. She is also patroness of artisans and weavers, and taught crafts to mankind.

**Atreus** [Greek]. King of Argos, he became involved in a blood-feud with his brother Thyestes and butchered Thyestes' children. In revenge, Thyestes cursed his brother's line. This curse passed down to Orestes. (See p. 89.)

**Atropos** [Greek]. One of the three Moirai or Fates. Atropos is called 'the cutter' because she severs the thread of fate which ends a mortal life.

**Attis** [Phrygian]. Son and lover of the great fertility goddess Kybele, he is a vegetation god and is analogous to Tammuz and Adonis. He was unfaithful to Kybele and in revenge she struck him with madness, and he castrated himself. Kybele then changed him into a fir tree.

**Atum** [Egyptian]. A form of the sun god Ra.

**Baldur** [Teutonic]. The most beautiful of the gods of Valhalla, everyone loved him for his radiance and wisdom. The goddess Frigg begged every living thing on earth, animal, vegetable, mineral, to swear an oath never to harm Baldur. All took the oath except the mistletoe, which was too young. Loge, the fire god, was jealous and plotted Baldur's death. During a contest one of the other gods hurled a branch of mistletoe at Baldur, which instantly killed him.

**Bast** [Egyptian]. Originally a lion goddess, her sacred animal later became the cat. She is a goddess of sensual pleasure and also a patroness of sorcery and witchcraft. She is related to the Greek Artemis–Hekate.

**Castor** [Greek]. One of the pair of twins associated with the constellation of Gemini, Castor was the immortal twin, fathered by Zeus. His brother Polydeuces (Pollux in Latin) was mortal, fathered by King Tyndareos of Sparta. Castor and Polydeuces fought another pair of twins, called Idas and Lynceus, and Polydeuces was killed. Castor mourned so bitterly that Zeus promised to allow them alternate periods in the underworld and on Mount Olympus so they might be together.

**Cerberus** [Greek]. The monstrous three-headed dog who guards the gateway to the underworld.

**Charon** [Greek]. The ancient ferryman who ushers the souls of the dead across the river Styx into the underworld. He must be paid his coin, or the soul of the dead person will be left to wander eternally on the far bank.

**Cheiron** [Greek]. King of the centaurs, he is a sage and healer, who taught earth-wisdom and the healing arts to the young sons of kings. He was accidentally wounded in the thigh by an arrow dipped in the poisonous blood of the Hydra. All his wisdom could not cure him, and because he was immortal he could not die. He hid in his cave in agony until the Titan Prometheus offered his own boon of death in exchange so that the centaur could find peace in the underworld.

**Clotho** [Greek]. One of the three Moirai or Fates, Clotho is the spinner who weaves the thread of mortal destiny.

**Cocytus** [Greek]. One of the rivers of the underworld. The name means 'wailing'.

**Cronus** [Greek]. Also spelled Kronos, he is the equivalent of the Roman Saturn. Son of Ouranos and Gaia, he is an earth deity and a god of fertility. He led the rebellion of the Titans against his father, castrating him with a sickle and becoming king of the gods. Eventually he was overthrown by his own son Zeus. He is portrayed as an old man, and devoured his own children in order to keep them from usurping his power.

**Dactyls** [Greek]. The dwarf gods, servants of the Great Mother. They are smiths, artisans, and tenders of animals and plants.

**Daedalus** [Greek]. The master craftsman of Crete, he was hired by King Minos to build a labyrinth to house the monstrous Minotaur. See *Minos*.

**Demeter, Ceres** [Greek]. Daughter of Kronos and sister to Zeus, she is the goddess of agriculture and of the harvest. She is an earth goddess, usually portrayed with her virgin daughter Persephone but with no husband or consort.

**Dia** [Greek]. Another name for Gaia or Rhea, the earth goddess.

**Dike** [Greek]. Another name for Astraea, the goddess of justice. Dike embodies the justice of nature, and the orderly round of the seasons.

**Dionysos, Bacchus** [Greek]. A complex and multifaceted god, he is at once both a deity of life, ecstasy and sexuality, and a god of death. The son of Zeus by Semele, he is portrayed as youthful and vaguely androgynous. He was driven mad by Hera, and wandered all over the world teaching the art of viticulture and initiating men and women into his orgiastic mystery rites. As a child he was dismembered by the Titans and brought to life again. His nature has great cruelty, but he is a redeemer god who vouchsafes the mystery of eternal life.

**Dis** [Roman]. Another name for Pluto, the god of the underworld. The name means 'rich'.

**Ea** [Babylonian]. A water god, he is also a creator god of supreme wisdom. He is portrayed as a goat with a fish's tail, from which image the Capricornian goat–fish is derived. He is also patron of magic, and the creator of man, whom he fashioned out of clay.

**Eileithyia** [Greek]. A goddess of childbirth, she is the patroness of midwives. She is the Greek equivalent to the Egyptian Nekhebet, protectress of childbirth, who is portrayed with a vulture's head.

**Enki** [Sumerian]. The god of fire, he is also a creator god. He is analagous to the Greek Hermes and the Teutonic Loge.

**Epimetheus** [Greek]. The brother of the Titan Prometheus, his name means 'hindsight' or 'he who learns from the event'. He was given as a wife Pandora, a woman fashioned by the gods to plague man. As her dowry she brought the famous box which contained all the woes which now plague mankind – sickness, old age, death, depression, strife and fear. Also contained in the box was hope.

**Erda** [Teutonic]. The earth goddess. Erda or Urd is also the name of the oldest of the Norns, analagous to the Greek Moirai or Fates.

**Ereshkigal** [Sumerian]. The terrible goddess of the underworld. Her name means 'Lady of the Great Place Below'. Her vizier is called Namtar, which means 'fate'.

**Erinyes**, Erinnyes [Greek]. Called the 'dogs of Hades', the Erinyes are the goddesses of vengeance, punishing those who have shed familial blood or broken oaths. In Hesiod's cosmogony they sprang from the blood of the castrated god Ouranos when it fell upon the earth. In Aeschylos they are the daughters of Nyx, the goddess of Night. Usually three in number, they are sometimes portrayed in a noxious swarm, armed with torches and whips with snakes on their heads. Their punishment is madness.

**Eros** [Greek]. Represented in classical Greek art as a chubby boy with a bow and arrow who inflicts mortals with the wounds of love, he was originally a great primal creator god whose passion formed the manifest universe. He is also a death god, whom Plato called a 'great *daimon*' (*daimon* means a dispenser of fate).

**Eumenides** [Greek]. A euphemism for the Erinyes or goddesses of vengeance, the name means 'the kindly ladies'.

**Europa** [Greek]. A mortal woman with whom Zeus fell in love. He carried her off to Crete and raped her, in the form of a white bull. She bore him three sons – Sarpedon, Rhadamanthys and King Minos.

**Eurynome** [Greek]. One of Zeus' lovers, she was the daughter of Okeanos. She bore Zeus the three Graces.

**Fafner and Fasolt** [Teutonic]. Two giants who quarrelled over a hoard of gold stolen from the Niebelungen or dwarfs. Fafner murdered his brother Fasolt and then turned himself into a dragon to guard the hoard. He was eventually killed by the hero Siegfried.

**Gaia** [Greek]. The goddess of earth. She was sister and lover of Ouranos, the god of heaven. Their union created the manifest universe.

**Ganymedes** [Greek]. A beautiful youth, he was the son of King Tros of Troy. Zeus desired him and, in the form of an eagle, abducted him and took him to Mount Olympus, where the boy was made immortal and installed as cupbearer to the gods.

**Gorgon** [Greek]. There were three Gorgons, Medusa, Stheino and Euryale. They were once beautiful, but because Medusa offended the goddess Athene by coupling with Poseidon in Athene's sacred precinct, all three sisters were turned into winged monsters with glaring eyes, huge teeth, protruding tongues, brazen claws and serpent locks. Their gaze turned men to stone.

**Graiai** [Greek]. Three withered old women with one eye and one tooth between them. With the single eye they could see everything in the world. The hero Perseus had to seek their cave and obtain from them the secret abode of the Gorgon Medusa whom he had to slay.

**Hades** [Greek]. Lord of the underworld, he is the son of Kronos and the brother of Zeus. He is a stern, dark god who wears a helmet which renders him invisible in the upper world. He is best known in myth for his abduction and rape of Persephone.

**Hapi** [Egyptian]. The god of the Nile, he is portrayed with great jugs of water which he pours into the river to cause its inundations. He is shown as a fat, jolly deity with a woman's breasts.

**Hathor** [Egyptian]. A fertility goddess, she is also a deity of battle. She is shown with a cow's head, and is analagous to the Greek Aphrodite.

**Hekate** [Greek]. Ruler of the underworld, she is also a moon goddess. She is connected with Artemis, the virgin huntress and mistress of beasts. Hekate is also the goddess of witchcraft and magic, and sends demons to earth to torment men. She has a retinue of infernal dogs, and is sometimes portrayed with three heads. She is also the goddess of crossroads, where her shrines were erected.

**Helen** [Greek]. The daughter of Zeus and Leda, a mortal woman, she became the wife of King Menelaos of Sparta. She was reputed to be the most beautiful woman in the world. Paris, a Trojan prince, abducted her, thus initiating the Trojan War.

**Helle** [Greek]. With her brother Phrixus she fled the wrath of her wicked step-mother, the queen of Iolkos, on the back of a golden ram which Zeus provided for their rescue. On the way to Colchis, Helle fell into the sea, which was called Hellespont after her.

**Hephaistos** [Greek]. The divine smith and artisan, he was the parthenogenous son of the goddess Hera. When he was born, his mother, shocked by his ugliness, hurled him down from Mount Olympus into the sea. Thetis the sea goddess cared for him until he was invited back to Olympus. Zeus threw him out again during a family squabble, and on this second occasion he landed on the earth and broke both his legs; he was lame ever after. He was married to Aphrodite, who was perpetually unfaithful to him. He was responsible for the creation of all the tools and weapons and emblems of power for the other Olympian gods.

**Hera**, Juno [Greek]. Wife and sister of Zeus, her name means 'the mistress'. She is queen of the gods and patroness of marriage, and is known in myth primarily for her violent jealousy of Zeus' lovers and her incessant persecution of his illegitimate children.

**Herakles** [Greek]. Called Hercules by the Romans, his great heroic achievement was the accomplishment of the Twelve Labours. The son of Zeus by a mortal woman, he was the subject of the goddess Hera's virulent enmity. Among the Labours were the destruction of the Hydra, the Nemean Lion, the Cretan Bull and the Stymphalian Birds.

**Hermes** [Greek]. The god of thieves, liars and merchants, he is also the guide of dead souls and the messenger between Mount Olympus and mortal men. He rules crossroads and is the patron of the traveller and of those who are lost. He is also a deity of luck and money, and is represented as brilliant and guileful. He is the son of Zeus and the nymph Maia, which is also another name for the goddess of Night.

**Hydra** [Greek]. A monster with nine poisonous snake-heads which, if they are cut off, each sprout another nine. The Lernaean Hydra lived in a cave in a swamp and preyed on the countryside until the hero Herakles destroyed it as one of the Twelve Labours.

**Ichthys** [Syro-Phoenician]. A youthful vegetation god, he is portrayed as a fish in company with his mother Atargatis, the great fertility goddess who is represented with a fish's tail. He is related to Tammuz, Attis and Adonis, and follows their characteristic death and resurrection pattern.

**Inanna** [Sumerian]. The goddess of heaven, she is analagous to the Greek Aphrodite and the Roman Venus. She is a fertility goddess, patroness of the arts of love, and also a goddess of battle. She descended into the underworld and was destroyed by her sister Ereshkigal, queen of the underworld, and resurrected.

**Io** [Greek]. Daughter of the river god Inachus, Zeus fell in love with her. Hera's enmity pursued her and she was turned into a white cow, over which the hundred-eyed Argus was placed as guard to ensure that Zeus did not steal her away. Hera, still not content, sent a gadfly to sting Io and chase her all over the world. Eventually she came to Egypt, where Zeus restored her to human form.

**Isis** [Egyptian]. A moon goddess, she was called 'Queen of Heaven'. She is a protectress of childbirth and a powerful magician and sorceress. She is also a goddess of fertility and sensual love. She restored her brother–lover Osiris to life after he was destroyed in the underworld by their evil brother Set.

**Ixion** [Greek]. Son of the king of the Lapiths, he unwisely planned to seduce Zeus' wife Hera, queen of the gods. Zeus, reading Ixion's intentions, shaped a cloud into a false Hera with whom Ixion, being too far gone in drink to notice the deception, duly took his pleasure. He was surprised in the act by Zeus, who bound him to a fiery wheel which rolled without cease in Tartaros, the bowels of the underworld.

**Jason** [Greek]. Son of the King of Iolkos, he was robbed of his inheritance when a child, by his wicked uncle Pelias. He was raised by the centaur Cheiron, and when he reached manhood went back to Iolkos to claim his kingdom. Pelias sent him off on a quest to find the Golden Fleece, hoping that he would be killed in the process. However, Jason retrieved the Fleece from the King of Colchis with the help of the king's sorceress – daughter Medea, and returned to become king of Iolkos. Jason then tired of Medea and planned to marry the daughter of the king of Corinth; but Medea, in a jealous fury, murdered the girl as well as her two children by Jason, and fled in a chariot drawn by winged dragons. She cursed Jason, and from that time his life went steadily downhill, until he was killed by a falling timber from his own ship, the *Argo*.

**Job** [Hebrew]. In the Old Testament, Job was God's good and loyal servant, but God, at the request of Satan, subjected him to severe suffering and loss to test his faith. Because Job's patience and love of God did not alter, everything that had been taken from him was ultimately restored.

**Kali** [Hindu]. Called 'the Black Mother', she is a bloodthirsty goddess of battle and death. She is portrayed with a necklace of human skulls, with a protruding tongue and blood-red eyes. She presides over disintegration and disease, yet she also restores life and grants boons to her faithful.

**Ketu** [Hindu]. A demon who devours the sun during the time of a solar eclipse. Astronomically, Ketu is equated with the moon's south or descending node.

**Klytaemnestra**, Clytemnestra [Greek]. Wife of King Agamemnon of Argos, she conspired with her lover Aegisthos to murder her husband upon his return from the Trojan War. In revenge, at the order of the god Apollo, her son Orestes in turn murdered her, and was driven mad by the Erinyes for his crime. (See p. 89.)

**Kybele**, Cybele [Phrygian]. One of the great fertility goddesses of Asia Minor, she is generally shown in a chariot drawn by lions. She was worshipped with particularly bloody rites, along with her son–lover Attis who castrated himself in a bout of madness inflicted upon him by his mother.

**Lachesis** [Greek]. One of the three Moirai or Fates, Lachesis is the measurer who decides the quality and length of a mortal life.

**Laios**, Laius [Greek]. King of Thebes, he was warned by Apollo's oracle not to have a son, or that son would become his murderer. His wife Iokaste bore him a child despite this warning, which Laios ordered to be exposed on a hillside. The child survived, however, and grew up to be Oidipus, who eventually killed his father unknowingly on a mountain road and then married his own mother, becoming King of Thebes. (For the complete myth of Oidipus, see p. 163.)

**Lamia** [Greek]. Sometimes portrayed as a swarm of vengeful underworld goddesses, Lamia was in the earliest version of the myth a queen of Libya who was loved by Zeus. She saw her children perish as a result of Hera's jealousy, and went mad with grief, devouring babies whom she tore from their mothers' arms. The underworld Lamia are responsible for the deaths of newborn children.

**Lethe** [Greek]. One of the rivers of the underworld. The word means 'forgetfulness'.

**Loge** [Teutonic]. Also spelled Loki, he is the trickster god and a god of fire. He is a thief and a liar, but offers wise and cunning counsel. He is analagous to the Greek Hermes.

**Maat** [Egyptian]. The goddess of justice. Her emblem is a feather, which is placed in the scales in the judgement hall of the underworld, and weighed against the heart of the dead person to assess his sins. If the heart is heavier than the feather of Maat, it is thrown to the monster Amemait to be eaten, and the soul is denied eternal life.

**Maenad** [Greek]. A woman follower of the god Dionysos. The Maenads dressed in animal skins and fell into ecstatic trances, during which they celebrated orgiastic rites on mountain-tops and tore wild animals in pieces.

**Maia** [Greek]. The mother of the god Hermes, she is usually portrayed as a nymph with whom Zeus fell in love. But Maia is also the name by which Zeus addresses the great goddess of Night, thus suggesting that the mother of Hermes is the darkness itself.

**Marduk** [Babylonian]. A fire god, he is roughly analogous to Yahveh as a creator god. He slew the sea-monster Tiamat, his mother, and out of her dismembered flesh created the physical universe.

**Mars** [Roman]. The god of war, he is equivalent to the Greek Ares.

**Medea** [Greek]. Daughter of King Aeëtes of Colchis, she was a sorceress who fell in love with the hero Jason when he arrived with his Argonauts to steal the Golden Fleece. She drugged the dragon which guarded the Fleece and stole away with Jason and the Fleece. When her father's fleet pursued them, she cut up her brother in pieces and threw them on the sea, knowing that Aeëtes would have to collect the pieces before he could continue his pursuit. When Medea and Jason returned to Iolkos, he abandoned her for another woman. She murdered the other woman and her own children, and fled to Athens, becoming the mistress of King Aigeus. Having tried unsuccessfully to murder Aigeus' son Theseus, she vanished.

**Mercury** [Roman]. The winged messenger of the gods, he is analagous to the Greek Hermes.

**Minos** [Greek]. A son of Zeus by Europa, he was King of Crete. He gained the kingship through the favour of the god Poseidon, who gave him a sacred bull to show to the people. Although he was required to sacrifice this bull to the god he coveted it and offered up a lesser bull instead. Incensed, Poseidon afflicted Minos' wife Pasiphaë with a passion for the bull. The union of woman and bull produced the monstrous Minotaur, with a bull's head and human body, which ate human flesh. This creature was eventually killed by the hero Theseus.

**Mithras** [Persian]. A redeemer god who bears many similarities to the figure of Christ, he is the messenger of the god of light, Ormuzd. He is portrayed as the slayer of the bull of earthly passion, and is ranged against the evil god Ahriman (Satan) in eternal battle. He was worshipped by the Roman soldiers as the protector of the Empire.

**Mnemosyne** [Greek]. One of Zeus' lovers, her name means 'memory'. She bore him the nine Muses who gave arts and sciences to mankind.

**Moira** [Greek]. The goddess of fate. The word means 'allotment'. She is portrayed as the oldest power in the universe, giving even the gods their circumscribed share of power. Sometimes she is represented as three women, Clotho, Lachesis and Atropos, the three Fates.

**Nemesis** [Greek]. Sometimes portrayed as a goddess and sometimes as an impersonal cosmic force, Nemesis is the inevitable punishment for *hubris* or too much arrogance and pride before the gods. Nemesis is a 'bad fate', and her punishments always fit precisely the nature of the crime.

**Nephele** [Greek]. A woman made of cloud, created by Zeus to fool the unwise Ixion who coveted Zeus' wife Hera. The cloud-woman was made in the likeness of Hera, and Ixion while drunk coupled with her. He was punished with terrible torments, but Nephele bore a child to him, the centaur Cheiron.

**Neptune** [Roman]. God of the sea, he is similar to the Greek Poseidon, but is solely a water god, while Poseidon is a fertility god and lord of earthquakes.

**Norns** [Teutonic]. The northern European version of the Moirai or Fates. They are sometimes portrayed as the daughters of the earth goddess Erda or Urd. Urd is also the name of the eldest Norn. Her sisters are called Verandi and Skuld. They sit at the roots of the World-Ash Yggdrasil, sprinkling the tree with water so that it does not wither.

**Nyx** [Greek]. The primal goddess of Night, she is an underworld deity.

**Odysseus** [Greek]. One of the heroes of the Trojan War, he is the subject of Homer's great poetic epic, the *Odyssey*, which narrates his long and circuitous journey from the wars back to his wife Penelope and his kingdom of Ithaca. He is called 'the wily one' because he managed to pass through many labours and dangers primarily through wit rather than brute force.

**Oidipus**, Oedipus [Greek]. The name means 'swell-foot'. He was the unwelcome child of King Laios and Queen Iokaste of Thebes. An oracle told him that he would slay his father and become the husband of his mother, and in his strenuous efforts to avoid this fate he invoked it. For the complete story of Oidipus, see p. 163.

**Olympus** [Greek]. A high mountain on the mainland of Greece, it was believed to be the abode of the gods. Like Valhalla in Teutonic myth, Olympus is a place too high for mortal man to reach.

**Orestes** [Greek]. The hero of Aeschylos' great trilogy of tragic plays, he was the son of King Agamemnon and Queen Klytaemnestra of Argos. Ordered by the god Apollo to avenge his mother's murder of his father, he was tormented by the Erinyes for his matricide until the goddess Athene and her court at Athens set him free. (See p. 89.)

**Ormuzd** [Persian]. The god of light and goodness. He is also called Ahura Mazda. He stands in perpetual contest with Ahriman, the spirit of darkness and evil.

**Orpheus** [Greek]. One of the saddest of Greek heroes, Orpheus was a poet and gifted musician. His beloved wife Eurydice was lost to him because Hades, falling in love with her, sent a snake to bite her in the heel so that she could enter the underworld to live with him. Orpheus wandered grieving over the earth, and his music made animals and stones weep. He was eventually torn to pieces by a group of wild Maenads, followers of the god Dionysos, who mistook him for a faun.

**Osiris** [Egyptian]. A god of life and death, he is both the judge of souls in the underworld and the redeemer of the spirit. Destroyed by his evil brother Set, he was mummified and the dismembered pieces of his body put back together by his sister–wife Isis, the moon goddess.

**Ouranos** [Greek]. The primal god of heaven. In Latin he is Uranus. Mating with his mother–sister Gaia, the earth goddess, he generated the physical universe.

They also produced the race of Titans and giants. He was overthrown and castrated by his son Kronos, who coveted the kingship of the gods.

**Pandora** [Greek]. A woman made by the smith god Hephaistos at the request of Zeus, she was sent as a gift to mankind, given as a wife to the Titan Epimetheus. The gift was meant to destroy, for she brought with her a box containing all the human ills – old age, sickness, insanity, fear, violence, death – which she proceeded to unleash upon man. Also included in the box was hope, the only compensation.

**Parcae** [Teutonic]. Another name for the three Norns or goddesses of fate. They were called Parcae, a Latin name, after the Romans had conquered Gaul and parts of Germany.

**Paris** [Greek]. The son of King Priam of Troy, he was renowned for his beauty and prowess with women. Because of these accomplishments he was asked by Zeus to judge a beauty contest between three goddesses, Hera, Athene and Aphrodite. He chose the goddess of love after she promised him as a reward the most beautiful woman in the world. This was Helen, whose subsequent abduction by Paris from her Greek husband King Menelaos of Mykenai resulted in the Trojan War and Paris' death.

**Parsifal** [Teutonic]. Later called Perceval in French and English versions, he is known for his place in the Arthurian tales, but is actually a much older and pre-Christian figure. He is the foolish and innocent knight who discovers the Holy Grail but neglects to ask the important question which would heal the sick Grail King and restore the land to health. He must then labour for twenty years before he can refind the treasure and ask the question which fulfils his quest.

**Pasiphaë** [Greek]. The wife of King Minos of Crete, she was afflicted by the god Poseidon with an unquenchable passion for the sacred bull which Minos had refused to sacrifice to the god. The result of the mating of woman and bull was the monstrous Minotaur, which the hero Theseus had to kill.

**Peleus** [Greek]. A mortal, he fathered the hero Achilles on the sea goddess Thetis. Thetis was in the process of burning her child to ensure his immortality when Peleus discovered her and dragged the boy out of the fire, thus leaving one limb mortal while the rest had been rendered immortal. It was through this vulnerable limb that Achilles was finally slain.

**Pelops** [Greek]. A king of Lydia, his father was Tantalos, who mocked the gods by killing his son and serving him up for dinner to the Olympians to see whether they would discover what they were eating. The goddess Rhea brought the child Pelops back to life again, but ever after he had a mark on his shoulder where the goddess Demeter had unknowingly bitten off a chunk. He founded the line of Atreus, upon which a curse hung until the hero Orestes broke the curse.

**Pentheus** [Greek]. A king of Thebes, he refused to permit the worship of the god Dionysos when that deity arrived with his train of wild followers. In revenge Dionysos drove Pentheus' mother mad, so that when she and her companions found him trying to spy on their rites they mistook him for a faun and tore him to pieces.

**Persephone** [Greek]. Her name means 'bringer of destruction'. A *kore* or maiden, she is the daughter of Demeter and Zeus, and is a goddess of spring. She was abducted from her mother and dragged into the underworld by Hades, where she was raped and bore him a child called Zagreus or Dionysos. She was worshipped as the Queen of the Dead.

**Perseus** [Greek]. The son of Zeus and a mortal woman, Danae, he was thrown out to sea with his mother locked in a wooden chest. They were rescued by King Polydectes, but the king wished to marry Perseus' mother against her will. Perseus was sent on a hopeless quest to kill the Gorgon Medusa, but with the help of the goddess Athene he accomplished his quest and returned to destroy Polydectes, rescue his beloved Andromeda, and live happily ever after.

**Phaedra** [Greek]. Daughter of King Minos of Crete, she became the wife of the hero Theseus, King of Athens. She fell desperately in love with his son, Hippolytus, but her advances were refused. In desperation she hung herself, leaving a suicide note explaining that Hippolytus had raped her. In rage Theseus cursed his son, only finding out the truth after the curse had been fulfilled and the god Poseidon had destroyed Hippolytus with a giant bull from the sea.

**Phlegethon** [Greek]. One of the rivers of the underworld. The name means 'burning'.

**Phrixus** [Greek]. A prince of Iolkos, he and his sister Helle escaped the wrath of their wicked stepmother on the back of a golden ram sent by Zeus. Helle fell off into the sea and drowned, but Phrixus arrived safely in Colchis at the court of King Aeëtes, where he sacrificed the ram. Its fleece became the Golden Fleece which the hero Jason later stole.

**Pluto** [Roman]. The god of the underworld, equivalent to the Greek Hades. His name means 'wealth'.

**Polydeuces** [Greek]. Called Pollux in Latin, he was the mortal twin of the pair associated with the constellation of Gemini. His brother Castor was immortal, being a son of Zeus. In a fight with another pair of twins, Idas and Lynceus, Polydeuces was killed and had to descend to the underworld. Castor mourned so bitterly that Zeus permitted them to spend alternate times in the underworld and on Mount Olympus together.

**Poseidon** [Greek]. Originally a fertility deity, he became the god of earthquakes and of the ocean depths. He is portrayed both as a horse and as a giant bull. He is called 'the husband of the Mother'.

**Prometheus** [Greek]. One of the race of Titans, he stole fire from the gods to give to man. He was punished for this crime by being chained to a rock in the Caucasus Mountains, where an eagle came every day to eat his liver. Eventually he was set free by the hero Herakles. Prometheus is a culture-hero, who taught the arts of mathematics, husbandry, agriculture, prophecy and architecture to man. In early versions of the myth he is said to have created man from clay.

**Proteus** [Greek]. A sea god, he is called 'the old man of the sea', and is portrayed with a fish's tail. He is a seer and can change his shape into any animal form. If he is securely bound and permitted to move through his transformations then he will eventually take his proper shape and offer an oracle.

**Psyche** [Greek]. A mortal woman with whom the god Eros fell in love. Aphrodite, Eros' mother, was furiously jealous of Psyche's beauty, and connived to destroy her. But Eros abducted her and married her, demanding only that she refrain from looking upon his face. Psyche's curiosity forced her to hold a lamp up to the sleeping god's face, and in revenge he left her. She pursued her lost love, but Aphrodite threw harsh labours and obstacles in her path. Eventually she passed these tests and was reunited with Eros and made immortal.

**Rahu** [Hindu]. A demon who devours the sun during the time of a solar eclipse. Astronomically, Rahu is equated with the moon's north or ascending node.

**Remus** [Roman]. One of a pair of twins fathered by the war god Mars, Remus was the 'bad' twin. He and his brother were suckled by a she-wolf and grew up to found the city of Rome. When the site had been chosen, however, Remus tried to murder his brother, and was himself killed.

**Rhea** [Greek]. One of the many names for the earth goddess, Rhea was a Titaness and wife–sister to the god Kronos. When Kronos swallowed his children to prevent them from usurping his power, Rhea hid the youngest, Zeus, and substituted a stone wrapped in swaddling clothes, which Kronos ate instead. Then Rhea armed Zeus so that he might lead a rebellion against his father, who was eventually overthrown.

**Romulus** [Roman]. One of a pair of twins fathered by the war god Mars, Romulus was the 'good' twin. He and his brother Remus were suckled by a she-wolf and grew up to found the city of Rome. When Remus tried to murder Romulus, Romulus managed to defend himself and killed his brother instead.

**Saturn** [Roman]. Analagous to the Greek Kronos, Saturn was a fertility god and patron of the harvest. His character in Roman myth is quite benign, and his Golden Age was a time of harmony and peace on earth when men enjoyed the fruits of the soil without strife. Each year he was celebrated by the Saturnalia, a time of license and abandonment, honouring the lecherous and fertile aspect of the god.

**Sekhmet** [Egyptian]. A solar goddess, she is portrayed with a lion's head. She was associated with the raging heat of the summer sun, and is a battle goddess and a goddess of vengeance. She is analogous to the Hindu Kali.

**Semele** [Greek]. One of Zeus' lovers, she was the mother of the god Dionysos. (In other versions of the Dionysos myth, his mother is Persephone.) Rashly extracting a promise from Zeus to give her whatever she wished, she demanded that he appear before her in his true form. Zeus manifested as thunder and lightning, and Semele was incinerated. Hermes saved the fetus in her womb and sewed it into Zeus' thigh until the nine months were complete and the child could be born.

**Set** [Egyptian]. The god of darkness and evil, he was responsible for the destruction of his brother Osiris. His sister Isis collected the dismembered pieces and brought the dead god back to life again. Set is sometimes portrayed as a serpent, with whom the sun god Ra fights each night in the bowels of the underworld; each morning the sun god rises victorious for another day, only to descend again to battle with Set the following night.

**Siegfried** [Teutonic]. Also called Sigurd, he is best known in Nordic and Teutonic sagas for his slaying of the dragon Fafner. Wagner made him the fearless hero of the *Ring*, where he is the child of an incestuous brother–sister union. Raised by the dwarf Mime, he slays the dragon Fafner and obtains the Niebelung gold and the ring of power. After pledging marriage vows to the Valkyrie Brunhilde, he abandons her for another woman and is murdered by treachery.

**Sisyphus** [Greek]. A mortal who betrayed Zeus' divine secrets and was punished in the underworld by being made to roll a great rock up a hill and having to watch it roll down again forever.

**Styx** [Greek]. One of the rivers of the underworld, Styx formed the boundary between the realm of mortals and the realm of dead souls. The name means 'poison'.

**Tammuz** [Babylonian]. A youthful vegetation god, he is associated with his mother–lover, the great fertility goddess Ishtar. He met his death while hunting, when a giant boar killed him. In company with Adonis, Osiris and Attis, he was worshipped as an eternally dying and resurrected god.

**Tantalos**, Tantalus [Greek]. A king of Lydia who offended the gods and was punished by being submerged in the underworld for eternity in a pool of water which he could not drink, tempted by fruit which he could not eat. (See p. 89.)

**Tartaros**, Tartarus [Greek]. Sometimes the name given to the underworld in its entirety, but more often the name for that special part of Hades' realm where crimes against the gods are punished by terrible torments.

**Teiresias** [Greek]. A blind seer, he warned Oidipus of his unwitting incest. In his youth, Teiresias was turned into a woman, and spent seven years in this form. Then his manhood was restored. Because of this unique experience, Zeus asked him to resolve an argument the god was having with Hera. Teiresias offended the goddess with his answer and she struck him blind. Zeus gave him the gift of prophecy in compensation.

**Tethys** [Greek]. Another name for Thetis, the goddess of the sea.

**Thanatos** [Greek]. The son of the goddess Night, he was the god of death, and served Hades by providing him with subjects. He is generally portrayed as a winged spirit. His brother Hypnos is the god of sleep.

**Theseus** [Greek]. Son of the god Poseidon by a mortal woman, he became King of Athens. Among his many adventures was the slaying of the Cretan Minotaur, which lived in the heart of a labyrinth and fed on human flesh. Theseus found his way into the labyrinth and out again with a ball of thread given to him by King Minos' daughter Ariadne, whom he later abandoned on the island of Naxos.

**Thetis** [Greek]. Goddess of the sea, she was the mother of the hero Achilles by a mortal man, Peleus.

**Thyestes** [Greek]. Brother of King Atreus of Mykenai, he avenged himself for Atreus' murder of his children by pronouncing a curse on his brother's line. (See p. 89.)

**Tiamat** [Babylonian]. The primal mother goddess, she is portrayed as a giant sea monster. Her son Marduk slew her and carved up her body to create the physical universe.

**Trojan War** [Greek]. The theme of Homer's great poetic epic, the *Iliad*, the Trojan War was an historical event as well as a mythic theme. The Greek city states, enraged by the kidnap of Helen, wife of King Menelaos of Mykenai, by a Trojan prince, used this incident as an excuse to invade Troy (located in what is now modern Turkey), which had long been envied for its gold and wealth. The Greeks managed to get their troops within the Trojan gates through the famous gift of the Trojan Horse, a huge hollow wooden horse in which the Greek soldiers were hidden. In the *Iliad*, the gods line up on either side of the conflict, and the human battle is reflected by a battle between Olympian deities. Troy's King Priam was slain and the city was razed to the ground.

**Uranus** [Roman]. Equivalent to the Green Ouranos, he is the original god of heaven.

**Valhalla** [Teutonic]. The abode of the gods, it is roughly equivalent to Mount Olympus in Greek myth.

**Valkyrie** [Teutonic]. A warrior goddess, daughter of the storm god Wotan. The Valkyrie follow battles and carry the souls of dead heroes up to Valhalla for an eternal round of partying and glorious fighting.

**Venus** [Roman]. Goddess of beauty and sensual love, she is the equivalent of the Greek Aphrodite.

**Vulcan** [Roman]. The divine smith and artisan, he is the equivalent of the Greek Hephaistos. Vulcan was married to the goddess Venus, who was perpetually unfaithful to him.

**Wotan** [Teutonic]. Equivalent to the Norse Odin and the Greek Zeus, he is a multifaceted deity. He is ruler of the gods and the lord of storm and chaos. He is also a magician and a battle god. He sacrificed one of his eyes to obtain wisdom from the sacred spring at the foot of the World-Ash, and has as his companions two ravens.who fly far and wide bringing him tidings of all that goes on in the world. He also bears a certain resemblance to the Hebrew Yahveh, for Wotan is also a god of covenants and laws, and exhibits a similar bad temper.

**Yahveh** [Hebrew]. Another name for Jehovah, the god of the Old Testament who is the God of Israel.

**Yggdrasil** [Teutonic]. The World-Ash. The world in Teutonic myth is imaged as a tree of prodigious dimensions. Its foliage is always green. Its roots reach down into the subterranean kingdom and its boughs rise to the heights of the sky and to Valhalla, the abode of the gods. Under one of its roots is the fountain of the Norns or Fates.

**Zagreus** [Greek]. The name means 'restored to life'. It is generally given as an epithet to Dionysos, who was dismembered by the Titans and brought back to life again. It is also sometimes used as a title for Zeus, king of the gods.

**Zethus** [Greek]. One of a pair of mythic twins, Zethus was the more warlike and aggressive, while his brother Amphion was a poet and musician. The twins fought constantly over these differences.

**Zeus** [Greek]. The name means 'lightener' or 'he who gives enlightenment'. King of the gods, he is the ruler of thunder and lightning and storm. He is the Great Father, giver of gifts, and is also portrayed as highly promiscuous, forever pursuing new erotic conquests. He is married to Hera, who is also his sister, and is the son of Kronos the Titan. Kronos received a prophecy that one of his sons would one day overthrow him, and so proceeded to swallow all his children. Zeus, the youngest, was hidden by his mother Rhea, and a stone was substituted instead. When Kronos eventually vomited up the stone and all the other children with it, Zeus led them in rebellion and became ruler of the gods.

# Index